Inside Intuition

What is 'gut feeling' and how can it be harnessed? To what extent should business decisions be informed by 'instincts' which may seem irrational or impossible to quantify?

Inside Intuition examines how the latest developments in social psychology and cognitive psychology, as well as exciting new insights from evolutionary psychology and cognitive neuroscience, can be used to explain the phenomenon of 'gut feeling' which has for decades been shrouded in magic and mysticism. The book provides a highly readable scientific explanation of 'gut feeling', and the sometimes profound effects it can have on decision-making in business, management and other professional contexts. Using examples ranging from Boeing to Buddhism it explains how managers and other decision-makers can make better use of this pervasive, involuntary and ubiquitous phenomenon in their personal and professional lives to support creativity, innovation and interpersonal functioning.

Inside Intuition is essential reading for all advanced students of business and management, and for managers and other professionals at all levels.

Eugene Sadler-Smith is Professor of Management Development and Organizational Behaviour in the School of Management, University of Surrey. He has researched and written extensively in the area of learning and development, and is the author of *Learning and Development for Managers: Perspectives from Research and Practice* (2006) and, with Dr. P.J. Smith, *Learning in Organisations: Complexities and Diversities* (2006). His work on intuition has appeared in a number of scholarly journals, professional magazines, *The Times* and on BBC Radio 4.

Inside Intuition

Eugene Sadler-Smith

Routledge
Taylor & Francis Group

LONDON AND NEW YORK

First published 2008
by Routledge
2 Park Square, Milton Park, Abingdon, Oxon OX14 4RN

Simultaneously published in the USA and Canada
by Routledge
270 Madison Avenue, New York, NY 10016

*Routledge is an imprint of the Taylor & Francis Group,
an informa business*

© 2008 Eugene Sadler-Smith

Typeset in Times New Roman by
RefineCatch Limited, Bungay, Suffolk
Printed and bound in Great Britain by
TJ International Ltd, Padstow, Cornwall

British Library Cataloguing in Publication Data
A catalogue record for this book is available from the British Library

Library of Congress Cataloging in Publication Data
A catalog record for this book has been requested

ISBN 10: 0–415–41452–0 (hbk)
ISBN 10: 0–415–41453–9 (pbk)
ISBN 10: 0–203–93207–2 (ebk)

ISBN 13: 978–0–415–41452–4 (hbk)
ISBN 13: 978–0–415–41453–1 (pbk)
ISBN 13: 978–0–203–93207–0 (ebk)

... A *seeming* somewhat more than *view*;
That doth instruct the mind
In things that lie behind,
And many secrets to us show
Which afterwards we come to know.

(Thomas Traherne, 1637–1674, *Shadows in the Water*)

Contents

Figures

Tables

Acknowledgements

This book is the outcome of an individual and a collective endeavour; that said I lay sole claim to the inevitable speculations, omissions and faults. My sincere thanks go to: Francesca Heslop at Routledge for commissioning *Inside Intuition*; students at the University of Surrey who have politely endured the excesses of my intuition classes; all of those people in the UK and elsewhere who have patiently sat through the various seminars and presentations on the subject of intuition that I have given (it helped to clarify my thinking – I hope they gained something also); colleagues at the School of Management, University of Surrey, UK (particularly the Management Learning group); Jane Mathison and Paul Tosey; colleagues at the Society for Organisational Learning (SOL) UK where we had many fruitful discussions about intuition and decision taking, and in particular the President of SOL (UK) Arie de Geus and its Executive Co-ordinator Eve Mitleton-Kelly; all the participants at the Advanced Institute of Management (Research) Symposium on Intuition in Management Practice, London, October 2006, and in particular Lisa Burke, Guy Claxton, Gerard Hodgkinson and Paul Sparrow, not only for making the event a resounding success, but for their impeccable scholarship in the study of intuition; Bill Lucas, not only for expertly facilitating the London Symposium and chairing the Talent Foundation and its intuitive 'thinking breakfast', but for being an inspiring, wise voice and motivator *par excellence*; participants at the Intuition Symposium at the Annual Academy of Management (AoM) Meeting in Atlanta, Georgia, August, 2006, and especially to the organizers of the event, Erik Dane and Michael G. Pratt, and my co-participants Gerard Hodgkinson and Marta Sinclair. My special thanks go to Erella Shefy whose big idea it was in the first place to have a book about intuition, and to whom I still say *ani lo mevina*!

Eugene Sadler-Smith, Surrey, July 2007

Photograph and image credits

My sincere thanks go to the following for their assistance with the photographs and other images ('what is the use of a book,' thought Alice, 'without pictures or conversations?'): Jonna Petterson at the Nobel Foundation for sourcing the photographs of the various Nobel laureates; George Kupczak at the AT&T Archives and History Center AT&T for the photograph of Chester Barnard; Sarah Thomas at Schott and Co. for the photograph of Sir Michael Tippett by Nicky Johnston; Alexander Zehnder at Lebrecht and Co. for the photographs of John Coltrane and Igor Stravinsky; Mark Jung-Beeman for the images of the insight fMRI scans and the EEG head model; Joanna Jarcho and Matthew Lieberman for the images of the 'C' and 'X' systems.

Abbreviations

AG	artificial grammar
aSTG	anterior superior temporal gyrus
CEST	Cognitive-Experiential Self-Theory
EEG	electro-encephalography
EI	emotional intelligence
ESP	extra-sensory perception
fMRI	functional magnetic resonance imaging
FOW	feelings of warmth
GP	general practitioner
IQ	cognitive intelligence
LH	left hemisphere
LI	latent inhibition
LTM	long term memory
MBTI	Myers-Briggs Type Indicator
NDM	naturalistic decision-making
OFC	orbito-frontal cortex
OR	operational research
PET	positron emission tomography
PR	pattern recognition
PRS	Perceptual Representation System
RB	ratio bias (phenomenon)
RH	right hemisphere
RPD	recognition-primed decision (model)
SCRs	skin conductance responses
SS	somatic state
SMH	somatic marker hypothesis
STM	short term memory
VMPC	ventro-medial prefrontal cortex
VOT	ventral occipito-temporal (region)
WM	working memory

1 The view from inside

> . . . The quick dreams,
> The passion-wingèd Ministers of thought.
>
> (Shelley, *Adonais*, 1821)

MAIN IDEA

Intuition is a phenomenon that recurs across languages, cultures, continents and history and throughout human endeavour from business to Buddhism. Intuition need not be 'magical' – it can be defined and explained scientifically. Understanding intuition contributes to more effective decision-making in professional and personal settings.

Everyone has intuition. It is one of the hallmarks of how human beings think and behave. It's impossible for us to function effectively without using 'gut feeling'. Intuition presents itself uninvited to us rapidly, and in many different guises, and under the right circumstances its effects can be life-changing and life-saving. Here are some examples.

Detecting illness

A small child at home develops a moderate fever and a sore throat – nothing unusual in that – it's happened before. Except that this time for some inexplicable reason an image invades the parents mind's eye, and an 'alarm bell' sounds off inexplicably and involuntarily in her body. The symptoms are checked out, medical help is sought immediately;

medics confirm that the parent's gut feeling was correct – the illness is far from trivial, it's scarlet fever. Luckily it was caught in its early stages and was treatable. Any delay and the outcome could have been much worse.[1]

'Sniffing-out' opportunity

In the 1950s an ex-food mixer salesman had risked everything on a nationwide franchise for 228 fast food restaurants but he was collecting less than 2 per cent of the turnover but turning over more than a quarter of it to the owners. He offered to buy them out, but the price was high – $2.7million dollars – an enormous sum of money in 1960. His lawyer warned him not to take the deal. He later recalled: 'I'm not a gambler and I didn't have that kind of money, but my funny bone instinct kept urging me on. So I closed my office door, cussed up and down, and threw things out the window. Then I called my lawyer back and said "Take it!" ' Fifty years later the company has hundreds of thousands of employees, feeds millions of customers every day, has restaurant locations in over 120 countries and is an emblem of 'globalization'.[2]

Split-second decision-making

One of the most famous sporting examples of intuition concerned the great Argentinean driver Juan Fangio in the 1950 Monaco Grand Prix. On lap two instead of maintaining speed as he exited a tunnel for an upcoming straight section Fangio inexplicably braked. By doing so he avoided a serious accident that had occurred just around the next corner. But quite why he'd braked just didn't make sense. The key was Fangio's intuitive perception of the scene, which he only later figured out. Spectators in the stands, alerted by the deafening sound of the cars' engines, usually had their faces turned towards them to see them roaring out of the tunnel exit. On this lap, however, they weren't looking at Fangio; they were looking up the track. Fangio's straight-ahead vision was focused on the road, but in his peripheral vision saw a subtle change in the colour of the stand area. Because the spectators had turned their heads away a normally light section in the field of view from their faces had become dark from the hair on the back of their heads. Fangio, concentrating on his driving, noticed this change and processed in split seconds without it having the chance to register. As a result he automatically braked, avoided the accident and went on to win the race.[3]

Choosing a mate

In a speed-dating experiment involving 156 undergraduates, researchers from Northwestern University and Massachusetts Institute of Technology found that in the space of a four-minute interaction daters exercised a highly-tuned ability that enabled them to sense whether a person 'desperately' desired a large proportion of the potential partners in the experiment or whether they were actually being more 'picky'. Researcher Eli Finkel commented that if you're a speed dater it seems like you're 'not only able to pick up something about the degree to which that person likes you, but you're able to pick up – in four minutes – the degree to which that person likes you more than their other dates. It's amazing.' Speed daters who were intuitively perceived as being 'unfussy' didn't generate the 'magical' mutual attraction and tended to be given the 'cold shoulder' by potential partners.[4]

INTUITION IS EVERYWHERE

Homo sapiens – the *wise* ape – reasons and makes decisions analytically and rationally, but also takes decisions emotionally and intuitively. The word 'intuition' comes from the Latin *intueri* which is often roughly translated as meaning 'to look inside' or 'to contemplate'.[5] In everyday English we frequently use terms like 'hunch' or 'gut feeling' to express intuition's bodily character, and not surprisingly we find equivalent phrases cropping up in other languages and across cultures. For example, in Chinese 'direct feeling' is *zhí jué* (直觉); in Hebrew 'intuition' is *intuizia*, and 'gut feeling' is *tchushat beten*; in Greek 'intuition' is *diaisthisi* (διαίσθηση), and 'hunch' is *proesthima* (προαίσθημα); in German to make a decision 'out-of-the-stomach' is *Eine Entscheidung aus dem Bauch heraus fällen*. Italians are more concise, and a single word suffices – *intuito*.[6]

But is intuition relevant in the world of business? It would seem to make sense that managers rely on intuitive judgement, and research certainly seems to back this up. When senior managers in US business were asked in a survey how often they used intuition in making decisions 12 per cent said 'always', 47 per cent said 'often', 30 per cent said 'sometimes' and the remaining small minority (one in ten) said they 'seldom' or 'rarely' used it.[7] The circumstances under which managers used intuition ranged from sensing when a problem exists, performing well-learned complex behaviour patterns rapidly, synthesizing isolated bits of data into a coherent whole to checking on the results of their rational analyses, or by-passing in-depth analysis altogether.[8] In a global survey of over one thousand managers the three most popular accounts of 'what is intuition' were: a perception of decision without recourse to logical or rational methods; an inexplicable comprehension that arrives as a feeling 'from within'; and an integration of accumulated knowledge and previous experiences.[9] Managers, it seems, are very 'switched-on' to intuition.

So, what is it that singles out intuitions? First, intuitions don't enter our conscious awareness as fully-formed answers; instead they appear as 'judgements'. Second, they come laden with feeling (affect), so much so that we often detect intuitions through changes in bodily sensations. Third, gut feelings are fast – they arise spontaneously and involuntarily; moreover we can't will them to happen, but equally nor can we 'block' them out. And finally, perhaps the most perplexing thing about an intuition is that it's almost impossible at the time to articulate the non-conscious perceptions and thoughts that lie behind it. We feel that we 'know', but we don't know 'how' we know.

INTUITION IS PERPLEXING AND POWERFUL

Intuitions enable us to recognize, judge or predict people's intentions and situations with certitude, speed and often, but not always, accuracy. What goes on beneath the surface is an enigma to the thinker; almost as if there is 'something else' doing the thinking – all we are allowed is a glimpse and the feeling that we 'know', but we aren't made privy to *how* we know. If challenged to explain we may frustrate our questioner with responses such as: 'Don't ask me why I just know it's wrong!', or 'I don't know why, but something tells me that . . .'. One of the perils of intuition is that these perceptions and compelling judgements can get mixed up with biases, fears and wishful thinking. Blindly following gut feelings is ill-advised; being intelligent about intuition requires being on-guard against subtle and invidious sources of error that can bias intuitive judgements.

From our standpoint in the early part of the twenty-first century intuition is a concept whose time has certainly come in terms of its popular appeal, for example, the best-selling book *Blink* by Malcolm Gladwell certainly de-mystified the concept in the public understanding.[10] In parallel with Gladwell's efforts research is helping to illuminate not only its scientific basis, but the powerful influence intuition has in areas as diverse as entrepreneurship, innovation, business management, education and training, and health care.[11] In our working lives the sensations that accompany an intuition can warn us away from or compel us to follow a particular judgment or course of action, and the consequences of our intuitive choices can be significant for ourselves, our colleagues and the organizations and social institutions of which we are a part.

The experiences of artists, scientists, inventors and business people testify that when it is given the conditions to flourish, intuition is one of the cornerstones of human artistic, scientific, technical and commercial ingenuity. Intuition has been a potent force in human culture, civilization and organization for millennia. History is replete with examples ranging from the poets and philosophers of Classical antiquity to major scientific figures of the modern age and multi-millionaire business people who have recognized the importance of intuition in their works:

> the soul is only able to view existence through the bars of a prison, and not in her own nature . . . philosophy received and gently counselled her, and wanted to release her, pointing out to her that the eye is full of deceit, and also the ear and other senses . . . and to trust only to herself and her own intuitions
>
> (Plato, 428–347 BC, *Phaedo* 66)

> The intellect has little to do on the road to discovery. There comes a leap in consciousness, call it intuition or what you will, and the solution comes to you and you don't know how or why.
>
> (Albert Einstein, 1879–1955)[12]

> Leaders have the courage to make unpopular decisions and gut calls[. . .]You have to rely on your gut, does the person seem real, does she openly admit mistakes [. . .] You have to rely on reference checks, reports and most of important gut [. . .] Your gut defies a technical rationale.[13]
>
> (Jack Welch, Former Chairman and CEO of General Electric, business 'guru' and author of *Straight from the Gut*)

INTUITION IS PART OF THE COGNITIVE UNCONSCIOUS

Intuition's power can be so convincing as to be mistaken for clairvoyance, extrasensory perception or some other paranormal phenomenon. At the transcendent and transpersonal end of the spectrum it has been suggested that intuition can connect us to the spiritual aspects of our beings and to a 'supra-consciousness'.[14] At a more mundane level our

Figure 1.1   Albert Einstein, Nobel Laureate in Physics (1921) and 'intuitive scientist' without parallel. Copyright The Nobel Foundation (reproduced by permission).

personal experience attests to the fact that without intuition it would be difficult to make everyday decisions and function effectively in a social world which, as the most gregarious of all the primates, we inhabit and are an active part of. Whether, as reasoning, rational beings we like it or not, the capability to intuit is integral to the condition of being *Homo sapiens*.

Research in cognitive and social psychology reveal the origins of intuition to be within the non-conscious aspects of our thought, reason and judgment. The capability to intuit is an outcome of human evolution and occupies a 'border state' that stands on the threshold between our thoughts and our feelings, and between our conscious and non-conscious thinking. Modern brain-imaging techniques such as functional magnetic resonance imaging (fMRI) allied to emerging insights from neurology and cognitive neuroscience are beginning to identify specific brain regions that are implicated in intuitive judgement processes. We not only have a better idea of what intuition is but we are also beginning to understand where in the brain it happens.

A fundamental precept of getting inside intuition is that there are non-conscious mental events to which we do not have direct access. The evidence that non-conscious thought (non-conscious cognition) plays a critical role in human memory, reasoning and judgement is overwhelming.[15] For example, when writing we are aware of the words as they occur visually as text on the page or screen. But if we stopped to think about every letter . . . every word . . . every phrase . . . every possible meaning . . . every aspect of the grammatical structure of sentences . . . we would not get very far at all . . . things would slow down pretty quickly. By devoting conscious awareness to the apparently simple act of writing or speaking things would move so slowly that it would become laborious, effortful and extraordinarily inefficient. On the other hand, if I let things 'flow' words and phrases seem to simply emerge, so much so that I, by which I mean my conscious self, am sometimes pleasantly surprised at what has 'appeared' on the page. We are aware of *what* we are writing or speaking as it happens; however, *how* we speak or write with fluency is more difficult to account for in conscious terms.[16] The seemingly simple act of writing or speaking seems to be more automatic and non-conscious than controlled and conscious, but paradoxically, is also an extremely complex process. There are numerous other examples of the ways in which we can 'think' in highly complex ways outside of conscious awareness.

The concept of unconscious cognition extends to the processes of subliminal perception (for example, images flashed so quickly that they do not register in consciousness but have an effect on behaviour) and implicit learning[17] (acquiring knowledge without conscious awareness of how or what was learned); we need think only of the ways in which we acquire our first language or social skills to see the power of implicit learning. Recent developments in neuroscience are also shedding light on possible brain mechanisms which support 'learning-without-awareness'. In the early 1990s a group of Italian neuroscientists (including Giuseppe di Pellegrino and Giacomo Rizzolatti) made an extraordinary discovery: they observed single neurons that fire in the brains of monkeys not only when the monkey grasps a piece of food such as a grape with its own hand but also when it simply sees a human experimenter or other monkey doing the same action. These 'mirror neurons' are not merely concerned with imitation learning and the creation of neural pathways to imitate the action, they may also transform visual information relating to an act of non-verbal communication into an implicit knowledge and understanding of that act. So for example, the action done by another individual, such as a hand or facial gesture, because of the firing of the mirror neurons, becomes understood by the receiver without conscious, effortful cognition playing a role. Not only that, Rizzolatti has also suggested the existence of 'echo-neurons' which are activated when an individual listens to verbal material.[18]

If we re-wind a century or so, Freud's notion of the unconscious was of a primitive part of personality that pursues pleasure and gratification prompted by basic motivational forces (the *id*).[19] The 'cognitive unconscious' is quite different. Modern cognitive science provides strong and compelling evidence that most thought is unconscious (in a non-Freudian sense) and governed by mental processes that are inaccessible to conscious awareness but which have a powerful influence over judgement, feeling and behaviour. Social psychologist Timothy D. Wilson likens the cognitive unconscious to the vast workings of the Federal Government that goes on out of view of the President.[20] Every now and again one of these Federal Government departments files a report that ends up on the President's desk – the spotlight of consciousness falls upon what is happening behind the scenes. By and large the Federal Government is a backstage, invisible hand running the show.

Linguist George Lakoff and philosophy professor Mark Johnson in their book *Philosophy in the Flesh: The Embodied Mind and its Challenge to Western Thought*, state without equivocation that 'Thought is mostly unconscious' and that 'reason is not dispassionate, but emotionally engaged [and] shaped by the body'.[21] They describe conscious thought as the tip of an enormous iceberg – the vast majority of which is below the threshold of conscious awareness – and that the 'rule-of-thumb' amongst cognitive scientists is that 95 per cent of all thought is unconscious. Intuition is a manifestation of this; it is a 'Minister' from the unconscious which serves to guide thought, judgement and action. To return to Wilson's 'executive control' metaphor: intuitive judgements are high-priority 'files' stamped with feelings and sent up to the President's desk and offering advice on an issue of which he may or may not be aware, and which advice he can choose to heed or ignore.

Why should that supremely rational, 'big-brained', bipedal primate, *Homo sapiens*, unique amongst the great apes in its abilities to use language and make complex tools, concern itself with intuition? After all, for decades intuition has been shrouded in mystery and magic, seen by many as being of the fringes of scientific inquiry, as having no place within the doctrine of positivism[22] and the rationalist practices of science, business, and management.[23] Why should professional decision-makers, such as managers, doctors, lawyers, and teachers concern themselves with intuition when they have the power of their highly-trained and finely-tuned rational minds at their disposal to guide their judgement? The concept of rationality as having limits (being 'bounded') is one of the central tenets of the decision theories which have dominated administrative science in the twentieth century and management as taught in the business schools.[24] It is a topic that will be examined in more depth in Chapter 3, but the reality is that far from being a rare occurrence in management and professional practice, it is actually quite likely that managers and other professionals may have little choice but to rely upon their intuitions in many situations. Sometimes their intuiting may be overt, and this may be particularly so amongst powerful groups such as senior managers and executives who may not need to provide rational justifications for their decisions to the same extent as their more junior colleagues, and who may be also expected to run their firms with a unique 'business instinct' that justifies a large pay cheque. At other times and under different circumstances intuitive decision-making may be covert, consigned to the 'closet' and justified by *post hoc* rationalization. Intuition is 'the elephant in the room'[25] of management and professional practice: most people are well aware that they, and many of their colleagues, rely upon it to greater or lesser extents; fewer are willing to admit openly that they use it, or to discuss it – and if it does get discussed it is likely to be in hushed tones, in private conversations behind closed doors rather than in the meeting room or executive suite.

INTUITION IS IMPORTANT

More often than not education and training inadvertently allow professional decision-makers to remain unaware of what intuition is, let alone how to make better use of it in decision-making, problem-solving and creativity. This is in spite of the fact that managers, doctors, nurses, lawyers, teachers and many other occupational groups will meet and no doubt rely upon intuition at some stage in their day-to-day practice. Moreover, managers and other professionals are constantly being exhorted to be more creative, innovative, entrepreneurial and ethical – areas where intuition has an important if not invaluable role to play. The outcomes of major strategic decisions shape destinies and fortunes, but can rest upon whether intuition is used appropriately, and whether it's handled well or badly.

The flawed use of intuition is likely to be a result of ignorance of what it is, how it operates and how it might be improved (or at minimum better handled). But it seems that there is little desire on the part of institutions to develop the intuitive awareness of key members of society. As intuition pioneer Daniel Cappon noted over a decade ago 'everyone has an opinion on intuition but no one does very much about it'.[26] This oversight is a serious weakness in the education and training of decision-makers. Why? Because:

1 *Intuition happens*: intuition is involuntary, ubiquitous, and pervasive across work and personal contexts and therefore is unavoidable;
2 *Rationality is not enough*: as we shall see rationality is not 'demonic'[27] in its powers. Successful decision-making doesn't hinge on rationality alone, but involves a judicious mix of rational analysis and creative intuition. The ability to 'switch cognitive gears' from analysis to intuition and *vice versa* is a vital decision-making competence;[28]
3 *Experts use intuition*: effective use of intuition is one factor that distinguishes expert practitioners from novice practitioners. Developing informed intuitive judgement through intense, focused practice is an important step in the acquisition of expertise and professional development;
4 *Intuition is powerful and perilous*: in the right hands informed intuition can be a powerful, creative decision-making and problem-solving tool – conversely if handled badly it can be potentially dangerous and damaging;
5 *Balance is an art*:[29] relying exclusively and indiscriminately upon a purely 'mechanistic' rationality *or* uninformed intuition is naïve and unwise; seeking a harmonious balance of rationality *and* intuition is prudent and wise, moreover aesthetic qualities which intuitively feel 'right', such as 'balance', are important factors in the selection and refinement of creative ideas, inventions and innovations[30] and in the 'art' of excellent management and leadership;
6 *Cartesian dualism has suffered a demise*:[31] in the view of many, if not most, cognitive scientists the mind does not exist separately from and independent of the body.[32] Intuitions are constructions of our embodied minds, and understanding them in these terms may challenge certain preconceptions, but may also contribute to a better appreciation of how and why we think, feel and behave in the ways we do.

There are exceptions to the general lack of attention give to intuition in education; for example an executive training course in creative intuition was offered at one major US business school from the 1980s onwards incorporating discussions with individuals who claim to use intuition in their decision-making and reflective techniques such as mediation.[33] In the 1980s and 1990s a number of pioneering books for managers were published including Rowan's *The Intuitive Manager*, Parikh's *Intuition*, Agor's *Intuition in Organizations*, Cappon's *Intuition and Management* and Goldberg's *The Intuitive Edge*. Perhaps the greatest contribution to educating intuition in business has come from Bill Taggart, formerly Professor of Management at Florida International University. Taggart's argument (over two decades ago) was that we live in a highly rational culture which means that paying attention to intuition in our professional and personal lives is certainly a big challenge, but nonetheless he believes that it is essential if we are to restore a sense of balance of balance to the overly rational style in contemporary society.[34] I am reminded of the ancient Sufi story recounted by Peter Senge in his book *The Fifth Discipline* (1990):

> A blind man who was wandering lost in a forest tripped and fell. As he rummaged about on the forest floor he discovered he'd fallen over a man with only one leg. The two struck up a conversation. The blind man said: 'I've been wandering in this forest for days and I can't seem to find a way out'. The man with one leg said: 'And I've been lying on the forest floor for days unable to walk to get out'. Then the one-legged man had a 'Eureka!' moment: 'What if you hoist me up onto your shoulders and I'll tell you where to walk, that way we can get out of the forest together!'

The blind man symbolized rationality, the one legged man intuition, and Senge argued that managers and other decision-makers won't find a way out of their own forests until they learn how to integrate the two.[35]

Intuition is especially important in business, management and other areas of professional practice in the twenty-first century for a number of reasons: first, economic, business and organizational environments are as complex and dynamic as they have ever been; second, the world we inhabit appears to move ever-quickly, and in business organizations many of the most important decisions have to be acted upon speedily for fear of losing out on opportunities, being overtaken by competitors, or in response to a crisis. And finally, we live in an age where the amount of available information is potentially overwhelming, to the extent that it is often difficult for managers and other professionals to see 'the wood for the trees'. At other times strategic decision-makers and entrepreneurs are required to move into 'uncharted waters' with a blank sheet of paper as their only map of the territory.

Computing and information technology has made a global database of facts, information, advice and opinions instantly available to managers. As a result, managers and other professionals are faced with an information deluge; they have more alternatives to choose from than was ever the case in the past. A survey in the late 1990s found that three-quarters of communication is electronic, the average manager communicates with 24 people daily, receives six interruptions per hour, and over half of those sampled had difficulty responding to all of the messages they received.[36] One thing we can be sure of is that the situation is unlikely to have eased in recent years.

Faced with these challenges managers may simply be subject to a veritable onslaught, an information overload with too little time to analyse all the facts and figures. Where a fast decision is needed decision-makers need to be able to take in as much information as possible and use their experience and expertise to process the 'big picture', to quickly 'sniff out' viable options and know how to act without getting bogged down in minutiae. For example, in financial markets important investment decisions are often made 'on the run', and if an experienced financial analyst is unable, on the basis of contextual awareness gleaned from years of practical and market experience, to weigh up the situation and summarize an investment case in a few bullet points then there probably isn't one.[37] At Boeing, as the sophistication of air and space platforms becomes ever greater, it's harder for even experienced pilots to use system data, in this situation 'their senses, intuition and experience' have to be called upon to compensate for this.[38]

There is the alternative scenario of the uncertainty that comes with 'information under-load'. When moving into uncharted territories such as a completely new business venture (witness Virgin's forays into the world's first 'space-line' with 'Virgin Galactic'[39]), or when proactively marketing a new product or service on the basis of customers' 'latent needs', managers may have few precedents and little hard data to go on. Time spent in too much deliberation and over-extensive data collection, research and analysis may mean that a business idea may lose its currency, or the gap in the market might be filled by one's competitors.

In these situations entrepreneurial managers have to make judgements on the basis of their informed intuition, and accept the attendant ambiguity and uncertainty. This often necessitates taking a risk as Starbuck's CEO, Howard Schultz, noted in his recollection of the role that gut feeling played in his decisions to try to bring coffee house 'ritual and romance', and eventually the $3 cappuccino, to North America in the mid-1980s:

> I left [the original] Starbucks to start my own company. I decided that if I did not seize the opportunity and take a risk, my moment

would pass and I would regret it forever. It was a tough decision, but I knew I had to take a leap of faith and believe in myself. It took courage. It was like deciding to jump off the side of a building with no net.[40]

The anecdotes offered by many successful entrepreneurs lay claims to the possession of a business 'instinct' or 'entrepreneurial intuition' that enables them to 'sniff out' opportunities and judge rapidly whether they hold promise as commercially viable business ventures. And the reality is that leaders and managers may have little time to devote to the decision-making process, they may have to act quickly and decisively[41] with too much or too little information. In twenty-first-century business organizations 'fast', decisive, intuitive decision-making is not only necessary, it is often seen as an absolute requirement of effective entrepreneurial and transformational leadership.

INTUITION SNAPSHOTS

Intuition pervades numerous aspects of human activity, and diverse interpretations of it are encountered across the realms of philosophy, scientific discovery, the expressive arts, professional work, Eastern philosophies and practices, spiritual and mystical ways of knowing, and in

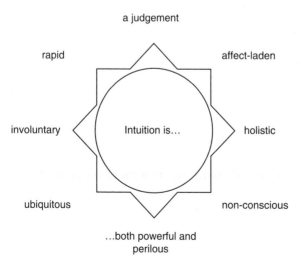

Figure 1.2 Eight essential characteristics of intuition.

magical systems of thought and belief. On the pages that follow some glimpses of these different manifestations of intuition are presented.

Intuitionism and intuition in philosophy

The concept of 'intuitionism' in moral philosophy asserts that 'good' is of itself indefinable, and that there are basic objective moral truths. The English philosopher John Locke (1632–1704) defined intuitive knowledge as that which is immediate and which does not depend upon other knowledge (for example, we intuit with immediacy that 'white is not black' without recourse to any other knowledge because 'black' and 'white' are simple and irreducible ideas). In Locke's words: '. . . sometimes the Mind perceives the agreement or disagreement of two ideas immediately by themselves, without the intervention of any other: and this, I think, we may call *Intuitive Knowledge*.' (John Locke, *Essay*, IV, ii, 1, original emphases).[42]

In Locke's philosophy certain fundamental or self-evidential truths are revealed to us as *de facto* intuitions.[43] The Scottish philosopher David Hume (1711–1776) argued that we are fundamentally creatures of instinct and habit whose mental lives are dominated by 'passion over reason'.[44] A contemporary of Hume was another Scottish 'commonsense' philosopher, Thomas Reid (1710–1796), who argued that what is 'right' is indefinable, that we understand what right is by means of an original power of the mind and that this inherent moral faculty provides us with a set of first principles for how to judge whether an act is right or wrong.[45]

In the early years of the twentieth century the English philosopher G.E. Moore (1873–1958) asserted that moral judgements are based upon an infallible intuitive knowledge, for example 'moral' things are intrinsically 'good' and cannot be further defined and analysed because a moral thing (like 'good' or 'bad') is a simple idea that cannot be broken down into smaller ideas and cannot (or need not) be proved empirically.[46]

> There is no intrinsic difficulty in the contention that 'good' denotes a simple and indefinable quality. There are many other instances of such qualities. By far the most valuable things, which we can know or imagine, are certain states of consciousness which may be roughly described as pleasures of human [interaction] and of beautiful objects.
>
> (G.E. Moore, *Principia Ethica*, 1903)

In Classical antiquity Plato's 'middle period' philosophy is based on the 'theory of Forms', a conception of the universe in which the world of our ordinary experience is illusory and transitory, and the real, stable and permanent part is that of the Forms.[47] The Forms are ideal realities, such as 'Justice', 'Equality' or 'Beauty' that exist outside of space or time.[48] Within Plato's system, the highest kind of knowledge is 'rational intuition' which is directed towards the Forms themselves. The Forms are perfect ideas, whereas 'sensible (i.e. sensed) objects' are imperfect – they never exclusively possess one property (for example, a person can be 'just' in some respects but 'unjust' in others).[49]

Intuition in musical creativity

Musical composition in the classical tradition – as well as being based upon a very exacting and rigorous training, requiring expert knowledge and skills in harmony, rhythm and counterpoint – also draws upon subconscious, intuitive modes of thinking in two ways:[50]

1   *Origination*: composition and the inspiration that underpins it cannot take place at purely the conscious level because inspiration often arises subconsciously;
2   *Judgement*: intuition gives a felt sense of 'rightness' about a composer's inspiration and therefore an inspiration can be judged intuitively.

The twentieth century French composer Edgar Varèse (1883–1965) called by some the 'father of electronic music' and an influence on The Beatles, Charlie Parker and Frank Zappa, remarked that 'the composer knows as little as anyone else about where the substance of his work comes from'. The English composer Frederick Delius (1862–1934) in similar vein commented that he was 'entirely at a loss to explain how I compose – I only know that I first conceive a work suddenly through a *feeling*'[51] (emphasis added).

One of the most famous examples of the role of intuition and the unconscious in musical composition is the case of the Russian twentieth-century composer Igor Stravinsky (1882–1971) and his most celebrated work, *Le Sacre du Printemps* (*The Rite of Spring*) – a work so shocking and revelatory that it caused both sensation, uproar and a riot at its premiere in Paris in 1913. Stravinsky himself described the 'source' of *Le Sacre* thus:

> I had a fleeting vision which came to me *as a complete surprise*, my mind at that moment being full of other things. I saw in imagination a solemn pagan rite: sage elders, seated in a circle, watched a young

Figure 1.3 Igor Stravinsky in 1913, the 'vessel' through which *The Rite of Spring* passed. Photo Lebrecht and Co.

girl dance herself to death. They were sacrificing her to propitiate the god of spring.[52] (italics added)

Some years later the composer went on record (literally) to say that: 'Very little immediate tradition lies behind *Le Sacred du Printemps*, and *no* theory. I had only my ear to help me. I "heard", and I wrote what I heard. I am the vessel through which *Le Sacre du Printemps* passed'.[53] Subconscious, creative compositional processes were also significant in the methods of the English twentieth-century composer Benjamin Britten (1913–1976). One of Britten's collaborators, Eric Crozier, suggested that formal planning of a composition went on whilst Britten was asleep: 'He had considerable faith in the ability of his unconscious mind to solve daytime problems while he slept: perhaps for that reason his favourite reading before going to bed was poetry'. As well as understanding the wisdom of 'sleeping on a problem', other colleagues of Britten noted how he was disinclined to be analytical, and in fact resented analysis as a kind of 'prying'. He felt that there was a 'special secret' about composition and creative flow that would be spoiled by

Figure 1.4 Sir Michael Tippett, who felt that his art reflected elements of a collective unconscious. Photo by Nicky Johnston.

over-analysis. Like the poet T.S. Eliot who had practically finished his set of poems the *Four Quartets* before he had written a word on paper, Britten usually had the music complete in his mind before he put pencil to paper.[54]

In the 1970s transpersonal and humanistic psychologist Frances E. Vaughan argued that at any given moment a person can only be conscious of a small portion of what they know and that intuition allows not only to draw on this personal knowledge but also 'the infinite reservoir of the collective or universal consciousness, in which individual separateness and ego boundaries are transcended'.[55] These non-conscious mental processes and the idea of an intuitive supra-consciousness were important features of the personal psychology and the Jungian archetypes which underpinned the music and inspiration of another English composer, Sir Michael Tippett (1905–1998). In a talk for the BBC in the late 1950s Tippett remarked that intuition is way of accessing the 'infinite reservoir': 'I know that my art might form a tiny fragment of the great mirror in which we see our unconscious longings reflected as images that have the power to change us, and where we might go'.[56]

One of the most famous philosophers of science of the twentieth century Sir Karl Popper (1902–1994) argued that if we go back to more and more primitive theories and myths we shall in the end find 'unconscious, inborn expectations'.[57] Visual images such as cycles, geometric forms and motifs are also important in artistic, psycho-analytical and mystical interpretations of intuition. For example, Jung argued that a 'mándala'[58] with its basic motif of the disc or circle symbolizes a central point within the psyche (the 'in-side') and that this manifests itself 'out-side' in architecture, religious art, and other human artefacts.[59] There is a parallel with what the Oxford historian and Leonardo da Vinci scholar Martin Kemp refers to as 'structural intuitions'[60] which he describes as 'the recurrence of decorative motifs in very different civilisations, such as spiral formations,[61] polygonal patterns and diverse symmetries' which endure across ages, cultures and different modes of expression. For Kemp it is inevitable rather than surprising that human 'mental landscapes' across art and science should share these structural intuitions.

Figure 1.5 A mándala-like pattern. Such forms are often interpreted in Jungian terms as symbolizing the centre of the 'psyche'.

Intuition and insight in scientific discovery

Intuition (and its close companion insight) has played a vital role in scientific enquiry and discovery. Numerous scientists have testified to the deeper understandings that intuition can reveal. For example, Einstein is often quoted as saying that 'The really valuable thing is intuition'.[62] However, such intuitions do not appear 'out of the blue' as an unpremeditated and effortless spark of creativity or genius in an unprepared mind. Instead they are an outcome of extensive learning, effort, experience, the acquisition of deep knowledge structures and the development of high levels of expertise in a particular field of activity or domain of knowledge.[63] Einstein is a case in point supporting the importance of prior knowledge in intuitive judgement: 'My intuition was not strong enough in the field of mathematics . . . In [physics], however, I soon learned to scent out that which was to lead to fundamentals and to turn aside from everything else, from the multitude of things that clutter up the mind and divert it from the essential'.[64]

As well as extensive prior learning and experience as a necessary precondition for accurate intuition, visual images also have been known to play an important role in science as well as art. The inventor of the Polaroid camera, Edwin Land used 'fantasy' and visualization. Again, Einstein[65] is reputed to one day have been riding in a streetcar and in looking back at a clock tower imagined what would happen if the streetcar raced away from the clock tower at the speed of light. The realization came to him that the clock would appear stopped, since the light from it could not catch up to the streetcar; on the other hand his own clock in the streetcar would pulse normally. His realization, via this concrete image, that time passes at different rates depending on how fast an observer is moving contributed to the development of the theory of relativity. The Nobel prize-winning physicist Richard Feynman commented that Einstein may have in fact failed later to develop a unified field theory because he 'stopped thinking in concrete images'.[66] These and other accounts suggest that intuition has an imagistic, nonverbal (not expressible in words) or at least pre-verbal (not currently expressed verbally) quality.

Others who have pointed to the crucial role that intuition can play in science include Jonas Salk, the discoverer of the polio vaccine. He remarked that: 'Our subjective intuitional responses are more sensitive than our objective reasoned responses'. Moreover, he was of the view that intuition is 'trainable': 'Intuition is an innate quality but it can be developed and cultivated'.[67]

In the early stages of his career the French mathematician Henri

Poincaré (1854–1912) was a supreme mathematical analyst but later underwent something of a conversion. He moved towards an extreme intuitionist stance highlighting the importance of the progression from 'arduous work', leading to a 'compression of thought' and, once the 'scaffolding' is removed, the eventual 'intuitive grasp' that may be attained by a mathematical 'master-builder'.[68] Like many, Poincaré's accounts testify to the crucial importance of prior learning and experience in building an informed, as opposed to a naïve, intuition.

The role of intuition in business management

In the field of management Chester Barnard (1886–1961), AT&T executive and author of one of the most original and influential books on business administration, *The Functions of the Executive* (1938), championed what he described as the 'non-logical processes', and criticized the 'over-stressing' in business of logical processes (and the consequent inhibiting of intuition). Barnard was one of the first management thinkers to make the distinction between conventional logical analysis and 'the handling of a mass of experience or a complex of abstractions in a flash [i.e. intuition]'.[69] Moreover he makes the telling observation that managers would be unable to function effectively without intuition. For example an experienced accountant may rely upon her or his ability to:

> take a comparative balance sheet of considerable complexity and within minutes or even seconds get a significant set of facts from it. These facts do not leap from the paper and strike the eye. They lie *between* the figures and are the part filled in by the mind out of *years of experience and technical knowledge*. (italics added)[70]

Barnard is careful not to dismiss rationality, arguing three crucial points instead: first, neither logical (rational analytical) nor non-logical (intuitive) processes are infallible; second, both kinds together are better than either alone; third, that it is important for managers to be able to select the right mental process for the task; and finally, that managers should have the courage to follow their intuitions.[71] Since Barnard's original and ground-breaking work entrepreneurs, managers and management researchers, perhaps because of the strong connection to creativity, invention, innovation and strategic visioning, have shown and keen and burgeoning interest in the role of hunch and gut feeling in business.

Chester Barnard and Steve Jobs are generations apart. Jobs is the CEO of Apple which he founded in 1976 and is also the co-founder of Pixar Animation (*Toy Story, A Bug's Life, Finding Nemo*, etc). Like

Barnard, Jobs puts a very high premium on the value of intuition in business. In an address at Stanford University is 2005 he placed it at the heart of personal ambition and self-actualization:

> Your time is limited, so don't waste time living someone else's life. Don't be trapped by dogma – which is living the results of other people's thinking. Don't let the noise of other's opinions drown out your inner voice. And most important, have the courage to follow your heart and intuition. They somehow already know what you truly want to become. Everything else is secondary.[72]

Managers who have what Peter Senge refers to as a high levels of 'personal mastery' do not set out to integrate intuition and reason, they achieve it naturally, nor do they choose between intuition *or* rationality any more than they would choose to 'walk with one leg or see with one eye'.[73] Senge and his colleagues also argued that the rational model of decision-making, which is the norm in organizations, pays little attention to the inner state of the decision-maker and that that only by retreating and reflecting can an 'inner knowing'[74] emerge. Reg Revans, the pioneer of 'action learning' (an innovative training and development technique) and an immensely influential figure in management in the UK, once said that 'intuition, the unremembered urges of the past, must always be the first weapon of the manager, he must be able to grasp the underlying structures of situations that challenge him'.[75]

Intuition in the classroom

School teachers and college and university lecturers, like managers, doctors and other professionals, are members of a select occupational group who have unique access to specialized bodies of advanced learning or knowledge. Moreover, the professions are crucial to the effective functioning of society, whether it is through educating the next generation, curing diseases, ensuring the rule of law, or managing organizations.[76] Autonomy and judgement based upon learning and experience *in situ* are critical elements of professional practice which according to Donald Schön is characterized by ' "Situations of indeterminacy and value conflict" where decision-makers and problem solvers have to apply their knowledge and learning to "choose among multiple approaches to practice or devise [their] own way of combining them" '.[77] In both the UK and the USA the professional autonomy of groups such as teachers and lecturers has become more regulated and even challenged by a multiplicity of policy initiatives from state and national governments.

In education this manifests itself in external (usually governmental) controls on curriculum content and design, assessment strategies and processes, as well as the structural organization and management of schools and colleges.[78] This shift has been reflected in increasing systematization, standardization and bureaucratization – the role has become more 'technicized'. One outcome of this is an increasing discrepancy between how experienced teachers and lecturers take many of their decisions in the classroom or lecture hall (i.e. intuitively) and how they are being required, ostensibly at least, to engage in their day-to-day practice (i.e. analytically).

In response to these issues, and in particular the issues of standardization, rationality and external scrutiny of school teachers' professional judgement and autonomy, researchers in the USA explored the role that intuition actually played in the decision-making approaches of school principals. They found that over 90 per cent of principals in their sample almost always used intuition when making 'difficult decisions' in areas such as 'hiring and firing', dealing with conflicts and difficult situations with parents, and when trying to handle change policies and programmes.[79]

These situations are precisely the complex, contentious and ambiguous problem settings referred to by Donald Schön as the 'swampy lowland' of professional practice where the decision-maker is often confronted by a confusing 'mess' often incapable of being solved through by means of a purely technical solution.[80] The accounts of experienced practitioners suggest that these problems may prove more amenable to the skilful practices and intuitive processes which they are able to bring to situations of uncertainty, complexity and instability[81] and which often have to be solved immediately. Rather than relying solely upon intuition or rationality, experienced and effective educational decision-makers use intuition to support rationality, often to hone down multiple options into a manageable number that can actually be analysed in-depth.

Medical intuition

The clinical judgement exercised by healthcare professionals is another example of an area of practice in which it is difficult to account for effective performance in purely technical and rationalist terms. In medicine and healthcare, as in management and teaching, deliberative rational analysis and the application of rules and procedures without cognisance of the uniqueness of each case are more typical of the behaviour of a trainee. Novices cannot exercise informed intuition because they do not have the deep knowledge structures to fall back on, especially when called upon to make decisions under difficult, uncertain conditions or severe constraints. Experienced healthcare professionals, on the other hand, tend to respond to clinical judgements based upon previous experiences they have encountered with patients in the past[82] in subtle, context-dependent ways. However, the 'grooves' in our thinking etched by learning and past experience should not be followed 'blindly'; as the American educationalist John Dewey cautioned: 'Spontaneous intuitions . . . have to be entertained subject to correction, to confirmation and revision, by personal observation of consequences and cross-questioning of quality and scope'.[83]

In healthcare settings the interplay of knowledge, experience and expertise interact in complex ways with the personalities of the medical practitioner and the patient, and with the clinical setting. For example, research in Australia[84] revealed that many experienced nurses considered the establishment of a relationship with a patient to be crucial before they could make intuitive judgements about that person. Similarly, the clinical setting could itself set a positive or negative tone for intuition by either supporting or suppressing its use. Sometimes, under the right conditions the synergy between knowledge, experience, expertise, personality, patient relationship and environment may combine to produce the bodily (somatic) response termed by many nurses 'gut feeling', 'hunch' or 'sixth sense'.

Although these intuitive judgements appear to lack explicit conscious cognitive processes and are difficult to explain in an analytical way, it is likely that they are underlain by a number of key factors including pattern recognition, judging by similarity, spotting trends, and a keen but difficult to articulate sense of the importance of the clues which present themselves in the environment.[85] In informed intuition a holistic pattern recognition process operates in which the various elements in the 'constellation' of clues come together, are evaluated below the level of conscious awareness. They can suddenly 'pop' into conscious awareness as a bodily sense which may guide decision-making.

Intuition and insight in Buddhism

The concepts of insight and intuition are important in Buddhist teachings[86] in which the term *vipassana*[87] is used to describe a flash of insight heralding a sudden intuition of a 'truth'.[88] One route to such insights is via a process of meditation (mind training) in order to calm the mind,[89] practised over a long term and to the point at which intuition arises. Therefore, from the Buddhist perspective intuition may be seen as the outcome of a deliberate process engaged in through highly-disciplined meditation and founded upon the teachings of the Buddha ('the enlightened one') and the traditions of Buddhist practices.

The Tibetan word for Buddhist is *nangpa* meaning 'in-sider' (recall that the etymology of the English word 'intuition' is from the Latin to 'contemplate' or 'look inside'). *Nangpa* is a person who through teachings and trainings seeks truth within the 'single point' of the nature of the mind:[90]

> We are so addicted to looking outside ourselves that we have lost access to our inner being almost completely. We are terrified to look inward, because our culture has given us no idea of what we will find. We may even think that if we do we will be in danger of madness. This is one of the last and most resourceful ploys of the ego to prevent us discovering our true nature.

Buddhist practices employ the trained observation (through meditative contemplation) of the interplay between mind and bodily sensations.[91] The aim of meditation (of which there are many different kinds) is the quieting of an agitated and ever-discriminating conscious mind and the liberation of 'the intuitive mind'.[92] By attending to mental and physical sensations Buddhist insight practices enable experienced meditators to observe their own minds[93] and achieve an integration of mind (cognition) and body (including changes in feeling states). Vipassana (seeing things as they really are) is one of the most ancient techniques of meditation discovered by the Guatama Buddha over 2500 years ago and handed down through a chain of teachers since then.[94] A growing number of cognitive scientists (witness for example James Austin's huge tome, *Zen and the Brain*) acknowledge the insights that Buddhism has for their work, Francisco Varela and his colleagues have gone as far as to assert that the re-discovery of the Buddhist tradition is a 'second renaissance' in the cultural history of the West.[95]

Intuition and dreams

The notion of intuition as a form of 'inner wisdom' occurs in a variety of cultural settings. Dreams which bring forth intuitions are a feature of many traditional cultures (for example, Australian Aboriginals, the *So* people of north eastern Uganda, Tibetan lamas and Navajo healers[96]), and aspects of more recent 'New Age' cultures in the West have often absorbed and adapted these ancient teachings. In traditional societies such as the North American Indians, religious belief systems involve rituals in which incantation, fasting, isolation and other techniques are used as a means of inducing dreams, often with the mediation of a Shaman,[97] to facilitate various rites of passage for example, from childhood to adulthood. The imagery and symbolism which are generated in induced dreams are a means of accessing 'inner wisdom' which may be used as an indicator of various portents, including a person's life calling.[98] In Australian aboriginal culture *wiringins* ('medicine men' or 'clever men') have access to a body of esoteric and spiritual knowledge which gives them the ability to interpret dreams and make conscious use of their unconscious mind. Techniques of 'inner search' using mind-stilling and totems (usually of animals) are not unusual amongst Aborigines of modern-day Australia[99] for direction-finding and bush navigation, and obviating any need to rely on a conventional analytical system of reasoning.

In Western culture, as well as being an important element of the theories and practices of the influential Swiss psychologist and psychoanalyst Carl Gustav Jung (1875–1961), the interpretation of dreams and dream consciousness is offered by some as a way of tapping into an 'unconscious wisdom'. Much of this approach takes Jung's ideas as its foundation; for example, one of the pioneers of the resurgence of interest in intuition in the 1970s, Frances Vaughan, described dreams and their interpretation as 'a form of intuitive, non-rational experiential knowing'.[100] The rationale for this was based upon the argument that the 'voice' of the intuitive mind can be heard more clearly when the brain's 'logical thinking apparatus' (rational analysis) is 'shut down' (referred to by some as 'mind by-pass'[101] or 'giving your rational mind a reprieve'[102]). Vaughan and others argue that sleep is one occasion during which the intuitive voice can be heard and when insightful or 'intuitive messages'[103] may be received. Anecdotes from the history of the creative arts and scientific discovery add credence to this claim.

Researchers have recently postulated another reason for dream states: they evolved and were selected for in the evolution of *Homo sapiens* was because they provided the opportunity in a safe 'virtual' environment (the dream state) for what amounts to a mental rehearsal or simulation of a potentially threatening situation.[104] The beneficial effect of mental rehearsal also occurs outside the dream state, for example many stage performers and sports people (including one of the greatest golfers of all time – Jack Nicklaus) testify to the positive effects on performance of visually imagining the actions involved in a repetitive motor task[105] such as playing a stroke in golf. So it is with dreams. Since non-real information appears to be treated in similar ways to real information in the brain's visual cortex the activation thus induced provides 'exercise' and 'practice' for the neural pathways involved. Threat rehearsal may enhance an individual's capabilities to make effective decisions and predictions if confronted with the threat in a real situation. The 'dreams-as-threat-rehearsal' hypothesis has been challenged on the grounds that we do not always remember our dreams, thereby obviating any beneficial effects. However as has been argued many times, simply because we cannot recall something does not mean that it cannot exert an influence upon our behaviours.[106] It seems that 'dreams-as-intuitions' have generative (creative) and mental rehearsal (simulation) functions.

Magical intuition

The magical-paranormal perspective on intuition is nothing if not eclectic (covering areas as diverse as medical intuition and precognition). A view among a number of the magical-paranormal protagonists is of intuition as a special power akin to a species of precognition or clairvoyance. Intuition has been described as a 'knowing without precedent' which permits the accomplishment of feats ranging from the mundane (such as knowing the name of somebody you never met before, or knowing who's on the phone before it rings) to the impressive (such as engaging in 'remote viewing').[107] This has been given a specific label by some – 'psychic intuition'.[108] Others make more exacting and utilitarian claims for their powers; for example, some 'medical intuitives' declare that they can give accurate readings of a person's health based on no more information than a client's name and age.[109] The fictional detective Sherlock Holmes was able to make deductions which amazed his friends and enemies alike; Holmes put it down to a 'kind of intuition' the functioning of which he explained to his friend Dr. Watson thus:

HOLMES: You appeared to be surprised when I told you, on our first meeting, that you had come from Afghanistan.
WATSON: You were told, no doubt.
HOLMES: Nothing of the sort. I knew you came from Afghanistan. From long habit the train of thoughts ran so swiftly through my mind that I arrived at the conclusion without being conscious of intermediate steps. There were such steps, however. The train of reasoning ran:

'Here is a gentleman of a medical type, but with the air of a military man. Clearly an army doctor, then. He has just come from the tropics, for his face is dark, and that is not the natural tint of his skin, for his wrists are fair. He has undergone hardship and sickness, as his haggard face says clearly. His left arm has been injured. He holds it in a stiff and unnatural manner. Where in the tropics could an English army doctor have seen much hardship and got his arm wounded? Clearly in Afghanistan.'

The whole train of thought did not occupy a second. I then remarked that you came from Afghanistan, and you were astonished.[110]

'Cold reading' involves a process of deduction: looking for subtle clues in a subject's clothing, jewellery, physical appearance, demeanour, etc. and using these as the basis for observations.[111] Of course it is entirely feasible that many people engage in a skilful 'reading' of others intentions – a form of social intuition – without consciously realizing they are doing so. The fictional character of Holmes was a skilled exponent of a form of 'cold reading', and a similar technique is often used by television psychics. That said, coming to what seem to be accurate judgements about people need to involve anything so elaborate as a cold reading; for example, in the 'Forer effect' (named after the American psychologist B.R. Forer) people are known to exhibit a tendency to accept generalized descriptions which purport to be of them, in spite of the fact that the same description could apply to almost anyone else. It's a fact that people are prone to seeing vague and what turn out to be quite general personality descriptions as applicable to them, when in fact they could apply to just about anyone.[112]

The possibility of extra-sensory perception (ESP) as a means of intuitively predicting future events was investigated in the UK by psychologists Richard Wiseman and Emma Greening. Using a computer-based device called 'The Mind Machine' which toured public venues all over the UK, volunteer participants were asked to complete ESP tasks configured as precognition or clairvoyance[113] which involved predicting the outcome of four randomly generated electronic 'coin tosses'. The fact that the size of the sample was very large (over 27,000 members of the public took part) meant that even small ESP effects if they existed stood a very good chance of being detected. Participants correctly guessed the outcome of the coin toss in 49.9 per cent of the 110,959 tosses. In other words there was no evidence of ESP; the results were entirely consistent with chance prediction. Believers in the paranormal tend to attribute what appear to be remarkable coincidences ('the phone rang and it was Sarah, just as I was expecting her to call me!') to paranormal causes rather than chance.[114]

Regrettably, a magical-paranormal perspective of intuition has a number of difficulties. The first of these is in relation to the scientific method:

the magical-paranormal view is likely to be generally perceived as unscientific (as opposed to non-scientific) and therefore it has a credibility gap to bridge before its claims will be taken seriously by psychologists and management researchers. This is an issue that the proponents of the magical view must address, and the struggle is likely to be an uphill one. A second major difficulty lies in the infallibility that is sometimes attributed to intuition. It is sometimes recommended that we ignore intuition ('the language of the soul'[115]) at our peril.[116] However, scrutiny of the ways in which successful business people, for instance, have used their intuitions (i.e. in concert with rationality) would suggest that even successful 'intuiters' do not presume its infallibility. As we shall see, effective decision-makers and problem-solvers in business and other settings often switch between, and integrate, intuition and analysis, for example by using intuition to sift through the range of available options and sort the 'wheat from the chaff'. Shrewd business people are unlikely to place and exclusive reliance upon intuition or analysis, given that neither is utterly infallible.

INFORMED INTUITION AND THE BIOLOGICAL ALARM BELL

Intuitive judgements arise spontaneously and rapidly, and are accompanied by feelings of certitude so much so that some critics have remarked, perhaps acerbically, that intuition is 'sometimes wrong but never in doubt'.[117] Our capability to successfully intuit in a professional decision-making context depends upon significant and substantial prior learning and experience in that context (it is a capability that is context- or *domain-specific*). Anyone can make a guess on any topic, but to be able to make 'smart guesses' a number of conditions need to be in place; principal amongst these is the necessary expertise. 'Mental models' of people, objects and situations are developed as result of experience and learning, and these enable decision-makers to quickly 'weigh-up' situations, run 'mental simulations', make predictions and take decisions.[118] Even if the 'hardware' (the neural circuitry) is in place the 'simulation' cannot run without the necessary structure being built-up or the necessary data being in place –successful intuitive judgements are based on *informed intuition*.

A corollary of this is that it's much more risky and difficult to make intuitive judgements in areas where we lack expertise (i.e. where the basis of the mental model – its structure and data – is not robust). For example, I as someone with no knowledge of the stock market could guess, but I could not intuit, what a particular company's share price will do over the next few days or weeks. However, as someone with considerable knowledge of the history and behaviours of my relatives and close friends I could in all probability intuit their behaviours with a much greater degree of accuracy, but without necessarily being able to explain how I can make such predictions. By 'weighing up' the situation and running a 'mental simulation' I could judge whether or not certain actions or behaviours might be consonant with the mental model that I hold of my family members or friends and their likely behaviours.[119] My prior analyses are held as a large number of patterns that enable me to 'weigh up and predict'. This does not prevent me being surprised by behaviours on their part that do not fit with any of the large repertoire of patterns I hold or are not predicted by the current model of them that I hold. Our mental models are approximations and rarely are they unerring in their fidelity. *Intuition is not infallible.*

The idea of 'informed intuition' is based in large part on an information processing view for example, as a manifestation of the 'compression' of lots of relevant experiences and prior analyses[120] and stored on the 'hard disk' (long term memory) of a 'biological computer' (the brain) ready to be uploaded and be processed as the situation demands. The cognitive view is useful, but is only a partial view of intuition. But as we have seen intuition is synonymous in many languages and cultures with bodily signals ('hunches' or 'gut feelings'), and the accounts that people give of their intuitions often feature a bodily (somatic) component. Neurologists have identified a specific region of the brain's frontal lobe as being implicated in the somatic component of decision-making, and when the functioning of this part of the brain is compromised through damage or disease the individual concerned may experience significant difficulty in making effective decisions. They may be frozen into indecisiveness by 'analysis paralysis', or be capricious and inconsistent in their decision-making. This research, which will be examined in more detail in Chapter 9, has identified a complex set of neural mechanisms which operate below the level of conscious awareness and which serve as a biological 'alarm bell'. Feeling (or 'affect') manifests itself in our conscious awareness as a bodily signal,[121] commonly referred to as 'gut instinct'. It forces our attention on how undesirable or desirable a potential outcome is. The great leap in understanding which comes from this very significant body research is that feeling (Shelley's 'wingèd passions'), as well as learning, knowledge, experience and expertise, is an essential component of human decision-making, and that this has a neurological basis.

DEFINING INTUITION

Intuition is at the crossroads of thinking and feeling – the nexus of cognition and affect. So how might it be defined?

1   *As expertise?* Cognitive science and decision theory describe it in terms of a manifestation of learning, expertise or tacit knowledge (the Nobel Prize winner Herbert Simon referred to this as 'analyses frozen into habit'). Certainly intuition draws upon thinking processes which are largely non-conscious, but there's more to it.

2   *As feeling or 'affect'?* Social psychology and neuroscience emphasize its emotional aspects (the role of 'gut feeling'). Intuition is undoubtedly a manifestation of bodily processes which are activated below the level of conscious awareness (and which involve recognition processes based on prior learning and habit) that appear in conscious awareness as a feeling state.

3   *As a mental simulation?* Intuition can be the basis for 'a window into a possible future' that operates in conscious awareness as a 'DVD-in-the-head' – we can fastforward particular scenarios and gauge how we feel about certain outcomes or their likelihood (but the rules by which we arrive at these feelings or judgements may remain unclear).

4   *As instinct?* Not really – in the rhetoric of the business world intuition has been loosely described as a 'management instinct'.[122] Daniel Cappon has described intuition as a coalescence of ancestral instincts and adaptive behaviours,[123] nevertheless in an area that has a surfeit of 'Is' (insight, instinct, intelligence, impulse, implicit, intuition, etc.) it's probably simpler to confine the term 'instinct' to biological reflex actions and other uncontrolled behaviours of this type.

5   *As insight?* No – the terms 'insight' and 'intuition' tend to occur in similar contexts, sometimes are equated, and are often used interchangeably (a 'solution that appears all-at-once'[124]), however, as we shall see in Chapter 3 they are by no means synonymous;[125]

6   *As ESP?* Some accounts depict intuition as shrouded in a 'magical' aura with connotations of the paranormal and the precognition. The scientific explanations of intuition which have emerged recently are not only simpler and easier to comprehend than magical explanations they also, arguably, make them redundant.

So how may intuition be defined? Intuition is:

Table 1.1 The three Is: instinct, insight and intuition. Definition of intuition.

Instinct	Automatically reacting in a relatively fixed way to a stimulus in ways that have an innate biological, reflexive origin.
Insight	Seeing the solution to a specific problem and being able to verbalize or otherwise articulate this knowledge – for example, having an 'aha' experience or a 'eureka moment' often after reaching an *impasse* and a period of incubation away from the problem.
Intuition	An involuntary, difficult-to-articulate, affect-laden recognition or judgement, based upon prior learning and experiences, which is arrived at rapidly, through holistic associations and without deliberative or conscious rational thought.

Source: Adapted from E.I. Dane and M.G. Pratt, 'Exploring intuition and its role in managerial decision-making', *Academy of Management Review*, 2007, 32(1).

1 an involuntary, difficult-to-articulate, affect-laden recognition or judgement based upon prior knowledge which appears to be ubiquitous across languages, cultures and human history;
2 arrived at rapidly, through holistic associations and without deliberative or conscious rational thought;[126]
3 part of *Homo sapiens* evolutionary inheritance and is a product of cognitive systems and processes that most likely evolved in the human animal before rational analytical systems emerged.

When exercised in an informed way, intuition is a powerful mechanism for arriving at judgments and taking decisions in uncertain and time-pressured situations, but equally, is potentially perilous if exercised indiscriminately and in an uninformed way. This book is not advocacy for 'gut feeling'. Neither intuition nor rationality for that matter should be employed exclusively or indiscriminately – both are needed. Which begs the question: 'when to use intuition?' The answer to this depends on the features of the decision and the context in which it is to be taken (i.e. whether or not it lends itself to an intuitive judgement) and the prior knowledge and experience of the decision-maker (i.e. the extent to which she or he is able to exercise informed intuition). Life and business opportunities may be squandered or missed if intuitions are overlooked, ignored or practised covertly in an uneducated fashion. Moreover, when – not if – a decision-maker encounters a situation where rational analysis is inappropriate, ineffective or impossible, informed intuitive judgement presents a viable alternative to paralysis-by-analysis, 'groping in the dark', or passive inaction.

TAKE-AWAYS FOR CHAPTER 1

Key ideas

The English word 'intuition' comes from the Latin *intueri* which is often roughly translated as meaning 'to look inside' or 'to contemplate'. Intuition occupies a *border state* between thoughts and feelings, and between the conscious and unconscious mind. Intuitions recur across art and science, across ages and cultures, and across a spectrum of social settings, both personal and professional. An intuition, according to Erik Dane and Mike Pratt, is a rapid, involuntary, *affect-laden judgement* that is arrived at through holistic pattern recognition without deliberative or conscious rational thought.[127] *Informed intuition* built up through time, learning and experience is a powerful mechanism for arriving at judgments and taking decisions in uncertain and time-pressured situations.

Intuition quote: Robert M. Pirsig, author of *Zen and the Art of Motorcycle Maintenance* (1974)

'Traditional scientific method has always been at the very *best* 20–20 hindsight. It's good for seeing where you've been. It's good for testing the truth of what you think you know, but it can't tell you where you *ought* to go. Creativity, originality, inventiveness, intuition, imagination – "un-stuckness", in other words – are completely outside its domain.'

Action point

The first, most decisive and most important step on 'tuning-in' to intuition is *paying attention*. Improved attentiveness to 'gut feeling' and 'hunch' starts with conscious observations of sensations in the 'body landscape'. 'Action point #1' is to introspect and reflect on the basis of this question: 'what happens when *you* intuit?'[128]

FURTHER READING

Gladwell, M., *Blink: The Power of Thinking Without Thinking*. London: Allen Lane 2005.
Vaughan, F.E., *Awakening Intuition*. New York: Doubleday 1979.

2 Analysis paralysis

Humpty Dumpty sat on the wall;
Humpty Dumpty had a great fall.
All the King's horses and all the King's men
Couldn't put Humpty together again.

(*Mother Goose Rhymes*)

MAIN IDEA

Rationality is not omnipotent either in management decision-making or other areas of personal and professional life. Thinkers and researchers in business and management from the 1930s onwards have come to recognize increasingly rationality's limits and role that feelings play in decision-making. More recently decision researchers, social psychologists, cognitive scientists, neurologists and others have provided compelling scientific evidence why this should be so.

Charles Darwin was indisputably an impeccably accurate observer and data recorder,[1] who as an ever practical man in the highly competitive and entrepreneurial environment of Victorian England, thought of the living world as if it was a financial 'balance sheet'.[2] As a result of his logical, analytical mentality Darwin often produced lists of attributes of things to help him clarify his thinking and make decisions. For example, he wrote out a reasoned list of the attributes his father raised in objection to his Voyage on the *HMS Beagle* ('accommodations uncomfortable', 'a wild scheme' and so forth). He adopted a similar approach in identifying the attributes of whether to marry or not. In 1838 at the age of 29 he constructed a balance sheet for this important reasoning and decision-making task. On a piece of paper headed 'This is the question' he produced a list of multiple attributes 'for' marriage on the left hand side and multiple attributes 'against' marriage on the right hand side, noting such things as:

> Marry: children; constant companion; home; charms of music and female 'chit-chat'; nice soft wife on a sofa with good fire and books, and music perhaps;
>
> Not Marry: Freedom to go where one liked; conversation of clever men at clubs; not forced to visit relatives; expense and anxiety of children; loss of time.[3]

After weighing up the advantages and disadvantages the attributes of 'Marry' outweighed those of 'Not Marry', and Darwin's final written remarks were: 'Marry – Marry – Marry Q.E.D[4] and he shortly afterwards married his first cousin, Emma Wedgwood, in 1839.

Benjamin Franklin (1706–1790) adopted a similar multiple attribute

Figure 2.1 Charles Darwin.

decision-making approach but was more sophisticated in this respect than Darwin; in a letter to Joseph Priestley he advocated factoring in the worth or 'utility' of each identified attribute:

Divide half a sheet of paper by a line into two columns; writing over the one *Pro*, and over the other *Con*. Then, during three or four days consideration . . . when I have got them all together in one view I endeavour to estimate their respective weights . . . and though the weights or reasons cannot be taken with the precision of algebraic quantities when . . . the whole lies before me I think I can judge better and am less liable to make a rash step[5]

By identifying the 'pros' and the 'cons', Darwin and Franklin were exercising a reasoned, analytical method to aid their decision-making.

THE RATIONAL PRACTITIONER

The rational decision model which managers are taught, trained or learn by trial and error is based on the process of establishing the parameters of the problem and its potential solution, assembling the necessary data, and reasoning the decision through by a process of analysis. For example, a rationalist view of consumer behaviour would suggest that potential buyers identify multiple attributes of products in making purchasing decisions. When buying convenience foods a consumer might identify cost, nutritional value and anticipated satisfaction as attributes relevant to their decision.[6] When selecting a holiday the likely weather, suitability of available accommodation, the range of cultural attractions, anticipated exchange rates, and distance to travel might figure as attributes to compare alternative destinations. Curiously, feeling doesn't seem to figure. There are many different approaches to rational choice, but most of them are variations on a basic theme[7] in which a decision is a reasoned choice made from the available alternatives on the basis of analysis. By following a rational choice model a decision-maker aims to select an alternative from those with which they are faced via a logical sequence of steps with the aim of optimizing outcomes.[8]

Breaking down a decision into its component parts allows for the identification of the foreseeable courses of action, the events that might flow from these, the likelihoods for each event (in technical terminology their 'subjective probabilities', P) and the 'worth' or 'value' of each event to the decision-maker (its 'utility', U). The components may be mapped

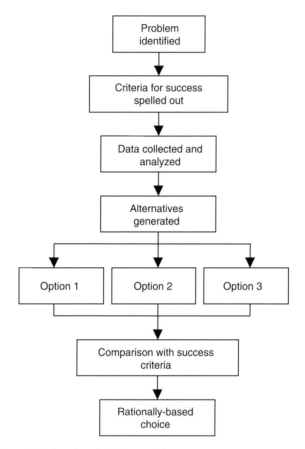

Figure 2.2 A rational choice model.

out as a decision tree and the outcomes (as subjective expected utilities) for alternative actions calculated[9] to give an objective quantified summary statement. The result is a 'bottom-line' figure along similar lines to those suggested by Benjamin Franklin to his friends. The results appear not only objective and unambiguous, they look impressive too.

Undoubtedly, the rational choice model has many attractive features, including:

1   *Consistency*: It allows for consistency of decision-making (i.e. it is repeatable);
2   *Generality*: It is a general decision aid (i.e. it can be applied across many different situations);

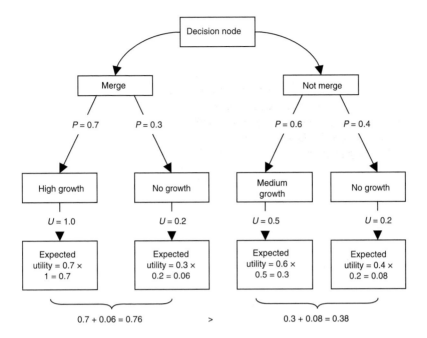

Figure 2.3 An example of a decision tree for company merger decision.
Adapted from H.R. Arkes and K.R. Hammond (eds), *Judgement and Decision-making: An Interdisciplinary Reader* (Cambridge: Cambridge University Press, 1958) p. 6.

Notes: P = probability associated with outcome, e.g. 'merge' has a 0.3 probability of resulting in no growth; U = utility to company of each outcome, e.g. 'medium growth' is 'worth' 0.5; high growth is 'worth' 1.0 (the maximum); and no growth has a low utility of 0.2 (the minimum would be zero). The sum of the expected utilities for the decision 'merge' are (0.7 + 0.06 = 0.76) and are greater than the sum of the expected utilities for the decision 'not merge' (0.3 + 0.08 = 0.38). Other outcomes (and their associated utilities) of 'merge' and 'not merge' are left out for the sake of clarity.

3   *Training*: It helps novices to learn how to solve problems and make decisions (i.e. it is a rigorous training tool);[10]
4   *Transparency*: It forces the decision maker to make explicit the bases for a decision (i.e. is open to scrutiny and can be verbalized).[11]

However, one problem that's often encountered with rational models such as the decision tree is the difficulty and subjectivity involved, not in the decision process itself, but in the design of the model. As the decision researchers Hal Arkes and Kenneth Hammond noted, subjective probabilities and utilities are often not easy to assess, and because the usefulness of a decision tree is based in large part on the accuracy of probabilities and utilities it is really important that good estimates for these are obtained.[12] And where do these come from? Usually from experts' judgements. There's a further complication: as well as being dependent upon the judgement of experts for the accurate design of decision aids, the rational choice model also makes a number of assumptions (see Table 2.1). Contrast this with reality of organizational life. Managers' and other professionals' roles are often concerned with taking decisions to ensure the smooth and efficient running of modern, technologically complex, organizations operating in dynamic and difficult-to-predict economic, social and political environments. Common responses to deal with sluggish decision-making are 'change the structure', 'change the culture', or 'change the people', but rarely 'change the mindset'. Organizational culture (sometimes defined as 'the way we do things around here') is based in large part upon unwritten norms and expectations of how decision-makers ought to behave. Against this backcloth managers and other professional groups are empowered with authority which stems from the organization they work for (firms, hospitals, schools and so forth), from institutions (governments, professional bodies, etc.) or from society itself to take decisions.

Table 2.1 Features, assumptions and problems of the rational approach

Feature	Assumption	Problem
Quantifiable data	Data which are needed to make the decision actually exist in a tangible and, ideally, quantifiable form	Data may be in short supply
Outcome prediction	Outcome is such that it can be envisaged and predicted	Outcomes may be unknown and unpredictable, but nevertheless are worthy of being, or have to be, pursued
Sufficient time	Decision-maker has the luxury of the necessary time to go through a sequential process in order to optimize the outcome	Pressure in the real world may be to act decisively
Mental capacity	Human decision-makers have brains that are capable of performing the necessary analyses objectively and within the required timescales	Perceptually and computationally they may be unable to do at all or in the timescale

Naturally, in a rationalist world the cultural expectation is that, as a trusted professional group, managers will exercise unemotional, impersonal and objective logic – since the cultural perception is that rational analysis is a safe way to make effective decisions. As a result managers and professional groups may feel compelled by the expectations of their peers, organizations and society at large to reason analytically and to be accountable in rational terms. But such high expectations can create tensions, which may be asking too much. For example, what if:

1 in reality decisions taken are not, or cannot be, based squarely upon rational analysis?

2 rational analysis is an inappropriate or insufficient tool for the problems being faced for example where a creative solution is required?

3 feelings exert as strong, if not a stronger, hold upon decision-making than does rational analysis?

4 the problem is too complex, ambiguous, uncertain or time pressured for a detailed, time-consuming, calculative approach?

In many business organizations to go 'against the grain' of the rational decision model might, for many managers especially at junior and middle levels, be greeted with the surprise, disdain and even alarm of their colleagues and bosses. But if we look across at medicine the problem faced in justifying management decisions on 'gut feeling' are similar to those that a nurse might have in trying to get a doctor out of bed in the middle of the night to attend to a sick patient on the grounds that they felt that the patient 'just wasn't quite right for some reason'. Would it happen? Not always, but the fact is that many such judgements are reached by intuition.[13] In midwifery for example the 'gut feeling' of an experienced and empathetic midwife may often turn out to be the basis of an accurate judgement:[14]

> Many [midwives] told us that the trick, each time their inner voice speaks, is how to know whether or not it is a real intuition, and the struggle is to learn the difference between the inner doubt and debate that accompanies ratiocinative[15] thinking [the process of reasoning], and the true voice of intuition

In the early days of nursing intuition was played down on the basis that only the 'rational, scientific and objective mind' was valid as a form of reasoning in medical practice.[16] This situation has changed to the extent that in nursing and other aspects of clinical decision-making the 'gut feeling' of an experienced professional is an important component of judgement[17] and has its place alongside the tools and techniques of medical diagnosis and treatment. Professor of Primary Health Care, Trisha Greenhalgh, in addressing the UK's Royal College of General Practitioners summarized the position when she declared that: 'Intuition is not unscientific. It is a highly creative process, fundamental to hypothesis generation in science. The experienced practitioner should generate and follow clinical hunches as well as (not instead of) applying the deductive principles of evidence-based medicine.'[18]

In support of this view she cited the case of a general practitioner (GP) who got a call from a mother saying that her three-year-old daughter had had diarrhoea and was behaving strangely. The doctor knew the family well, and was concerned enough to break off his morning surgery and visit the child immediately. It was extremely fortunate that he did so: the GP's hunch led him, on the basis of nothing more than two non-specific symptoms reported over the telephone, to diagnose correctly, and treat successfully, a case of meningococcal meningitis.

RATIONALITY RE-CONSIDERED

The rational choice model of decision-making is justified on a number of grounds[19] including the following:

1   *Managers are rational*: managers and other professionals are inherently rational decision-makers who seek to maximize outcomes.

2   *Business environments are knowable*: the business environments in which managers make their decisions are objective entities.

3   *Planning guarantees success*: successful plans and strategies are the products of deliberate planning.

What does this mean in practice? Well, taken to its extreme it could be taken to mean that: first, 'more is better' – the more 'hard' facts and figures that are to hand the better; second, 'factor-out feelings' – managers gain approval when they don't debase 'cool and calm' strategic thinking with feelings; third, 'subjugate emotion' – logical thinking and rational behaviours must be called upon to subdue emotions whenever they intrude. In other words, good organizations manage employees' feelings (for example, with employee assistance programmes or counselling), or design them out of the decision-making process as much as possible by using flowcharts, algorithms and computer-based modelling for decision-making.[20] These assumptions are open to challenge because in the real world they raise at least three potential difficulties:

1   *Consensus on goals*: being exclusively rational requires agreement about goals and their relative priority, since this will determine what information should be collected, how it should be analyzed and how outcomes will be judged. However, important goals are rarely un-contentious; from the Cabinet room and boardroom to the factory floor battles and 'turf wars' are a fact of political, organizational and working life.

2   *Cause and effect relationships*: being overt and unambiguous about cause and effect relationships is also important since this will aid planning, prediction and control and the ability to manage future actions and their outcomes. However, uncertainty and ambiguity are all too often the order of the day, and debates about cause and effect can rumble on for weeks, months and years. There is the old joke that when Mao Tse Tung was asked what he thought had been the effects of the French Revolution he replied that 'it was too early to tell'!

3   *Passion and reason*: There is an inherent and culturally-biased assumption in many organizations that data are more 'valuable' when they are explicit, untainted by feelings, i.e. when they are 'hard', and open to conscious thought and introspection, i.e. when they are explicit. Human cognition is infused with affect and reason can, whether we like it or not, be a 'slave to the passions',[21] added to which we also know a lot more than we actually choose or are able to tell.

Rationality is not omnipotent – it has its limits, and decision-makers' behaviours, and their power, are 'fenced in' (bounded) by these limits. The limits of rationality, the use of cognitive shortcuts in decision-making, the role of intuition and emotions and the underlying biological and neuro-physiological mechanisms have been discussed, analyzed and critiqued from the early decades of the twentieth century to the present day by writers, researchers and scholars, including at least one Nobel Prize winner. The remainder of this chapter will explore the seminal contributions made to our understanding of the limitations of rationality and the importance of intuitive judgement by five key thinkers – Chester Barnard, Herbert Simon, Donald Schön, Gary Klein and Antonio Damasio.

CHESTER I. BARNARD: THE ROLE OF NON-LOGICAL PROCESSES IN BUSINESS MANAGEMENT

Chester Barnard (1886–1961) worked for nearly forty years in the American Telegraph and Telephone Company (AT&T), where he began his career as an employee in their statistical department and rose to the presidency of the New Jersey Bell Telephone Company. Barnard's most famous book was *The Functions of the Executive* published by Harvard University Press in 1938. The significant event in Barnard's career as far as the study of intuition is concerned occurred on 10 March, 1936 when he gave the Cyrus Fogg Brackett lecture to the Engineering Faculty and Students at Princeton University.

Figure 2.4 Chester I. Barnard (President of New Jersey Bell).
Photo courtesy of AT&T Archives and History Center.

It is in the content of this lecture,[22] entitled inauspiciously 'The mind in everyday affairs', where we find some of Barnard's most original and thought-provoking writing on what he termed the 'non-logical processes' in management. Barnard was writing in the wake of classical 'scientific management' as espoused by Frederick W. Taylor and others, but Barnard lies within a more 'humanistic' tradition in management and organization theory.[23] The starting point of his lecture was a discussion of two difficulties that he personally experienced in the workplace: one was the adjustment to a new kind of work or new position; the second was attaining mutual understanding between persons or groups. His great insight, given that the prevailing orthodoxy in the psychology of the time was behaviourism,[24] was to attribute both of these difficulties to differences in mental processes (he called it 'the way the mind works'). With great insight Barnard subdivided mental processes into two groups – logical and non-logical (see Figure 2.5).

1   *Logical mental processes*: he described this as conscious thinking expressible in words or other symbols. In Barnard's view this mental process is a major characteristic of the work of a mathematician or an 'exact scientist', but is not evident in high pressure tasks or in the work of 'businessmen [*sic*] or executives'.[25]

2   *Non-logical mental processes*: these, on the other hand, are not capable of being expressed in words because they are so unconscious, complex and rapid that they cannot be analyzed by the person within whose brain they take place. He attributed their sources to unspecified 'physiological' conditions and other (unspecified) factors in the physical or social environment. Barnard's view was that the knowledge which underlies the non-logical is impressed upon us non-consciously or without conscious effort and that the potential harmfulness of logical processes lies in their misuse and in the 'knock-on' effect on the non-logical processes (i.e. their deprecation).

Barnard made a direct reference to intuition in his writings defining it as 'the handling of a mass of experience or a complex of abstractions in a flash'.[26] He went further and cited at length an illuminating description of intuition from the 1930 edition of the *Encyclopaedia Britannica*:

> It consists of a vague feeling, or intuition, that certain things are relevant and others are not. This feeling 'in our marrow' is probably an outcome of previous experience that has not yet emerged into articulate thought. Its very vagueness shields it from critical scrutiny.

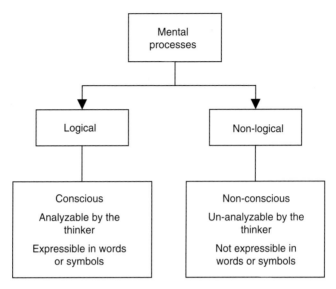

Figure 2.5 Barnard's distinction between two different types of mental process.

He also speculated on the distinction between the types of mental processes required in different job types. For example, for the scientist, mastery of logical reasoning especially mathematical reasoning is essential, but 'able and great' scientists also possess non-logical and highly intuitional mental processes (this view concurs with many of the anecdotes from the history of scientific discovery as we shall see in Chapter 3). Barnard argued that paradoxically, it is logical reasoning processes which can be disadvantageous for senior managers if they are not in subordination to highly developed intuitional processes. In what he termed the 'world of affairs' (what we would call business and management) a decision often has to be made quickly 'on the spot' – the practical necessities of this demand the use of the rapid intuitional, non-logical processes by experienced decision-makers. He concluded his lecture with a plea for greater recognition of the importance of the non-logical processes and their accompanying 'inspirational' mental energy and enthusiasm, and the dismantling of the intellectual 'snobbishness' that surrounds the logical processes (see Box 2.1).

Barnard was a practitioner rather than a scholar (a fact that adds weight to, rather than detracts from, his insights), and he appealed to the biology and psychology of his day as a basis for his explanations which are remarkably ahead of their time. He was one of the first management

---

Box 2.1

Nor should non-logical processes, even when they are the only kind really possible, be confused with snap judgement. Most people whose judgement I respect take plenty of time on major problems and make time if possible. They do not decide until it is necessary to do so. They 'think it over' carefully but not necessarily logically. What I have tried to emphasise is the insufficiency of logical processes for many purposes and conditions and the desirability of the development in intelligent coordination with the on-logical, the intuitional, even inspirational processes, which manifest mental.energy and enthusiasm. This is by no means easy. To rely upon 'feeling', to give weight to first impressions, to reject logical conclusions and meticulous analysis in favour of an embracing sense of the whole, involves an inconsistency of attitudes. It means developing the artistic principle in the use of the mind, attaining proportion between speed and caution, between broad outlines and fineness of detail, between solidity and flexibility. As in other arts, the perfection of subsidiary techniques and their effective combination both require constant practice.

That the increasing complexity of society and the elaboration of technique and organisation now necessary will more and more require capacity for rigorous reasoning is evident; but it is a superstructure necessitating a better use of the non-logical mind to support it. 'Brains' without 'minds' seem a futile unbalance.

Source: Chester Barnard, *The Functions of the Executive* (Cambridge, MA: Harvard University Press, 1938/1968) p. 322.

---

writers to articulate what intuition is, to speculate upon its nature and origins and upon the circumstances and particular job roles in which it is relevant. Moreover, in his writing we see the calling into question of the pre-eminence of analytical reasoning and a plea for the logical (analysis) and the non-logical (intuitive) to be placed on an equal footing.

Perhaps most remarkable of all is that these deliberations on the logical versus non-logical mental processes were at a comparatively early stage in the history of management as a field of professional practice and academic study. In one sense, for writers such as Barnard, perhaps intuition had an essence which meant that it spoke to his keen common sense and that in itself it had an intuitive appeal which endowed it with a normative[27] quality. Barnard's writings set the scene for much of the subsequent work by the next generation of researchers who explored, through a programme of rigorous scientific investigation, the limitations of the logical (rational analytical) processes and the potential of the non-logical (intuitional) processes.

HERBERT A. SIMON: BOUNDED RATIONALITY

In our exploration of intuition we will meet several Nobel prize winners, the first of these is Herbert Simon (1916–2001), a towering intellectual figure who has had a major impact in several fields of research, scholarship and practice, including cognitive psychology, computer science, artificial intelligence (AI), economics and public administration. Much of his work was devoted to the 'de-mystification' of human thinking and decision-making;[28] indeed his motto in relation to human thinking might be 'wonderful but not incomprehensible'.[29] In the field of business administration he is most famous for his work on decision-making processes in organizations, for which he was awarded the Nobel Prize in 1978. There is continuity with Barnard's work: *The Mind in Everyday Affairs* is acknowledged explicitly by Simon as offering a persuasive account, and Barnard wrote the Preface to Simon's most famous and enduring decision-research book – *Administrative Behavior: A Study of Decision-making Processes in Administrative Organization* (1945). From the perspective of an understanding of intuition, Simon's writings have two related facets which have had a profound effect upon the way the subsequent generation of researchers have thought about decision-making: first, the notion of the limits of rationality, i.e. that rationality is 'bounded'; and second, the role of intuition and emotion in management decision-making, i.e. to 'discover the reason that underlies unreason'.[30]

Bounded rationality

To be perfectly rational within the rational choice models which were discussed earlier in this chapter would be to behave in such a way that one's pursuit of rationality knew no bounds:

- The search for complete information would need to go on indefinitely.
- The consequent demands upon the brain's information processing

resources and time would be insatiable (in a sense rationality would be 'unbounded').

Clearly this is impossible. Herbert Simon (and others at the time including James March) recognized that organizations can never be perfectly rational since managers' choices are always exercised with respect to a limited, approximated and simplified model of reality.[31] By asserting that in the real world human behaviour is *intendedly* rational but only *boundedly so*, Simon's work endeavoured to place psychology rather than economics at the heart of a theory of organization.

A key concept in bounded rationality is 'satisficing'. Satisficing behaviour involves approaching a problem or decision by setting an aspiration level, searching until an alternative is found that is satisfactory by the aspiration level criterion and then selecting the alternative which emerges.[32] An example of satisficing is a manager selecting from a large group of applicants the first employee to be interviewed who meets the basic requirements for the job and thereby truncating further

Figure 2.6 Herbert Simon (1916–2001). Copyright The Nobel Foundation (reproduced by permission).

search at that point. By taking the first candidate who meets the aspiration level in terms of experience and qualifications a manager would be taking the alternative that is at least as good as the cut-off value (the aspiration level). Better candidates may have come along later but the approach was to take the one who met a threshold level rather than some ideal maximal level[33].

We live in a highly complex and dynamic world and given the limitations of conscious thought relative to the complexity of our environment it is unsurprising that human behaviour is in most cases restricted to satisficing. Rationality is therefore bounded by the complexity of the world we live in relative to our cognitive abilities. Managers ('administrators'), unlike an unboundedly rational 'economic man' (*Homo economicus*), settle for satisficing because in Simon's words human beings 'do not have the wits to maximize'.[34]

Individuals and organizations of which they are a part settle for a world of bounded rationality in which managers adopt satsificing behaviours (resulting in performance that is considered acceptable rather than maximal) on the basis of what is 'good enough', but in

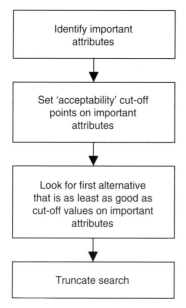

Figure 2.7 Satisficing.

Source: R. Hastie and R.M. Dawes, *Rational Choice in an Uncertain World: The Psychology of Judgement and Decision-making* (Thousand Oaks, CA: Sage, 2001) p. 233.

Table 2.2 'Administrative man'-versus-'Economic man'

Administrative man	Economic man
Satisfices	Maximizes
Looks for course of action that is 'good enough' (for example: reasonable profit, fair price, etc.)	Selects 'best' alternative from those available
Recognizes that the perceived world is a drastically simplified model of reality	Deals with the 'real world' in all its complexity
Seeks simplification	Seeks fidelity
Recognizes limits imposed by cognitive demands	Assumes cognitive demands do not impose limits

Source: H.A. Simon, *Administrative Behavior: A Study of Decision-making Processes in Administrative Organisations* (4th edn) (New York: The Free Press, 1997).

doing so run the risk of overlooking better options[35] and also being open to sources of bias. Satisficing reduces the cognitive demands placed upon the decision-maker's scarce mental resources and results in a solution that is reasonably acceptable under the circumstances in which the decision-maker is working.[36]

The role of intuition and emotions in management decision-making

Simon was somewhat troubled by Barnard's work because it did not give any clues as to what subconscious processes go on while judgements are being made. In spite of this he (Simon) was convinced that a theory of decision-making was needed which gave an account both of the conscious and non-conscious processes. Simon invoked the notion of expertise as a means to understand the way in which intuition works. Indeed one of his most famous quotations is that: 'Intuition and judgement – at least good judgement – are simply analyses frozen into habit and the capacity for rapid response through recognition'.[37]

Simon's view is of intuition as a compression of prior knowledge, learning and experience into a capability to respond in ways that do not appear to use an overt rational reasoning process. This perspective has sometimes been referred as a view of 'intuition-as-expertise', and it goes a long way in explaining the ways in which experienced managers and other expert decision-makers are able to respond quickly, effortlessly and accurately. This apparently non-rational reasoning and decision-making process is not the same as 'guessing', nor is it the same as irrational decision-making. Indeed Simon is careful to distinguish between the non-rational intuitive decisions which experts are able to make and 'pure guesswork', and what he saw as the irrational decisions which may be induced by stressful situations where there is an excess of emotion (see Box 2.2).

None of this is to deny the value of rational analysis. The 'hard' tools of decision theory, management science and operational research (OR) have had an undeniable and significant impact upon decision-making that is deliberative, well structured and quantitative. And indeed there are many situations in which decision-making machines (i.e. computers) outperform humans, but such methods have had less of an impact on decision-making that is judgemental, loosely structured and qualitatively based. For example, can a machine identify a business opportunity with minimal hard data in the way successful entrepreneurs do? Can a machine intuit a creative idea or can a machine

---

Box 2.2

Non-productive responses are especially common when actions have to be made under time pressure. The need to allay feelings of guilt, anxiety and embarrassment may lead to behaviour that produces temporary personal comfort at the expense of bad long-run consequences for the organisation. Behaviour of these kinds is 'intuitive' in a very different sense from the intuitive action we discussed earlier. It is 'intuitive' in the sense that it represents response without careful analysis and calculation . . . The intuition of the emotion-driven manager is very different from the intuition of the expert whom we discussed earlier. The latter's behaviour is the product of learning and experience, and is largely adaptive; the former's behaviour is a response to more primitive urges and an emotion-narrowed span of attention, and is more often than not inappropriate. We must not confuse the 'non-rational' decisions of the experts – the decisions that derive from expert intuition and judgement – with the irrational decisions that stressful emotions may produce.

Source: H.A. Simon, *Administrative Behavior: A Study of Decision-making Processes in Administrative Organisation* (4th edn) (New York: The Free Press 1997) p. 139.

envision a desirable future? The intuitive process in Simon's theory does not operate in isolation from rational analysis, rather rationality and intuition are complementary components of an effective decision-making approach. In practical terms Simon doubts that there are successful managers who are able to rely solely upon rational analysis or intuition, but instead:

> every manager needs to be able to analyse problems systematically. Every manager also needs to be able to respond to situations rapidly, a skill that required the cultivation of intuition and judgement over many years of experience and training. The effective manager does not have the luxury of being able to choose between 'analytic' and 'intuitive' approaches to problems.[38]

Simon emphasized that the structure of the everyday problems that professionals face – whether it's an engineer building a new bridge, an architect designing a house or a manager deciding where to locate a new store – are characterized by many ill-defined components. Consequently the practitioner in organizational and professional life is a boundedly rational human being who satisfices rather than maximizes. By placing the concepts of subconscious pattern recognition and expertise at the heart of organizational decision-making Simon was one of the first researchers to demystify intuition and reveal it as comprehensible rather than 'magical'.

DONALD A. SCHÖN: FROM THE 'LOFTY HEIGHTS' TO THE 'SWAMPY LOWLANDS'

Donald Schön (1930–1997) was born in Boston, graduated from Yale in 1951 and went on to postgraduate studies at Harvard. He was an accomplished musician who studied clarinet and piano at the Paris Conservatoire. His seminal contributions are in two books: *The Reflective Practitioner: How Professionals Think in Action* (1983) and *Educating the Reflective Practitioner: Towards a New Design for Teaching and Learning in the Professions* (1987). He argued that professionals, such as managers, teachers, engineers and doctors, know more than they can put into words and that they rely to a large extent upon informed improvisation in their real-world, day-to-day practice. Schön's contribution to our appreciation of the role that intuition plays in decision-making lies in the critique that he offered the rational model, or more correctly the 'technical rational model', which dominates professional practice and the schools that feed it (such as the university and college law, engineering and business schools of today).

One of the precepts of Schön's critique of rationality is that in fields such as medicine, management and engineering some problems are complex and inherently unstable to the extent that they often resist the skills and techniques of 'technical rationality'. The latter was defined in *The Reflective Practitioner* as 'instrumental problem solving made rigorous by the application of scientific theory and technique'.[39] Schön made two crucial points as far as real-world practice is concerned:

1   *Reality is messy*: problems do not present themselves neatly packaged as 'givens', rather they (like their 'solutions') have to be constructed from the puzzling and sometimes 'messy' material of the real world situation.

2   *Problem-setting precedes problem-solving*: problem-setting is not in itself a technical problem, rather it is an activity by which the practitioner makes sense of and names the things to be attended to and frames the context in which they will attend to them.

Decision-makers with different views of the world may attend to and make sense of a situation in quite different ways – two individuals' awareness of the same situation may be vastly different. As a result of differences in their learning, experience or level of expertise, an expert will see a problem in quite a different way to a novice. For example, an entrepreneur with a capacity for 'entrepreneurial alertness' will see opportunities and possibilities that others overlook. Schön summarized the key issue when he argued that:

From the perspective of Technical Rationality, professional practice is a process of problem-solving. Problems of choice or decisions are solved through the selection from available means, of the one best-suited to established ends. But with this emphasis on problem-solving, we ignore problem-setting, the process by which we define the decision to be made, the ends to be achieved, the means which may be chosen.[40]

In other words many of the situations of practice that confront doctors, engineers, teachers, entrepreneurs, inventors, managers and others are less like problems to be solved with easy to identify and clear-cut criteria for success, and are more like problematic, judgemental situations which are characterized by uncertainty, disorder and indeterminacy.[41]

From an entrepreneurial perspective for instance, if an individual cannot identify an opportunity to be exploited then no problem exists which requires a solution. In this respect effective high-level practice, when placed in the context of rational analysis and positivist doctrines,[42] is a puzzling anomaly since it resists attempts at reduction to pure analytical description (see Box 2.3).

Professionals can, to draw on an oft-quoted phrase from Michael Polanyi, 'know more than they can tell'.[43] To this extent Schön is not advocating intuitive approaches as such (witness the very few references to this concept in his book). However, in common with those who hold the view of intuition as being founded in expertise, he articulates a view of effective practice in the real world of uncertainty, dynamism and time pressure as being founded upon:

1 *sufficiency of knowledge*: an established knowledge base such as that taught in the professional schools, universities and colleges;

Box 2.3

When we go about the spontaneous, intuitive performance of the actions of everyday life, we show ourselves to be knowledgeable in a special way. Often we cannot say what it is that we know. When we try to describe it we find ourselves at a loss, or we produce descriptions that are obviously inappropriate. Our knowing is ordinarily tacit, implicit in our patterns of action and in our feel for the stuff with which we are dealing. It seems right to say that our knowing is *in* our action.

Every competent practitioner can recognise phenomena – families of symptoms associated with a particular disease, peculiarities of a certain kind of building site, irregularities of materials or structures – for which he cannot give accurate or complete description. In his day-to-day practice he makes innumerable judgements of quality for which he cannot state adequate criteria, and he displays skills for which he cannot state the rules and procedures. Even when he makes conscious use of research-based theories and techniques he is dependent on tacit recognitions, judgements and skilful performances.

Source: Donald Schön, *The Reflective Practitioner: How Professionals Think in Action* (Aldershot: Gower, 1983) pp. 49–50.

---

2   *artistry of application*: the conversion of this into an approach to practice tailored to the unique requirements of the situation.

This calls upon the individual's experience and expertise and is 'implicit in the artistic, intuitive processes which some practitioners do bring to situations of uncertainty, instability, uniqueness and value conflict'.[44] By reflecting 'in the midst of doing' or by reflecting 'after the fact' decision-makers can build better mental models of reality to fuel their intuitive judgements. In this sense professional practice is more 'art' than 'science' and in the words of one of our other key thinkers (Barnard), 'involves attaining proportion between speed and caution, between broad outlines and fineness of detail, between solidity and flexibility. As in the other arts, the perfection of subsidiary techniques and their effective combination both require constant practice'.[45]

One of the most direct references to intuition in *The Reflective Practitioner* follows Schön's discussion of Chester Barnard's *The Mind in Everyday Affairs*, where he notes that we can often recognize when something is out-of-kilter but that we usually cannot describe how we know that there is a 'bad fit' because it is based upon learning that we are unaware of (which is implicit) and draws upon a form of knowing which cannot be articulated (which is tacit). Here Schön is alluding to the finely-tuned 'situational awareness' that experts have, and which some years later manifested as one of the central features of the recognition-primed decision (RPD) model of Gary Klein and his colleagues.

GARY KLEIN: DECISIONS MADE IN REAL-WORLD 'LIFE-OR-DEATH' SETTINGS

Herbert Simon's concept of satisficing – the search for a choice that will work, rather than an exhaustive search for the best choice – emerges again in the decision-making research of Gary Klein (born 1944). Klein trained as a psychologist and was one of the pioneers of the field of naturalistic decision-making (NDM). Klein and his colleagues researched extensively the decision-making processes in a number of areas of real-world professional practice (as opposed to in the laboratory) including the armed forces, the emergency services and healthcare. The breakthrough in his research came through a critical examination of the classical rational choice model of decision-making based on the proposition of two earlier researchers (Lee Beach and Terry Mitchell) that there are times in decision-making when analysis is appropriate, but there are other times when intuition is better (see Box 2.4).

Box 2.4

So how do we make decisions? Well, largely through a process based on intuition. Think about the times when you had a sense about something, even though you couldn't quite explain it. Can a subordinate handle a tough project? You can't imagine it working out without some disaster. Better give the job to someone else. Why is a customer late with a payment? You have a hunch that the customer may be having a cash flow problem. Is the contract going well? The reports and expenditure rates look fine but you aren't picking up any signs of excitement from the project team? Maybe you should look more deeply into it. What is it that sets off alarm bells inside your head? It's your intuition, built up through repeated experiences that you have unconsciously linked together to form a pattern.

Source: Gary Klein, *Intuition at Work* (2003) p. 11.

How can an expert decision-maker under intense pressure when lives may be at risk weigh-up all the 'pros' and 'cons'? In order to explore this question Klein focused upon the strategies that decision-makers use when they don't have the opportunity to engage in deliberative, reasoned analysis. In one of his research projects he examined the decision choices made by highly experienced firefighters in the US Army who have to make life-or-death decisions in time-pressured situations. Klein's hypothesis was that the firefighters would not be following a rational choice model and comparing lots of options at each stage in the process – they couldn't. Instead they would be comparing only two options at each decision point. To appreciate Klein's perspective consider some examples of decision-making upon which his model is based, described in his ground-breaking book *Sources of Power*:

> *Fire-fighters in a one storey building which is on fire*: the commander and his team spray the fire with water but the fire roars back at them. This just doesn't fit with experience. They try again – and again dousing with water doesn't work – the fire flares back. The commander senses something is not right. He decides to order his team to leave the building immediately. Seconds later the floor they had been standing on collapses – unbeknownst to them the

building had a basement and this is where the fire was emanating from.

The commander didn't have a magical ability to foresee future events or ESP. He did however because of his experience, have a sufficiently large store of knowledge which he accessed non-consciously to enable him to recognize the clues which presented themselves in this complex and pressured scenario. This highly-tuned awareness of the situation gave him enough of a 'sense of unease' that things were 'out of kilter' (for example, the fire was hotter than expected and much too quiet) that he had no choice but to evacuate the building – all accomplished within a matter of minutes if not seconds.[46] Consider another example:

> *British Warship HMS Gloucester under possible attack by Iraqi Silkworm missile in the Gulf War*: The anti-missile battery commander on board HMS Gloucester had seconds to decide if the blip on his radar screen was an Iraqi Silkworm missile (a single-decker bus-sized projectile filled with high explosives headed straight for his ship) or whether it was a friendly American A6 warplane. He judged within a few seconds that it was a missile. He watched it for a full 40 seconds before taking his decision to open fire. Fortunately it was a Silkworm and not an A6.

But what was it that gave him the sense that the blip on the screen was definitely not friendly, especially when other experts seeing the data afterwards said there was no way to tell the Silkworm and the A6 apart? Again, like the firefighter in the previous example, the anti-missile battery commander did not have magical powers or ESP. The answer lay in the fact that through experience he had developed a highly-tuned situational awareness (an intuitive 'muscle power') which enabled him to reason, without knowing how, that the blip was life-threatening.

In each of these examples Klein's hypothesis that only two options would be considered at each decision point did not hold true – in this respect he was incorrect. Rather than comparing several or even just two options, the decision-maker(s) in each case did not appear to be comparing any. The experienced firefighter and the anti-missile battery commander arrived rapidly at one course of action (they chose to 'evacuate' and to 'fire') and trusted it. In its simplest form the process is one in which the decision-makers use their experience to size up the situation, get a sense of its typicality, recognize a course of action that matches the typical situation, and implement the course of action[47] – Klein calls this the 'simple match' situation. Decision-makers may also

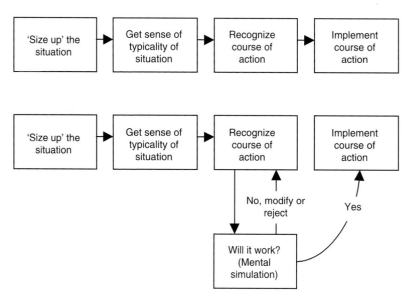

Figure 2.8 The recognition-primed decision (RPD) model: 'simple match' (top), similar to Simon's 'analysis frozen into habit'; evaluation of course of action via mental simulation (bottom).

Based on G. Klein, 'The recognition-primed (RPD) model: looking back, looking forward', in C.E. Zsambok and G. Klein (eds) *Naturalistic Decision-making* (Mahwah, NJ: Lawrence Earlbaum Associates, 1997) pp. 286–7.

use a mental rehearsal akin to a 'DVD-in-the-head' to assess the feasibility of the course of action prior to implementation, and on the basis of their mental simulation may need to adjust or reject it.[48]

The general pattern that Klein observed was that under certain sets of circumstances experts generate one course of action, whereas novices compare a number of different approaches.[49] Experts appear not to get paralysed by analysis because they are able to use their informed intuition, based on prior learning and previous experience, to weigh up the situation, generate realistic and viable options one at a time, evaluate these quickly through mental simulations (if necessary) and make an acceptable choice. The theory is called the RPD model, and in it Klein takes the concept of satisficing, develops a new angle on it and provides empirical evidence to support this view. Moreover RPD offers the combined processes of pattern recognition, situational awareness and mental simulation as highly plausible explanations of how experienced managers and other professionals are able to avoid succumbing to 'analysis paralysis'.

ANTONIO DAMASIO: THE NEURAL CIRCUITRY OF DECISION-MAKING

So far we have looked at contributions to our understanding of the limits of rationality mainly from the fields of management, administrative science and decision research. Antonio Damasio (born 1944), by contrast, is a neurologist. Neurology is the scientific study of nerve systems (including the brain). It may seem a strange choice to include a neurologist in a discussion of the limits of rationality, but as we shall see the research by Damasio and his co-workers has significant implications for the ways in which we understand how the brain's neural circuitry affects human beings' decision-making processes and how this impacts upon their daily lives and behaviour. On a broader front, the work of Damasio and his team, as well as more recent research in social cognitive neuroscience,[50] demonstrate how far we have come in a relatively short space of time (50 years) in shedding light upon the brain's intuitive – or 'non-logical' as Barnard called them – decision-making processes (see Box 2.5).

Much of the clinical work of neurologists involves treating patients who have experienced some form of damage to specific parts of their

---

Box 2.5

From an evolutionary perspective, the oldest decision making device pertains to basic biological regulation; the next to the personal and social realm; and the most recent, to a collection of abstract-symbolic operations under which we find artistic and scientific reasoning, utilitarian-engineering reasoning, and the developments of language and mathematics. But although ages of evolution and dedicated neural systems may confer some independence to each of these reasoning/decision making 'modules', I suspect that they are interdependent. When we witness signs of creativity in contemporary humans, we are probably witnessing the integrated operation of sundry combinations of these devices.

Source: Antonio Damasio, *Descartes' Error: Emotion, Reason and the Human Brain* (New York: Quill, 1994) p. 191.

brain due to illness, injury or other causes. This type of research helps to shed light upon the deleterious effects of such damage on normal brain functioning and the patient's consequent behaviours in their personal and professional lives, including the way they make decisions. Damasio's work includes poignant case studies of specific individuals, for example one such patient did indeed seem to be almost literally frozen into inaction by 'analysis paralysis'.

The patient in question had incurred damage to a part of his brain's frontal lobe called the ventro-medial prefrontal cortex (VMPC), one of a number of brain sites involved in inducing emotions (other sites include the hypothalamus, basal forebrain and amygdala).[51] Damasio explained the case in his book *Descartes' Error: Reason, Emotion and the Human Brain*:

> The patient had undergone his regular consultation and was discussing his next visit to the neurology laboratory. Two dates were suggested to the patient. However, rather than being a fairly routine and uncomplicated decision task it prompted behaviour on the part of the patient which Damasio described as nothing less than 'remarkable'. The patient conducted a lengthy and laborious cost-benefit analysis invoking every conceivable reason for and against each date, not only for a few minutes, but for a full half hour (including a consideration of his other commitments, the proximity of the pro-

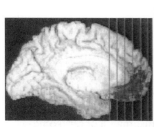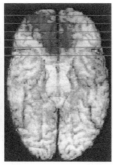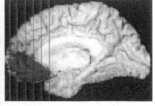

Figure 2.9 Location of the ventromedial sector of the prefrontal cortex (darker region within lines). Damage to this region results in abnormalities in the processes of emotion and feeling, and in impaired decision-making.

Reproduced by permission of Oxford University Press: A. Bechara *et al.*, 'Emotion, decision-making and the orbitofrontal cortex', *Cerebral Cortex*, 2000, 10: 297–307 (p. 296).

posed dates to other engagements, the likely weather conditions and so forth). Eventually, and politely, Damasio and his fellow researchers coolly and calmly chose the second of the two dates on behalf of the patient to which his response was that it was 'fine'.[52]

This example from Damasio's work is a vivid illustration of the limits of a purely rational choice approach (the unbounded consideration of all the possible 'fors' and 'againsts'). It also illustrates the ways in which many of us take for granted the capability to infuse our rational choices with feeling. Not only that; it also shows the potential consequences of not having the necessary automated emotional mechanisms and underlying intact neural circuitry which aid rational choice. In this case, Damasio argued that emotions might have helped the patient to see a number of issues more clearly, such as: the overall problem, and put this into context (the choice between the two dates was really very marginal); the indulgent and time-wasting nature of his actions in spending too much time on a trivial task (not sensing its sheer wastefulness); that the simple task might have been solved equally well by 'going with his gut', tossing a coin or asking the clinicians to choose.

But in general when emotions are lacking, because of disease or damage to the neural circuitry which induces them, the effect on decision-making and social functioning is quite profound, resulting in amongst other things paralysis-by-analysis. Damage to the neural circuitry that underpins decision-making may mean that reasoning by analysis reaches its natural limits, becoming in the end dysfunctional.

DECISION-MAKING IS NOT DISPASSIONATE

There is more to reasoning and decision-making than rational analysis alone can provide. As we have seen multiple attribute identification of the kind that Darwin and Franklin exhorted us to employ is logical, and provides a sound basis for analysis. Attributes can be assigned a 'worth', and attributes and utilities may be combined to come up with a 'bottom line' figure upon which the alternative courses action may then be juggled.

But do managers always stick to a logical mode of thought? At what point does a decision-maker truncate the search for attributes? Can the value of an attribute always be assigned objectively or dispassionately? Can a human being make a complex judgement in a real world setting using analysis alone? Is it desirable to do so? What happens in situations where there is not the luxury of time to conduct a lengthy, in-depth analysis? And finally, what happens when the neural circuitry that mediates our decision-making is compromised? The seminal contributions of our five key thinkers help to answer these important questions:

1   *Barnard*: decision-makers use both analytical and intuitive thinking processes, and in managerial and professional work the intuitive approach is often called upon as much as the analytical approach.
2   *Simon*: human beings lack the cognitive capabilities to maximize utility in complex situations. They will often settle for satisficing by setting an aspiration level and searching until an alternative is found that exceeds this level. Not only that, emotion is a source of motivation in itself which serves to direct our powers of attention and thought to the goal.[53]
3   *Schön*: many of the problems that confront decision-makers in organizational settings are complex, uncertain and unstable, often requiring value judgements to be made. Such decisions are not always amenable, nor will they yield, to 'technical rational' solutions, and instead they require the application of a 'professional artistry' born out of experience, expertise and intuitive judgement.[54]
4   *Klein*: Experts use pattern recognition, situational awareness and mental simulation to make fast, effective judgement calls in complex and pressured situations – as a result they avoid becoming paralysed by analysis and learn when and where to trust their intuitions.
5   *Damasio*: emotion is an inherent part in human decision-making. The neural circuitry that evolution has endowed us with produces what are sometimes referred to as 'gut feelings' and these help us to sift through the choices which are available to us and provide positive and negative signals which guide our selections.

Research since the 1950s demonstrates that: rationality has its limits; that affect is an indispensable component of human decision-making processes; and that rationality and affect are both required if human beings are to function as effective decision-makers. We sometimes have no alternative but to acknowledge uncertainties and be more tolerant of ambiguities. The consequences of failing to do so can be the mortifying 'analysis paralysis' described by Sylvia Plath in her novel *The Bell Jar*:

> I saw myself sitting in the crotch of this fig tree, starving to death because I couldn't make up my mind which of the figs I would choose. I wanted each and every one of them, but choosing one meant losing all the rest, and, as I sat there unable to decide, the figs began to wrinkle and go black, and, one-by-one, they plopped to the ground at my feet.[55]

Decisions may have to be taken speedily and with cognitive economy in the face of a dearth or a plethora of information, against tight deadlines and a pressure to act. Under such conditions experienced decision-makers often draw upon informed intuitive judgments rather than on non-existent or not-yet-invented plans, procedures or routines to guide their decisions and actions in a timely fashion.

TAKE-AWAYS FOR CHAPTER 2

Key ideas

Rationality is not omnipotent – it has its limits, and decision-makers' behaviours are 'fenced-in' (*bounded*) by these limits. Logical reasoning processes by themselves can be disadvantageous for senior managers if they are not used 'in concert' with highly-developed intuitional processes. The ability to *recognize patterns* based upon deep knowledge structures enables decision-makers to judge situations rapidly and intuitively. Many *real world decisions* are problematic, judgemental situations which are characterized by uncertainty, disorder and indeterminacy. *Experts* are likely to be less frozen by 'paralysis by analysis' than non-experts because they are able to use their informed intuition to weigh-up the situation, generate a small number of realistic and viable alternatives and evaluate these quickly. *Neural circuitry* in the central nervous systems exists which infuses decision-making with feeling and probably has evolved as to assist human judgement in social settings and other complex situations.

Intuition quote: Akio Morita, co-founder of Sony

'Machines and computers cannot be creative in themselves, because creativity requires something more than the processing of existing information. It requires human thought, spontaneous intuition and a lot of courage.'

Action point

Think of an occasion in the past in which you relied on your intuitive judgement in making a tough decision where the outcome was *positive* for you. What were the circumstances; what was the outcome? Think of an occasion in the past in which you relied on your intuitive judgement in making a tough decision where the outcome was *negative* for you. What were the circumstances; what was the outcome? Would you say that intuition has been your *friend* or *foe* when making tough decisions?

FURTHER READING

Barnard, C.I., *The Functions of the Executive*. Cambridge, MA: Harvard University Press 1938/1968.

Damasio, A.R., *Descartes' Error: Emotion, Reason and the Human Brain*. New York: Quill 1994.

Klein, G., *Sources of Power: How People Make Decisions*. Cambridge, MA: The MIT Press 1998.

Schön, D.A., *The Reflective Practitioner: How Professionals Think in Action*. Aldershot: Gower 1983.

Simon, H.A., *Administrative Behaviour: A Study of Decision-making Processes in Administrative Organisations* (4th edn). New York: The Free Press 1997.

3 Eureka! moments

Phantasy, or imagination, is an inner sense which doth more fully examine the species perceived by common sense, of things present or absent, and keeps them longer, recalling them to mind again, or making new of his own. In time of sleep this faculty is free, and many time conceives, strange, stupend, absurd shapes. His organ is in the middle cell of the brain.

(Robert Burton 1577–1640, *The Anatomy of Melancholy, Subsection VII. Of the Inward Senses*)

MAIN IDEA

Insight and intuition are related in that they both rely upon non-conscious mental processes. There are however important distinctions between them. Intuitions may lead to insights which can result in major creative breakthroughs and commercial innovations, and there are numerous examples of these phenomena in science, technology and business.

The two problems shown in Table 3.1 are of a type that tends not to succumb very easily to logical analysis. Often in trying to solve them the problem solver reaches an impasse, only to find that the solution pops up 'all at once' when least expected, as an 'insight'* in a 'Eureka!' moment.

---

* The answers can be found at the end of the chapter (see page 102) but you might choose to wait to see if the solution 'pops' into your conscious awareness suddenly and unexpectedly.

Table 3.1 Two insight problems

Problem 1	Problem 2
Consider the following scenario: A man walks into a bar and asks for a glass of water. The bartender takes out a gun and points it at the man. The man says 'Thank you so much!' and then walks out. Can you explain the events that took place?	Consider these three seemingly unrelated words: Pine-Tree-Crab What is the linking word* that can be added to each one and still make sense?

* So, for example 'palm' could be added to 'tree' to make the compound 'palm-tree' but would be nonsensical when added to 'pine' and 'crab'.

'Eureka!' is a Greek word meaning literally 'I have found it!'[1] and it is most often associated with the apocryphal story of Archimedes' reaction when he solved the problem of King Hiero's crown.

Archimedes of Syracuse (287–212 BC) was the greatest mathematician of his age. Story has it that his King, Hiero II, was given as a gift a wreathed crown purportedly of pure gold but which he suspected of being adulterated with silver. Who better to enlist than Archimedes to help to solve the problem? Archimedes knew the weight per unit of volume of gold and of silver, and had the crown been a pure block of either metal the volume calculation would have been easy. But the crown was not only a very elaborate ornament, it was also a sacred object which could not be melted down or hammered into a regular block shape. So the problem was how to measure the crown's volume non-destructively.

   One day whilst climbing into his bath, Archimedes' attention was drawn to the familiar sight of the rise in water level, but unusually on this occasion it occurred to him quite suddenly that this rise was proportionate to his own body's volume. If he could use the displacement of water to measure the volume of his own body he could do the same with the crown to calculate its volume and thereby verify whether or not it was pure gold. Archimedes was so delighted with his insight that he allegedly leapt from his bath and ran through the streets crying 'Eureka!'.[2]

For Archimedes the bathing experience gave his thinking the jolt it needed – the water was an external cue which precipitated his sudden understanding of how its displacement could be used to calculate the density of an object. The parts of the problem suddenly came together and led to the forming of an integrated whole that eventually led to a generalized principle relating to the displacement of liquids. The solution was clear enough in Archimedes' mind for it to be explicable to anyone he cared to tell; all that remained was for him to empirically verify the solution.

Archimedes' story is the archetypal 'Eureka!' moment. Whether or not the story is true (and no less a figure than Galileo raised doubts about its plausibility)[3], it illustrates the concept of insight: a sudden and able-to-be-articulated conscious awareness of the solution to what was a perplexing problem, which usually occurs after the problem solver has taken some kind of mental 'reprieve'. It has several distinguishing features all of which are to be found in the Archimedes story, including:

1   *Spontaneity*: the solution occurs suddenly and unexpectedly, often after a time away from the problem;
2   *Clarity*: the problem solution is understood clearly, so much so that the solution can be explained in logical terms;
3   *Satisfaction*: solving the problem induces feelings of satisfaction (the 'aha!' experience) or even elation at the moment when the elements suddenly come together.[4]

When insight takes place the problem solver shifts from 'not knowing how to solve the problem to a state of knowing how to solve it'.[5] Moreover, since there is no intermediate process that is detectable in conscious awareness[6] the problem solver is often unaware of the incremental progress being made towards the solution.[7] Described by the English humorous writer P.G. Wodehouse as the 'unsealing of the fount of memory': 'One moment the mind a blank: the next the fount of memory spouting forth like nobody's business. It often happens this way'.[8] Like its close neighbour intuition, insight has a non-conscious quality, which gives it an aura of mystery in the eyes of some. Insight is vitally important because it leads to technical and scientific breakthroughs which are the bases of innovation. In recent decades the accounts of several Nobel laureates attest to the fact that a number of them placed considerable reliance upon their intuitions:

> As we did our work, I think, we almost felt at times that there was almost a hand guiding us. Because we would go from one step to the next, and somehow we would know which was the right way to

go. And I really can't tell how we knew that, how we knew that it was necessary to move ahead.

(Michael S. Brown, Medicine, 1985)[9]

I consider that I have good intuition and good judgment on what problems are worth pursuing and what lines of work are worth doing. I used to say (and I think this was bragging) that whereas most scholars have ideas which do not pan out more than, say, four percent of the time, mine come through maybe 80 percent of the time.

(George Stigler, Economics, 1982)[10]

To me it is a feeling of . . . 'Well, I really don't believe this result' or 'This is a trivial result' and 'This is an important result' and 'Let us follow this path', I am not always right, but I do have feelings about what is an important observation and what is probably trivial.

(Stanley Cohen, Medicine, 1986)[11]

A better understanding of insight's psychological mechanisms opens up the possibility of creating the conditions in organizations for discovery, creative intuition, invention and innovation to flourish.[12] There are other reasons why the study of insight is important in a book about intuition:

1 *Insight is not intuition*: although insight and intuition both involve the non-conscious processing of information, they are not the same.[13]
2 *Intuitions can presage insights*: intuition may sometimes play a role in the process of insight, for example when a problem solver has a sense that a solution to the problem is to be found but cannot yet articulate the solution (referred to as 'intimation').

The insight-intuition distinction is evident in the way in which Paul McCready, winner of The American Society of Mechanical Engineers 'Engineer of the Century' Award, described the 'Eureka!' moment in 1976 that led to his design for a machine that would enable 'man-powered' flight. His insight occurred as he was driving along the freeway and happened to notice a flock of large birds circling overhead. By estimating the birds' bank angle and timing their circles, he calculated their speed. His mind then turned to comparing the birds with hang-gliders and sail-planes, and back to the basic physics and aeronautics he'd been taught at Yale and Caltech.[14] As a result he was able to explicate the

Figure 3.1 Some Nobel laureates who used intuitive judgement. Copyright The
Nobel Foundation (reproduced by permission).

Top left: George Stigler, Economics, 1982, for his seminal studies of industrial structures,
functioning of markets and causes and effects of public regulation. *Top right*: Michael S.
Brown, Medicine, 1985, for discoveries concerning the regulation of cholestrol metabol-
ism. *Bottom*: Stanley Cohen, Medicine, 1986, for discoveries of growth factors in cell
growth and definition.

reasoning behind the insight in very precise terms: 'If you triple the size of a hang-glider-size plane and triple its wingspan to 90 feet while keeping its weight the same, the power needed to fly it goes down by a factor of three, to about 0.4 horsepower ... what a trained cyclist could pump out for several minutes at a stretch.' On the basis of his creative Eureka! moment a year later McCready and his colleagues built the *Gossamer Condor* and successfully flew it around the mile long figure of eight course needed to claim the $100,000 Kremer Prize for man-powered flight.

INSIGHT IN SCIENTIFIC DISCOVERY

There are numerous examples of scientists and others who, having reached an impasse with a problem, report being jolted by a sudden cognitive 'shift' in which the parts of the problem come together and the solution becomes clear. One of the most famous examples of insight in science, as much because it is very well documented as for the discovery itself, is the story of the discovery of the physical structure of the benzene molecule. Benzene is a substance found in crude oil and used in the production of plastics, nylon and other polymers. Its structure was discovered by the nineteenth-century German chemist Friedrich Kekulé (1829–1896) and has been labelled a 'landmark' that ushered in the science of organic chemistry.[15]

Benzene is one of a class of hydrocarbon compounds – molecules of varying degrees of complexity composed of hydrogen atoms and carbon atoms. The chemical composition of benzene (C_6H_6) was already established. The problem which was perplexing nineteenth-century scientists, including Kekulé, was its physical structure, and specifically how carbon atoms (valence four) and hydrogen atoms (valence one) could be combined together in the formula C_6H_6? The bonding just didn't work out; a string of six carbon atoms should have more hydrogen atoms – fourteen to be precise, not six as it in fact has.[16]

The story, as recounted by F.R. Japp in 1898 from a speech made by Kekulé in 1890, goes something like this:[17] Kekulé was staying in London, and one evening in 1854 when travelling home on the bus fell into a daydream:

> and lo, the atoms were gambolling before my eyes! Wherever these diminutive beings appeared to me, they had always been in motion; but up to that time I had never been able to discern the nature of their motion. Now ... I saw how, frequently two smaller atoms

united to form a pair; how a larger one embraced two smaller ones; how still larger ones kept hold of three or even four of the smaller; whilst the whole kept whirling in a giddy dance. I saw how the larger ones formed a chain dragging the smaller ones after them, but only at the ends of the chain.[18]

Unfortunately at this point the London bus conductor intervened with the shout of 'Clapham!' which, not unsurprisingly, awakened Kekulé who then spent the night capturing on paper his 'dream forms'. The images had revealed to him the concept of a molecular chain structure – a major insight and the first step on the path to uncovering benzene's structure. The story didn't end there. Kekulé had a second reverie in his room in 1865 in which he 'turned his chair to the fire' and dozed:

Again the atoms were gambolling before my eyes. This time the smaller groups kept modestly in the background. My mental eye, rendered more accurate by repeated visions of the kind, could now distinguish larger structures of manifold conformation: long rows, sometimes more closely fitted together; all twining and twisting in snakelike motion. But look! What was that? One of the snakes had seized hold of its own tail, and the form whirled mockingly before my eyes. As if by a flash of lightening I awoke; and at this time spent the rest of the night in working out the consequences of the hypothesis.[19]

Kekulé's insight was that benzene is indeed a chain but, more importantly, it is a chain that is folded back on to itself thereby forming a ring structure – this was the major leap of understanding. 'Seeing' this highly unusual physical form involved a shift in perception which took Kekulé out the cognitive 'rut' of thinking of molecules only as linear chains and enabling benzene's chemical formula of C_6H_6 to now make perfect sense as a ring molecule (see Figure 3.2).

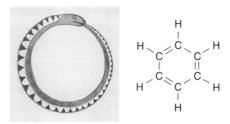

Figure 3.2 The *uroborus* and the benzene molecule (C_6H_6).

Psychologists have interpreted these accounts in a number of ways. Some have suggested that Kekulé was in a 'hypnagogic state'. Hypnagogic phenomena are vivid visual images experienced in the stage between wakefulness and sleep but which, unlike dreams, are under some degree of conscious control. Arthur Koestler in his book *The Act of Creation* referred to this as the most fertile of the mind's 'regions': 'the marshy shore, the borderland between sleep and full awakening where the matrices of disciplined thought are already operating but have not yet sufficiently hardened to obstruct the dreamlike fluidity of the imagination'.[20]

Other inventors and innovators in more recent times have testified to the 'fertility' of the region between sleeping and waking as a source of creative ideas: 'Sometimes you just kind of like float away, in the mind, so deep. It's just a matter of how much you can insulate yourself from anything else around. And then as deeper you can go into that, somehow you just go and [start] picking up those ideas.'[21]

A degree of conscious awareness is necessary if this state is to be maintained – any excessive drowsiness may be quickly followed by sleep and the loss of valuable ideas. There is no suggestion in Kekulé's own account and its subsequent interpretations that he was actually dreaming. Because of the conscious control which can be exercised by the subject in this condition it is possible for the 'dreamer' to describe the images immediately after their occurrence. Other inventors have been known to deliberately 'up-load' problems before they go to sleep with the intention of allowing their unconscious minds to work on them. Ray Kurzweil is the originator of numerous inventions including optical character recognition, text-to-speech synthesis and electronic keyboard instruments and was the winner of the USA's most prestigious prize for innovation, the $500,000 Lemelson-MIT Prize. In an interview in 1987 he described taking a two-pronged approach to idea generation: first, he 'seeds' his unconscious mind in advance with a vexing problem immediately before going to sleep; second, he deliberately cultivates a quasi-conscious state where he feels he can merge together the logical and censoring function of his conscious mind with the inventiveness and 'free-wheeling' of his unconscious.[22] Amongst Kurzweil's technological inventions credited to this method are a reading machine for the visually impaired and an electronic synthesizer capable of recreating the sound of an orchestra. Kurzweil's more recent writings push the boundaries of innovation and cover topics such as 'How to build a brain', 'Will machines become conscious?' and 'The sustainable brain'.[23]

A century before Kurzweil's innovation-oriented cognitive strategies, Kekulé is also thought to have deliberately engaged in modes of thinking which would help him solve scientific problems. Earlier in his career he trained as an architect and was used to visual and spatial thinking in two and three dimensions. It's been speculated that the 'visions' he had were not at all unusual for him but were a special kind of imagery that he had deliberately cultivated as a thinking and problem-solving tool.[24] The final point which mustn't be overlooked is that Kekulé was engaged in a conscious and enduring purpose to solve a specific problem (eleven years elapsed between the two episodes related above). It was not a capricious, 'flash-in-the-pan' endeavour. Kekulé's immersion in the field of chemistry gave him the prior knowledge and skills, what some have referred to as 'deep, vertical expertise',[25] which he drew on both consciously and non-consciously.

There was also a role for serendipity in all of this as well – his bus ride, his dozing off by the fire, his prior knowledge, his use of imagery – all came together at particular moments in time to eventually create a novel, insightful and organized conceptual whole. This was not an intuition – no judgement was involved characterized by a vague but compelling sense of 'rightness'; instead a crystal clear understanding was achieved.

An intriguing aside to these debates is the significance that some have accorded to the image of the snake in the second episode, interpreted as visual metaphor for the closed carbon ring in benzene's structure. The image of the snake swallowing its own tail is an alchemical symbol, the *uroborus* (from the Greek *oura* for 'tail', and literally meaning 'eating one's own tail'). This image has its origins in Classical antiquity; for example, it is found in Greek manuscripts from 300 BC. The Swiss psychoanalyst Jung interpreted dream forms and symbols such as the *uroborus* as products not of memory, but as archetypal material that arises from a collective unconscious: 'I have found again and again in my professional work that the images and ideas that dreams contain cannot possibly be explained solely in terms of memory. They express new thoughts that have never yet reached the threshold of consciousness'.[26]

Whether or not the snake symbol is one that is shared by all human-ity as an element of some 'collective unconscious' which manifests itself in dreams, myths, fairy tales and religious phenomena is open to debate. But as was noted in Chapter 1, one of the themes in the more mystical accounts of intuition revolves around its supposed connection to a 'supra-consciousness'.[27]

GRAHAM WALLAS'S MODEL OF CREATIVE INSIGHT

The chain of events leading up to creative breakthroughs and discoveries was captured by Graham Wallas in his influential book *The Art of*

Thought (1926). Wallas (1858–1932) was an Oxford-educated political theorist and psychologist who taught at the London School of Economics from 1895 to 1923. He described the creative problem-solving process as consisting of several clear-cut stages (see Figure 3.3), and in so doing he created one of the most persuasive accounts of insight and creativity. The stages in Wallas' model are to be found in the many of the accounts left by famous scientists and inventors; one in particular is the writing of the great French mathematician Henri Poincaré (1854–1912)

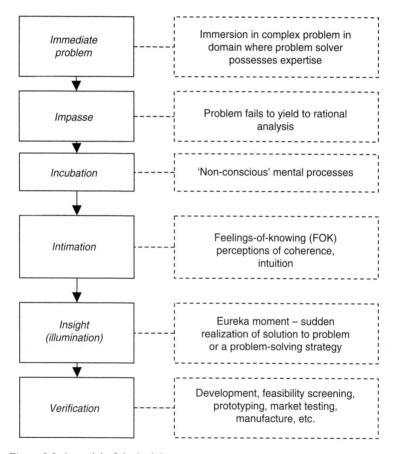

Figure 3.3 A model of the insight process.
Based on G. Wallas, *The Art of Thought* (New York: Franklin Watts, 1926).

Preparation stage

Poincare's writings illustrate the mental discipline he brought to his work and the frustration of reaching an impasse: 'For fifteen days I strove to prove that there could not be any functions like those I have since called Fuchsian functions. I was then very ignorant; everyday I seated myself at my worktable, stayed an hour or two, tried a great number of combinations, and reached no results'.[28] Preparation involves immersion in the underlying concepts, rules and principles of a particular field which become embedded in an elaborate cognitive architecture. Preparation also gives the problem solver a familiarity with the field which enables them to judge which problem-solving strategy is likely to be effective. Problems which can yield to routine, laborious analytical methods (sometimes called 'grind-out' problems) have solutions whose general shape can be envisaged in advance. For example: students can be taught a routine technique to solve quadratic equations by following a logical process involving various mathematical operations; technicians can fault-find on equipment by methodically tracing a route through an electrical circuit diagram; and a manager can solve an accounting problem by applying arithmetical rules. The shape of the outcome is known in advance – 'equation solved', 'fault found', and 'books balanced'. Problems which are non-routine are more challenging. A difficulty which confronts innovators and entrepreneurs who operate in uncharted territories outside the bounds of what is 'routine' is the absence of objective criteria by which the most novel ideas can be judged as 'viable' or 'not viable'.[29] This makes sorting the 'wheat from the chaff' in non-routine problem solving a real challenge, and the difficulty is exacerbated if the necessary preparatory experiences and expertise are lacking.

Incubation stage

Following his mental blockage Poincaré later wrote: 'Disgusted with my failure, I went to spend a few days at the seaside, and thought of something else'. In spite of the application of cognitive effort, certain problems will fail to yield to intentional analyses. In this situation the problem solver may reach an impasse at which point retreat and temporary disengagement is an advisable course of action. Wallas recommended two forms of disengagement:

1   *undertaking alternative mental work*: turning one's energy to other mental activity (for example, doing a crossword puzzle, working on an unrelated project);

2 *relaxation from mental work*: turning one's mental energy away from problem solving entirely (for example, relaxing, reading, physical exercise).

This is the 'incubation' stage in which it was proposed by Wallas that conscious thought about the problem is fully or partly suspended, and instead it is subjected to 'the free working of the unconscious or partly-conscious processes of the mind'.[30]

Intimation stage

An element of Wallas' model which is often overlooked is the stage when, in his own words, a 'fringe consciousness of an association-train is in the state of rising consciousness which indicates that the fully conscious flash of success is coming'.[31] The verb 'intimate' is from the Latin *intimare* which means 'to announce', and intimations are intuitions to the extent that they are feelings, but no more than that, that something is about to happen. Intimations are, because they are momentary phase, a transient intuition. The fully-fledged solution which follows hot on the heels of intimation can be put into words, articulated and clearly understood. Many intuitions remain as judgments laden with feeling which may or may not be verified through subsequent experiences, and this is where they and insights part company.

Illumination stage

It was proposed by Wallas that during incubation 'a series of unconscious and involuntary mental events take place' which end in a 'flash of illumination' as a result of 'the culmination of a successful train of association, . . . probably preceded by a series of tentative trains [of association]'.

> Most striking at first is this appearance of sudden illumination, a manifest sign of long unconscious prior work. The role of this unconscious work in mathematical work appears to me incontestable.
>
> One morning, walking on the bluff, the idea came to me, with . . . brevity, suddenness and immediate certainty.
>
> (Henri Poincaré)

Wallas speculated that 'tentative solutions' may be reached in the unconscious mind. This view is supported by more recent evidence which suggests that solutions to insight problems do arise gradually, but that this is a process which is outside of the problem solver's conscious awareness.[32] The autobiographical accounts of Kekulé, Poincaré, Einstein and others suggest that moments of insight may occur in a variety of states both wakeful and half-wakeful. For example, in Poincaré's account his 'Eureka!' experience occurred when he was fully alert, albeit distracted from mathematics whilst walking along the cliffs at the seaside; whereas Kekulé's 'aha!' moment occurred whilst he was in a *reverie* somewhere between wakefulness and sleep. There does not seem to be any hard and fast rule.

Verification stage

> Returned to Caen, I meditated on this result and deduced the consequences. I set myself to form all these functions. I made a systematic attack upon them and carried all the outworks one after another.
>
> (Henri Poincaré)

Having arrived at the point of illumination and the generation of a potentially valuable idea, the hard, conscious work begins in earnest. In a business context this is likely to involve the following stages in the innovation process:[33]

1   *Concept development*: getting the idea off the 'drawing board';
2   *Feasibility screening*: judging whether the developed concept will work and/or sell;
3   *Prototyping*: designing and developing a fully-functioning prototype;
4   *Consumer testing*: testing the market to see if anyone will buy the product and exploring with customers how it could be improved;
5   *Commercialization*: manufacturing, marketing, distribution, retailing and so forth.

The importance of the verification stage was well understood by Thomas Edison who, with over one thousand patents to his name, was one of the most prolific and successful inventors of all time. Edison's approach to creativity was deliberate, managed and strategic. Here are some creativity lessons that researchers[34] have gleaned from the mass of notes and sketches he left behind and which now reside in the vaults of the Edison Archive:

Stage	Poincaré's account
Preparation phase and impasse	'For fifteen days I strove to prove that there could not be any functions like those I have since called Fuchsian functions. I was then very ignorant; everyday I seated myself at my worktable, stayed an hour or two, tried a great number of combinations, and reached no results'
Incubation space	'Disgusted with my failure, I went to spend a few days at the seaside, and thought of something else'
Intimation presage	'Most striking at first is this appearance of sudden illumination, a manifest sign of long unconscious prior work. The role of this unconscious work in mathematical work appears to me incontestable'
Illumination event	'One morning, walking on the bluff, the idea came to me, with … brevity, suddenness and immediate certainty'
Verification	'Returned to Caen, I meditated on this result and deduced the consequences. I set myself to form all these functions. I made a systematic attack upon them and carried all the outworks one after another'

Figure 3.4 Wallas's model of insight with illustrative quotes from French mathematician Henri Poincaré.

1 *Set idea quotas*: for himself Edison set the quota at one minor invention every ten days and a major one every six months. He also set idea targets for his workers.

2 *Challenge assumptions*: the story goes that before hiring research assistants Edison would take the applicant out to lunch and if they seasoned their soup before tasting it they didn't get the job because, in Edison's view they had an assumption that the soup needed seasoning which they did not bother to challenge (i.e. by tasting the soup first).

3 *Learn from mistakes*: instead of regarding failures as failures, to discover something that did work, Edison regarded failures more positively – as discoveries of things that didn't work.

4 *Capture ideas*: Edison was an obsessive note-taker and recorder, so much so that in the Edison Archive there are around 3500 note books which he actively used as his 'paper-based memory'.

INSIDE THE 'BLACK BOX'

The model offered by Wallas, and recounted many times, is based upon introspective, autobiographical accounts and describes phenomena that are likely to be familiar to many of us. However, given that Wallas was working in the 1920s and was more political scientist than psychologist, it is unsurprising that apart from the notion of 'trains of associations' and speculations on the unconscious, he appears to have largely avoided any detailed discussion of the psychological processes which precipitate illumination and insight. Like Chester Barnard, who by 1938 had developed a keen awareness of the significance of intuitive, non-logical processes in management but couldn't explain them very well, Wallas left unanswered the question of what happens inside the 'black box' of insight. The first significant steps in this direction took place in the 1940s when insight researchers focused upon a number of mechanisms, centred mostly upon the role that perception plays in hindering (by imposing constraints) or helping (by relaxing constraints) the route to the problem's solution. This early work offered a number of different explanations for insight:

1   *Visual restructuring*: seeing the problem in a different way;
2   *Problem reformulation*: putting the question in a different way;
3   *Removing mental blocks*: getting over 'functional fixedness';
4   *Using analogical reasoning*: going from the known to the unknown;
5   *Completing schemas*: filling in gaps.[35]

As an illustration of 'visual restructuring' (1), take a look at the geometry problem in Figure 3.5a. If the diameter, d, of the circle is ten centimetres, how long is line x?

Seeing the problem in a different way (visual restructuring)

On the face of it the geometry problem might appear mathematically challenging, and a non-mathematician might be forgiven for arriving at a mental blockage and giving up. But no complex geometrical calculations or trigonometry are required; the impasse may be breached by a very simple visual re-organization of the problem.

Insight into the problem comes through simply flipping the line x horizontally as in the Figure 3.5b. What should now be clear is that x is the same as the radius (r), which is half the diameter (d) of the circle – so the length of line x is $d \div 2$, (i.e. 10 centimetres $\div$ 2) – five centimetres. The problem becomes immediately solvable as a result of,

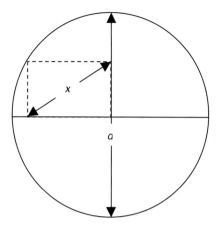

Figure 3.5a A geometry insight problem.

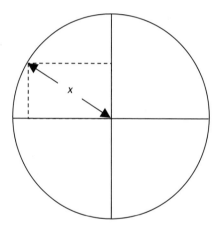

Figure 3.5b A geometry insight problem – solution.

literally in this case, a visual restructuring achieved by flipping the line over. The solution 'pops out' and insight is achieved.

Problem-solving in general and insight in particular were extensively researched by a group of European psychologists called the 'Gestaltists' (*gestalt* is a German word meaning 'organized whole') in the first half of the twentieth century. Gestalt theories of perception were based on the idea that organized structures are built up and cohere to form a particular visual configuration (Figure 3.6). The Gestaltists put forward the 'reorganizing of visual inputs' as an explanation of insightful and creative thinking.[36] By literally looking at the visual representation of a problem from a different angle or in a different way (in Figure 3.5 by flipping the line) the solution may become immediately obvious. Another example that can be solved by looking at its visual configuration in a different way is shown in Figure 3.7. The challenge in this case is to say what the area is of the jigsaw piece on the left of the diagram.*

Putting the question in a different way (problem reformulation)

An influential contribution to the understanding of insight came from Karl Duncker (1903–1940) who wrote *On Problem Solving* – described as one of the 'single most important publications on insight'.[37] Duncker

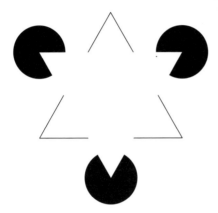

Figure 3.6 Example of the Gestalt grouping law in visual perception.

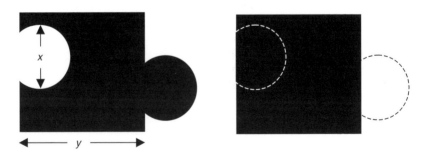

Figure 3.7 'Area of puzzle' problem.

Source: M.A. Schilling, 'A "small world" network model for cognitive insight', *Creativity Research Journal*, 2005, 17(2&3): 135.

* The area is simply y^2 (no calculations involving x are required).

argued that problems may be solved through a succession of steps in which the task is 'reframed' or 'reformulated' either from the 'bottom-up' (in terms of reformulating the elements of the problem) or from the 'top-down' (in terms of redefining the goal).

Bottom-up reformulation

An example of bottom-up reformulation occurred in the hint given by the investigators in Maier's famous 'two string experiment'.[38] Participants were requested to try to tie together two cords that were hanging from the ceiling, but which were wider apart than the human arm span and therefore could not be reached simultaneously. The room in which the experiment took place also contained various seemingly irrelevant objects on the floor. The solution was derived by reformulating from 'bottom-up' the available elements of the problem (the cord and a suitable object from the floor) not as isolated elements ('cord' and 'object' as separate) but in combination as a new integrated element – cord and object as a pendulum. The pendulum can then be used to swing the cord to bring it closer to the other and previously out of reach cord. The experimenter sometimes gave a hint by walking across the room and 'accidentally' brushing against one of the cords to set it swinging. Most subjects who solved the problem were not consciously aware of the intentionally-given hint but did solve the problem soon afterwards.[39]

Top-down reformulation

An example of top-down reformulation is Duncker's 'radiation problem' in which participants were required to try to devise a way for administering radiotherapy to treat a tumour located deep within the abdomen of a patient. The challenge was to do so without destroying the healthy tissue that surrounded the tumour. The solution to the problem typically involves a series of reformulations of the goal from 'avoid damaging healthy tissue' at all (leading to an incorrect solution, for example 'send rays down through the oesophagus') through to one of 'lower the intensity of the ray it passes through healthy tissue' (not feasible) leading eventually to the correct solution of sending many weak rays (rather than a single ray) from all angles but focused through the tumour (rather than the commonly used method of sending one strong ray from a single point; see Figure 3.8).[40] Some healthy tissue would be affected, the ray is of constant strength (and low) but the concentration of the rays at the point where the tumour is located is sufficiently large to give the required high dose.

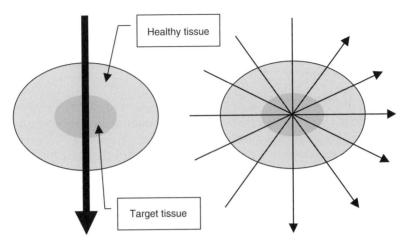

Figure 3.8 Schematic representation of the radiation problem (arrows represent radiation beam).

Getting over functional fixedness (removal of mental blocks)

Familiarity breeds 'functional fixedness'. Functional fixedness occurs when an object is seen only in terms of the ways in which it is tradition-ally used. It is a kind of automatic processing in which accepted ways of doing things are internalized and automatically applied without ques-tion. Overcoming functional fixedness removes mental blocks. The tech-niques associated with 'lateral thinking' (made famous by Edward de Bono in the 1960s) are ways of getting round this kind of mental rigid-ity. Duncker used the 'box problem' to investigate the extent to which perceptions can focus upon a single and well accepted function for an everyday object and limit its creative application. It goes as follows:

> Given three boxes each containing a candle, a tack and a match, mount three lighted candles on a wooden door at eye level.

To get to the correct solution participants in the experiment were required to think of the box not as being fixed in its function as a 'box' but as having some other possible function related to the problem, for example, as an improvised 'shelf'. Functional fixedness is overcome when the box is not seen exclusively as a container but as, when inverted and tacked to the door, a shelf for the candles to stand on (the problem solver needs to literally 'think outside the box').

Other examples of overcoming functional fixedness are the experiments that the Gestaltists performed in which chimpanzees were given the task of obtaining bananas that were just out of reach (by being attached to the ceiling or being outside of their cage) but where the potential solution was available. Crates in the cage could serve as a 'ladder' to enable the chimps to reach the bananas, or sticks could be used to reach outside the cage and drag the bananas in. In the stick example the chimpanzees were allowed to explore the range of possible functions for the sticks by playing with them for several days prior to the experiment. As a result of this exploratory play they were much more likely to solve the problem correctly. Past experience or pre-conceived notions about the function of an object have a self-persistence which may constrain novel thinking and block creative and productive uses for objects or ideas.

Filling in gaps (completing schemas)

Consider this perplexing insight problem:

> Two men were walking through a desert. They discovered on the sand the body of man. The dead man had with him a small pack containing fresh food and water. He had a larger pack on his back and a large ring on the index finger of his right hand. The two men puzzled over the man's death but were unable to fathom what had happened.

> There was no obvious explanation for how the man had met his end. With nothing more they could do the travellers continued on their way.

> Some miles further on one of the men accidentally dropped his handkerchief whilst mopping his brow and watched it float to earth. Eureka! He suddenly realized how the man had died.[41]

> How did the man die?*

Problem-solving requires the elements of the problem to be fitted together into a coherent mental structure or schema. A schema (*pl.*

---

* The large pack on the dead man's back was his unopened parachute, and the large ring on his finger was the ring pull for the parachute's opening cord. The ring pull had failed to open the man's parachute causing him to fall to earth and be killed on impact with the ground.

schemata) is a mental framework plan, or outline which internally represents some aspect of experience.[42] The 'body in the desert' problem is an example of the way in which filling in gaps to give a coherent whole (or schema completion) can give rise to a sudden, spontaneous and unexpected problem solution. The elements for the problem outlined above did not fit together until one of the men dropped his handkerchief, and up to this point the schema was incomplete. The man had stored a partial schema of the unsolved problem; the accidental encounter with the relevant external cue (the fluttering handkerchief) gave him the piece of the 'jigsaw' that was missing and the gaps could be filled in.

Using an analogy (analogical reasoning)

Two problems are analogous if there are shared features in the pattern of relationships amongst their respective elements. For example, a computer with its memory systems and information processing capacity has been offered as an analogy for the human brain. A base, or source, analogue consists of 'elements' and 'relationships' that are familiar and better known than those of the target analogue (the unsolved problem). Source analogues can be used to generate inferences about the target analogue.[43] The application of the source analogue's features (familiar) to the target analogue (unfamiliar unsolved problem) can trigger insight. Consider the 'fortress capture story'[44] below:

> A large army wishes to capture a fortress but to do so they need to converge at the fortress in sufficiently large numbers. The army is approaching the fortress from the north. The fortress has many roads leading to it from all sides. All of the roads leading to the fortress are narrow, too narrow to allow the army to converge simultaneously at the fortress. What is the leader of the army to do?

The army should split into smaller divisions and come together at the fortress from all sides along the many narrow roads that converge on the fortress. The fortress capture story is a base or source analogue for the tumour problem encountered earlier:

> A sufficiently large number of soldiers can come together simultaneously at the fortress
>
> If they split into smaller concentrations
>
> And come at it from different routes which converge at the fortress.

Similarly, in the tumour problem (which is the target analogue):

A sufficiently large dose of radiation can be brought to bear on the tumour

If a large enough number of weaker rays is deployed

And is directed at the tumour from all sides.

The relevant mappings between concepts are:

Army – Rays
Fortress – Tumour
Many roads – Multiple angles
Capture – Destroy

Many people solve the fortress problem much more easily than they solve the tumour problem, but both problems are underlain by the same abstract and general schema – a focal point with several narrow routes converging upon it. Because schemata can have general features that go across different problems (they can be generic representations) they can be utilized to solve novel problems that have similar structures and guide future problem-solving.

Analogies can work forwards or backwards (prospectively or retrospectively). Unsolved problems encountered previously may be stored and spontaneously accessed and mapped onto a later encounter with an analogous problem that has a solution[45] (this is 'backward mapping' onto the unsolved problem is one explanation for the phenomenon of incubation). The generalized use of analogous reasoning across different problems and contexts distinguishes experts from novices[46] and explains how they are able to solve a much broader class of problems than a novice can.

In the context of scientific discovery, invention or creative innovation, the discovery of what Philip Johnson-Laird refers to as 'profound analogies' is unlikely to depend upon pre-existing rules. Instead profound analogies depend upon the creation of new mappings inside an extensive domain of knowledge. The important point about extensive prior knowledge is that within it the number of possible mappings increases exponentially with the number of links between concepts. The tail-biting snakes in Kekulé's dream by the fire was an analogical representation, the structure of which he was able to match to the thing it came to represent[47] (benzene's structure) and hence interpret the fantastical 'dream forms' in a profound and insightful way. It is not surprising that the task of discovering profound analogies usually defeats all but a small number of exceptional thinkers[48] who have the necessary expertise and large repertoire of schemata with which they can see the relevance of an analogy and judge its suitability. For non-experts a profound insight may simply pass them by un-noticed because they may not be alert to its significance.

EXPLAINING INCUBATION

At a deeper level what are the processes which may be occurring within the brain of the problem solver during incubation? Several inter-related mechanisms have been suggested.

Random recombination

Insight can arise through chance associations of ideas, concepts, recollections, emotions, sensations and other 'mental elements'.[49] According to this view problem solvers may search through a bank of concepts and ideas which undergo haphazard combinations and re-combinations outside of conscious awareness. The combinations are filtered by mechanisms such as latent inhibition (see below) and those ideas which hold promise are selected for further processing.[50] 'Chance favours the prepared mind' (*'Le hasard favorise l'esprit préparé'*) is an aphorism often

Table 3.2 Problem-solving strategies based on insight

Visual restructuring *Seeing the problem in a different way*	Physically moving around and re-arranging the visual elements of a problem can help to re-combine them in different ways.
Problem reformulation *Putting the question in a different way*	Problems can by re-formulated by: (1) searching for available elements that might help solve the problem and exploring ways in which they can be combined in novel ways; (2) by re-stating goals in alternative ways (e.g. 'bring sufficiently large dose of radiation to bear on the tumour').
Removing mental blocks *Getting over 'functional fixedness'*	Functional fixedness can be overcome by: (1) using lateral thinking techniques; (2) engaging in exploration and playfulness.
Using analogical reasoning and completing schemas *Using an analogy and filling in gaps*	Visual mapping of the elements of a problem and their relationships may help to create a general schema onto which analogical situations may be mapped.

attributed to the French chemist and microbiologist Louis Pastuer (1822–1895). In-depth knowledge of a particular subject area (having a 'prepared mind') does two things:

1 supplies the relevant knowledge upon which random combination may operate;
2 helps in judging the potential value or viability of novel combinations.

Many of the examples of invention and innovation in business attest to this fact – Thomas Edison (with thousands of inventions to his name), Edwin Land (Polaroid), Art Finn and Spencer Silver (3M), and many others were well prepared for the innovations for which they are now famous. Random combination is much more likely to lead to insights and creative breakthroughs if the problem solver is an expert rather than a novice. An expert is able to make unusual and fruitful connections between ideas but also recognize the significance of novel combinations.

In 'random recombination' the incubation phase is a 'space' or 'melting pot' for allowing combinations to occur through incidental exposure to problem-relevant stimuli in the environment. Recombination may happen, as it did with the handkerchief in the 'body in the desert' problem, because of pure chance, or it may not. 'Opportunistic assimilation' theory[51] claims that if the problem solver does not encounter problem-relevant random cues the problem remains unsolved (if the handkerchief hadn't have been dropped the man's death would have remained a mystery).

Latent inhibition

One way in which the brain reduces the cognitive load being placed upon it is through the process of 'latent inhibition' (LI), which filters out information before it can consume the valuable processing capacity demanded by conscious awareness.[52] Lower levels of LI are associated with the personality trait of openness to experience (one of the 'Big Five' personality dimensions) which in turn is associated with divergent thinking (i.e. random, informal thinking around and away from the problem). It may be therefore that creative individuals somehow lower (attenuate) their LI in order to make more mental elements available which may be combined in novel ways.

Research at Harvard University suggests that creative individuals have lower levels of latent inhibition and this reduced level of LI is associated with creative achievement, creative personality and divergent thinking. High creative achievers in a specific field (such as those whose work had won prizes at juried art shows) were seven times more likely to have low rather than high LI. It appears that people with low LI don't filter out as much information as people with high LI and therefore have a larger pool of disparate ideas with the potential to be integrated together in novel ways.[53]

Spreading activation

Another explanation that has been offered for incubation is the spread of neural activity through networks in long term memory (LTM).[54] This activation may occur in a number of ways. First, without any further contact with cues in the environment where a 'train' of activation is set off and runs it natural course (this is called 'autonomous activation'). Second, with further contact with environmental cues which connect with concepts in LTM that have been 'primed' by partial activation (this is called 'interactive activation').

Autonomous activation

A period of inactivity allows for activations across neural networks to simply accumulate. The incubation 'space' allows the time for neural activation to spread to nodes that are relevant to the problem and its solution.[55] When researchers gave problem solvers on a visual restructuring task 'no break', a 'short break' (four minutes) or a 'long break' (12 minutes) they found that once an impasse had been reached a short or long break resulted in a problem-solving performance that was between two and half and four times better than if no break was given.[56]

Having been diverted from the problem, returning to the problem presented the problem solvers with a brief moment of release from the blocking false assumptions and allowed them a 'free-floating mind'. This lowered the chance of the previously-held false assumption getting a stranglehold on their thinking. Simply sitting and engaging in 'no activity' not only provided a break from effortful processing, it also served to direct attention away from incorrect assumptions. In a sense they were 'doing by not doing'.[57]

Interactive activation

Activation in the incubation phase heightens problem solvers' sensitivities to chance encounters with relevant external stimuli[58] – they become 'primed'. In the mysterious case of the 'body in the desert' the problem solver's sensitivities to problem-relevant cues (such as freely falling objects) was heightened through non-conscious activation of associated cognitive networks. When problem-relevant information is encountered (the handkerchief fluttering to Earth) it is assimilated into the problem solver's cognitive system and facilitates schema completion. Koestler[59] cites the experience of Gutenberg, the inventor of the printing press, who happened to be at a wine harvest and realized (from the cues which presented themselves, and towards which his sensitivities were heightened) that the steady pressure used to crush grapes could also be useful for imprinting letters: 'In the trivial routines of thinking we are exploring the shallows on the twilight periphery of awareness, guided by a more or less automatised scanning procedure. In creative thinking we are exploring deeps, without any *obvious* guidance' (added emphasis).

The problem-relevant mental framework (schema) is geared-up by activities below the threshold of conscious awareness,[60] then problem-relevant information in the environment (perceived consciously or non-consciously) is directed along the necessary cognitive pathways. One mechanism by which this occurs is through 'failure indices' – these are special markers that remain active but below the level of conscious awareness after an impasse in solving the problem has been reached and which remain vigilant for sought-after information.[61]

It is likely that both the accumulation of neural activity (autonomous activation) and heightened sensitivity to relevant cues (interactive activation) combined with low latent inhibition in the incubation stage are involved in insight. If autonomous incubation alone doesn't produce a solution, interactive activation through exposure to cues in the environment may provide an additional impetus.[62]

Individual differences

Differences between individuals in the way they process information (their 'cognitive style' or 'thinking style') can result in differences in problem-solving and creativity. For example, some individuals' attention and activation is narrowly-focused (they attend to a comparatively small number of items at any one time) while for others their attention and activation is widely-focused. Widely-focused attention can generate leaps and combinations and which may give rise to novel associations; in narrowly-focused attention on the other hand such leaps may not occur.

Narrowly-focused attention is associated with a smaller 'semantic field' (for example, in a remote word associate task such as (crab, pine, sauce) the focus is upon a few concepts related to the input words) and lower levels of creativity.[63] Similarly, individuals who generate only a few closely-related words in response to a stimulus (e.g. 'chair' in response to 'table') have a quicker falling-off in their responses (they have a steeper associative hierarchy) than those who generate a larger number of unusual ones. For example, responding 'leg', 'food' and 'Mabel' and so on, in response to 'table' gives a much slower tailing-off in responses (the associative hierarchy is shallower). How steep or shallow is your associative hierarchy? Try this question:

How many uses can you think of for a brick?

We may be familiar with some people for whom this challenge to an almost incessant stream of suggestions (they have a shallow associative hierarchy) whilst others quickly exhaust their list of possibilities after one or two of the more obvious suggestions (for example, 'build a house', 'break a window') – their associative hierarchies are steep (see Figure 3.9).

A flatter associative hierarchy is related to a wider spread of activation, larger semantic fields (encompassing a larger number of concepts including those only distantly related to the input word) and more novel, unusual or bizarre combinations.[64] Widely-focused (or de-focused) attention and flatter associative hierarchies are properties of the cognitive processes that occur in dreaming and reverie (referred to by Erich Fromm as 'primary process' cognition), whereas more abstract, logical, conscious and less associative modes of thinking are properties of Fromm's secondary process cognition (see Figure 3.10).[65]

There are tried and tested thinking strategies which can be used to generate novel associations and which can help to give flatter associative hierarchies. Table 3.3 shows one such technique that can be used for idea generation.[66]

EXPERTISE AND INSIGHT

Coming up with a significant creative insight without ever having been deeply involved in an area is not impossible but it is improbable.[67] The picture which emerges is one of insight as a process of the 'prepared mind' drawing consciously or non-consciously upon problem-relevant information ('domain-specific knowledge'). The role that expertise plays in insight is illustrated by the seemingly mundane example of solving anagram puzzles. Look at the following arrangement of letters. Try rearranging them to make a common English word:

suoeh

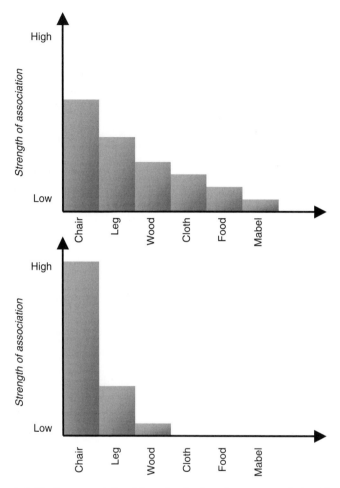

Figure 3.9 Shallow associative hierarchy (top) and steep associative hierarchy (bottom) for the stimulus word 'table'.

There are a number of possible ways to solve this problem. One is by systematically rearranging the letters. By following this approach the anagram can be solved in three step-by-step moves. But some people report being able to solve such problems involuntarily – the solution comes to mind suddenly 'out of nowhere' without any awareness of having done anything particularly effortful to get to the answer (the solution 'pops out').

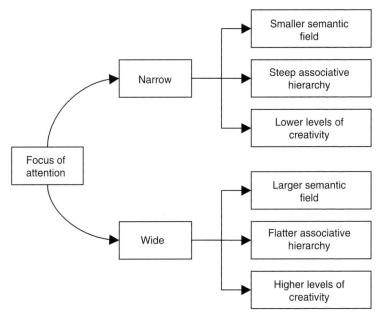

Figure 3.10 Focus of attention, semantic field width, associative hierarchies and creativity.

Table 3.3 Structured word association

Round	fish	hotel	coin
#1			
#2			
#3			
#4			
#5			

Source: M. Michalko, 'Lights on!', *Across the Board*, 1998, 35(7): 32.

Notes: In the Table three words ('fish', 'hotel' and 'coin') are listed. For each one write down the first association that comes to mind and go across the row (this is Round #1). Do the same for Round #2 but this time give a word which has a different association than on Round #1. For example, if you gave 'sea' (a fish's habitat), think of a non-habitat association, such as 'silver' (an appearance association) rather than 'tank' (another habitat association). This forces a greater diversity of associations.

To try to unravel this phenomenon Laura Novick and Steven Sherman conducted a series of experiments which examined the speed and accuracy of anagram solution and the strategies that people used in solving such puzzles. They compared the performance of highly-skilled anagram solvers and less-skilled anagram solvers and observed a 4:1 difference in the proportion of solutions that occurred within the first two seconds of exposure to the problem in favour of the expert anagram solvers. The experts were much more likely to generate 'pop-out' solutions than were the less-skilled anagram solvers.[68]

In another experiment Novick and Sherman asked expert anagram solvers to give a subjective solution report for each puzzle they solved to say how they thought they got there. Almost half (47 per cent) of the solutions generated were 'pop-outs', and these occurred on average 1.9 seconds after exposure to the problem.[69] Non-expert anagram solvers appear to engage in 'grind-out' solutions, whereas 'pop-outs' appeared to be a hallmark of expertise in anagram solving.

It may prove more difficult for a problem solver or decision-maker to have a profound insight or make an informed intuitive judgement when she or he is lacking extensive knowledge, experience and prior learning. The chess masters researched by Herbert Simon (see Chapter 4) had internalized tens of thousands of patterns, the firefighters in Klein's decision-making studies were experienced and seasoned professionals, well used to recognizing subtle cues in the environment, and Kekulé and the other scientists we encountered earlier in this chapter were all deeply immersed in their own particular field of study.

That said, marginal intellectuals or 'polymaths' (thinkers who participate in multiple domains but are central to none) may be in a privileged position to make connections across different domains and yield up novel solutions.[70] Individuals extolled as highly creative in science or art sometimes turn out to be polymathic. Einstein, for example, was an accomplished musician especially on the violin, and had he not been a scientist he may well have become a musician. Einstein's passion for music affected his life and work; for example, his second wife Elsa is quoted as saying: 'Music helps him when he is thinking about his theories. He goes to his study, comes back, strikes a few chords on the piano, jots something down, returns to his study'.[71] Unfortunately, being an effective polymath is increasingly difficult given the huge explosion of knowledge that has taken place since the early 1900s. Polymaths run the risk of being 'jack of all trades' but 'master of none'. This has meant that creative individuals in most domains have had to become more and more specialized.[72]

Along with expertise the suspension (but not abnegation) of judgment and a tolerance of ambiguity may be important factors in facilitating insight and creative intuitions. Whilst certain individuals may be more tolerant of ambiguity than others and able to suspend judgement and avoid premature closure, there are techniques by which anyone's judgement may be suspended and the censoring function of the rational mind 'turned off'. As psychologist Guy Claxton has argued there are some problems which 'will not succumb to an increase in expertise . . . To deal with such problems, we need access to those slow ways of knowing . . . called rumination or contemplation; mental modes which deliver, it is claimed, forms of *creativity* and *intuition*'[73] (original emphases). Meditative and contemplative practices are tried-and-tested strategies for giving one's rational mind a 'reprieve'.[74] These approaches serve to de-focus attention, create an 'incubation space', and stop stronger rational thoughts overwhelming weaker but more creative insightful or intuitive thoughts. Clearly many of the tasks which require insights and creative intuitions differ markedly from those tasks requiring rapid intuitive decisions under time constraints or other forms of pressure where rumination and contemplation may be neither appropriate nor viable (a meditative firefighter may be less than effective!).

The contemplation exercise in Table 3.4 is one way to clear the mind

---

Box 3.1   A 'sitting' practice for contemplation

Traditional postures for sitting are the lotus or half-lotus position, or kneeling back on your heels (but sitting on a chair is also acceptable). Your head and spine are held very upright: your hands are in your lap with the back of your left hand resting on your right palm, thumbs together. Your eyes stay open. 'Once your posture is in order regulate your breathing. Your attention follows the breath. If a thought arises take notice of it and dismiss it. If you practice this way for a long time, you will forget all attachments and concentration will come naturally'. The technique itself appears extremely simple and requires no rituals or complicated mantras. Beginners should concentrate on their breathing, counting cycles of ten breaths for the duration of 10 minutes on the first occasion, practised twice a day. Build-up to 40 or 50 minutes after some practice over a period of weeks and following breaths without counting them. The most difficult form does not employ any focus (not even the breath), and advanced 'sitters' face a plain wall. Pushed to its limits this deceptively simple technique is very demanding both physically and mentally.

Source: E. Chaline, *The Book of Zen* (Gloucester, MA: Fair Winds Press, 2003) pp. 90–1.

of rational thoughts and allow intuitions to surface and insights to happen.[75] It's not always possible to 'sit' during a busy day and a number of successful business leaders have developed their own tactics as they revealed in interviews for *Management Today* in 2003:[76]

> *Gerry Mulvin, global business consulting firm Bain & Co.*: 'I go running nearly every day. I run for more than an hour, before work, first thing in the morning. I think about what I'm working on, about the problems that I face, and ways of sorting them out. I have all my bright ideas when I'm running – I do all my problem-solving between Regents Park and Hyde Park. When I'm running, my mind is freed up to think more laterally; it broadens my horizons.'

> *Bryan Sanderson, speaking in 2003 as Chairman of BUPA*: 'I don't go anywhere in particular when I need space to think, I just need somewhere peaceful. That's the key driver, it's not location. I prefer to think somewhere that's very quiet. I spend a lot of time on the road, and have the luxury of a chauffeur-driven car, so I sit back, put on Classic FM and think. I'm a keen gardener and there's a particular area of my garden that has a Japanese feel; it has a courtyard and fountain. It's amazingly quiet and very conducive to thinking.'

The same article revealed that not all workers are able to create the mental space even though they feel the need to do so: 56 per cent of workers surveyed in the June 2003 'Workspace Satisfaction Survey' wanted break-out areas as refuges from their desk space, but only a fifth have access to such areas.

Until recently much of the evidence for the effects of meditation on cognition came from religious, spiritual or mystical writings, based upon a paradigm which is valid in its own terms but does not emphasize a scientific approach.[77] Evidence is beginning to emerge from studies using the scientific method that mediation can help to break fixed and habitual modes of thinking.[78] For example, alternative health practitioners have used meditation in experimental settings to interrupt habitual and automatic ways of responding. De-automatization of thinking was observed to occur immediately after meditation but was not sustained, and hence left intact the ability to respond habitually.[79] Techniques and strategies for the de-automatization of response have considerable potential in work settings for creating the conditions conducive to creative insight and intuition.

NEURO-PHYSIOLOGY, INSIGHT AND INTUITION

Insight comes upon the problem solver suddenly and unexpectedly, with few indications of progress towards the illuminative moment. A number of psychologists have tested this idea using the concept of 'warmth ratings'[80] by comparing problem solvers' estimates of how close they felt they were to a solution on insight problems (sometimes called 'pop-out' solutions) with their estimates on non-insight ('grind-out') problems.[81] During the experiment participants were asked to give subjective ratings at regular 15-second intervals of how close they felt they were to a solution (on a warm-cold interval scale, with 'warmer' meaning 'closer to solution'). Researchers found that participants:

1   could predict with reasonable accuracy at the outset if they could or could not solve the non-insight problems;
2   had a more incremental growth in their 'feelings of warmth' (FOWs) as they worked through non-insight problems than they did when working on insight problems.

Insight problems tended to show a very sudden increment in FOWs once the solution state was reached or about to be reached. Other research shows that in the final minute of insight problem solving heart rate shows a rapid increase especially in the last 15 seconds leading up to the solution state. No such step change in heart rate for non-insight problems is observed (indicating controlled mental activity).[82] Moreover, the feeling which accompanies the 'Eureka!' moment is likely to be related to the unexpectedness of the connections made.[83]

Experimental findings, anecdotal accounts and introspection confirm that insight is accompanied by a strong affective response. Archimedes is alleged to have called out 'Eureka!' as he leapt from his bath and Kekulé's account was similarly exclamatory '. . . lo, the atoms were gambolling before my eyes!' Some psychologists have argued that the only real substantive difference between insight and non-insight problems is the emotional intensity which accompanies the solution.[84] Their argument is that there is 'nothing special' about insight and that there is little reason to believe that solutions to problems do come 'in a flash'.[85] If this were to be the case we might expect to see no differences in neural activity when insight and non-insight problems are solved. There are two ways that this has been looked at in lab settings:

1   *Electro-Encephalography (EEG) studies*: EEG is based on the principle that when large populations of neurons are active

simultaneously (such as when a problem is being solved) they produce electrical signals large enough to be measured by electrodes on the scalp.[86]

2 *functional Magnetic Resonance Imaging (fMRI) studies*: fMRI does not measure neuronal activity directly, instead it relies on the fact that the more active neurons are, the more blood they need. fMRI and other techniques such as Positron Emission Tomography (PET) track changes in blood flow (hemodynamics).[87] From the patterns of blood flow it is possible to indirectly infer which neural circuitry is 'firing' (and thereby consuming oxygen from the bloodstream which shows up on the scan) during particular mental activities.

In psychology lab. settings remote word association tasks have been used as problems in various fMRI and EEG studies of brain activation. For example:

> What single word can be added to each of these words to make a familiar compound word?
>
> Fence / Card / Master*

The basis of the argument is familiar. If, when prompted with the 'fence/card/master' stimuli, the problem solver initially has a narrow focus of attention concentrated within a small semantic field (i.e. upon a few words closely related to each stimulus) the solution is unlikely to be found. To solve the problem a wider spread of activation is required across a larger semantic field since this has a greater likelihood of encountering the common word. The 'incubation space' provides the opportunity for inactivity, and by the suppression of deliberate mental work activations across neural networks accumulate. The non-conscious activation that occurs in the mental incubation space also heightens the problem solvers' sensitivities to encounters with relevant external stimuli (by priming).

Mark Jung-Beeman and his colleagues used remote word associate problems of the crab/pine/sauce†-type in their fMRI studies of insight problem-solving.[88] They compared the pattern of neurological activity when the problems were solved by insight (where there was an 'aha!' moment) with the neurological activity that occurred when problems were solved non-insightfully (no 'aha!' moment). The researchers

---

* The answer is 'post': fencepost; postcard; postmaster.
† The answer is 'apple'.

observed an increase in neural activity in the anterior Superior Temporal Gyrus (aSTG)[89] of the right hemisphere (RH) when insight occurred (see Figure 3.11). Their explanation for this was that the aSTG region is specialized in facilitating the integration of information across wide semantic networks thus enabling problem solvers to make connections

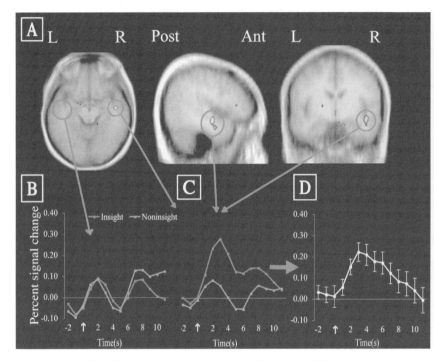

Figure 3.11 fMRI (brain scan) images of the activations which took place in the right hemisphere aSTG when problems were solved with insight. (A: the three images from left to right are views from the top, side and back of the head). Graphs B and C are average signal change for non-insight and insight solutions for left hemisphere (LH) aSTG (B) and right hemisphere (RH) aSTG (C). Short vertical arrow on time axis represents time at which button pressed by participants to indicate an insightful solution. Per cent signal change shown in C indicates burst of activity in RH aSTG at around 2 seconds after button press. Graph D is insight solution change minus non-insight solution changes in RH aSTG (i.e. amount of additional activation associated with insight solution in RH aSTG). Reproduced by permission of the authors.

Source: M. Jung-Beeman *et al.*, 'Neural activity when people solve problems with insight', *Public Library of Science (Biology)*, 2004, 2(4): 500–510.

that had previously eluded them. The neural circuitry in the same region of the left hemisphere (LH) on the other hand produces more discrete fields of activation, compared to that in the aSTG of the RH which is more diffuse and overlapping.

The researchers further speculated that because wide semantic processing in the RH is weak it may remain non-conscious and is perhaps overshadowed by the conscious processing of irrelevant or misdirected information in the LH. Recall that one of the supposed functions of meditation is to 'quiet' the rational mind or give it a 'by-pass'[90] and loosen the stranglehold of analytical thinking. The decay or suppression of the misdirected LH processing (such as that which may occur when the problem solver withdraws from conscious effort) may allow the weaker non-conscious RH processing to emerge suddenly into conscious awareness. Moreover, environmental cues (like Archimedes 'getting into the bath', or the floating handkerchief or the nudged pendulum in the examples we met earlier) combined with decay and suppression of the narrowly focused processing may further increase the chances of the insight solution emerging fully-formed into conscious awareness.

A supplemental EEG finding from Jung-Beeman's experiments was in relation to the alpha wave patterns produced in participants' brains. As noted earlier, simultaneous activation of large populations of neurons produces electrical signals large enough to be measured on the scalp[91] – this is the basis of the EEG technique. In general terms the presence of alpha activity is associated with a quiescent, meditative state, whilst its disappearance is due to attention and arousal. Jung-Beeman and his colleagues observed a burst of alpha waves over the right posterior parietal-occipital region of participants' brains (part of the visual cortex) in insight problem-solving. Alpha activity in the visual cortex may indicate that visual information from this brain region was subject to 'idling' (witness the burst of alpha activity) in order to protect fragile insight processes from interference by stronger visual information. Jung-Beeman *et al.*, by their own admission, describe this interpretation as 'provocative', nonetheless it offers intriguing possibilities for the role that meditative states may play in the 'idling' of strong cognitive processes that may otherwise interfere with insight.

Notwithstanding the speculative EEG results, the main fMRI findings of this research suggest that the quite specific cognitive functions and neural circuitry are involved in insight. 'Eureka! moments' are associated with neural processes which are absent when problems are solved in a regular analytical and narrowly-focused way. The diffuse patterns of activation which occur below the level of conscious awareness during incubation contribute to the creation of novel solutions which may be

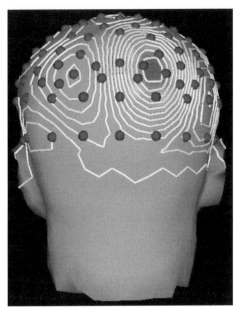

Figure 3.12 Head model (rear view) showing alpha band power in right parietal occipital region for insight solution. Diagram shows the increase in alpha band power between −1.31 and −0.56 seconds before 'Eureka!' moment. (Numerous black circular dots are EEG electrode locations; white lines are 'topographic maps' of scalp current density). Reproduced by permission of the authors.

Source: M. Jung-Beeman *et al.*, 'Neural activity when people solve problems with insight', *Public Library of Science (Biology)*, 2004, 2(4): 500–510.

Table 3.4 Comparison of insight and intuition

Intuition	Insight
Precedes insight	Builds on intuitive processes
Detected affectively in conscious awareness	Appears fully-formed into conscious awareness
Consists of a hypothesis	Consists of a solution
Broader (i.e. is holistic)	Narrower (i.e. is problem-specific)
A spontaneous conscious perception of a 'sense of coherence'	A slower non-conscious accumulation of activation during incubation

presaged by an intimation or intuition that the problem is close to being solved. Allowing space for incubation is one way of establishing the pre-conditions for creative intuitions to occur and for insights to emerge and flourish and, in the words of Robert Burton in *The Anatomy of Melancholy*, for 'phantasy, or imagination' to 'conceive, strange, stupend, absurd shapes' which are available to that 'inner sense'. On other occasions however, intuitions may occur which will remain as judgements rather than fully-formed insights. Whether or not the degree of conviction that accompanies an intuitive judgement is justifiable can be tested out by subsequent experience (i.e. may be verified empirically). As the intuition researcher Kenneth Bowers and his colleagues noted, intuitive judgement involves the generation of hunches (akin to 'hypotheses') that require further testing before they can be accepted as valid.[92] Time may tell if an intuition – which is an 'affectively-charged' hypothesis 'posted' into conscious awareness – was 'right' or not. The reasoning which leads to insight involves non-conscious processes, the outcomes become conscious. Intuitive reasoning on the other hand leads to judgements in which we have confidence but for which we unable to articulate any explicit reasoning – the reasoning if it is such tends to be below the level of conscious awareness.

TAKE-AWAYS FOR CHAPTER 3

Key ideas

As a result of 'insight' a problem solver shifts *rapidly* and *unexpectedly* from not knowing how to solve a problem to knowing how to solve it without any intermediate processes being detectable in conscious awareness. Insight is not the same as intuition – intuitions are *affect-laden judgements*, insights are *clear-cut solutions*. Creative problem-solving is process consisting of several *stages*, for example: preparation, incubation, intimation, illumination and verification. *Incubation* occurs through the connecting together of mental elements (which may be affectively 'tagged') by a number of mechanisms including *chance associations* and spread of neural activity through networks of *common associations*. Coming up with a significant creative insight without deep knowledge is improbable because insight is a process of the 'prepared mind' drawing consciously or non-consciously upon *problem-relevant information*. Insight processes appear to be associated with a burst of neural activity in the right hemisphere (RH) anterior Superior Temporal Gyrus (*aSTG*) and also with the *idling* of activity in the visual cortex to 'protect' fragile insight processes from interference by stronger visual information. Organizations can create and support the *conditions* which may allow insight and intuition to arise and flourish.

Intuition quote: Sir Karl Popper, philosopher of science

'There is no such thing as a "logic of creation", instead every discovery contains an "irrational element" or a "creative intuition".'

Action point

What things will you do in your personal or professional life to *create conditions* which are conducive to insight and intuition and which allow them the space to flourish and to provide *direction* for your analytical mind to follow?

FURTHER READING

Boden, M.A., *The Creative Mind: Myths and Mechanisms*. London: Routledge 2004.
Claxton, G. and Lucas, B., *Be Creative: Essential Steps to Re-vitalise your Work and Life*. London: BBC Books 2004.
Sternberg, R.J. and Davidson, J.E. (eds), *The Nature of Insight*. Cambridge, MA: The MIT Press 1995.

Solutions to insight problems (page 65):
Problem 1: in pulling a gun the bar tender gives the man a fright which cures him of his hiccups.
Problem 2: apple.

4 Intuitive expertise

> Time and education begets experience; experience begets memory;
> memory begets judgement and fancy; judgement begets strength and
> structure, and fancy begets the ornaments of a poem.
>
> (Thomas Hobbes, 1588–1679, *The Answer to Davenant's*
> *preface Before 'Gondibert'*, 1650)

MAIN IDEA

Human beings are equipped for fast pattern recognition and to
be able make judgements on the basis of the thinnest 'slices'
of data. More often than not the ability to make fast accurate
judgements is borne of an extensive period of intensive prior
learning, experience and practice.

Some university and college lecturers may not always think of their
students as being experts. However, students are likely to be expert in at
least one thing – judging their lecturers. Moreover it is something which
they appear to be able to do with considerable accuracy from glimpsing
the 'thinnest slices' of lecturers' behaviours. Why should this be so?
In any social setting it is important for humans to be able to rapidly
execute a wide variety of judgements, including the perception of the
character and motives of another person.

'THIN SLICES': STUDENTS AS INTUITIVE EXPERTS

In an educational setting it is advantageous for students to be able to come to rapid judgements about the effectiveness, or otherwise, of their lecturers. The judgement they arrive at might then be used to inform their learning and studying behaviours (for example, whether 'Professor X's' 9 a.m. classes really are worth attending or not). In the 1990s two Harvard researchers looked at how accurate these perceptions of 'thin slices' of lecturers' behaviours can be. Nalini Ambady and Robert Rosenthal[1] of Harvard's psychology department aimed to investigate the relationship between students' judgements of video clips of lecturers and the actual ratings by class members of lecturer performance in classroom settings. The key variable they chose to focus on was overall end-of-semester ratings of lecturers by students. The observers giving the ratings of the video clips were student raters but were not members of the lecturers' classes (in this sense they were 'strangers').[2]

In the first experiment the nine female undergraduate student raters (females were used because they were deemed better judges of non-verbal behaviour) were shown silent video clips of the first, middle and last ten seconds of a class (three clips of 13 lecturers, making 39 clips in all) and asked to score the lecturers on 15 non-verbal behaviours (for example, 'accepting', 'enthusiastic' and 'warm'). The researchers were looking to see if there was a relationship between the ratings of non-verbal behaviours based on these 'thin' ten second video 'slices' and the ratings of lecturers' performance given after a whole semester by the actual class members. Of the fifteen non-verbal behaviours no fewer than ten of them correlated highly with the independent ratings of lecturer effectiveness. Lecturers' 'confidence' and 'optimism' correlated most strongly with effectiveness,[3] and the results showed a remarkably accurate correspondence, given how short the video clips were.[4]

In other words the ratings by people who were in effect strangers, based on very thin slices of video-taped behaviour (consisting of a matter of seconds) predicted with remarkable accuracy the ratings by students who had a semester-long, face-to-face interaction with those same lecturers. Ambady and Rosenthal concluded that their results highlight two significant findings:

1   Thin slices of behaviour convey a wealth of information about interpersonal and affective behaviours – we unwittingly communicate a very great deal about ourselves in a very short space of time.
2   Strangers' judgements of behaviour based upon exceedingly short observed segments can be remarkably accurate, or to put it another

way – our intuitive judgements based upon the thinnest of slices of visual data can be unexpectedly precise.[5]

This finding, that students possess a high level of intuitive skill in forming impressions of their lecturers is perhaps not all that surprising: evolution has equipped human beings with the capability to make rapid and accurate judgements and predictions. From birth we are engaged constantly in social interactions and in learning from experience about the character and behaviours of others through what amounts to 'trial and error', imitation and social learning. This capability combined with the appropriate experiences in the right kind of learning environment and feedback[6] endows each of us with the potential to develop the expertise that underpins intuitive social judgement – or social intuition. Important, and quite likely long-lasting, judgements about other people are arrived at within only several seconds of first meeting with them. The intriguing possibility exists that human beings come 'pre-loaded' as a result of evolutionary adaptations with the 'software' to make intuitive social judgements – a kind of 'social expertise' or 'social intuition'.

FAST PATTERN RECOGNITION

As an illustration of the power of expertise William Chase and Herbert Simon performed a simple experiment. Here is a much simplified representation of it. Experts and novices were presented with chessboards, with the pieces arranged much as they are in the photographs in Figure 4.1. Participants studied Chessboard A for a short period, and it was then removed from view. Their task was to recall the positions of as many of the pieces as possible. They then performed the same task with Chessboard B.

If a novice is pitted against a chess grandmaster in recalling the arrangement of pieces on Chessboard A they would most likely have been easily beaten since an expert would probably have been able to place around 90 per cent of the pieces correctly. So maybe chess grandmasters have great visual memories? No, because if a novice is pitted against a chess grandmaster in recalling the layout of Chessboard B both would have probably scored about the same (around six pieces correctly recalled). When chess non-experts take this simple test they manage to get about six pieces give or take a couple correct *in both tasks*. Chess experts score about 90 per cent on Chessboard A and about the same as a novice on Chessboard B. How can this be?

Figure 4.1a Chessboard A.

Figure 4.1b Chessboard B.

The difference is that on Chessboard A the pieces are arranged mean-ingfully in a pattern as they might be in a real game; on Chessboard B on the other hand the pieces have been arranged randomly in a pattern that would be very unlikely to be encountered in a real game. A chess grandmaster is an expert and as such sees Chessboard A meaning-fully, not as an arrangement of pieces but as a small number of familiar patterns that they have met in some form in previous learning and experience. Simon estimated that a chess grandmaster is likely to have internalized around 50,000 familiar patterns[7] and is able to respond in a game, if the need arises, accurately within a couple of seconds with apparent intuitive ease. The chess expert stores patterns in long term memory and it is likely that this is captured in their long term memory along with other associated information in a parallel affective system. For example a pattern or move may be emotionally-'tagged' with the level of danger or opportunity and the feeling of elation or disappointment which a particular pattern may have induced in past successes or failures. Where the same scenario is encountered again the affective response, but at a reduced level of intensity, may be instigated.[8]

Most of the readers of this book are unlikely to be chess grandmasters; indeed most readers are likely to be novices in this area and so cannot recognize the meaningfulness of Chessboard A as a set of patterns – to most readers A and B are an arrangement of individual chess pieces on an 8×8 board without any particular significance.

The ability to recognize patterns helps chess experts to play good chess very rapidly without consciously engaging in careful and deliberate analysis – they can play up to 50 opponents at once with little diminution in their performance levels. The inability to recognize patterns means that novices are unable to respond intuitively – they are of course able to guess wildly – but a wild guess is not an intuition. The ability to recognize patterns based upon deep knowledge structures enables experts in many different domains, not just chess (for example, firefighters, doctors and managers) to make decisions rapidly, intuitively and with cognitive economy – mental effort can be conserved by withdrawing from conscious thought those aspects of a decision or problem that are repetitive.[9] The advantage of doing so is that resource-intensive conscious thinking can be devoted to other processes.

Like chess grandmasters, experienced managers have in their long term memories an extensive database of knowledge held as chunks, patterns or 'mental models' (an internal representation of external reality) which they have gained from learning processes and exposure to problems. These patterns may be called up by 'recognition-and-retrieval' mechanisms which are largely non-conscious. An analogy that has been offered is that of a large static store of knowledge, such as might be held in an encyclopaedia, library or computer database, with access to it through rapid and elaborate cross-referencing and indexing.[10] For example, a naïve researcher set the task of finding out about the topic of '*Intuition* and its role in *decision-making* in *management*' would in a simple search of scholarly peer-reviewed journals find, to their dismay or delight, that a typical library data base would list 124,871 articles that contained 'intuition' or 'decision-making' or 'management' in their summary abstracts. However, by asking the database to search for a pattern which matches 'intuition' or 'decision-making' and 'management', the search is narrowed to a mere 5304, and asking for the pattern which matches 'intuition' and 'decision-making' and 'management' a paltry, but highly significant, 27 papers are all that are left to satisfy this criterion. So by a process of fast pattern-matching hundreds if not thousands of irrelevancies are eliminated almost instantaneously leaving only the most relevant pattern to be attended to saving much time and energy.

EXPERTISE AND INTUITION

Expertise, like insight and intuition, is neither magical nor mystical, nor is it a divine 'gift from the gods'. Becoming an expert in any domain from football, music or chess to running a business requires a strict regime of study and practice.[11] Experts are able to achieve consistently superior performance because they have relevant knowledge and the necessary skills.[12] One of the most influential contributions to the 'expertise debate' was made by the brothers Hubert L. Dreyfus and Stuart E. Dreyfus in their 1986 book *Mind Over Machine: The Power of Human Intuition and Expertise in the Era of the Computer*.[13] Originally the Dreyfuses were commissioned by the US Air Force to research the development of the knowledge and skills of pilots; they later studied the development of expertise in domains as diverse as chess, second language learning amongst adults, and driving an automobile.[14] They proposed a five stage model in which the progression from novice to expert involved the passage through the sequence of 'novice', 'advanced beginner', 'competent', 'proficient' and finally, 'expert performer'. The Dreyfus' Skill Acquisition Model (SAM) is summarized in Table 4.1.

At the 'expert level' decision-makers 'do what normally works' without consciously deciding;[15] and may not always be able to provide a reasoned rational explanation for their decisions. As well as being able to recognize patterns of clues and acting quickly, with intuition 'sweating away' doing the hard work in the 'back room', the expert is also attuned to spotting distortions in complex patterns and situations and to being able to recognize when things don't fit their expectations. The example from healthcare illustrates two things, first, how expertise can attune a decision-maker to spotting things that are 'out-of-kilter'; and second, to the ineffable quality that intuitive judgements may sometimes have:

Table 4.1 Summary of the Dreyfus' Skill Acquisition Model (SAM)

Stage	Description
Novice	Deploys detached, context-free, rule-following stance; does not take subtleties of the problem/decision into account
Advanced beginner	Uses more sophisticated rules acquired by observing the similarities between specific instances of a phenomenon in real-life situations
Competent	Coping with the 'crowdedness' of problem-solving and decision-making by conscious deliberate planning and analyzing manageable set of factors deemed important
Proficient	Associates newly-encountered situations with similar ones previously experienced and with plans that worked in past
Expert	Fluidity of performance and ability to discriminate between large number of contextual variables and situations based on deep knowledge structures
	Appears to 'do what normally works'; does not have to consciously decide what to do but may not find it easy to provide convincing rational explanation decision choice
	Able to 'vision' what might be possible

Sources: P. Benner, C.A. Tanner and C.A. Chesla, *Expertise in Nursing Practice: Caring, Clinical Judgement and Ethics* (New York: Springer, 1996); H.L. Dreyfus and S.E. Dreyfus, *Mind over Machine: The Power of Human Intuitive Expertise in the Era of the Computer* (New York: Free Press, 1986).

Her [the patient's] breathing was okay. However, once I walked in her room and thought: 'I'll look for her again'. A colleague of mine had the same thought and we went into the room together . . . I was looking at her and saying: 'I don't like her looks. She is breathing but I cannot say what . . .' I thought, 'Oh God, something isn't right'. Her blood pressure was okay, pulse was okay . . . *Everything was okay but something wasn't right.* (emphases added)[16]

In this example the doctor was called but didn't have the same bad gut reaction as the two nurses. Within half an hour the patient's condition deteriorated so badly that she ended up in intensive care. The bases of, in this case, the nurses' high level of intuitive skill are the abilities:

1   to perceive holistically and simultaneously a large number of clues in the environment;

2   of not needing to devote scarce cognitive resources to laboriously analyzing these clues, thereby freeing up working memory capacity for other tasks.

Unlike novices, who process details (not all of which may be relevant) and apply learned rules (in ways that may be insensitive to the specifics of the actual, as opposed to textbook, problem actually being faced), experts appraise situations holistically by abstracting summary information. They are then able to act in ways that are sensitized to the features of the context as they perceive it.[17] One media CEO explained in a *Harvard Business Review* interview the basis of his holistic judgement and the way in which 'gut feeling' and 'reason' are linked: 'reams of historical information about yourself that you remember from when you were a child pop into your mind. Gut instincts are the sum total of those experiences – millions and millions of them. And that sum total enables you to make reasonable decisions.'[18]

It's worth reiterating that as in the case of creative intuition, an expert's intuitive capabilities are 'informed' – they are borne out of many long hours of 'apprenticeship', even though to an outsider an expert may appear to engage in little conscious analysis, forethought and planning. The ability to be able to execute exceptional levels of performance requires tightly coordinated, sequentially focused practice activities (analogous to the long hours of practice that a virtuoso musician amasses).[19] Practice can take place in formal educational and training settings with expert guidance from teachers, but the role of coaching by an expert performer in workplace settings should not be underestimated – most of us spend 40 or more hours per week at work which presents abundant opportunities for several hours of intense, real-world practice per day. Unfortunately, but understandably, in organizations this tends to not happen; learning from exposure to problems and experts is sometimes more 'hit-and-miss' than 'managed-and-coordinated'.

At its maximal level expert performance shares a number of similarities with the concept of optimal or 'flow' experiences as described by the Hungarian psychologist Mihaly Csikszentmihalyi:

> A sense that one's skills are adequate to cope with the challenges at hand, in a goal-directed, rule-bound action system that provides clear rules as to how well one is performing. Concentration is so intense that there is no attention left over to think about anything irrelevant, or to worry about problems. Self-consciousness disappears and the sense of time becomes distorted.[20]

In the 'flow' condition thoughts 'bubble up' and arrange themselves in an order of their own making. 'Ecstasy' (from the Greek *ekstasis* meaning 'standing outside oneself') is a term that many performers use to describe what happens when they are in the 'flow condition'. Paradoxically, for the consummate performer, if conscious thinking intervenes the bond between the 'doer' and 'doing' gets broken,[21] flow may dissipate and performance suffers.

INTUITION, IMPROVISATION AND 'ALL THAT JAZZ'

On a different note, the organizational theorist Karl Weick draws our attention to the link between improvising and intuiting and the metaphor of jazz music. As Weick observes, *proviso* means to make some stipulation beforehand (as in 'provide'), whereas *im* negates this (as in 'im-possible'); *improviso* therefore means working without prior stipulation and in a sense anticipating, or at least leaving space for, the unexpected to occur. Weick and others have used the metaphor of jazz (the most improvisational of all music and referred to by the New York writer Whitney Balliett as 'the sound of surprise') to analyze the improvisational behaviours that occur in organizations.

In any field, be it jazz or management, the non-conscious processing of information and intuition guides improvisation and enables performance to proceed in a deceptively effortless fashion. However, because expertise born out of practice is at the heart of improvisation, whether improvisation is 'good' or 'bad' depends upon how well the performer or decision-maker can intuit on the basis of their expertise. For example, one way in which the ability to play effective improvised solos in jazz is developed is by playing phrases over and over again in a variety of different keys so that they can be used, via 'muscle memory', in any situation that happens to come up.[22] The jazz soprano and tenor saxophonist John Coltrane (1926–1967) for example, spent inordinately long hours practising obsessively and fanatically ('wood shedding')[23], and continued to do so throughout his career even when, in the mid-1960s, he was the most famous jazz musician in the world and at the top of his profession.[24] As a rule of thumb expert performers can sustain a maximum of about four hours of intense practice per day.[25] Paradoxically therefore, the freedom to improvise well comes through the strict discipline of practice.

Weick argues that the parallel with jazz is useful because expert 'practitioners'[26] (including managers) who, like highly skilled jazz musicians, are able to intuit and improvise around problems and decisions are

Figure 4.2 Jazz saxophonist John Coltrane; consummate performer, improviser and 'practicer'. Photo: Lebrecht and Co.

perhaps more accurately described as 'highly disciplined "*practicers*" '[27]. Jazz improvisers have through their laborious practising achieved a degree of compression of prior learning and experience that enables them to intuit automatically, accurately and rapidly. In management and other areas of professional practice similar levels of immersion and practice are necessary if decision-makers are to achieve the fluidity and intuitive ease of the virtuoso performer. Indeed management may have much to gain by learning from the ways in which its own exceptional performers and those in other fields achieve excellence. Perhaps the workplace as a space for intense practice has a lot to learn from the musical conservatories.

Rapid recognition and fast response depends on the availability in long term memory of large, well-organized knowledge structures and a complex set of rules that allow for quick and accurate judgements to be made.[28] These are analogous to the jazz improviser's 'execution in action' of internalized of riffs and phrases in response to the flow of the music. Many of the important problems and decisions that managers and other professionals face are complex, unstructured and judgemental; it is unsurprising therefore that they often rely upon their intuitions.[29] Informed intuitive judgement allows an experienced performer to respond to each situation based on prior learning and experience.[30] Viewed statically, expertise is like an extensive 'library of the mind', holding:

1   the books and the information contained in them (a set of elements);
2   their ordering on the shelves (information about the meaning or significance of the elements);
3   the indexing and cross-referencing rules, systems and short-cuts in databases and library catalogues which facilitate the bypassing of laboriously analyzing the content and location of each element[31] (pattern creation and recognition mechanisms).

Furthermore, a particular pattern may carry a 'significance rating' flagged up by the indexing and cross-referencing system (analogous to the role played by 'gut feeling' in decision-making) which serves to alert the user to its relevance to the problem at hand ('for' or 'against' its viability).

EXPERTISE IN BUSINESS AND MANAGEMENT

At higher levels in business organizations the ability to exercise intuitive, expert judgement is a vital skill – a point made by the CEO of a major multinational company in a *Harvard Business Review* interview:

> Very often, people will do a brilliant job up through the middle management levels, where it's very heavily quantitative in terms of the decision-making. But then they reach senior management, where the problems get more complex and ambiguous, and we discover that their judgment or intuition is not what it should be.

And when that happens, it's a problem; it's a *big* problem. (original emphases)

On the face of it this makes a lot of sense: we expect middle management decision-making to be routine and less complicated than the judgements demanded of an executive (for one thing they command higher salaries). This assertion is backed up by large scale surveys of managers in the UK which show that intuition is used more frequently by decision-makers who are higher up the organizational hierarchy.[32] Executives and senior managers who have the mastered the relevant knowledge and have the necessary skills are able to read situations quickly and holistically and tend not to consciously engage with the the the detailed aspects of a problem.[33] On the other hand, novice managers are more likely to have analyzed a situation painstakingly with the result that they may sometimes actually remember more specific details than an expert.[34] Did you for example, notice that the word 'the' occurred twice in succession a couple of sentences ago? A skilled reader is more likely to read sentences holistically rather than laboriously processing every word and examining its relationships with preceding and subsequent words in the sentence. Less proficient readers (and proofreaders) are more likely to notice the double 'the'.

Leading companies have learned to recognize the value of expertise and informed intuitive judgements. For example at Boeing, an engineering simulator is used for software development and familiarizing pilots with the new features and the handling characteristics of aircraft such as the Boeing 777. However, it is not a purely analytical approach; technicians take great heed of pilot's intuition when testing the system's functionality:

We'll take something they [pilots] notice that doesn't feel or look right and try to isolate it on the simulator. The pilots' intuition is incredible. They'll get a funny feeling that something is wrong but they don't know what it is. They'll point us in the right direction and we troubleshoot and, lo and behold, we validate there is a problem. We have learned not to discount their gut feelings.[35]

Education and learning allied to time and experience in occupational settings support the intuitions which experts, like Boeings' test pilots, use. For example, the ability of medics to perform effective clinical diagnoses shows marked improvements over the course of the transition from the novice medical student (who has had to 'cram' a vast amount of general medical knowledge) through to the medical expert who has highly structured, specialized clinical knowledge which supports accurate diagnoses.[36] Trish Greenhalgh, evidence-based medicine researcher and GP in her own right, illustrates the differences between experts and novices with examples of the 'clinical clerking' of a single patient, Mr Brown, adopted by health professionals at different stages of their careers:

> *Third-year medical student*: Mr Brown is a 38-year-old computer operator who attended the Accident and Emergency department with a bad feeling in his eye. The history of the presenting complaint was that it was there when he woke up at 7.15 am on Wednesday morning. When he was a little boy he had had an operation on his eyes for squint. He is up to date on his jabs [and so it goes on]
>
> *Experienced General Practitioner*: Rt conjunctivitis; Chloramphenicol drops; See S.O.S.

In turning to business and management, perhaps the role of undergraduate business degrees (Bachelors programmes) in universities should be, as Henry Mintzberg has forcefully argued, to educate students in general management and business knowledge (i.e. concepts and principles from the base disciplines of psychology, sociology, economics, philosophy and so forth) and in critical thinking. In Mintzberg's view business schools should 'get the applied material out of the undergraduate curriculum'.[37] If this were the case the equivalent of the 'clinical diagnostic skills' may then later be built upon the solid foundations provided by relevant social science knowledge and a critical and inquiring mind. As far as MBA programs go one astute executive in a US computer company noted that:

> Although people think that 'gut feeling' is not a rational decision-making method, many people fail to realise that 'gut-feeling' is actually a sub-conscious derivative of the accumulation of years of management experience. An MBA course may provide the tools to make better decisions, but it is no substitute for management experience. It is therefore important that decision-making be based on a combination of relevant information and 'gut-feeling'.[38]

Expert diagnostic and judgemental skills draws upon highly elaborated cognitive structures that have been built up over years if not decades, and it is these which allow experts to take complex and difficult decisions quickly. Experts, be they chess grandmasters, musical performers, firefighters, experienced nurses, teachers or managers, possess domain-specific knowledge which is situated in the context of practice and which can be drawn upon with little effort:[39]

> You've experienced something before, and it's there in your mind, but you don't know what it is. Yet it's there – something . . . You see a lot, and the thing is you remember what you see and look for it again. I don't know if I consciously look for it, but you remember . . . I think you develop it with experience.[40]

As this quote from a nurse illustrated, intuitive decisions involve making predictions based upon knowledge and past experiences which are woven together in complex ways, stored tacitly and not always open to introspection or available in conscious awareness. This is the basis of the notion of 'intuition-as-expertise'.[41]

INDIVIDUAL DIFFERENCES IN EXPERTISE

Learning when and when not to have confidence in an informed intuitive judgement calls is a, perhaps *the*, vital skill. Many successful entrepreneurs and business executives exhibit a propensity to recognize faint signals or patterns, but also have the confidence to assume that the missing elements of the pattern will take a shape they can predict or foresee. This anticipatory skill may enable them to keep ahead of potential competition[42] and envision beyond the present with strategic foresight as this quote from the multinational cosmetics company L'Oreal reveals:

> L'Oréal's success is due to Owen-Jones' [L'Oreal's Chief Executive Officer (CEO) is Lindsay Owen-Jones] acute market intuition. He instinctively knew that the world was ready for L'Oréal to duplicate the enormous success it had in France on a global level, by developing worldwide brands and by choosing the right brands to attack the right markets. Rapidity is also a big part of getting to number one: 'Being fast is sometimes more decisive than verifying every idea and validating every hypothesis', says Owen-Jones. 'The fact that intuition has regained such importance in the world of business is deeply gratifying to me'.[43]

This begs the question of how long it takes an individual to build up the elaborate cognitive architecture that supports improvisation, foresight and intuition. There is an oft-quoted 'ten-year rule' for the time it takes to acquire the necessary knowledge and skill to be able to perform expertly. For example, in chess, sports, arts and science, as a very general rule of thumb it requires around ten years of four hours per day intense practice, i.e. around 15,000 of hours of preparation and practice to achieve the higher levels of skill and performance.[44] In science the time interval between a scientists' first and their most important publication averages ten years or more.[45] In chess grandmasters' performance tends to peak in their mid-30s and decline gradually after that, but the good news for ageing chess players is that performance at age 63 years old is no worse than it was at 21 years[46] – so at least as far as chess goes you can always be 21.

Are there individuals, like Shakespeare, Mozart, Einstein and Picasso, who are born with exceptional 'talent' (a 'gift from the gods')? At a more mundane level the question of 'what role does innate ability play in expert performance?' in artistic, sporting and professional contexts is a huge and controversial issue. K. Anders Ericsson and Neil Charness' review of an extensive body of evidence suggests that differences between expert and non-expert performers reflect acquired knowledge and skills more than they do individual differences in innate ability. The retrospective accounts, biographies and diaries of musicians and athletes reveal relationships between the amount of deliberate practice undertaken, the age at which deliberate practice is engaged in and the eventual maximal level of performance.[47] Ericsson and Charness cite the examples of a number of exceptional individuals (including Einstein, Ghandi, Picasso and Stravinsky) whose achievements were associated with not only long periods of intense preparation (for example, Picasso produced many thousands of works of art not all of which were of 'genius' quality), but also with the coincidence of many favourable environmental and social factors. For example, the English artist David Hockney (born 1937) whose painting *The Splash* sold for over £2.5 million in 2006, had the support of his parents in his decision to leave the highly esteemed Bradford Grammar School at the age of 16 to attend to the local art college instead. This was despite financial concerns and the much 'safer bet' of continuing with a grammar school academic education.

Undoubtedly, there are differences between individuals in the factors which predispose them to engage in extensive and deliberate practice to reach the expert level of performance. Some of these individual difference factors may be environmental (for example a disciplined or nurturing home or workplace) but other factors (definable attributes such as temperament and preferred activity level) may have a genetic component.[48] Moreover, although psychologists have often confined their studies of expertise acquisition to areas such as chess, sport or music there is no reason to suppose that their conclusions do not similarly apply to occupational and professional settings, including decision-making, problem-solving and social functioning in business and management. In many fields of human endeavour it is likely that intensive, deliberate practice over a number of years account for differences in performance as much as innate 'talent' of itself.

THE LIMITS OF EXPERT PERFORMANCE

The idealized depiction of experts that we sometimes encounter should not be taken to imply that they somehow no longer need to think, are always right, or that learning stops when one reaches the lofty heights of being acknowledged as an 'expert'. For one thing experts can be wrong;[49] the psychologist Paul Meehl in his book *Clinical Versus Statistical Prediction* (1954) demonstrated the fallibility of human judgement in comparison to computational methods for certain types of problem. Another factor is that the decision-making environment that prevails in organizational settings is complex, dynamic and uncertain – which means both novices and experts alike have to learn, adapt and improvise. However, there are a variety of social and psychological reasons why experts may be resistant to new learning[50] (see Table 4.2).

Table 4.2 Some of the drawbacks of expertise

Image	If experts are seen to have a need to learn it might be interpreted that they are 'deficient' in some way.
Specialization	Being an expert implies occupying a very narrow intellectual or occupational niche. Specialization is essential if experts are to keep up with the explosion of knowledge that exists in society. One of the downsides of this is reduced versatility, flexibility and inability to synthesize across different domains.
Perceptual filters	Information that experts act on is attenuated because they may be exposed to a limited sub-set of information. Also they may only attend to a portion of the information that they are exposed to or which is needed.

Based on: W. Starbuck, 'Learning by knowledge intensive firms', in M.D. Cohen and L.S. Sproull (eds), *Organizational Learning* (London: Sage, 1996) pp. 484–515; G.P. Hodgkinson and P.R. Sparrow, *The Competent Organization: A Psychological Analysis of the Strategic Management Process* (Buckingham: Open University Press, 2002) pp. 161–2.

Although they are distinguished by a set of unique cognitive processes, experts like anyone else are not, nor can they afford to be, exclusively intuitive. When confronted by a situation for which there is no previous experience to fall back on, where the initial grasp of the situation is flawed as a result of a perceptual error or because the dynamics of the situation cause events develop an unexpected turn, an expert is likely to rely more on an analytic rather than an intuitive mode of cognition.[51] Experts, like non-experts, do engage in rationality and it would be extraordinary to think that they did not; but the types of rational analyses they are able to deploy differ:

1   Non-experts are more likely to engage in a 'calculative rationality' by applying and improving their concepts, theories, and knowledge of procedures.

2   Experts engage in a 'deliberative rationality' of detached, contemplative reflection (when time permits) which guards against 'grooved thinking' or 'tunnel vision' and provides an opportunity to challenge intuitions and literally re-cognize (re-think) one's understandings.[52]

From the perspective of cognition standard problem-solving approaches can reinforce particular activations along neural pathways. This can create benefits where the standard pathways lead to a viable solution to the problem; however in non-routine situations expertise which relies purely on existing approaches can be harmful.[53] Monitoring the interaction between the situation and one's own thinking processes and behaviours enables experts to deploy self-monitoring and self-regulative behaviours which enable them to reflect in the midst of action (Donald Schön referred to this as 'reflection-in-action') as well as after-the-fact (reflection-on-action).[54] These reflective processes help to build rich cognitive architectures upon which intuitive judgements can draw. Novices on the other hand may need to devote so much cognitive effort to perception, attention and analysis that little is left over for reflection. Expert performers in areas such as music, chess and medicine can generate better judgements than their less skilled counterparts even in situations they have never directly experienced.[55]

Many of the mental processes that operate our linguistic, perceptual and motor systems operate outside of conscious awareness[56] and the conscious and laboursome use of rationality can interfere with performance and result in a regression to merely competent or even novice levels. For example, it is sometimes better for an experienced public speaker to trust the form and content of what is being said to the implicit rules of grammar and mastery of content which may not be in conscious awareness (it is pre-conscious, i.e. can be recalled if necessary). Working memory can then be engaged in attending to more mundane matters such as time-keeping and audience attentiveness. The phenomenon of the breakdown of skill (sometimes called 'choking' or the 'yips') is to be found in a number of different fields, including golf and baseball. A stressful situation can also lead to an absorption in the step-by-step elements of a task and disrupt the flow and automaticity of skilled performance.[57] There is also evidence to suggest that this disruption is less likely if the skill has been learned implicitly.[58]

As practitioners become more expert they also are more likely to realize the limits of their knowledge and have a deeper appreciation of their ignorance – learning creates knowledge which itself creates questions, and more learning. The organizational behaviour researcher Karl Weick argues that wisdom can be defined in terms of both knowledge and ignorance; it is founded in a humility which stems from:[59]

1 *balance*: balancing confidence with caution – 'knowing without excessive confidence or excessive cautiousness';
2 *scepticism*: having a healthy tendency to doubt that one's abilities, knowledge and skills are necessarily true or valid;
3 *doubt*: doubting that ones' abilities, knowledge and skills are an exhaustive set of those things that could be known.

Weick summarized it succinctly when he made the point that in a dynamic and complex world extreme confidence and extreme caution destroy the things an organization needs most: 'curiosity, openness, and complex sensing'.[60] He illustrated the complex interplay of different ways of thinking with an example the traditional wisdom of the Naskapi Indians of the Labrador region of Canada and their use of caribou shoulder bones to decide the direction in which to hunt. The Naskapi hold old caribou bones over the fire until they crack from the heat; they then hunt in the direction in which the crack points. Weick argues that this seemingly arbitrary and almost irrational decision based upon ritual is effective because:

the decision is not influenced by the outcomes of past hunts, which means that the stock of animals is not depleted. More important, the final decision is not influenced by the inevitable patterning in human choice, which enables hunted animals to become sensitised to humans and take evasive action. The wisdom inherent in this practice derives from its ambivalence to the past. . . . The seasoned hunter 'reads' the cracks and injects some of his own experience into the interpretation of what the cracks mean.[61]

The practice confounds a rational strategy which would have exhausted caribou stocks by over-hunting the places where caribou were found in the past. The caribou hunters are sensitive in a complex and nuanced way to the past, the present and the future, and the decision is a delicate balance between the expert bone-reading skills of the shaman and the cracks themselves. This approach honours experience but also invites randomness. The Naskapi exercise a wisdom which blends a subtle rationality with the intuition of the shaman, rather than privileging one mode of knowing above the other. It draws upon complex, context-dependent patterns derived from extensive prior learning, advanced knowledge of a domain (hunting) and the natural environment and many years, not to say generations, of practice and experience.

Creativity depends upon expertise. It is possible for unskilled, naïve, non-experts to engage in self-expression or exploratory play, for example in an artistic medium such as painting, musical performance or composition, dance or literature. However, the products of such activity are unlikely to be judged as creative or even technically competent by expert judges. The vast majority of individuals who make major creative works or leaps forward have spent many years, sometimes decades, immersing themselves in the traditions, absorbing the prerequisite knowledge and mastering the necessary techniques which enable them to generate, select and justify better creative outcomes.[62]

The journey from novice to expert, and even to that extreme form of expertise 'wisdom',[63] involves a transformation in the overall sense of the task from being 'fragmented and disjointed' to 'holistic and integrated'. Similarly, the level of context-dependence in the ways knowledge is applied also changes. In the early stages of the journey novices apply rules and procedures in ways that are relatively insensitive to the context. For example, they may apply simple rules of thumb or heuristics in a 'mechanistic' way even when the rule doesn't quite fit the situation, but being novices they have little else to fall back on other than the taught rule. At the opposite extreme the expert has a powerful appreciation of the context and applies solutions and takes decisions that are highly nuanced and judgemental to the extent that the reasons they behave as they do are difficult to articulate.

The picture of the expert performer which emerges is one where theory and practice, and informed intuition and rational analysis co-exist seamlessly in a harmonious integration. The accounts of experts testify

to the fact that their decision-making is often practised without conscious awareness of the steps involved. Intuitive performers, even when
they know *what* they think, do not know *how* they think it.[64]

TAKE-AWAYS FOR CHAPTER 4

Key ideas

We can unwittingly communicate a very great deal about ourselves in a very short space of time, and judgements by strangers
based on these *thin slices* can be remarkably accurate. *Experts* are
able to achieve consistently superior performance over the longer
term because they have relevant knowledge and skills achieved
through a strict regime of study, practice and experience. Experts
appraise *situations holistically* by abstracting summary information, unlike *novices* who process details and apply learned rules in
ways that may be insensitive to the requirements of the situation
to hand. *Intuitive expertise* depends on the availability in long
term memory (LTM) of large, well-organized knowledge structures and a complex set of rules that allow for quick, accurate
judgements. Because the decision-making and problem-solving
environment in modern organizations is complex, dynamic and
uncertain, novices and experts alike have to learn and adapt in
order to guard against 'grooved thinking', 'functional fixedness'
and other forms of *cognitive inertia*.

Intuition quote: Gary Klein, decision researcher

'What is it that sets off alarm bells inside your head? It's your
intuition, built up through repeated experiences that you have
unconsciously linked together to form a pattern.'

Action point

If intuitive judgement *depends* on expertise, and expertise *depends*
on learning, and learning *depends* on experience, how will you
accelerate progress towards attaining and honing 'intuitive expertise'? *Who* and *what* will you learn from in your *physical* and *social*
environment? What objects and experiences will you be *open* to
and seek out? What sources of *good feedback* will you use to build
better intuitions?

FURTHER READING

Csikszentmihalyi, M., *Flow: The Classic Work on How to Achieve Happiness.* London: Rider 2002.

Dreyfus, H.L. and Dreyfus, S.E., *Mind over Machine: The Power of Human Intuitive Expertise in the Era of the Computer.* New York: Free Press 1986.

Goldberg, E., *The Wisdom Paradox: How your Mind can Grow Stronger as your Brain Grows Older.* London: Simon and Schuster 2005.

Weick, K.E., *Making Sense of the Organisation.* Oxford: Blackwell Publishing 2001.

5 All in the mind?

> ... all that inner space one never sees, the brain and heart and other
> caverns where thought and feeling dance their Sabbath
>
> (Samuel Beckett, *Molloy*, 1955)

MAIN IDEA

Human beings are able to learn without conscious cognitive
effort and to think in ways which are both rapid and complex
without being fully-conscious of the processes involved or the
outcomes achieved.

For managers and other decision-makers being consciously in charge
is 'part of the territory' – the control and deployment of resources
(physical or human) is necessary for effective and efficient performance.
Part and parcel of 'being in control' is the belief that not only can we
exercise control over resources external to ourselves but also that we are
in 'control' of ourselves and of the thing which makes us uniquely
human – our thinking processes. All may not be as it seems however:
research in cognitive science over several decades provides compelling
evidence that, although we are aware of the contents of our conscious
experience, we are far from fully aware of the processes that generate
and control not only our conscious experiences, but our feelings and
behaviours as well.

Many of our cognitive processes and much of the content of our
memories are inaccessible to conscious awareness. As was noted in
Chapter 1 there are some cognitive scientists who go so far as to say that

the majority of thought (they claim at least 95 per cent) is unconscious.[1] From the perspective of this book 'unconscious cognition' is vitally important in the processes of incubation, insight, creativity, invention and, of course, intuition. To understand intuition we need to appreciate the power that human beings' non-conscious mental processes have to influence both conscious reasoning and feeling and the ways in which people behave in social settings.

MEMORIES ARE MADE OF THIS?

Can human beings perceive, think and learn without realizing they have done so? Some clues to answering this question come from studies of memory loss. In anterograde amnesia events occurring after brain damage has set in are not transferred into long term memory. In retrograde amnesia it is the events occurring before (*retro*, meaning 'backwards') the onset of amnesia that cannot be recalled.[2] People who have sustained head injury, for example may incur retrograde amnesia, and hence be unable to remember events that took place before the injury was sustained.[3] Fortunately, this type of memory loss often shrinks to the extent that the individual is able to remember events that took place to within a few minutes of the onset of amnesia. Anterograde amnesia, on the other hand, involves impaired function of short term memory – in effect a short term memory loss. In the movie *Finding Nemo*, one of the fishes ('Dory') has a profound short term memory disturbance as a result of anterograde amnesia and experiences severe difficulties in learning and retaining any new information, recalling names and knowing where she is going. Dory gives a caricatured but touching portrayal of the difficulties caused by profound amnesic syndrome.[4]

LOW EFFORT LEARNING

We might conclude that profound short term memory loss might be a significant impairment to learning, but consider the case of the Swiss psychologist Édouard Claparède (1873–1940) and one of his patients, a 47-year-old female amnesic who had a severe memory loss for recent events (known as Korsakoff's syndrome). She could not recognize the doctors and nurses who had been treating her on a daily basis for several years. Claparède had to introduce himself anew each time he and the patient met. Other aspects of her cognitive functioning were unimpaired, for example she could recite the capitals cities of Europe, carry out mental calculations and form new procedural knowledge,[5] but on the other hand she did not know what day it was, or her age and she could not acquire new episodic memories.[6]

Claparède was interested in finding out if she could better retain information if it was linked to an episode with intense impressions involving a feeling (in this case pain). To test this Claparède decided to use a somewhat fiendish trick. When greeting the patient with a handshake:

> I stuck her hand with a pin hidden between my fingers. The light pain was forgotten as quickly as neutral perceptions; a few minutes later she no longer remembered it. But when I again reached for her hand, she pulled it back in a reflex fashion, not knowing why. When I asked her the reason, she said in a flurry, 'Doesn't one have the right to withdraw her hand?' and when I insisted she said, 'Is there perhaps a pin hidden in your hand?' To the question, 'What makes you suspect me of wanting to stick you?' she would repeat her old statement, 'That was an idea that went through my mind,' or she would explain 'Sometimes pins are hidden in people's hands.' But never would she recognise the idea of sticking as a memory.[7]

Claparède's patient had no recollection of how she acquired the knowledge that people sometimes 'hide pins in their hands', but nonetheless had acquired the knowledge that this may sometimes be the case. Her actions in withdrawing her hand on occasions subsequent to the pin-pricking episode was attributable to an event in the past of which she had no explicit memory, but for which she did have an implicit emotional memory.[8] The latter was acquired as a result of non-consciously learning that Claparède himself was a stimulus with a specific affective association – he could cause her pain, and therefore signified a danger to her.

Although its not possible to confirm of deny where the actual brain lesions were, since both Claparède and his patient have long gone, the brain scientist Joseph Le Doux speculated that the patient's amygdala was intact (she had the conditioned fear response) but her temporal lobe memory system was most likely damaged (she did not form an explicit conscious memory of the pin-pricking episode). Learning and the retention of new episodic and autobiographical information require an intact medial temporal lobe (principally the hippocampus),[9] and one effect of damage to this region is anterograde amnesia.[10] Le Doux also notes that non-amnesic individuals, had Claparède's trick been pulled on them, as well as having an implicit fear-conditioned 'emotional memory', would also (because of their intact temporal lobe memory system) have an explicit declarative 'memory of the emotion' associated with the episode of Claparède and his pin-pricking.[11]

Other historical evidence for implicit or non-conscious perception and 'low-effort' learning may be found in studies of the memories acquired by patients while anaesthetized. In a famous case in the 1960s B.W. Levinson staged a 'mock crisis' in the operating theatre whilst surgical patients were under a general anaesthetic. The mock crisis was created by reading aloud the following statement: 'Just a moment! I don't like the patient's colour. Much too blue. Her lips are very blue. I'm going to give a little more oxygen. There, that's better now. You can carry on with the operation.' If patients are not aware of events taking place whilst anaesthetized or are unable to recall post-surgery any events that take place under general anaesthetic they should not be able to recall any of the details of such a statement that has been read to them.[12] However, Levinson found that under hypnosis four out of the ten patients were able to give a word-for-word account of the mock crisis statement, whilst another four had some memory of it.[13] More recently it has been found that patients in surgery who have been given the suggestion whilst unconscious (under general anaesthesia) that they will have a quick recovery spend less time in hospital than those not given the same suggestion.[14] Although some of the research in this area has been questioned on the grounds that the subjects may not have been fully unconscious, the general findings from these and similar studies seem to indicate that unconscious patients perceive information during surgery and are able to recall the non-consciously-perceived information afterwards, especially if the information is personally relevant and meaningful.[15]

IMPLICIT COGNITION: KNOWING MORE THAN WE CAN TELL

There is an indisputable body of evidence that points towards the existence of learning processes and contents of memory that are implicit – we can quite literally 'know more than we can tell', a phrase coined by the Hungarian-born physical chemist-turned-social philosopher Michael Polanyi (1891–1976). He argued that there exists a knowledge whose contents are not part of one's normal consciousness or are open to introspection. Others before Polanyi including William James, one of the pioneers of psychology, readily admitted that there is 'an unconscious way' in which an idea can exist in the mind and not reach the threshold of conscious awareness. There is of course also the Freudian notion of the repression of instincts, wishes, desires and images into the darker and deeper recesses of the unconscious. In management the intuition pioneer Chester Barnard of AT&T declared in 1938 that 'the things that are seen are moved by the things unseen'.[16]

In the wake of the cognitive revolution in psychology, research and theorizing on the subject of learning and implicit knowledge gathered pace in the 1960s. One of the researchers who gave the idea of implicit learning a great deal of its impetus is the psychologist Arthur S. Reber. He chose the term 'implicit' (which is broadly equivalent to 'incidental' and 'learning-without-awareness') to distinguish it from the explicit learning that various cognitive theorists and other researchers at the time were focusing their attentions upon. Reber described implicit learning as the acquisition of knowledge that takes place:

1   largely independently of conscious attempts to learn;
2   without awareness of how learning took place;
3   in the absence of explicit knowledge about what knowledge or skill was acquired.[17]

Implicit learning plays an important role in unstructured 'real world' learning. It allows people to develop a 'feel' for how a particular situation works enabling them to perform well (explicit learning may be better at allowing transfer of learning between situations),[18] and is built-up over exposure and experience. For example, when actually throwing objects people are able to identify patterns of correct and incorrect motion through the implicit learning of motion patterns, but are less able to do so when making explicit judgements about height, speed and distance.[19] Moreover, things learned implicitly show a remarkable retention over weeks or even years, during which explicit knowledge gained at the same time has long faded away. Reber was interested in how two of our most important accomplishments – the acquisition of language and the process of socialization – can take place in early childhood apparently without awareness. More recently he has summarized implicit learning 'in a nutshell' as: '. . . the process through which knowledge about the world about us it picked up largely independently of awareness of both the process and products of that learning'.[20] Our everyday lives appear to be managed, if not controlled, by an implicit system of learning and memory. For example, the coordination skills needed to drive an automobile become largely automatic and implicit, as do the skills used in riding a bicycle, tying one's shoelaces, speaking in public, interacting in socially acceptable ways, etc. Moreover, the 'knower' is unable to completely articulate all they know[21] about how to perform these behaviours in these situations. If we delve beneath the surface of these well-known phenomena and unpack a more recent and all-encompassing term 'implicit cognition',[22] we find it to be made up of several overlapping and inter-related elements (see Figure 5.1).

IMPLICIT PERCEPTION

When we explicitly perceive a stimulus we are able to discern its presence, location, form and movement: for example I can see the cursor on the screen of the computer on the desk in front of me as I type this manuscript. There are other things, such as the door behind me which I know exists and that I could choose to attend to and perceive by merely turning around. However, certain objects or events may have an effect upon our experience, thought and action but fall outside of the spotlight of our conscious awareness of their existence. Such perceptions may be said to be 'implicit'.[23]

Stimuli presented visually for very brief periods have the power to influence our subsequent judgements. For example, in experiments in which a picture of an 'aggressive-looking' person or a picture of a 'non-aggressive, polite' person are displayed but at a rate too quickly to be consciously registered before a neutral picture of the person is displayed, the subliminally displayed picture (aggressive looking or non-aggressive) is likely to bias whether the neutral picture of the person is judged as 'aggressive' or 'not aggressive'. This phenomenon of

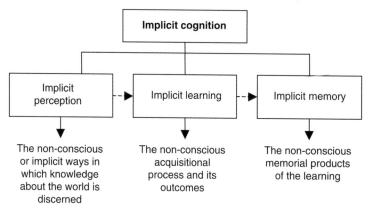

Figure 5.1 A simplified taxonomy of implicit cognition.

implicit perception is often referred to as 'subliminal perception'. It came to popular attention in the 1950s through the infamous 'eat pop-corn/drink Coke' messages allegedly flashed for 1/3000th of a second to cinema-goers in the USA in an attempt to subliminally influence them into consuming more popcorn and fizzy drinks.

Another well-known example is the so-called 'cocktail party phe-nomenon' in which we may switch at least part of our attention from a conversation we are earnestly engaged in to a nearby conversation if we hear something that grabs our attention (such as our own name being mentioned in the conversation we are not part of). Rather than being truly 'non-conscious', the partial monitoring through selective atten-tion that enables us to react to relevant stimuli in such settings may be better described as 'pre-attentive'. An analogy that has been offered is of the unconscious as a kind of cognitive 'internet search engine',[24] which we can leave to do its work while we multi-task with more pressing things that demand conscious attention and require working memory capacity.

As noted earlier, implicit perception researchers have investigated the effects of so-called 'mere exposure' to a stimulus. The pioneer of mere exposure studies, Robert B. Zajonc (pronounced 'Zy-unce'), examined how a subliminal emotional stimuli (a smiling or frowning face pre-sented for 5 milliseconds) affected participants' preferences for an

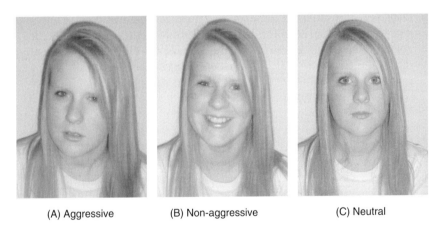

(A) Aggressive   (B) Non-aggressive   (C) Neutral

Figure 5.2 Subliminal perception: flashing the picture (A) Aggressive, or (B) Non-aggressive, can bias the judgement of the subsequently pre-sented neutral picture (C).

Adapted from M.S. Gazzaniga, R.B. Ivy and G.R. Mangun, *Cognitive Neuroscience: The Biology of the Mind* (New York: W.W. Norton and Co., 2002) p. 665.

innocuous stimulus (such as a Chinese ideogram). Participants' responses were affected by whether or not the ideogram had been preceded by a subliminally-presented smile or frown.[25] This programme of research began in the 1960s and spawned a series of related investigations over several decades. For example, in the early 1990s researcher Robert Bornstein found that faces which were subliminally pre-exposed as a priming stimulus were more positively rated when presented as a test stimulus than previously unseen faces[26] (the psychologist David Myers refers to this as 'familiarity-fondness').[27]

Implicit perception is a powerful means by which advertisers can get their message across without us realizing it; for example researchers gave two groups of participants a set of magazines to study to see if mere exposure to adverts in the magazines positively biased their attitudes towards them. The first group were given clear direction about how to study the magazines; the second group were told to simply browse through them. Both groups were then asked to say which of 50 adverts in the magazines they recognized. Not surprisingly the first group recognized about 60 per cent, whilst the second group recognized only 11 per cent. What was surprising though was that both groups showed the same positive bias in their attitudes towards the adverts they had been exposed to when compared to adverts they had not seen before.[28] The way we acquire our attitudes towards people and objects can be independent of our conscious recollection.

Significant steps toward determining the role played by different brain regions in implicit perception and implicit processing have taken place. Paul Whalen and his colleagues[29] used fMRI to study whether the amygdala[30] is activated in response to subliminally presented emotional stimuli in the form of pictures of human faces with fearful or happy expressions. The emotionally-charged facial expressions were exposed for 33 milliseconds and masked by 167 millisecond presentations of neutral faces. Although participants reported seeing only the neutral faces, the fMRI signal in the amygdala (as measured by blood oxygen levels[31]) was significantly higher during the viewing of masked fearful faces than during the viewing of masked happy faces.

Pawel Lewicki and his colleagues argued that not only is it possible for information to be acquired non-consciously (for example, as a result of the physical properties of the stimuli such as the 'flash' of a very short time-span of exposure, or masking by a subsequent stimulus) but also for procedural knowledge[32] to develop 'unknown' to conscious awareness by being encoded and entering into the memory system through channels that are independent of consciousness. Moreover Lewicki went further and argued that this information can have a more advanced and structurally complex organization than could actually be handled by consciously-controlled thinking.[33] Not only can we know more than we can tell, we may even be smarter than we ever could have imagined.

Table 5.1 Explicit/implicit distinctions in perception, memory and learning

	Explicit	Implicit
Perception	Conscious perception in which subject able to discern presence, location, movement, form and other palpable attributes of stimulus E.g. words on page in front of you	Effect(s) of stimulus event on experience, thought and action in absence of conscious perception of event E.g. picture of smile or frown exposed for 5 milliseconds can influence whether subsequent target stimulus is liked/disliked ('subliminal emotional priming')
Memory	Conscious recall or recognition of information, rules or events E.g. episodic memories – recalling what you were doing on Christmas day last year	Any effect on experience thought and action attributable to past events in absence of conscious recollection of those events E.g. driving home from work on familiar route Implicit memories can be available to conscious awareness (i.e. can be in pre-conscious state) Others may be unavailable to conscious awareness but may affect conscious thought and action
Learning	Knowledge and skill acquired as result of events that subject is consciously aware of and for which outcomes are available in conscious awareness E.g. acquiring procedural rules of arithmetic, or knowing of facts	Knowledge and skill acquired independently of conscious attempts to learn and in absence of explicit knowledge about what was learned E.g. recognizing and using rules of grammar in our native language; learning by mere exposure to role model

Sources: J. Dorfman, V.A. Shames and J.F. Kihlstrom, 'Intuition, incubation and insight: implicit cognition and problem solving', in G. Underwood (ed.) *Implicit Cognition* (Oxford: Oxford University Press, 1996) pp. 257–96; A.S. Reber, *Implicit Learning and Tacit Knowledge: An Essay on the Cognitive Unconscious* (New York: Oxford University Press, 1993).

IMPLICIT MEMORY

The term implicit memory was coined in the 1980s by Daniel Sachter to distinguish between the contents of memory that are accessible to conscious awareness and those that are not. For example, I can recall what I was doing on Christmas day last year (I have an episodic memory of the event). I can also recall trivial facts such as the date of the Battle of Hastings (1066), or who the winners of the football World Cup in 1966 were (the England team) – these are semantic (factual) memories. Memory of events and memory of facts (episodic and semantic memory) comprise our explicit (or declarative) memory (see Figure 5.3). Declarative memory is very large; it has been estimated that the average college-educated adult knows around 50,000 words (there are over 10^5 words in the English language), and that approximately twenty times more than this (i.e. 10^6 or $20 \times 50,000$) pieces of knowledge comprise a person's total declarative knowledge base.[34]

In order to impress people with my general knowledge, the relevant contents of my LTM have to be retrieved from beneath the threshold of conscious awareness and thereby become explicit memories in my conscious awareness. These retrieved memories can be used to perform actions or be communicated on demand to others. The explicit (declarative) component of LTM may be sub-divided into semantic and episodic sub-components (see Figure 5.3), but a moment's introspection may reveal that there are other types of memories. As well as being able to talk about my specific personal past experiences (using information from my episodic LTM) and recount trivial facts about the world (from my semantic LTM), I can also ride a bicycle. I can't explain particularly well how I do it and what the specific motor skills that I have are, but the memory stays with me and enables me to ride a bicycle even if I've laid off the pedals for many years.

The motor skills of bicycle riding are held in my implicit (nondeclarative) memory. Moreover, my implicit memory needn't be confined to motor skills; it includes the cognitive skills I possess as well. As I type this manuscript the words arise, I don't consciously follow explicit rules of grammar (and probably break a good few of them) – things tend, most of the time, to flow (after a fashion). The use of language, and in particular the use of the rules of grammar, is an example of the 'implicitness' of much of our mental processing. When speaking we execute these rules freely without thinking about what rule to use, or even being able to say what the rules are. They are held implicitly, and as a consequence are less available to conscious awareness than are, for example, other rules for carrying out an unfamiliar procedure such as operating a new piece of equipment, are executed slowly, intentionally and effortfully with constant reference to the necessary facts held in declarative memory or on the pages of the instruction manual.

Working memory

Finally a few words about 'working memory' (WM). Sometimes referred to as 'short term memory' (STM), working memory is a limited capacity storage and processing system. In his famous paper 'The magical number seven, plus or minus two' the psychologist George A. Miller suggested that the capacity of short term memory is limited to 7±2 items.[35] Information can be quickly displaced from working memory by new

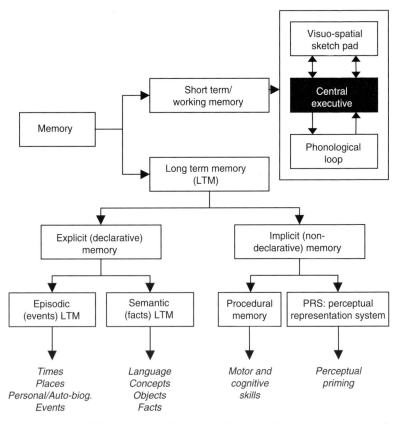

Figure 5.3 The different forms of memory (Adapted from: Gazzaniga *et al.*, 2002, p. 314).

incoming information. For example, the fragile nature of storage of information in working memory and the ease with which it can be displaced is easily demonstrated:

> Read through this list of numbers 314 965 151, close the book, and then write the numbers down in the same order.
>
> Now read through this list of numbers 781 454 362, close the book, count backwards from 10, and then try to write the numbers down[36].

The contents of working memory may originate from sensory inputs or retrieval from LTM.[37] Areas of the frontal cortex and a number of other brain regions form the neural basis of working memory.[38] We know about the present moment from what happens to be in working memory at a point in time (i.e. now). This has led a number of cognitive scientists to argue that 'consciousness' itself is the awareness of what is in working memory.[39] Others have argued against this view, for example as Timothy D. Wilson observes there are things that may not be in working memory at a particular moment in time as an object of attention (such as 'Australia'), but to say that Australia is part of my unconscious, rather than my pre-conscious, is stretching the notion of 'unconscious'. Wilson argues persuasively, however, that there are parts of one's mind that cannot be accessed even if one tries but which undoubtedly influence our judgements, feelings and behaviours.[40]

At a more practical level, working also memory plays a role in expert-novice differences: experts can plan solutions to problems rapidly and are able to do their complex planning in working memory; novices on the other hand plan slowly and concretely, one step at a time.[41] From a decision-making perspective working memory is where the analysis of the costs and benefits of various options are played out.[42] Working memory is relevant as far as intuition is concerned since it provides the 'stable playing field'[43] for coherent mental activity where gut feeling is registered and can do its job in marking a potential outcome as positive (potentially beneficial or desirable) or negative (undesirable).

A further point in relation to working memory and gut feeling is that, as was noted above, working memory is a limited resource, therefore the cost-benefit analyses that are played out in the arena of working memory need a mechanism that enables a decision-maker to sift through and narrow down the range of possibilities and to focus upon those that are worth pursuing or seem promising. A negative gut feeling restricts the range of opportunities by 'weeding-out' options,[44] whilst a positive gut feeling may serve to focus attention on those options worth following through. Moreover, by ignoring the 'gut feeling' signals offered by our bodies we inadvertently commit our conscious minds to the effortful, and possibly unnecessary, processing of information in working memory.

Controlled-versus-automatic processing

When I drive home from work, I often do so without a great deal of conscious cognitive effort. It is a skill that I can execute automatically after having made the trip many times (it has been 'over-learned'). Once established it becomes inflexible and difficult to modify; for example, I may automatically set out to travel home from work every day, even when I may have a different plan than to go home right away. Although often executed automatically, the route home can be reproduced and communicated on demand (as when I explain to another person how to get to my house) – it can become an explicit memory and under conscious control. 'Automatic processing' differs from 'controlled processing' in a number of ways. For example, controlled processing:

- requires attention;
- is subject to the limits of the cognitive capacity of the thinker;
- may be used flexibly when circumstances change.[45]

Automatic processing on the other hand:

- Is not subject to the same limitations of cognitive capacity;
- Does not reduce the capacity for performing other tasks;
- Does not require the same level of attention;
- Is difficult to modify once learned.[46]

As noted earlier, declarative memory consists of explicit knowledge of facts and episodes, but applying this knowledge *verbatim* to solve problems of the type that have already been encountered can be slow, laborious and cognitively taxing. Through experience and practice it is possible to automatically compile or compress declarative memory into procedural knowledge which may then be used with cognitive economy to solve problems.[47] The more efficient performance associated with automatic processing occurs as a result of:[48]

(1) *conversion*: the conversion of knowledge from declarative (slow) to procedural (fast).[49] For example, the knowledge of the layout of the pedals in a car (accelerator, brake, clutch – memorized as declarative knowledge by the mnemonic ABC) eventually becomes

procedural knowledge when the middle pedal is pressed automatically to slow the vehicle down;

(2) *chunking*: small, related pieces of knowledge are gradually combined together (chunked) to form large pieces of knowledge allowing a task to be accomplished with fewer mental elements[50] (for example, turning a corner involves the compilation of the separate knowledge associated with braking, gear changing, steering and indicating);

(3) *practice*: individual pieces of procedural knowledge can be executed more quickly with practice.[51]

As a result the learner may recall relevant sequences from memory and apply these to problems which are judged to have similar features, rather than 're-invent the wheel' each time. The execution of procedures on multiple occasions results in them being refined and streamlined, enabling faster and more reliable problem-solving to occur in routine situations. At this point in the learning process the skill is automatized to the extent that it can be executed without conscious awareness, without continual reference to declarative memory and with minimal impact on the capacity of working memory.[52]

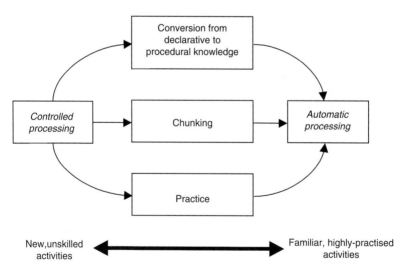

Figure 5.4 Automatic and controlled processing.

Based on K. Van Lehn, 'Cognitive skill acquisition', *The Annual Review of Psychology*, 1996, 47: 513–39; G. Underwood and J.E.H. Bright, 'Cognition with and without awareness', in G. Underwood (ed.) *Implicit Cognition* (Oxford: Oxford University Press, 1996) pp. 1–40.

Priming and implicit memory

Evidence for the ways in which implicit memory operates comes from laboratory studies involving priming tasks (as used in the Zajonc and Bornstein studies described above). Priming is a term used in experimental psychology for the improvement in identifying or processing a stimulus as a result of it being seen before. A prime, from the Latin *primus* meaning 'first', is a cue given to facilitate a particular response.

A test which uses priming might involve a word fragment completion task, such as '_ _ g _ o n' (for 'pigeon') or 'v _ o _ _ n' (for 'violin') following prior exposure to a list of words such as 'pigeon/animal/table/car/tree/camera/coin/boot'.[53] Under experimental conditions performance on the first word fragment completion task is likely to be significantly better than on the second word fragment task because subjects would have been primed by the prior presentation of the word (pigeon).

Psychologists have argued that in this situation the perceptual structure of the stimulus is stored in a Perceptual Representation System (PRS) which is part of implicit memory. The contents of the PRS do not lessen over hours or even days, are not better remembered if processed at the time of encoding (whereas the contents of explicit memory are) and rather than being conceptual in their representation, are structural, visual or auditory (if a word is presented auditorily and tested for visually the effect of the priming is reduced).[54]

Studies of amnesic patients have shown that while one group of patients with a particular type of brain lesion show impairment on implicit memory tasks, another group, with a different type of brain lesion, show impairment on explicit memory tasks. In the terminology of cognitive neuroscience, explicit and implicit memory can be 'doubly-dissociated' by brain lesion. These findings suggest that:

- separate brain areas are responsible for implicit and explicit memory systems;
- implicit memory is tied to the surface characteristics of stimuli.[55]

The PRS component of the implicit system is thought to develop earlier in life than the explicit system.[56] Moreover, on the basis that through natural selection nature builds on older structures that have yielded advantages to the organism, the explicit memory system that manifests itself in conscious awareness may be thought of in evolutionary terms as a comparatively late addition (Reber refers to it as an evolutionary 'Johnny-come-lately') given that evolution is accumulatory and conservative (new structures are built on older ones)

The implicit system is a system which was advantageous in that it enabled the human organism to acquire information about the world without the cognitive effort required by conscious awareness. It has continued to exist and function effectively from a time in our ancestors' evolutionary past when the phenomenon of consciousness did not exist.[57] This line of thinking is in keeping with that of a number of other researchers who have suggested that *Homo sapiens'* intuitively-based information processing system, like the implicit system, has a comparatively long biological history.[58] Similarly, the rational information processing system (which came later and in an evolutionary sense overlies the intuitive system) is, like the explicit system, a relatively recent arrival in the evolution of *Homo sapiens*.

IMPLICIT LEARNING

If information can be perceived and stored without conscious awareness, can complex learning also take place without conscious awareness? Some evidence for how 'smart' or 'dumb' our cognitive unconscious is comes from two different sources: experiments using artificial grammar (AG) and research into complex procedural learning tasks (the so-called 'Tulsa experiments' of the 1990s).

Artificial grammar experiments

Psychologists have used the concept of grammar (the rules for using the elements of a language), and more specifically artificial grammar, to research the ways in which implicit knowledge is acquired. AG employs complex rules devised by an experimenter that determine the sequence in which meaningless letter strings (for example, SRWR) can be formed. Participants in AG studies are required to study groups of letter strings which follow the complex rules of which they have no explicit knowledge. These are the 'learning stimuli' of which, in a typical experiment, there may be 10 or 15 that subjects are required to memorize. Participants are asked to judge whether letter new letter strings (the 'testing stimuli', for example, SRRWU) follow the same rules as the ones they have studied. They have no explicit knowledge of the rules upon which these letter strings are formed; not only that, the rules are complex and difficult to describe (the letter strings are actually generated by an algorithm – see Figure 5.5 for an example).[59]

The AG technique has been widely used by Reber and other implicit learning researchers. Their results reveal that participants can make

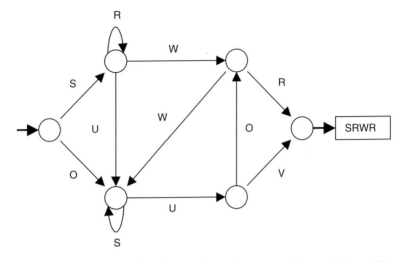

Figure 5.5 An AG algorithm (Adapted from Litman and Reber, 2005, p. 435).

Note: the algorithm generates letter strings (a well-formed string is SRWR) by following the arrows from the input on the left to the output on the right. An example of a string with a single-letter violation is: SRRWU. Subjects are required to detect violations.

reliable judgements quite quickly (for example, by the end of the first day of a four-day experimental trial – a surprising finding in itself given the complexity of the grammatical rules involved).[60]

In a more elaborate version of an AG experiment Mathews and his colleagues[61] had participants at the end of the first day articulate the rules they felt they were following, which then were written down (transcribed). These transcribed rules were then given to a parallel ('yoked') group to study – the argument being that if the experimental group were able to effectively articulate (make explicit) the rules they were following these rules should be learnable by the yoked group and they also should be able to make accurate judgements in the AG task. When using the information provided by the participants at the end of the first day (the transcriptions of the rules they felt they were following) the yoked group were unable to make decisions that were any better than chance judgments. The significant implication of this is that the experimental group were able to make judgements based on complex rules but were unable to articulate the rules that they were following. However, by the end of day four the yoked group could perform as well as the experimental group on the basis of the transcripts presented to them.

The implication of this is that the experimental group were, by day four, able to articulate their knowledge (even though their own performance did not improve beyond day one). A more general implication is that the implicit knowledge system (which as has already been noted, served by a memory system that is separate from that which serves explicit memory) is able to acquire highly complex rules comparatively quickly. Moreover, bringing the rules into conscious awareness in a form that can easily be expressed verbally takes time and effort.[62]

The Tulsa experiments

Imagine a computer screen divided into quadrants in which a target, let's refer to it as 'X' (e.g. a number or a letter), may appear in any of the quadrants in a sequence based upon an algorithm which includes the following rules:

1   ' "X" never appears in the same box twice in succession' (sounds easy?);
2   'Third location of "X" depends upon its second location' (getting harder?);
3   'Fourth location of "X" depends upon its locations in the preceding two trials' (pretty impossible?), and so forth.[63]

The task of tracking the target's position as it jumps from quadrant to quadrant of the screen in each trial sounds mind-bogglingly difficult. This was the basis of the experimental setting used by Pawel Lewicki and his colleagues at the University of Tulsa.[64] They wanted to study the acquisition of procedural knowledge based on rules which are so complex that it is exceedingly difficult, if not impossible, to be articulated (i.e. the rule for where the target will appear next).

Over a number of trials participants' non-conscious acquisition of the algorithms steadily improved; they performed better and better in the task as time went by until by the seventh trial they could recognize quickly in which quadrant the target would appear. What was surprising was that the participants were able to learn the algorithm and make accurate predictions; but more surprising than that was the fact that they were unable to explain what they had learned:

* Participants learned complex rules for predicting the target's position but they could not verbalize what the rules were.
* When the complex rule was replaced by a random sequence their performance declined[65] and although participants were aware of

this decline in performance they were unaware that they had learned rules that no longer applied.

- Participants in a similar study were unable to uncover the hidden pattern they had non-consciously learned even with a very generous inducement of a $100 reward.

It is also worth noting that the participants in the main study were college professors who tried hard to figure out the experiment but none of them came close; some attributed the decline in their performance to them 'losing the rhythm' or to distracting stimuli being subliminally flashed on the screen.

Other research by Lewicki with his colleagues Maria Czyzewska and Thomas Hill demonstrated that complex algorithms can be easily and non-consciously acquired even by pre-school children.[66] They summarized the potential significance of these findings: 'Most of the real work, both in the acquisition of cognitive procedures and skills and in the execution of cognitive operations, such as encoding and the interpretation of stimuli, is being done at the level to which our consciousness has *no access*' (emphasis added).[67] The tasks used in the Tulsa experiments would be fiendishly difficult to learn deliberately; however, the results seem to suggest that our non-conscious 'mind' can sometimes outperform our conscious mind.[68] The view of Lewicki and his colleagues is that the inaccessible regions of our cognition are not simply assigned the routine and mundane operations but are involved in much more sophisticated processing which are traditionally associated with consciously-controlled thinking.[69]

Ap Dijksterhuis in his Unconscious Thought Theory (UTT) argues that the amount of information that can be kept under conscious scrutiny and processed at any one time is limited. One result of this limitation is that the demands of complex decision-making may simply be too much for consciousness to handle. Dijksterhuis and his colleagues have presented evidence to support their view that when people are faced with complex decisions (such as judging the attractiveness of a place in which to live, or attitudes towards potential room-mates) unconscious thought can lead to superior decisions.[70]

Human beings have a natural, and sometimes excessive, tendency to 'dichotomize' things – to divide or polarize them into two opposing groups, kinds, types, classes, categories, etc.; it is a natural way of simplifying our thinking. In the same way, it is often tempting to pigeonhole particular aspects of human information processing as being based on either implicit processes or, their presumed opposite, explicit processes, as though the complex cognitions and behaviour that emanate from them are either one thing or the other. Arthur Reber and his colleague Leib Litman cautioned against treating the explicit system and the implicit system as being at the opposite poles of a continuum where 'never the twain shall meet' (they cite this as example of a 'bi-polarity fallacy').[71]

> Human memory has distinct systems with distinct evolutionary histories and separate, although only partly understood, neurological underpinnings that map, on the one hand, into conscious, subjective experience and, on the other, into a nexus of encoding, storage and retrieval systems that function largely independently of awareness and consciousness.[72]

Instead Reber and his colleagues emphasized that in human information processing there is likely to be a delicate balance between the implicit system and the explicit system, in the same way that effective decision-making is a process based upon informed intuition and rational analysis.

THE 'SMART' UNCONSCIOUS

It isn't only in laboratory settings using comparatively artificial tasks where the power of implicit learning has been observed. Behaviours, such as helping, cooperation and aggression control, are learned through observation[73] and imitation in social settings. It is in these contexts where implicit learning is likely to be especially powerful and relevant in the development of social intuitions. For example, researchers have investigated the role of implicit memory in the learning of business-relevant tasks, such as the key skill of the art of negotiation. Nadler and her colleagues[74] conducted an experiment using over one hundred participants to compare the effectiveness of learning how to negotiate by observation and imitation with three other training methods[75] (participants were divided into four experimental groups according to the training method).

The observational learning group watched a videotape of a 'win-win' negotiation and when tested they achieved the highest outcomes of all the groups. However they were unable to articulate the learned principles that are involved and which they'd actually practised in successful negotiation. They had acquired implicit knowledge of how to negotiate successfully by the observation of videotaped performance, it helped them to perform well, but they were unable to articulate why or how.

The observational learners not only 'knew more than they could tell', they could not say how they learned what they had learned.

The picture which emerges from this brief survey of implicit cognition is far removed from the conventional view in management and other professional contexts of knowledge as a tangible, explicit entity, thought as mostly conscious and of learning as a controlled and often laborious process. Conventional management education and training concerns itself in the main with learning that is explicit and classroom-based, and tends to fixate on tangible outcomes.[76] There are two main problems with this approach:

(1) Learning processes and their outcomes may be implicit as well as explicit – we can know and learn more than we are able to tell and are able to behave in ways that demonstrate mastery of knowledge and skill but which cannot easily be put into words. It becomes tangible only in the act of doing.

(2) Conventional educational and training programmes may overlook the learning (good or bad) that takes place through the very powerful mechanisms associated with observation and imitation, and also undervalue the plethora of opportunities for intense, disciplined practice that exist in workplace settings and which are the keys to developing high levels of expertise and excellent performance (including the ability to make effective, informed intuitive judgements).

What is clear is that memory can exist in both explicit and implicit forms, and that learning is not always an explicit, observable or indeed, arduous phenomenon under conscious control. From the perspective of business management and professional practice, implicit learning is one of the most important aspects of non-conscious cognition.[77] Our unconscious mind has the power to internalize and execute highly complex rules, algorithms and cognitive skills to the extent that it may be, on occasions, able to outsmart its conscious counterpart with reasons that only it is privy to. We are allowed glimpses into its reasoning processes when we become aware of the bodily signals (gut feelings) that accompany implicit cognitions and which may be used to guide judgement and decision-making. However, the unconscious is far from omnipotent in its 'smartness', nor are these low-effort cognitive shortcuts without serious limitations of their own in certain settings.

TAKE-AWAYS FOR CHAPTER 5

Key ideas

Many of our cognitive processes and much of the content of memory are *inaccessible* to conscious awareness (some cognitive scientists argue 'at least 95 per cent of thought' is unconscious). It is possible to learn *independently* of any conscious attempt to learn, *without awareness* of how learning took place and without being aware of the knowledge or skill was *acquired. Homo sapiens'* implicit learning system probably has a comparatively long biological history; it enabled the human organism to acquire information about the world *without* the cognitive effort required by conscious awareness. Non-conscious cognition is involved in *sophisticated* levels of processing and is not simply assigned the routine and mundane mental operations.

Intuition quote: Albert Einstein, Nobel prize-winning physicist

'The intellect has little to do on the road to discovery. There comes a leap in consciousness, call it intuition or what you will, and the solution comes to you and you don't know how or why.'

Action point

Practice may or may not 'make perfect', but it's more than likely that it will improve your expertise and your intuition. What are the things that you find '*tough-going*' at the moment in your work? Why do you find them tough-going? What new knowledge or skills do you need to increase your *speed, accuracy* and *performance* in these areas? Where will you get the necessary space, time and resources to *practise, make mistakes* 'safely' and *experiment*, preferably not with reality, but in a simulated environment, supportive circumstances and where there's *good feedback*?

FURTHER READING

Lakoff, G. and Johnson, M., *Philosophy in the Flesh: The Embodied Mind and its Challenge to Western Thought*. New York: Basic Books 1999.

Reber, A.S., *Implicit Learning and Tacit Knowledge: An Essay on the Cognitive Unconscious*. New York: Oxford University Press 1993.

Underwood, G. (ed.), *Implicit Cognition*. Oxford: Oxford University Press 1996.

Wilson, T.D., *Strangers to Ourselves: Discovering the Adaptive Unconscious*. Cambridge, MA: Belknap Press 2002.

6 The 'least effort' principle

I wouldn't have said off-hand that I had a subconscious mind, but I suppose I must without knowing it, and no doubt it was there, sweating away diligently at the old stand, all the while the corporeal Wooster was getting his eight hours.

(P.G. Wodehouse, *Right Ho, Jeeves*, 1934, Ch.12)

MAIN IDEA

Some of the intuitive mental 'short cuts' that human beings unwittingly and routinely employ can result in erroneous and biased judgements. There are other types of mental 'shortcuts' which can be fast and cognitively economical, as well as accurate, under particular sets of circumstances.

When people make judgments relating to chance occurrences they often rely upon mental 'short cuts'. And whether it's tossing a coin, choosing the lottery numbers or betting on the spin of a roulette wheel, gut feeling is a commonly-used, sometimes daring and cognitively undemanding short-cut way of making a decision. As a test of your 'gambler's intuition' which one of the sequences of coin tosses in Figures 6.1a and 6.1b do you feel is more likely, Pattern A or Pattern B? Often, when called on to make judgements based on random sequences, research suggests that more people feel that Pattern A is more likely, and that the run of heads in Pattern C is more likely to be followed by a tail than by a head on the seventh toss. 'Pattern A' and a 'tail' seem intuitively to make sense as the more likely alternatives.

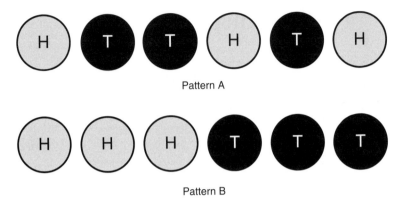

Pattern A

Pattern B

Figure 6.1a Which of the above patterns A or B is more likely?

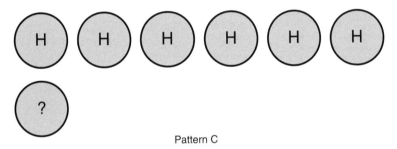

Pattern C

Figure 6.1b What is more likely on the seventh toss, a head or a tail?

Sadly in this situation our intuition is likely to let us down: Pattern A and Pattern B are equally likely, and the seventh toss of Pattern C is just as likely to be a head or a tail even though the first six tosses yielded a head.

You may have succumbed to a short cut in reasoning another name for which is a 'heuristic'. The word itself comes from the Greek *heurisko* meaning 'to find' and is related to the Greek word *heureka* meaning 'I have found it' which we met in Chapter 3 in connection with Archimedes' insightful bath-time experience. This chapter will begin by exploring the ways in which the types of cognitive short cuts we often, wrongfully, employ in making judgements related to chance occurrences (so called 'intuitive probabilistic judgements') can lay traps for the unwary. But cognitive short cuts are not always bad, and we will examine a more positive view of a particular type of cognitive short cut – one that is both quick and mentally economical (so-called 'fast-and-frugal heuristics').

PROBABILISTIC JUDGEMENTS

One problem of relying upon intuition in probability or chance-related (i.e. probabilistic) judgements, such as the coin toss examples, lies in the fallacy that 'short sequences in a random process represent the essential characteristics of that process' (i.e. that heads and tails are equally likely even in the short run). The error of logic is that any deviation from this essential characteristic (the equal likelihood of a head or a tail), such as the seemingly-anomalous pattern in B or the unexpected run of heads in Pattern C will in the short term somehow self-correct with a run of 'luck' in the opposite direction. This 'rule of thumb' is one of the common misconceptions which many novice gamblers follow. For example, roulette wheel players betting on black after a long run of red, or lottery players persisting with a chosen set of numbers in the belief that they are 'bound to come up soon' are committing this error of judgement.

Dice, coins and roulette wheels do not exhibit the same pattern of outcomes in short sequences as they do in long sequences – the 50:50 outcome is maintained in an infinite number of throws of the dice, tosses of the coin or spins of the roulette wheel.[1] In pointing out these and other common misconceptions Daniel Kahneman and Amos Tversky summarized the general point as follows: that people expect that the essential characteristics of a process will be represented not only 'globally' in a complete sequence, but also 'locally' in each of its parts.[2] The problem lies in the lack of representativeness of the data available at the time. Intuitively we expect to see 50:50 represented even in a relatively small sample of observations because that is all we have to go on.

In a mere six tosses of the coin, or the hour's play on the roulette wheel or in the weeks or months of persistence with a chosen set of lottery numbers we are observing only a small (a 'local') part of the random sequence (incidentally, according to the UK's National Lottery the chances of matching 'six main numbers' is 1:13,983,816[3]). Any deviation in one direction, for example in favour of heads, is not self-corrected as the chance process unfolds but instead is merely diluted[4] over the longer term. In the examples that opened the chapter the probability of a head or a tail is being assessed from a small sample in relation to its representativeness of the overall probability of 50:50 which would be observed in an infinite number of tosses of the coin. If you thought that Pattern B was less likely than A and that a 'tail' was more likely on the seventh toss your judgements were being insensitive to the small sample size and falling foul of what Kahneman and Tversky called the 'representativeness heuristic'.

HEURISTICS

'Representativeness' is one of a number of cognitive shortcuts ('heuristics') which people routinely, but largely unwittingly, employ when required to make such judgements (there are several more of these heuristics, for example the 'availability heuristic' and the 'anchoring and adjustment heuristic', which are discussed later). Because they are economical ('frugal') in terms of the conscious cognitive effort required, heuristics can be a low-effort and efficient way to solve problems. Sometimes however the errors of logic upon which these shortcuts are based can result in oft-repeated biases and serious errors of judgement.

The errors derived from heuristics are not only confined to seemingly trivial probability exercises: managers need to be wary of intuitive judgements inferred from a small sample of occurrences in many different business settings. For example, making intuitive decisions based on only handful of previous good 'intuitive judgement calls' is no basis for adopting intuition as one's sole and exclusive decision-making style – in this case the sample size (a 'handful') is simply too small and the intuition is unlikely to be very well informed. Nonetheless, when they do occur intuitive runs of success can be flattering and beguiling.

THE FALLIBILITY OF INTUITIVE PROBABILISTIC JUDGEMENTS

Imagine you've just briefly met 'Jake' at a party. He weighed in at about 120 kilos, his hands were the size of baseball gloves, his biceps were tattooed and he expressed no interest in 'culture'. At the party he drank rather more than was good for him and came across as a little on the aggressive side towards the end of the evening. If you were asked to judge if Jake made his living as a school teacher or as a boxer, what would your 'gut feeling' tell you?

Putting 'gut feeling' aside for one moment, there are some pre-existing (prior) probabilities that could be taken into account in deciding if Jake is more likely to be a professional boxer than a teacher. These typically get overlooked, but they might be helpful in making a more logical and rational judgement about Jake's occupation. Given the data in Box 6.1, do you think Jake is more likely to be a school teacher or a boxer?

If you judged Jake to be a boxer before taking these data into account you are likely to have fallen foul of a phenomenon known as the 'base rate fallacy'. The 'base rate'[5] in this context is the pre-existing ('prior')

Box 6.1

There are about 770 registered boxers in England (this is about 0.005 per cent of the adult male population*).

There are about 270,000 male teachers in England (this is about 1.7 per cent of the adult male population).

The proportion of boxers is about 1 in 21,000.

The proportion of teachers is about 1 in 60.

Boxer or teacher?

* There are about 16,000,000 adult males in the population of England.

---

probability which needs to be taken into account in judging the likelihood of an event. The prior probability that Jake is a teacher is much higher than the prior probability that he is a professional boxer (or rugby player, wrestler, or night club bouncer for that matter in spite of the prototypes we may hold for these).

The 'base rate fallacy' is a tendency to under-use or even to ignore the prior probabilities. The judgements that we make, such as that of Jake's occupation, are often made not on the basis of prior probabilities, but on the basis of the degree of match between the description of, in this case, Jake and the prototypes that we hold to be representative of 'boxers' and 'teachers'. Jake may resemble our prototype of a boxer, but given the base rates for the population as a whole we are much more likely to meet a teacher than a boxer.

THE POWER OF STEREOTYPES: 'THE REPRESENTATIVENESS HEURISTIC'

The error of judgement which occurs in typical responses to questions like that of 'what is Jake's occupation?' is because the base rate of the respective groups, teachers and boxers, in the population is not taken into account. It's easier to overlook this information. The cognitive short cut which is used instead is based on the extent to which Jake appears representative of boxers (or teachers) in terms of how these two groups are stereotyped or pre-conceived. The base rate fallacy and the associated errors and biases are key features of the 'representativeness heuristic'.

The 'Linda problem'

Another example of this heuristic is to be found in the famous 'Linda problem', a judgement task used by heuristics and biases researchers in the 1970s and 1980s to investigate what are termed 'conjunction effects'.[6] The 'Linda problem' is based on eight statements about a hypothetical female.

> Linda is 31 years old, single, outspoken, and very bright. She majored in philosophy. As a student she was deeply concerned with issues of discrimination and social justice and also participated in anti-nuclear demonstrations. Please rank order by probability (highest to lowest) the following:
>
> 1   Linda is a teacher in an elementary school.
> 2   Linda works in a book store and takes yoga classes.
> 3   Linda is active in the feminist movement.
> 4   Linda is a psychiatric social worker.
> 5   Linda is a member of the League of Women Voters.
> 6   Linda is a bank teller.
> 7   Linda is an insurance sales person.
> 8   Linda is a bank teller and active in the feminist movement.[7]

When confronted by this task most people rate the probability that Linda 'is active in the feminist movement' (3) higher than the probability that 'Linda is a bank teller' (6). But more significantly, 86 per cent of people who participated in the original study rated the probability that 'Linda is a bank teller and active in the feminist movement' (8) higher than the probability that 'Linda is a bank teller' (6). In effect they were judging:

Probability ('Bank teller' & 'Active in feminist movement')
> Probability ('Bank teller')

If we stop to think, this is a surprising judgement to arrive at, for number of reasons. First, an elementary logical analysis tells us that the probability of Statement (8) cannot be greater than the probability of Statement (6). It's analogous to believing that the chances of meeting a '50-year-old long-haired motorcyclist' are greater than the chances of meeting a '50-year-old motorcyclist'. Why? Because 50-year-old motorcyclists with long hair are a subset of 50-year-old motorcyclists (some of whom will be bald, others will have short hair and some will have long hair and perhaps even a pony tail) – there must be less of them. Nonetheless, we may hold a prototype which we believe to be representative of 50-year-old motorcyclists (for example, 'ageing biker') a feature of which may include long hair, and this image may exert so strong a hold as to bias our thinking and override logic.

Feminist bank tellers are a subset of both bank tellers and of feminists; there must therefore be fewer feminist bank tellers in the population than there are bank tellers or feminists. The probability of Linda being a feminist bank teller must be lower than her being a bank teller or a feminist. In the Linda problem those people in the study who rated the probability of (8) higher than (6) fell foul of the 'conjunction fallacy'.

Second, the description of Linda suggests a prototype (or even stereotype), and the category that it is most similar to in many people's minds is (3) – someone who is likely to be active in the feminist movement. The decision researcher Robin Hogarth argued that a powerful cognitive mechanism is at work here in which the description we are given facilitates an image of Linda and thereby activates an intuitive rather than an analytical mode of judgement[8]. One of the reasons for this is that our 'intuitive system' operates in more concrete visual terms than does our abstract, verbal, symbolic rational system of reasoning. Paradoxically, given that vivid visual imagery may be a contributory factor to the biasing step which takes place, one way to overcome errors in judgement in the Linda problem is by using imagery in the form of a Venn diagram (see Figure 6.2). The judgements which are often employed in tasks such as the Linda problem are based upon illusions derived from prototypical thinking rather than from the laws of probability and logic.

Representativeness and cognitive functioning

One problem with making judgements based on probabilities is that they are quite abstract. A more vivid (and arguably realistic) way to present such problems, is in the form of a frequency – for example the statement '1 person in 1000 will die from disease X' is easier to picture and likely to have a greater emotional or affective 'charge' than the statement 'the probability of death from disease X is 0.001'.[9] When probabilities of the type used in the 'Linda problem' are replaced by estimates of frequencies, a greater proportion of people avoid the conjunction fallacy, they assign a higher probability to (6) rather than (8).

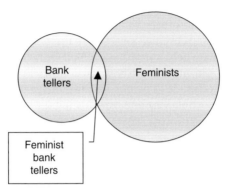

Figure 6.2 Venn diagram for the Linda problem which 'seems certain to reduce the rate of Linda problem errors to zero'.

Adapted from R. Hastie and R.M. Dawes, *Rational Choice in an Uncertain World: The Psychology of Judgement and Decision Making* (London: Sage, 2001) p. 186.

Robin Hogarth suggested that this and other evidence may be interpreted as to suggest that human beings' cognitive systems have evolved to process information in the form of frequencies (which are more concrete) rather than in the form of probabilities (which are more abstract).

Daniel Kahneman and his colleague Shane Frederick argued that couching problems in the language of a frequency format enables the irrational and erroneous inferences drawn (which may occur as a result of judgement by representativeness) to be corrected.[10] The evolutionary biologist Stephen Jay Gould offered the view that our minds are not built to work by the rules of probability but operate by abstracting salient features and engaging in a matching-to-type process that usually serves us well but may fail us in crucial instances:

> We abstract what we consider to be the 'essence' of an entity, and then arrange our judgements by their degree of similarity to this assumed type. Since we are given a 'type' for Linda that implies feminism, but definitely not a bank job, we rank *any* statement matching the type as more probable (emphasis added).[11]

Other researchers have observed that people create stories or narratives based on a holistic interpretation of their reading of the problem – for example: Linda is more likely to be a bank teller and a feminist because as an active feminist she has, nevertheless 'got to make a living'.[12] The fact that many of us still feel a conflict even when confronted with irrefutable mathematical or logical evidence attests to the power that our interpretive, narrative, similarity-seeking, pattern-based thinking holds over us.[13] When making probabilistic judgements people appear to routinely engage in heuristic shortcuts that systematically depart from basic principles of probability, for example 'judgement by representativeness' or the 'law of small numbers' (small samples are erroneously viewed as highly representative of the population from which they are

Figure 6.3 Daniel Kahneman pioneer, along with Amos Tversky (1937–1996), of the seminal programme of research on the role of heuristics and biases in judgement and decision-making. Kahneman was awarded the Nobel Prize for Economic Sciences, 2002 for having integrated insights from psychological research into economic science, especially concerning human judgement and decision-making under uncertainty. Copyright The Nobel Foundation (reproduced by permission).

drawn – as in the coin examples we met earlier), to arrive at what seems like a plausible judgement. As we shall see in the sections that follow, these are not the only sources of error and bias uncovered by Tversky and Khaneman which our reasoning is prone to.

THE POWER OF EASY RECALL: THE AVAILABILITY HEURISTIC

Read through the following list of twelve names:

Anne Wade	Sean Connery
Condoleezza Rice	Derek Burgess
Julia Roberts	Margaret Thatcher
Matthew Bates	Mother Theresa
Princess Diana	Steve Smith
Arthur Allen	Timothy Hughes

Now look away and estimate within five seconds whether the list contained more men's names than women's names.

This experiment has been conducted many times, with the typical result that people usually estimate that the list contains more females than males (the genders are actually equally balanced with six of each). The gender of the famous people (females) is more available for recall than is that of the obscure people (males) so we judge them to be more frequent. The same effect is observed if famous men are intermingled with obscure women. This simple experiment demonstrates the power that ease of retrieval can exert over our judgement. What we witness in this example is the 'availability heuristic' in action: objects or events are brought to mind by retrieval and judged accordingly.

If asked about the safety of our streets from crime or about the hazards of air travel our response is likely to be guided by the vividness of our mental snapshots for muggings and plane crashes, and the feelings that they engender in us. People invariably judge the likelihood of such events as being higher than they actually are. Death as a result of suicide is more frequent than homicide, diabetes is a more common cause of death than the dreaded botulism, and more people die from electrocution than they do as a result of the effects of natural disasters such as floods or tornadoes.[14] Homicide, botulism and natural disaster make dramatic news stories ('if it bleeds, it leads',)[15] they grab our attention and inevitably, help to boost viewing figures and newspaper sales. Inflated judgements of the frequency of events such as these are the result of two sources of bias:

1 They are more available in our environment: dramatic events such as muggings and plane crashes, because they make better news, are more widely reported. Therefore, the sample of data that we have available to base our estimates upon is biased to begin with (deaths from suicides, diabetes and from electrocution in the workplace and the home, tragic though they are, tend not to make the headlines).

2 They are more emotionally charged: vivid and dramatic events are more easily retrieved from memory than are mundane events, and as a result of emotional arousal may exert a strong influence upon our judgements.

People commit errors in judgements of the probability or frequency of events as a result of how easy or difficult it is to imagine or recall relevant instances.[16] This gives rise to unrepresentative and biased samples from which to make inferences or predictions. Retreivability is also affected by the personal significance and the recency of the instance. Imagine that you actually saw a plane crash – the impact upon your subjective judgement of the probability of such an event occurring is likely to be greater because of the emotional 'charge' of seeing the plane coming down, than if you only ever heard about air accidents indirectly through reports in the media. Similarly, seeing an overturned vehicle by the side of the road is likely to affect the subjective probability you attach to the frequency of occurrence of car accidents.[17]

THE 'JUDGEMENT BY ANCHORING AND ADJUSTMENT' HEURISTIC

The place that we start from can exert a strong influence on the judgement that we eventually arrive at. Consider these two examples from Tversky and Kahneman's research:

> Give yourself five seconds to compute an estimate for this multiplication problem:
>
> $1 \times 2 \times 3 \times 4 \times 5 \times 6 \times 7 \times 8$

When researchers gave a group of students the problem as an ascending sequence (as above) their median estimate for the product of the eight digits was a mere 512. However, another group of students were give the problem in reverse (descending) sequence (i.e. $8 \times 7 \times 6 \times 5 \times 4 \times 3 \times$

2 × 1); their mean estimate was a whopping 2250. The actual answer is 40,320 (336 × 120). Here's another frequency judgement task posed by the same group of researchers:

1   'Do you think the proportion of African countries in the United Nations (UN) is more or less than ten per cent?'
2   'On the basis of the response you just gave, what percentage of African countries would you estimate make up the UN?'

When one group of subjects in this experiment were given the above starting point ('more or less than ten per cent?' Question (1) – a meaningless figure randomly chosen by spinning a wheel) and the subsequent 'what percentage?' (Question 2) their median estimate of the percentage of African countries in the UN was 25 per cent. However, a separate group in the experiment who were given the random starting point of 65 per cent (a figure again generated by spinning a wheel) and asked to give their actual figure by moving upwards or downwards from 65 per cent resulted in a median estimate of 45 per cent. The correct answer to the problem in 1972 when the study was conducted was 35 per cent.

Subjects' estimates were initially anchored by the randomly selected value and then insufficiently adjusted upward or downward away from

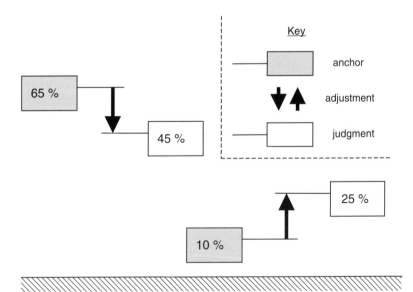

Figure 6.4 Anchoring and adjustment (adapted from Tversky and Kahneman, 1986).

this value – hence the name for this heuristic: 'judgement by anchoring and adjustment'. The phenomenon has been widely observed in situations ranging from share values and political attitudes to real estate prices. Initial values, which we may derive ourselves through partial calculation or which may be presented to us, result in estimates that are anchored by and adjusted in relation to the initial value.[18]

"IF ONLY I'D . . .!": THE SIMULATION HEURISTIC

Mental reconstruction of events (their 'mental simulation') is another way we can bring things to mind but without the need for the recall of an actual event. The simulation heuristic is a way in which people judge the extent to which something 'nearly happened' – how close they came to a particular outcome.[19] Moreover, the interpretation of 'what-might-have-been' affects not only how situations are judged, but also how we feel about them. Consider this example adapted from heuristics and biases research:

> Miss A is flying from London's Heathrow airport at 9.30am to attend an important business meeting in New York. Mr B is flying from London's Gatwick airport at the same time, also to travel to New York for a meeting. They each decide to travel by cab and they leave their respective apartments in good time; unfortunately they both get delayed by heavy traffic on the motorway. They eventually arrive at their respective airports at 10.00am.
>
> When Miss A gets to the check-in at Heathrow she's told the flight left on time at 9.30am.
>
> When Mr B gets to the check-in at Gatwick he's told that he just missed the flight which itself was delayed and left only a few minutes ago.
>
> Who's likely to be more disappointed Miss A ('far miss') or Mr B ('near miss')?

When a similar scenario was given to a group of people, 96 per cent of them said that a 'near miss' person (Mr B's position) would be more disappointed. But why should this be so – in objective terms they both missed their flights and their meetings, and on the face of it surely they ought to be equally disappointed?

Kahneman and Tversky suggested that an emotional 'script' is activated when Miss A and Mr B conduct mental simulations of what happened. For example, Mr B might envisage that if the traffic lights had been green not red, if he'd not stopped to wait for his change from the cab driver or if he'd have ran up the escalator he may just have made it. Consequently he has regrets that these things did not happen and thereby increased his chances of making the flight. Miss A has no such regrets because even if the traffic lights had been green all the way, if she'd have bounded up all the escalators and not stopped to wait for her change from the £20 she gave the cab driver she still had no chance of getting to her flight on time. Scenarios like these may result in counterfactual thinking (the alternative ways in which events may have turned out) which exert an effect upon the perceiver's judgements of what might have happened and the emotions that are aroused (such as regret).[20]

One of the useful functions of mental simulation is that it allows emotions to be re-experienced and processed, which in turn helps with coping and regulation and the restoration of our self-esteem. It also has an estimation function. For example, the probability of an event occurring may be judged by the ease with which the sequence that might bring it about can be imagined.[21] Mentally simulated retrospective thinking ('counterfactuals') has enormous power to create feelings of regret ('*if* only I had done X, *then* Y would have followed') and to influence subsequent judgements. There are two types:

1   *Inaction*: regrets of inaction focus on what should have been done following a failure to obtain a valued outcome, for example: '*If* I'd have studied harder *then* I would have passed the exam'.
2   *Action*: regrets of action focus on what shouldn't have been done, for example: '*If* I hadn't been speeding on the icy road *then* the accident wouldn't have happened'.[22]

Comparing reality with a favoured event may generate regrets which give rise to particular affective states, for example they can induce sadness or relief.

The simulation heuristic focuses upon ways in which the past can be 'undone', explained and come to terms with, however mental simulation is also a powerful means by which people can mentally construct 'what might be' and make predictions that help to inform their decisions. Its power is illustrated by advertising research which indicates that if potential customers imagine themselves 'in' the products with favourable consequences they may be more likely to buy the product than if they were to evaluate a product purely dispassionately and analytically.[23] People who in response to an advertisement imagine themselves

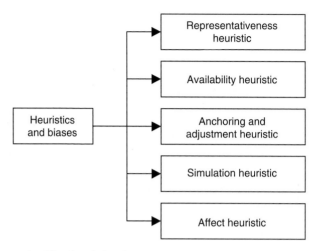

Figure 6.5 Five heuristics from the 'heuristics and biases' programme of research.

winning the lottery may feel luckier and hence buy more lottery tickets. Mental simulations, usually in the form of stories or narratives, enable us to re-run events in their original or altered state and to project one or more versions of future events. In other words mental simulations as well as having an emotional or affective function also have a preparative function in generating alternative scenarios. They can be our personal 'mental DVD' which can be fast-forwarded.

IT DEPENDS WHAT YOU KNOW: SOME RESERVATIONS ON 'JUDGEMENT-BY-HEURISTICS' RESEARCH

How the Linda problem is answered can depend on how much statistics the person being asked the question knows.[24] For example, in the 'Linda problem' a number of the original eight alternative items were 'fillers'. A pared-down version of the problem is:

> Linda is 31 years old, single, outspoken, and very bright. She majored in philosophy. As a student she was deeply concerned with issues of discrimination and social justice and also participated in anti-nuclear demonstrations. Please rank order by probability (highest to lowest) the following:

1   Linda is a bank teller.
2   Linda is active in the feminist movement.
3   Linda is a bank teller and active in the feminist movement.[25]

Linda may resemble what we might think a 'feminist bank teller' would be like, but as we know she cannot be more likely to be a feminist bank taller than a bank teller.[26] In fact when a shorter version of the Linda problem was given to people who were statistically naïve their performance was essentially the same as with the eight-item version. However, knowledge and expertise can play an important role. When a shorter version was given to people who had some statistical knowledge the number of people who made the conjunction error ('Linda is a bank teller' is more probable than 'Linda is a bank teller and active in the feminist movement') fell away dramatically. Their statistical expertise enabled them to follow logic rather than a cognitive short cut.[27] The shorter format makes it easier to see that (3) is a subset of (1) or (2). These and other findings have led some to the view that judgement biases, such as that associated with the representativeness heuristic, are somewhat 'artificial' and 'fragile'.[28] Kahneman and Tversky made two points in response:

1   *Flawless performance is possible*: the theory does not preclude sometimes flawless performance for example, by people with statistical expertise.
2   *Lots of people are statistically naïve*: the fact that flawless performance is possible is not an argument against the role of heuristics in the predictions[29] which are made by the large numbers (perhaps the vast majority) of people (who are statistically naïve).

The heuristics and biases research suggests that the fast, low-effort principle that our intuitive system sometimes adopts may be disadvantageous when processing abstract, probabilistic information of the kind that we often have to deal with in the modern world. Because the onconscious intuitive analysis is fast it also tends to be somewhat crude[30] when dealing with statistical and probabilistic judgements, and will sometimes make mistakes. Our intuitive processing system did not evolve to process this kind of information, and it therefore finds itself at a disadvantage. Where it comes into its own is when the information is presented in more concrete, narrative forms.

THE 'UP-SIDE' OF COGNITIVE SHORT CUTS

Whilst Kahneman and Tversky acknowledged that heuristics can have some utility, their research focused principally upon the 'down-side' which is stated simply as: relying on cognitive short cuts, such as representativeness, can produce less than optimal decisions. Some psychologists have argued that research on human judgement which has exploited the ignorance of experimental subjects has discredited intuition and led to premature pessimism.[31] Alternative ideas about heuristic problem-solving and decision-making have emerged in recent decades and these place greater emphasis on the 'up-side' of cognitive short cuts in processing.[32] One such approach developed by Gerd Gigerenzer and his colleagues[33] is the notion of special type of heuristics which are not only fast and 'frugal' but can also be effective as a means of making judgements in real world situations.

Recall that Herbert Simon proposed the concepts of 'bounded rationality' and 'satisficing' on the precept that an 'unbounded' rationality is not possible because it would:

1   require decision-makers to search for complete information, which would need to go on indefinitely;
2   impose exceedingly taxing demands upon the decision-makers' information processing capacities and other resources.

These things could not happen because in real-world settings time is often at a premium (choosing cannot go on forever) and decision-makers may not have the cognitive capacity to handle the computational requirements.

Arguably the requirements of unbounded rationality are for an 'omnipotent mind' capable of computing with endless complexity and dexterity in an environment which will, if we search long and hard enough, eventually yield up the necessary information. As we know, this is a fiction; human beings have cognitive limitations (witness the limitations of working memory for one), and the world they inhabit is complex, dynamic and often highly ambiguous. Rationality is bounded by the complexity of the environment relative to the cognitive capabilities of the human mind.

'FAST AND FRUGAL' HEURISTICS

Fast and frugal heuristics take bounded rationality a step further: they are ways in which decision-makers can make effective decisions using

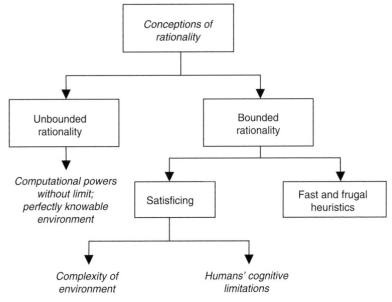

Figure 6.6 Different conceptions of rationality.
Adapted from Gigerenzer *et al.*, 1999, p. 7.

mental mechanisms which exploit the relationships between those objects in the environment for which inferences need to be made.[34] For example, the recognition heuristic[35] is a 'less-is-more' fast and frugal judgement mechanism which, paradoxically, relies upon a comparative lack of knowledge for the making of a decision. The recognition heuristic is stated as follows: 'If one of two objects is recognized and the other is not, then infer that the recognized object has a higher value.'[36] But what does this mean in practice? Supposing the 'value' that you are being required to assess is the population size of two US cities:

> Which US city has more inhabitants, San Diego or San Antonio?

We might expect Americans to be better at answering this question than non-Americans. When Gigerenzer and his colleagues gave this task to US students at the University of Chicago, 62 per cent of them made the correct judgement. When they gave the same question to German students 100 per cent made the correct judgement. The recognition heuristic is based upon there being a relationship between whether or not an object is recognized ('city heard of' or 'city not heard of') and the criterion variable (in this case, population size). Without this it doesn't work: it can only be applied successfully where one of the objects being compared is recognized by the person making the judgement and the other is not.

Gigerenzer and his colleagues argue that in some areas such as identifying kin or avoiding food poisoning organisms are genetically programmed to employ the recognition heuristic, but that in other domains they learn the predictive power of recognition through their experiences. The recognition heuristic is one of a number of decision tools which come within a category that Gigerenzer and his colleagues refer to as 'ignorance-based decision-making'. This mode of decision-making is based on the adaptation of human beings to be able to recognize stimuli such as faces, objects and so forth (i.e. recognition is 'hard-wired' into *Homo sapiens*). But for the recognition heuristic to be 'ecologically rational' and for it to work there must be some correlation between a recognizable feature of an object (for example, brand) and a criterion (such as, quality).[37]

THE EFFECTIVENESS OF FAST AND FRUGAL HEURISTICS

But can such a simple heuristic as 'recognition' be effective? Gigerenzer and a number of his colleagues examined how well the recognition heuristic performed in compiling company stock portfolios. They asked nearly 500 people in the USA and Germany which out of 500 US and 298 German companies they recognized. The US participants' responses then were used to form a portfolio of the ten most recognized German companies; similarly, the German participants' responses were used to form portfolios based on their ten most recognized US companies. These portfolios were then trialled in 1996–7 (the researchers themselves 'put their money where their heuristic was' and bet a 'non-trivial' amount on the stocks recognized by the Munich laypersons.[38])

The surprising finding was that the portfolios generated by means of the recognition heuristic outperformed not only those chosen at random (which we might expect) but also those chosen by highly-trained ('expert') fund managers using all the information available to them (which we might not expect). Two conclusions can be drawn. First, the recognition heuristic couldn't be used with experts because they would have heard of the companies, or complete ignoramuses because they wouldn't have heard of any. It relies upon a 'beneficial degree of ignorance'.[39] Second, it provides evidence not that people use the recognition heuristic, but that a heuristic designed to be as 'fast and frugal' as possible in its information requirements ('how well-known a company was') can be used to make effective judgments in a complex and uncertain environment.

The power of recognition as a predictive tool was taken to support the idea that, paradoxically, a lack of recognition can contain implicit information which may be in some instances as powerful as knowledge explicitly held by experts. For example, where there is a positive relationship between a business' core competence, which makes the company name pretty ubiquitous – such as engine production for Honda whose engines are used in products from lawn mowers to power boats, and its profitability.[40]

Companies use the recognition heuristic to promote awareness of their brand on the basis that recognition is associated with quality. Advertisers are paid huge sums of money to devise ways of placing a brand in the recognition memory of the public – carried on sometimes to the extent that they seek only to achieve recognition (on the assumption that recognition of a brand is related to choosing that brand). The re-make of the James Bond film *Casino Royale* in 2006 was noted for its use of 'product placement' of, amongst other things, Sony lap top computers and Virgin Atlantic Boeing 747s (and including a 'cameo' role for Sir Richard Branson). Gigerenzer and his colleague cited the advertising campaign by Benetton in the 1980s which placed the company's brand image ('United colors of Benetton') next to irrelevant but emotionally powerful images (including an AIDS victim, a guerrilla holding a Kalashnikov and a human thigh bone, and a ship dreadfully overcrowded with refugees) without attempting to convey anything at all of the brand itself.

'Recognition' is a fast and frugal heuristic in its simplest form, and there are more complex types. For example the decision heuristic developed by Breiman and his colleagues for emergency care in hospitals consisted of a simple algorithm with three sequential 'yes/no' questions that could be used in order to classify heart attack patients as either 'high risk' or 'low risk' (see Figure 6.7. Conventional approaches to this diagnostic judgement may employ as many as 19 steps, and clearly may not be executable in the time that an emergency room doctor has available to treat the patient – to delay could literally be fatal.

These various fast and frugal heuristics are part of a larger set of 'tools' or psychological mechanisms[41] which Gigerenzer argues we have in our mind's 'adaptive toolbox'; the metaphor is explained thus:

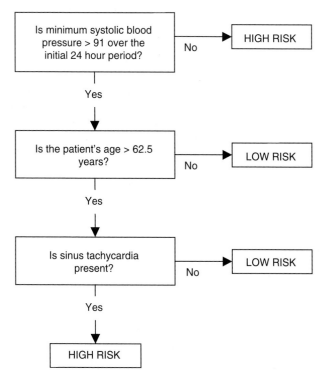

Figure 6.7 A simple decision-tree heuristic for classifying cardiac victims as being high risk or low risk.

Source: Gigerenzer & Todd, 1999; adapted from Brieman *et al.*, 1993.

Just as a mechanic will pull out specific wrenches, pliers and spark-plug gap gauges for each task in maintaining a car's engine rather than hitting everything with a large hammer, different domains of thought require different specialized tools. This is the basic idea of the adaptive toolbox: the collection of specialized cognitive mechanisms that evolution has built into the human mind for specific domains of inference and reasoning, [and] including fast and frugal heuristics.[42]

The necessary tool is selected on the basis of the task (and because the tools are so specialized there may not be so much room for choice), the knowledge of the decision-maker him or herself and external factors such as time pressure. The metaphor of a toolkit is based on the assumption that the human brain comprises a series of 'modules' each designed to execute specific cognitive functions built into the mind through evolution. The necessary tool is selected from the adaptive toolbox depending upon the nature of the judgemental task at hand – i.e. they are selected to suit the situation. The components of the tools themselves are simpler, more primitive and probably quite early-evolved building blocks – basic components from which new tools can be fashioned through learning.[43]

Gigerenzer and his colleague Peter Todd speculate about the evolutionary advantages of the 'less is more' axiom of the fast and frugal school of thought. They suggest that simple heuristics with their speed and robustness had an inherent advantage over more complex approaches and that the ability to use these simpler judgemental strategies 'required the evolution of no more than a certain limited amount of cognitive capacity necessary to execute those heuristics'.[44] Their argument is speculative and perhaps controversial – one implication of it is that simple decision mechanisms underlie, at least in part, the emergence of bounded rationality and the limits of human information processing capacity. By following Gigerenzer and Todd's argument through, the conclusion can be reached that human beings may not have the 'wits to maximize' in Simon's terms, because their ancestors never needed to. On average and in general the human brain does not appear to deal all that well with the reasoning problems which the heuristics and bases researchers used in their experiments. The neuroscientist Michael Gazzaniga and his colleagues suggest that a reason for this may be because our brains are adapted for a different life on the savannahs of Pleistocene Africa. In this environment our ancestors would have had to been adroit at defending themselves, detecting cheats, recognizing kin, reading other peoples' body language, facial expressions and intentions[45] and weighing up situations and making necessary predictions upon which to make decisions.

TAKE-AWAYS FOR CHAPTER 6

Key ideas

Heuristics can be a *low-effort* way to solve problems; however the errors of logic on which some heuristics are based can result in biased judgements. Small samples are often viewed as being *overly representative*; they may lead to what seem to be plausible judgements but which turn out to be biased. How easy or difficult it is to *imagine* or *recall* relevant events or instances can give rise to unrepresentative and biased samples from which inferences or predictions are then made. Where we *start from* may result in final estimates that are anchored by and adjusted in relation to the initial value and therefore be biased. *Mental simulations* (for example, in the form of stories or narratives) enable us to re-run events in their original or altered state and to project one or more versions of the future. The recognition heuristic is an example of a *fast and frugal* heuristic. Fast and frugal heuristics may be genetically pre-programmed (such as recognizing kin). Decision-makers need to be aware of the potential sources of error and bias that heuristics can be prone to and, wherever possible, take steps to *guard against* them.

Intuition quote: John Dewey, educationalist

'Spontaneous intuitions . . . have to be entertained subject to correction, to confirmation and revision, by personal observation of consequences and cross-questioning of quality and scope.'

Action point

Next time you're confronted by a tough decision and you get a gut feeling: treat it as a hypothesis; play *'devil's advocate'*; ask stiff and searching questions; try to uncover your *prejudices*; be on-guard against *'wishful thinking'*; and *bounce* your hunch off a sympathetic colleague or friend.

FURTHER READING

Gigerenzer, G., Todd, P.M. and the ABC Research Group (eds), *Simple Heuristics that Make us Smart*. Oxford: Oxford University Press 1999.

Hastie, R. and Dawes, R.M., *Rational Choice in an Uncertain World: The Psychology of Judgement and Decision Making*. London: Sage 2001.

7 Intuitive 'muscle power'

Buddy Willard went to Yale, but now I thought of it, what was wrong with him was that he was stupid. Oh he'd manage to get good marks alright, but he didn't have one speck of intuition. Doreen had intuition. Everything she said was like a secret voice speaking right out of my own bones.

(Sylvia Plath, *The Bell Jar*, 1963)

MAIN IDEA

Accurate intuitive judgement depends upon good situational awareness which is developed through experience, learning and feedback; it can be exercised with or without conscious awareness of the processes involved.

In contrast to the 'magical' view that pervades some 'New Age intuitionism', the decision researcher Gary Klein advocates a 'muscular' view of intuition which sees it as a mental strength that can be acquired[1]. Rather like a body-building exercise programme in a fitness club, 'intuitive muscle' can be built up through experiences, especially if those experiences are managed effectively and channelled in the right direction, and if intuitive judgements become more refined through good feedback. Intuitive muscle can be in evidence in many different complex and uncertain decision scenarios ranging from war zones to neonatal wards. Consider this incident described by Klein[2] in his 1998 book *Sources of Power*. It involved two nurses, Linda (an experienced nurse but new to neonatal care) and Darlene (six years experience in neonatal care) and their sick infant patient 'Melissa'.

The incident occurred towards the end of a fairly uneventful night shift. Melissa was a little less fussy than usual (maybe a sign she was getting better?). She had seemed lethargic (but who wouldn't be at that time in the morning?) and the spot on Melissa's heel where her blood sample had been taken was still bleeding a little (a good 'heel stick' closes up almost instantaneously). Melissa was Linda's patient and so Darlene left the routine checking to her less-experienced colleague:

> But when Darlene walked past Melissa's isolette near the end of the shift, something caught her eye. Something about the baby 'just looked funny', as she later put it. Nothing major, nothing obvious, but to her the baby 'didn't look good'. Darlene looked closer, now noticing specific details . . .

The details that Darlene noticed were on closer inspection that the heel stick was still weeping, Melissa was a little off-colour and mottled and appeared bloated; moreover a check on her temperature profile showed that it had been dropping consistently over the shift. Piecing all these clues together sounded Darlene's internal 'alarm' and she immediately called the emergency doctor. They ordered antibiotics and a blood test simultaneously and immediately. Some time later the blood test confirmed their suspicions – sepsis (blood poisoning) and the fact that they administered antibiotics right away rather than waiting for the results of the blood test probably saved the baby's life. What was the difference between Linda and Darlene? Linda noticed the symptoms but didn't piece them together; the more experienced neonatal nurse Darlene on the other hand saw, as Klein described them, a 'particular constellation of symptoms' that when interpreted in the light of her six years neonatal experience together rang a loud alarm bell.

'Heuristics and biases' research often concerned itself with controlled experiments in laboratory settings, contrast this with the 'Linda and Darlene' scenario in which:

1   the problem as very real (it was not an artificial 'psychology lab' problem);
2   the consequences of a bad decision were significant (the stakes could not be higher);
3   the situation could have changed at any moment (circumstances were not static and stable);

4   the decision had to be made quickly (there was not the luxury of time).

Compared to the judgements that decision-makers are required to make in field settings some of the problems we looked at in Chapter 6 (such as ranking alternatives, performing mental calculations and making estimates), although cognitively demanding, are comparatively unpressured and stress free. The fast and frugal heuristics research moved beyond these intellective types of judgement tasks to examine how certain types of cognitive short cuts were consciously employed to make decisions in settings that were closer to reality. The fast and frugal programme was also concerned with how better decision aids (for example, the cardiac arrest algorithm) might be designed on the basis of their 'real world' relevance and validity.

A number of the key experiments in the 'heuristics and biases' and the 'fast and frugal' research programmes were concerned with the judgements made by people who were statistically naïve (as in the case of the representativeness heuristic experiments), or by lay persons (as in the case of the recognition heuristic researchers' stock market studies). The design of these studies meant that it was important that participants lacked experience and expertise in the domain in which the judgement was to be made (for example, the errors in the 'Linda problem' were ameliorated when participants knew some statistics). A missing piece in our jigsaw is an explicit consideration of the ways in which people intuitively employ their experience and expertise in real-world settings and take advantage of this to make difficult and time-pressured decisions in complex situations. For this we turn to the field of naturalistic decision-making (NDM) research and in particular the recognition-primed decision (RPD) model developed by Gary Klein and his colleagues.

MAKING IMPORTANT DECISIONS IN THE 'REAL WORLD'

NDM refers to the ways in which people use their experience to make decisions in real world (what might be called 'field') settings. The term NDM first appeared in 1989 at a conference of researchers who dared to step outside the traditional decision research paradigm. It is worth remembering what the latter stood for: it was typified by advice to decision-makers that they should assess the nature of the situation, determine the options available and ideally, in the view of

Irving Janis and Leon Mann in 1977[3], generate large option sets, evaluate the risks and benefits of each alternative and select a response that best fits the demands of the situation[4]. This is not a million miles from the balance sheet or multiple attribute approach that Benjamin Franklin in the offered to his friends in the eighteenth century. It works very well in certain types of intellective and computationally complex situations.

Contrast the high aspirations of the rational decision model with a narrative borrowed from one of Klein's case studies encountered previously in Chapter 2. It concerned a team of firefighters who were attending a simple one storey house fire. The fire was being unresponsive to being hosed with water which did not fit with what the expectations of the experienced lieutenant who was leading the team. The fire didn't 'feel' right, so much so that the lieutenant decided to evacuate his team from the building no sooner had he done so than the floor where they had been standing collapsed. Had they lingered a moment longer they would have plunged into the fire below.[5]

One of the most striking things about this example is that no multiple options and attributes were generated in response to the feeling that something was 'out-of-kilter'. The lieutenant's expectations of what might occur were violated (he expected that the fire would respond to being hosed with water), but at the time he could not explain this violation occurred. In spite of being unable to rationalize or verbalize any reasoning he relied on his affect-laden judgment ('he just doesn't feel right') which was, fortunately, to evacuate his team moments before the floor collapsed.

The crucial issue in this time-pressured, life-or-death situation was that the balance in the way the lieutenant weighed up the situation was front-end loaded (his main concern was with sizing up the situation) rather than back-end loaded as it might have been in the traditional 'choose-among-many-options' approach. The lieutenant, an experienced firefighter, on the basis of the way this fire in this context was behaving quickly weighed up the situation and didn't compare any options, he acted on the first tactic he generated – evacuate. A similar phenomenon has been observed in experiments with chess players – the first moves the players generated tended to be judged by grandmasters as 'strong moves'.[6] We also saw it with Darlene, she didn't weigh up whether to ask for a blood test, wait for the results, and then ponder whether to administer antibiotics; she and the doctor acted on the first tacit they generated – antibiotics and blood test simultaneously. Darlene's and the lieutenant's decisions:

1 were taken in a naturalistic setting and as a result they were highly context-dependent;
2 weren't made on an indiscriminate 'one-size-fits-all' basis (as a novice may have done);
3 were attuned to the clues in the situation that the experienced decision-makers perceived consciously and non-consciously;
4 were used to generate behaviours based on a finely-honed awareness of the total problem scenario.

Both the lieutenant and Darlene were keenly aware of a particular constellation of clues that made up the whole picture; some of these were perceived and processed consciously (they could be verbalized), and others were perceived and processed beneath the level of conscious awareness and only drawn out in the subsequent in-depth analyses that the researchers conducted.

As the research into expert-novice differences reveals, the use of experience by experts to make rapid judgements *in situ* is under-pinned by:

1 *perception*: a holistic process of recognizing patterns in the clues present in the environment;
2 *deriving meaning*: the matching of these to patterns and scripts in long term memory;
3 *detecting mismatch*: having enough of a highly tuned awareness to be able to detect when a pattern does not fit one's expectations.

Sizing up a situation is often referred to as a 'situation awareness'. It's based upon the perception of relevant clues enables decision-makers to adopt responses that are appropriate to the situation without devoting scare cognitive resource to irrelevancies. They don't waste time and mental effort in going down blind alleys and are able to adapt what they have learned to fit the situation that faces them at the time. Good situation awareness is founded on the ability to attend to relevant environmental information, exclude irrelevant information, and syn-thesize the relevant clues into a plausible overall assessment.

RECOGNITION-PRIMED DECISION (RPD)-MAKING

RPD model was formulated in the mid 1980s by Klein and his col-leagues and was an outcome of a project for the US Army Research Institute for the Behavioral Sciences. It looked at the ways in which experienced people made decisions in under time pressure and how the decision-makers who were unable to engage in a comparative evaluation of the costs and benefits and deliberate upon various alternative courses of action actually behaved. RPD is the prime example of NDM.[7] In their Army research project Klein and his colleagues set out with a number of expectations one of which was the 'two-option' hypothesis: 'Under time pressure fire ground commanders could not think of lots and lots of options. Instead, they would have to consider only two options, one that was intuitively the favourite, and the other to serve as a comparison to show why the favourite was better.'[8] A surprising thing about this hypothesis is the way in which it went against the grain of traditional decision analysis (the principle of generating several alternative courses of action). Even more striking is Klein's finding that this hypothesis itself was overly-cautious – in point of fact the research revealed that fire-ground commanders did not consider two options, instead they appeared not to be considering any options at all. The two option hypothesis was unsupported by the data. The key to effective decision-making seemed to be that experience enabled decision-makers to see situations as prototypes for which they knew a typical course of action pretty much immediately – this meant that there was often no need to think of other courses of action. The process is more complex than this suggests, but the essence of RPD consists of:

- *sizing up* (situation awareness) matching the situation to a prior experience to determine a singular course of action;
- *imagining* (mental simulation): evaluating the consequences of the proposed action through a mental simulation to see if it is likely to run into difficulties (imagining the course of action). If the mental simulation suggests potential problems they move on to another singular course of action.[9]

Much of the research in this area has focused on decision-making behaviour on the flight decks of aircraft. One of the main findings of this programme of research is that aviation experts and aviation novices differ in the number of important cues they are able to recognize in the environment and are able to report. In this context situation awareness is defined as: 'a pilot's continuous perception of self and aircraft in relation to the dynamic environment of flight, threats and mission, and the ability to forecast, then execute tasks based on that decision'.[10] In one research study expert pilots under time pressure were able to report 15 relevant cues; novices on the other hand were only able to report about nine relevant cues.[11]

Klein and his colleagues studied a total of 156 cases and documented the type of decision strategy they found in each case. Their results are summarized below – they looked almost in vain to find evidence of comparative evaluation, but they found instead plenty of evidence of the singular evaluation strategy:

1   *0 per cent*: choosing from pre-selected options given by someone else;
2   *12 per cent*: comparative evaluation (most of these were from cases where the decision-makers were novices);
3   *7 per cent*: novel option (new and creative ideas were initiated and not based on any previous examples);
4   *81 per cent*: singular evaluation, i.e. decisions based upon recognition (the case studies were somewhat atypical and it is likely that the proportion of singular evaluations found would have been even higher for routine decisions).[12]

The 'sizing up' of the situation in the cases of the lieutenant in command of the single story building with the basement fire ('he just doesn't feel right about being in that house') and of Darlene on the neonatal word ('Something about the baby "just looked funny" ')

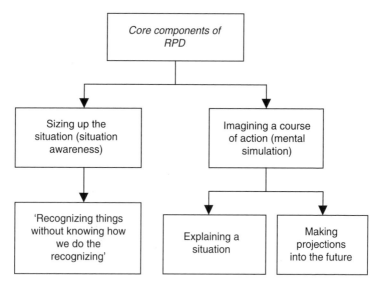

Figure 7.1 The core components of RPD – 'sizing-up' and imagining a course of action.

Adapted from Klein, 1998.

occurred intuitively and attest to the power of situational awareness in recognizing the prototypes and detecting deviations. Klein offers a very succinct definition of intuition: 'recognizing things without knowing how we do the recognizing',[13] based on RPD's two core elements: non-conscious pattern recognition by situation assessment; and projection into the future based on mental simulation.

ESP OR 'INTUITIVE SITUATION ASSESSMENT'?

Klein and his colleagues conducted much of their research fieldwork by means of in-depth interviews.[14] One of the curious features of some of their reported findings is that the interviewees often appear convinced that they made their decision using some special skill or power such as ESP. One case in point is a Royal Navy Lieutenant ('R') who was in command of an air defence battery on the British destroyer *HMS Gloucester* in the Gulf in 1992 (see Chapter 2). Lieutenant R shot an 'object' down that was headed for the fleet at a speed of about 650 knots and before the correct identification procedure had been carried out. He strongly believed that:

(1) it was a hostile missile and not a friendly American A–6 aircraft;
(2) he needed to act as quickly as possible before the threat escalated any further.

He could have been seriously in error with disastrous consequences. Lieutenant R – having no apparent objective basis for his judgement – confessed to Klein and his colleagues that he thought it was ESP that enabled him to recognize the radar blip as a hostile Iraqi Silkworm missile and not an A–6.

Through a series of probing questions and meticulous analyses the researchers 'boiled it down' to a more scientific explanation: Lieutenant R perceived the blip to be accelerating as it came off the coast, some-thing contrary to the behaviour of an A–6 which always travelled at a constant speed as they came off the coast. The apparent acceleration of the blip appeared to be the answer to how R was able to recognize the missile and solved the 'mystery'. All except for one small point: it would be impossible to work out the acceleration on only one radar sweep – two sweeps (which take more than five seconds) are needed to compare two velocities (acceleration is the rate of change of velocity). Lieutenant R based his five second decision on one sweep only – so perhaps he did have ESP after all?

Sadly, for proponents of the magical view of intuition, ESP was not the explanation – the answer was much more fascinating. The blip only appeared to be accelerating, in reality it was not. More detailed probing by the researchers and other experts revealed that Lieutenant R had non-consciously inferred the altitude of the object on the basis of how far from the coast the radar blip had been picked up. Ground clutter meant that the low-flying Silkworm wasn't spotted by radar until later than it would have been had it been a higher-flying A–6 (giving the impression of great acceleration); a Silkworm flies at 1000 feet whereas an A–6 flies at 3000 feet. The lieutenant's highly-tuned situation awareness was able to intuitively recognize the blip as a missile without knowing how he did the recognizing. Like the people in Pawel Lewicki's Tulsa experiments Lieutenant R's recognition was as a result of a complex interplay of implicit perception and non-conscious cognitive processing of the data.

PATTERN RECOGNITION (PR) AND PERCEPTION OF COHERENCE

Naturalistic decision-making researchers are strongly wedded to the idea that intuition involves 'pattern recognition' (recognizing an implicit coherence in a set of clues). A number of researchers in personality and social psychology have offered explanations of the ways in people are able to make intuitive judgements based upon the 'perception of coherence'. Pattern recognition involves a non-conscious perception of coherence in the available clues – their structure and meaning[15], whether things 'fit' or whether they are 'out of kilter'. 'Coherence' in this context refers to the degree of connectedness between concepts; for example, if a person is presented with a word triad (for example: 'pine', 'tree', 'crab') an implicit perception of coherence (a feeling that the words 'somehow' are linked) or incoherence would enable them to rate the triad of words as being 'coherent' or 'incoherent' without being able to state what the common word is which links them (these words happen to be coherent – the linking word is 'apple'). Psychologists have used so-called 'dyads of triads' (DOTs) problems to explore how the coherence in clues is intuitively judged.

Take a moment to look at the word triads below. Does your intuition tell you that Triad 1 is coherent or incoherent? What about Triad 2 – coherent or incoherent?

Triad 1: 'Goat' 'Pass' 'Green'
Triad 2: 'Bird' 'Pipe' 'Road'

Kenneth Bowers and his colleagues found that people are able to judge Triad 1 as coherent even without being able to explicitly state why; Triad 2 is more likely to be judged as incoherent (the common word in Triad 1 is 'mountain').[16] The phenomenon of 'perception of coherence' is based upon a principle (perhaps familiar to us by now) that information that is not in conscious awareness is nonetheless able to have an effect upon judgement. Each clue word automatically activates a host of associated words and a non-conscious process of spreading activation occurs. The psychologists Nicola Bauman and Julius Kuhl argue that extended associationistic networks are activated automatically on exposure to a stimulus (for example the word triads). Parallel processing of information occurs which is holistic and implicit and this gives rise to the immediate intuitive judgement of the word triad as being coherent or incoherent.[17] The neural activation spreads but remains below the threshold of conscious awareness until such time as the problem is solved. Kuhl calls the extended semantic networks which enable these judgments to arise 'extension memory'. Following the intuitive judgement of coherence and the spread of activation through networks of association neural activation may fully cross a threshold of awareness. At this point non-conscious thought becomes explicitly available to conscious awareness and an insightful 'Eureka!' moment is likely to be experienced. The spread of activation between the initial intuitive judgement and the occurrence of insight is often referred to as the incubation stage[18] (see Chapter 3).

People are able to not only to judge accurately the coherence of word triads; Bowers and his colleagues also has their experimental subjects judge the coherence of visual stimuli in the form of 'Gestalt closure stimuli' (they called it the 'Waterloo Gestalt Closure Task'). These were meaningful pictures of common objects (e.g. a camera, see Figure 7.3A) paired with a displacement of the elements of the meaningful gestalt ('organized whole') into a non-meaningful pattern (B). As with the word triads, people were able to detect coherent gestalts even if they were unable to say what they were. It's also worthy of note that it is very hard to conceive of someone being able to detect coherence in the DOT or Waterloo Gestalt Closure Tasks without the necessary prior knowledge upon which to draw (e.g. the English language and having previously seen the everyday objects upon which the gestalt tasks are based). This reinforces a fundamental principle – that intuition is informed judgement based for the most part upon prior knowledge, learning and experience.[19]

Cognitive neuroscientists have used a variant of Waterloo Gestalt Closure Task in fMRI studies which aimed to identify the brain regions

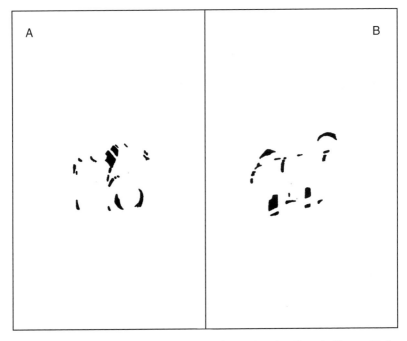

Figure 7.2 Sample gestalt closure stimulus from Waterloo Gestalt Closure Task.
Source: K.S. Bowers, G. Regehr and C. Balthazard, 'Intuition in the context of discovery', *Cognitive Psychology*, 1990, 22: 83.

involved in intuitive judgement of visual coherence (their 'neural substrates'). Kirsten Volz and Yves von Cramon found that the orbito-frontal cortex (OFC), the amygdala and other brain regions (including the ventral occipito-temporal regions, VOT)* were activated in coherence judgements even when participants were unable to name the object concerned.[20] It has been suggested that the role of the brain's frontal cortex is to provide an initial 'guess' at visual recognition which limits the number of options that need to be considered; this activation occurs before activation in the brain regions involved in

---

* The human orbito-frontal cortex (OFC) is divided into a more central part – the ventromedial prefrontal cortex (VMPC) and a more lateral portion – the lateral orbito-frontal cortex (Gazzaniga, Ivry and Mangun, 2002, p.546). Its primary functions are related to the processing of emotions, and as we shall see in Chapter 9, damage to the VMPC region of the OFC can profoundly impair decision-making. The visual cortex is located primarily within the occipital lobe (Gazzaniga *et al.*, 2002).

object recognition.[21] This enables a quick response to be generated in situations with time pressure and/or insufficient information which signals the most likely interpretation[22] which can then be used by downstream brain regions.[23]

Research by Kuhl and others suggests that positive affect ('feeling good') opens up access to extension memory whilst negative affect closes down access. If this is the case creative and other 'high level' intuitions are more likely to arise if a person is in a state of 'positive affect'. Positive mood supports the spread of neural activation to remote associates in memory (a holistic processing mode), whilst negative mood restricts the spread of activation (an analytical processing mode).[24] Cognitive neuroscientists have also suggested that the extended and overlapping semantic networks necessary to make intuitive judgements of word triads are located in the cerebral cortex of the right hemisphere of the brain.[25]

Much of this research is based on an 'associative network' model of semantic memory in which activation along 'associative links' occurs automatically, but whether this mechanism applies to the kinds of tasks which NDM researchers are concerned with is an open question. Judging the semantic coherence of word triads or the coherence of a visual pattern is a very different judgemental task from assimilating and assessing clues in complex, time-pressured real-world situations. Nonetheless the spread of activation and the consequent generation of a

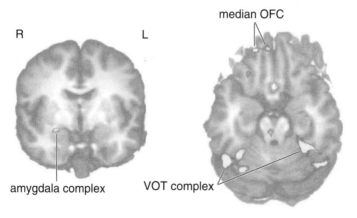

Figure 7.3 Brain regions activated during Waterloo Gestalt Closure-type Task.

Source: K.G. Volz and D.Y. von Cramon, 'What neuroscience can tell about intuitive processes in the context of perceptual discovery', *Journal of Cognitive Neuroscience*, 2006, 18(12); 2077–2087. Reproduced by permission of MIT Press.

feeling of certitude about 'knowing without knowing why' suggests one potential mechanism which may go some way in explaining the cognitive processes which underpin pattern recognition.[26]

MENTAL SIMULATIONS

In addition to situation awareness based on PR the second of the two core elements of the RPD model is conscious 'mental simulation'. Previously we met Kahneman and Tversky's concept of the 'simulation heuristic' (a mental reconstruction of events without the need for the recall of actual events). A mental simulation is an imitation of events that have already happened (e.g. 'what should have been said in an argument'), or the construction of hypothetical scenarios (e.g. 'how to conduct oneself in an up-coming sales presentation').[27] Mental simulations are used by athletes and other performers when they imagine themselves making a record high jump or going out on set before the cameras or an audience. The golfer Jack Nicklaus described the way in which vivid mental simulations helped him to play better golf:

> Before every shot I go to the movies inside my head. Here is what I see. First I see the ball where I want it to finish, nice and white and sitting up high on the bright green grass. Then I see the ball going there; its path and trajectory and even its behaviour on landing. The next scene shows me making the kind of swing that will turn the previous image into reality. These home movies are the key to my concentration and to my positive approach to every shot.[28]

Klein describes mental simulation as a 'heuristic strategy' which decision-makers use to explain situations and make projections into the future (essentially predictions) based upon 'the ability to imagine people and objects consciously and to transform those people and objects through several transitions, finally picturing them in a different way than at the start'.[29] In order to mentally simulate events in ways that will support good judgement and problem-solving a decision-maker needs to have a robust mental model of how the system or process under consideration actually works. For example, I could mentally visualize the landing of an aircraft in bad weather; the fact that I could imagine this event does not mean that my visualization has any fidelity whatsoever as a mental simulation. One reason for this is because I do not have any experience as a pilot; hence I do not possess anything approximating to a mental model. Although my visualization could be vivid, my mental simulation would be ignorant and naïve. However, a skilled and experienced pilot would have a high fidelity mental model of how the various parameters affect how to safely land an aircraft in bad weather (the interaction of aircraft, weather, topography, and so forth). Because the pilot's cognitive processes are based upon a robust mental model grounded in learning, experience and expertise it would have a better correspondence with reality, and hence would have a much better fidelity than a visualization I could conjure.

That said, mental simulations are approximations which take into account a number of important constraints. Reality can be highly complex and dynamic, and the amount of information in the environment and the speed with which it can be processes are limited by the cognitive capacities of the human brain. Mental simulations are conscious (hence their description as heuristic 'strategies') and effortful, and are subject to a number of 'rules of thumb' which Klein and his colleagues derived inductively from their case studies. One of these cases was the effects of political, economic and social liberalization in the 1990s on the Polish economy. Through interviews with a number of experts Klein and his co-researchers were able to ascertain an expert mental model of how the Polish economy would fare in the post-Soviet era (see Figure 7.4). The model was based on:

- comparatively few variables (three in number): rate of inflation; unemployment figures; foreign exchange rates;
- a small number of transitions (six): rapid inflation; reduced level of inflation; gradual rise in unemployment; improved employment; loss in exchange rate; stabilized exchange rate.

This pattern of three variables and six transitions was one that Klein and his colleagues met on a number of other occasions in the various cases they studied and perhaps represents the optimum level of complexity for a mental simulation.

Another important feature of the ways in which people build mental simulations is the role that evaluation plays in the construction of the model. In his research Klein observed that people assess a mental simulation on the bases of:

1 *coherence*: 'does it make sense?' (its 'face validity');
2 *applicability*: will it deliver the results that are desired?
3 *completeness*: is it under- or over-specified?

As well as passing these various tests the mental simulation must

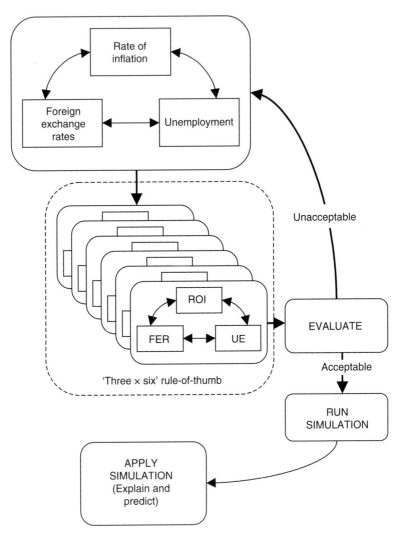

Figure 7.4 The components of a mental simulation – the example of the Polish economy.

Based on G. Klein, *Sources of Power: How People Make Decisions* (Cambridge, MA: MIT Press, 1998) pp. 54–7.

also 'pass muster' on a trial run – if difficulties become apparent the construction of the simulation may need to be re-examined. If the simulation provides an acceptable explanation it may be deemed suitable as a simulation – this does not, as Klein warns us – mean that it is correct. There may be other alternative explanations than the one that the simulation turns up – a simulation can generate an explanation much more easily than it can generate a proof.[30] Indeed one of the dangers of mental simulations is that they can be used to reinforce pre-existing views, and contrary evidence can be readily explained-away by merely 'tweaking' the simulation to fit preconceived notions or support wishful thinking.

THE PERILS OF THE CONFIRMATION BIAS

An 'intuitive experience' for many people is the 'phone call phenomenon' – thinking about a person and then suddenly 'out of the blue' receiving a phone call from them. At the time it seems a very strange coincidence; how can this be explained other than some kind of 'intuitive clairvoyance' where we tuned into the fact that this special person was about to call? Well, there may be an alternative explanation.

In the 1960s the English cognitive psychologist Peter Wason (1924–2003) designed an elegantly simple test to explore whether people approached reasoning tasks by trying to confirm or disconfirm a hypothesis.[31] The problem Wason devised is often referred to as the '2–4–6 problem'. The task is to work out the rule used to generate the series of numbers '2–4–6'. In the experiment people were invited to generate their own sequence based upon what they thought the rule for the '2–4–6' sequence might be. The experimenter would then tell them whether or their sequence conformed to the rule. If you were asked to generate a sequence of numbers that conformed to the same rule as the 2–4–6 series, what might your three numbers be?

The participants in Wason's experiments tried out many examples such as:

4–6–8

If you'd offered this triad as an example which might conform to the same rule as the '2–4–6' sequence and were told that this did indeed conform to the same rule as '2–4–6', what other sequence of numbers might you offer as your next triad?

The participants in Wason's experiments offered sequences such as

20–22–24
100–102–104

Happily, both of these also conform to the same rule as the 2–4–6 sequence, and so things are looking good. Now if you were asked to state the rule, what would you say it was? Many of Wason's participants offered the following rule:

The rule is 'any series of numbers increasing by two'

Unfortunately this is incorrect. The correct rule was simply: 'numbers of increasing magnitude', so 6–7–8 would have worked as would 17–23–51.

Could Wason's participants have tested their hypothesis in a different way? Yes, they could have suggested a negative instance of their hypothesized 'increasing by two rule', for example 1–2–3. Had they proposed this they would have been told that this too was a sequence that conformed to the rule. This sequence served the vital purpose of having the power to falsify their 'increasing by two' rule.[32]

Most of the participants in Wason's study adopted a strategy of trying to confirm rather than disconfirm (refute or falsify) their hypothesized rule.[33] Wason took this as evidence of a general bias in human reasoning, namely that people tend to fixate on a hypothesis and then try to confirm it. The general pattern seems to be that when people generate hypotheses they try to gather evidence that is consistent with their hypothesis and find it very difficult to consider alternate hypotheses. One reason may be because of the limited capacity of working memory. Considering more than one hypothesis in a memory store of such limited size is not easy and given the limits of working memory capacity it is doubly difficult to switch hypotheses in the face of inconsistent evidence[34] especially if significant cognitive resource has to be devoted to perceiving and processing information from the environment. In the case of mental simulations it appears that novice decision-makers are more prone to the confirmation bias than experts. Experts are more inclined to search for evidence that may be incompatible with their interpretations[35] and which may eventually reveal their assumptions as unreliable and cause their intuitive judgment to be abandoned.

We could test our 'intuitive clairvoyance' hypothesis for the 'phone call phenomenon' by checking out the correlation between the number of times we think about that person and the number of times they actually call when we happen to be thinking about them.[36]

In general terms Wason's findings suggest that there are dangers when people fixate on a hunch and then look for evidence to confirm it rather than for evidence to falsify it. An intuitive judgement (unlike an insight) is a hypothesis. A hypothesis or an intuition is a proposal made as a basis for reasoning ('my gut feeling tells me that this business venture is likely to succeed', 'I have a hunch that this person is the one we are looking for', etc.). Therefore, even though we may feel a high level of confidence in an intuitive judgement, we cannot assume that logically it is true. An intelligent decision-maker may be able to distinguish between an intuition and a wild guess, the distinction between an intuition and wishful thinking is less easy to discern. If our intuitive hypotheses are nothing more than desires or wishes that we hope will be true we are likely to fall foul of the confirmation bias. It's a source of bias we must be wary of because of the basic tendency in human reasoning to search for evidence that will confirm. One way of guarding against merely searching for evidence that will confirm is to look for contrary evidence for why it should not be true. If an intuition stands up to this kind of scrutiny this strengthens it as a hypothesis. Seeking disconfirmation is consistent with the theory of science proposed by one of the most famous philosophers of science of the twentieth century, Sir Karl Popper (1902–1994): namely that science advances by producing theories for which it constantly seeks evidence of falsifiability. In Popper's terms a genuine scientific theory can therefore only ever be considered 'provisional', and in one sense every scientific theory is 'sitting in the waiting room of refutation' waiting to see if it is to be called forward.

One of the differences between intuitions and falsifiable scientific hypotheses is that intuitions are not dispassionate scientific propositions; they are affectively-charged judgments which may contain a more than a dash of our wishes and desires ('If only it were true', 'I'd really like this deal to work out', 'Something tells me this is my big chance', etc). Our perceptions and our memories are both emotionally filtered and weighted[37] (intuitions are 'affect-laden' judgements). The neural activation which energizes implicit memories, to the extent that they can enter into conscious awareness and influence our conscious thoughts and our behaviours, relies upon affective as well as a cognitive process. Human beings are not dispassionate decision-making machines; instead we are species that evolution has equipped with a unique and complex cognitive-affective system which benefited the survival of our evolutionary ancestors. Whether we like it or not, this system still exerts a profound influence upon our behaviours in the twentieth century. Indeed much of the power of our 'intuitive muscle' derives from the feelings which accompany the non-conscious pattern recognition processes which are a principal feature of recognition-primed decision-making.

TAKE-AWAYS FOR CHAPTER 7

Key ideas

The 'muscular' view of intuition sees it as a mental strength that can be built up through *relevant experiences* and *good feedback*. Good *situation awareness* is founded on the ability (implicitly or explicitly) to perceive relevant environmental information, exclude irrelevant information, and synthesize the relevant information into a plausible overall assessment. From an RPD perspective intuition is simply 'recognizing things without knowing how we do the recognizing' on the basis of non-conscious *pattern recognition* (PR) by situation assessment, and projection into the future by *mental simulation*. An intuitive judgement (unlike an insight) is a *hypothesis* and there are dangers when people fixate on a hunch and then look for evidence to *confirm* it rather than for evidence to falsify it.

Intuition quote: Reg Revans, pioneer of 'action learning'

'Intuition, the unremembered urges of the past, must always be the first weapon of the manager; she must be able to grasp the underlying structures of situations that challenge her.'

Action points

What is it that makes your tough decisions *difficult*? What kinds of *errors* do you or other people make in these tough decisions? How do the *experts* you're familiar with make these tough decisions differently from people who are *novices*?[38]

FURTHER READING

Klein, G., *Sources of Power: How People Make Decisions*. Cambridge, MA: MIT Press 1998.

8   In two minds?

Two of these fellows you
Must know and own; this thing of darkness I
Acknowledge mine.
    (Shakespeare, *The Tempest*, Act 5, Scene 1)

MAIN IDEA

Human beings process information in two complementary
ways, intuitively (processing is automatic, quick, holistic and
affect-laden) and rationally (processing is slower, analytic and
relatively affect-free). Effective decision-making and problem-
solving across a range of tasks and situations depends upon a
harmonious blend of intuition and analysis.

Figure 8.1 represents two trays, A and B, each of which contains mix-
tures of red jelly beans and white jelly beans spread out in a single layer
(no jelly bean is hidden). Imagine you are to be blindfolded and offered
a reward of £100 if you can blindly pick a red bean from one of the
trays. On the basis of your gut feeling, which tray would you choose to
select from – the small Tray A, or the large Tray B?

Now imagine that you have the choice to be able to pay £1 to choose
which of the trays you select from, but if you don't pay the tray you
are to choose from will be selected randomly for you. Would you be
prepared to pay £1 for the privilege of selecting Tray A or B?

The odds of winning £100 by selecting a red jelly bean from Tray A
are 1/10 (i.e. 10 per cent); the odds of winning a £100 by selecting a red

Tray A   Tray B

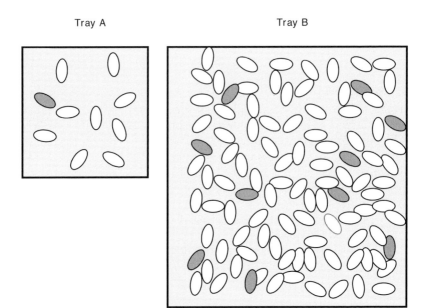

Figure 8.1 Schematic diagram of test trays for the ratio bias (RB) phenomenon.

jelly bean from Tray B are 10/100 (i.e. 10 per cent). The odds of choosing a red jelly bean are the same for Trays A and B – they offer the same probability of a favourable outcome (winning £100). Which tray did you choose?

When a similar experiment was conducted by the social psychologist Seymour Epstein and his colleagues amongst psychology undergraduates in the USA most participants expressed a preference for the larger Tray B which had odds of 10/100 (i.e. 1/10) of picking a red bean, rather than the smaller Tray A which had odds of 1/10. Not content with this surprising finding Epstein and his colleagues further manipulated the experiment by making it so that choosing from Tray B offered a lower probability of the favourable outcome of winning. A majority of respondents (61 per cent) still preferred Tray B when it offered a 9 per cent chance of winning (the odds of winning by selecting Tray A were kept at 10 per cent). When the odds were manipulated even further so that the large Tray B offered a five per cent chance of winning and the small Tray A still offered a ten per cent chance, a substantial number of participants (20 per cent) persisted in choosing Tray B.[1]

When the element of paying for the privilege of choosing between

trays that had equal odds was added to the experiments most participants continued to express a preference for Tray B (10/100 odds). Of
these a considerable majority were willing to pay to have the privilege
of choosing from a tray that had equal odds to the one they were
rejecting.

These surprising findings occur as a result of what Epstein refers to
as the 'ratio bias (RB) phenomenon'. It comes about when people judge
the occurrence of an event which has low probability as being less likely
when its probability is represented by a ratio of smaller (for example,
1 in 10) numbers than when represented as a ratio of larger (for
example, 10 in 100) numbers. In spite of appearances Tray B has no
probability advantage or disadvantage, but it has more target items, and
if you chose it over Tray A you were exhibiting the RB phenomenon.
But why should people exhibit this behaviour?

THE POWER OF 'EXPERIENTIAL THINKING'

One of the reasons Epstein gives for the power of the RB phenomenon
is the effect of the visual image of the beans in the tray appealing
directly to human beings' non-analytical, concrete mode of thinking.
Support for this view came when he and his colleagues performed a
similar experiment in which participants were asked either to vividly
imagine the jellybeans or to simply read a boring description of them.
The non-visualizing group behaved more rationally; whereas the visual-
izing group tended to behave as people do when confronted with real
trays (i.e. they exhibited the RB phenomenon).[2]

The fact that such modes of thinking can over-ride people's logical
analytical thinking processes, even when they have the capability to
arrive at the appropriate rational response (no complex statistics are
involved), is amply illustrated by some of the reasons that participants
gave for their choices. Even when the odds were literally stated and
stacked against them, one participant who went for the bigger tray said
that he picked the one with more jelly beans because it 'looked like'
there were more ways to win even though he knew that 'the percents
were against me'.[3] Epstein and his colleague Lee Kirkpatrick summarized the contradictions felt by participants who were willing to part
with their money to secure their favoured choice even though they knew
they were being 'foolish': 'many participants reported that they had
opposite views about how to proceed, one based on their knowledge
that the proportions in the two bowls were equal and the other based on
their strong intuitive impression that they were not'.[4] In other words

two contrasting modes of thinking appear to be at play, one based on analysis (revealing the odds to be the same for Trays A and B without any complex mathematical or statistical computations whatsoever), and the other based on strong intuitive impressions and feelings (against logic, the visual image of more red beans in the bigger tray is a compelling one).

The idea that human beings process information in two contrasting ways is very powerful and appealing, and what is more, has high face validity. For centuries scholars and writers have speculated on this 'duality'; for example, the ancient Eastern concept of 'yin' and 'yang', the Jungian notion of 'thinking-versus-feeling'[5] and the ever-popular notion of 'left brain' versus 'right brain' functioning. The psychologist William James (1842–1910) seemed in little doubt that the principle of 'rationalism' requires that the beliefs we hold must be based on four things:

- abstract principles;
- 'facts of sensation';
- hypotheses based on these facts; and
- inferences logically drawn.

However, James argued that if we look at human beings' mental life as a whole, in spite of the 'prestige' that rationality possesses it can only give a relatively superficial account, and there is something else at work as well:

> [I]t [rationality] has the loquacity; it can challenge you for proofs, and chop logic and put you down with words. But it will fail to convince you or convert you all the same, if your dumb intuitions are opposed to its conclusions. If you have intuitions at all, they come from a deeper level of your nature than the loquacious level that you rationalism inhabits.[6]

James is alluding to two types of information processing which may be distinguished on one level by the role played by language: rational analysis is verbal, or in James's florid vocabulary, 'loquacious' (from the Latin *loqui* meaning 'talk'); intuition on the other hand is non-verbal or pre-verbal, or in James' non-pejorative sense 'dumb'. We might argue that the 'intuitive mind' cannot speak directly to our conscious aware-ness in words, whereas the rational mind 'talks' directly to conscious awareness, often incessantly.

The concept of contrasting types of thinking or 'modes of information processing' are widespread in personality, cognitive and social psychology. They exist, for example, in the ideas alluded to earlier of Jung who drew distinctions between 'sensing' (S) and 'intuiting' (N), and between 'thinking' (T) and 'feeling' (F). This was subsequently used as the basis for the S-N and T-F dimensions of the personality inventory the Myers-Briggs Type Indicator, MBTI. In modern cognitive, personality and social psychology there are a number of theories, so-called 'dual-process theories', which describe this duality in human information-processing in a variety of ways (see Table 8.1).

COGNITIVE-EXPERIENTIAL SELF THEORY (CEST)

The RB phenomenon experiments conducted by Epstein and his colleagues were part of a much larger programme of work in which they developed a dual-process theory they referred to as the Cognitive-Experiential Self-Theory (CEST)*. In CEST Epstein and his colleagues advanced the idea that:

Table 8.1 A selection of dual process theories of cognition

Experiential	↔	Rational[1]
Intuitive cognition	↔	Analytical cognition[2]
Recognition primed	↔	Rational choice[3]
Implicit cognition	↔	Explicit learning[4]
Associative	↔	Rule-based[5]

Sources: [1] S. Epstein, 'Integration of the cognitive and the psychodynamic unconscious', *American Psychologist*, 1994, 49: 718; [2] K.R. Hammond, *Human Judgement and Social Policy: Irreducible Uncertainity, Inevitable Error, Unavoidable Injustice* (New York: Oxford University Press, 1996); [3] G. Klein, *Sources of Power* (Cambridge, MA: MIT Press, 1998); [4] Reber 1993; [5] S.A. Sloman, 'The empirical case for two systems of reasoning', *Psychological Bulletin*, 1996, 119: 3–22.

---

* Epstein and his colleagues contrast what they refer to as the 'experiential' system with the 'rational' system. The processes which emanate from the experiential system may be taken to be broadly equivalent to what has been referred to so far in this book as 'intuiting', 'intuitive judgements' and 'intuitions'. However, it must be stressed that Epstein does not explicitly refer to the system in these terms. Consequently, when discussing the Epstein's CEST the term 'experiential' will, by and large, be adhered to. It is also noteworthy that the decision researcher Paul Slovic, whilst drawing upon CEST to explain the role that affect plays in many human judgements, prefers the term 'analytical' to the term 'rational'. On this basis therefore, we might think of the 'rational-experiential' distinction in CEST as being broadly equivalent to 'analytic-intuitive'.

- human beings have two separate information-processing systems – one that is 'rational' and one that is 'experiential' (we might call this 'intuitive');
- the 'rational' mind and the 'experiential' mind interact with each other (harmoniously or conflictually) to produce behaviour that is a joint function of the two systems.[7]

Furthermore people differ in the extent to which they rely on the rational or the experiential system (i.e. there are important individual differences – sometimes referred to as 'thinking styles' or 'cognitive styles'). For example, Epstein and his associates found that sub-clinically depressed students engaged in less rational processing, and appear unable to control high levels of maladaptive experiential processing and undue negative thoughts and feelings.[8] In this situation the two systems do not appear to operate harmoniously. Epstein and his colleagues believe that the balance of influence shifts in favour of the rational system

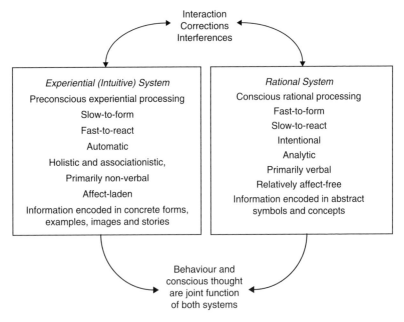

Figure 8.2 The 'rational mind' and the 'experiential (intuitive) mind' – the elements of Cognitive Experiential Self Theory (CEST).

Adapted from S. Epstein, R. Pacini, V. Denes-Raj and H. Heir, 'Individual differences in intuitive-experimental and analytical-rational thinking styles', *Journal of Personality and Social Psychology*, 1996, 71: 390–405.

through age, education and training (i.e. that we become more 'rational' as we get older) but not completely towards it (i.e. the experiential system still continues to exert an influence). The ideal state of development in terms of CEST would be high levels of experiential processing and high levels of rational processing, with a person being able to weigh up when and how to employ each when making a decision.[9] This fits well with the model of expert decision-making to be found in Klein's concept RPD. The decision-maker's rational system and hence the capability to recognise patterns has been fuelled by education, training and experience, but the actual pattern recognition processes appear to be more under the control of the experiential system. In RPD the two systems operate harmoniously (see Figure 8.3). This view is backed up by distinctions between the two systems in terms of their speed of operation and formation:

1   *Speed of operation*: the experiential system is automatic, effortless, and more rapid and is experienced passively (for example, we

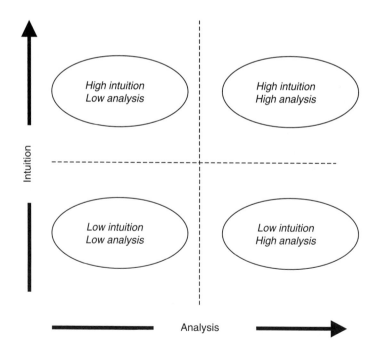

Figure 8.3 Two dimensions of human information processing. There are individual differences in degree to which people rely on each.

cannot 'will' an intuition to happen). The rational system is intentional, effortful, slower and experienced volitionally[10] (we consciously choose to engage in analytic thinking and can normally choose to 'switch' it off, for example by alternative mental work, relaxation, exercise, sleep or meditation).

2   *Speed of formation*: the experiential system involves learning from experiences in a cumulative fashion and hence is slow to build though exposure to sufficient real-life instances. The processing of the rational system on the other hand can be quickly adjusted and corrected, for example by explicitly learning a new fact, rule or procedure.[11] It takes considerably longer for such explicitly learned rules to become implicit, and this is usually achieved through practice and experience and manifests itself as exert performance and non-conscious pattern recognition.

Experiential thinking in everyday life

Epstein cites examples of behaviour from everyday life which he argues can be accounted for by the functioning of the more extreme manifestations of the experiential system ranging from fear of flying and of mice to superstitions:

* greater fear of flying than of riding in a car, in spite of widespread knowledge that the odds of an accident are heavily stacked in favour of car travel as the more risky alternative (the experiential system may be prone to some of the biases such as 'availability' which we met in Chapter 6);
* 'absurd' adult fears, such as being terrified of mice;
* the greater power of direct, personal experience in changing behaviour in therapeutic settings (a more implicit and intuitive form of learning) than 'intellectual knowledge' obtained by explicit learning processes from 'self-help' books or lectures;
* superstitious beliefs, such as the use of lucky charms by 'bingo' players and other gamblers, and extreme forms of non-rational thinking such as believing in ghosts, UFOs and ESP[12] – the paranormal view of intuition may itself also fall into this camp.

Epstein goes as far as to argue that the ubiquity of religion across history and cultures is explicable because of the fact that 'religion appeals to the experiential system through the use of narrative, metaphor, emotionally engaging messages, music and social relatedness'.[13]

The seemingly irrational behaviours and attitudes such as preferring car travel over air travel can be attributed to a non-verbal, affectively-charged influence on our decisions which is survival-oriented and which emanates from the experiential system. The basic mechanism that operates may indeed be inappropriate in some circumstances (for example in a world where air travel is very safe) but in other domains where threats may be very real it is an essential biasing mechanism in human decision-making[14] and most likely served our ancestors well in our evolutionary past.

Is experiential thinking irrational?

The risk researcher Paul Slovic and his colleagues, whilst drawing upon CEST in their research on the way humans perceive risk re-labelled the rational system the 'analytic' system. Their grounds for doing so were that there are strong elements of rationality in both the analytic and experiential systems. This is an important point that will be returned to later. It raises the question of whether experiential thinking or intuition is truly irrational or whether it is more appropriate to think of it of as a non-rational mode of information processing. Slovic's preference for 'analytic' rather than 'rational' as a label neatly avoids placing the experiential or intuitive system in opposition to rationality (opposing them has the unfortunate corollary of deeming experiential or intuitive judgements to be 'irrational'). As has been argued earlier, intuition is one of the hallmarks of human cognition and behaviour, and without it, effective functioning in personal and professional domains would be well-nigh impossible.

TWO MINDS IN ONE BRAIN

Epstein and his colleagues are by no means the only researchers to make a distinction between two systems of human information processing. Many other psychologists have proposed that we may sometimes be almost literally 'in two minds'.[15] Steven Sloman, for example, distinguished between the systems of 'rule-based' thinking and 'associative' thinking.[16]

1   *Associative thinking*: the associative thinking mode works on the basis of similarity-based retrieval and pattern recognition. In its more complex manifestations it supports the pattern recognition processes we met in Klein's recognition primed decision (RPD) model and the subtle ways experts make decisions based on

an 'intuitive situational response'.[17] Associative thinking can provide information quickly and automatically and operates pre-
consciously to the extent that we are only aware of the outcome
(i.e. the intuitive responses to objects or events that cross the
threshold into conscious awareness as 'hunches' or 'gut feelings')
but not of the process itself.

2   *Rule-based thinking*: on the other hand, the 'rule-based thinking'
mode[18] proposed by Sloman is formal, abstract and uses symbolic-
ally represented knowledge (such as language). Unlike the elements
of the associative system that draws on features built up slowly,
rule-based thinking can be acquired and built up relatively quickly,
from a comparatively small number of experiences[19] (such as in the
classroom);

We see rule-based thinking at play in the type of training in that goes
on in many organizations. It's comparatively straightforward to teach
trainees a new rule or procedure in the classroom and expect them to
apply it immediately; indeed this is one of the assumptions that underlie
the training programmes which business organizations provide for their
employees.[20] Employers often anticipate 'quick wins' (paybacks) for the
time and money invested in training on the basis of the rapid acquisition of explicit, formal, rule-based thinking. Implicit knowledge and
skill on the other hand may take longer to acquire through focused
repetition and practice and hence may not give the 'quick win' which
rational cost-benefit analyses are all-too-often hankered after. As a consequence management support for longer term programmes which
draw on implicit learning and develop intuitive judgement and expertise
may be less easy to secure.

The originator of the RPD model, Gary Klein, offered the analogy
of 'foveal' and 'peripheral' vision for the different modes of information processing. The fovea is the small area located at the centre of
the macula region[21] of the eye where the density of photoreceptor cells
is much greater than in other parts of the retina. It is only a very small
area of the retina (one per cent of the area) and it is surrounded by a
much larger area with a lower density of receptor cells. The fovea is
important in the kind of vision which requires visual detail, with it we
see about two per cent of the visual field but we do so in great detail (the
words on this page are being focused upon the macula region of your
retina). Peripheral vision on the other hand is adapted for detecting
movement and a wide, rather than narrow, field of view. Visually we
could not function effectively without both foveal vision (for precision)
and peripheral vision (for a 'wide-angle' view). Klein likens intuitive

processing to our peripheral vision (taking in the bigger picture enabling us to see the whole 'wood' rather than the individual 'trees'), and analytical processing to our foveal vision (taking in the fine details and enabling us to see the trees rather than the whole of the wood). As is the case with their visual systems, human beings need to be able to process information intuitively ('peripherally') and analytically ('foveally') in order to function effectively.

TWO SYSTEMS OF PROCESSING

A simple experimental task, the 'Wason selection task' (named after the English cognitive psychologist, Peter Wason*) provides as an important piece of evidence for dual-processing.[22] Figure 8.4 shows the Wason selection task. Take a look at it before reading on. The correct answer to the first task, which only between 10 and 20 per cent of people give, is to turn over cards A and 7 (not a 3). The statement can only be falsified by finding a card that has an A on its letter side and does not have a 3 on the other (the number side). The Wason selection task in this abstract form is very difficult and requires a brain with considerable 'computational prowess'. However, when the logically equivalent problem is expressed in more concrete terms as in the 'beer-drinking' version around 75 per cent of people are able to give the right answer.[23] Decision researcher Robin Hogarth offered an explanation for the commonly observed results of the Wason selection task; he argued that the beer-drinking version of the problem triggers intuitive (experiential) processing:[24]

- Concrete problems are easier to solve than abstract problems: familiarity of content (beer) and context (a bar) mean that it is easier to visualize both what is happening and what needs to be done in solving the problem.
- The information is meaningful: relevant information can be accessed quickly and with minimum effort and manipulated more easily in working memory.

The Wason selection task has been the basis of a number of important experimental findings in the field of evolutionary psychology. Leda Cosmides and John Toobey argued that because the problem is easy in

---

* You may recall that Wason also developed the 2–4–6 task used to research confirmation bias.

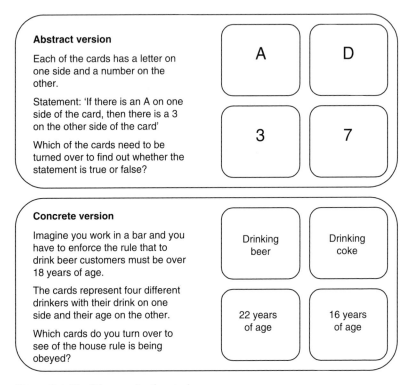

Abstract version

Each of the cards has a letter on one side and a number on the other.

Statement: 'If there is an A on one side of the card, then there is a 3 on the other side of the card'

Which of the cards need to be turned over to find out whether the statement is true or false?

A   D

3   7

Concrete version

Imagine you work in a bar and you have to enforce the rule that to drink beer customers must be over 18 years of age.

The cards represent four different drinkers with their drink on one side and their age on the other.

Which cards do you turn over to see of the house rule is being obeyed?

Drinking beer   Drinking coke

22 years of age   16 years of age

Figure 8.4 The Wason selection task.

Sources: J. St. B.T. Evans, 'In two minds: dual-process accounts of reasoning', *Trends in Cognitive Sciences*, 2003, 7(10): 456; R.M. Hogarth, *Educating Intuition* (Chicago: University of Chicago Press, 2001) p. 116.

the bar room context but much harder in the abstract context this suggests that the mind is not a 'general purpose reasoning device'[25] (otherwise they argue it would work equally well in both forms of the task). Instead, according to the 'modular view', originally developed by Jerry Fodor[26] and advocated by a number of evolutionary psychologists, the mind is like a 'Swiss Army Knife' composed of many independent, highly-specialized modules. In the case of the bar room version of the Wason selection task a finely-tuned, highly specific module – the 'cheater-detection module', is hypothesized as coming into play[27]. Perhaps there are other highly-specialized modules which human beings come ready-equipped with which enable rapid, involuntary social judgments, i.e. social intuitions the content of which does not need to be learned.

The cognitive psychologist Jonathan Evans makes the point that dual-process theories almost literally propose the existence of 'two minds in one brain',[28] and its not only Seymour Epstein's or Steven Sloman's models that make this claim – there is a multiplicity of dual-process theories which assert this in a variety of different ways (indeed it would be possible to go into the features of at least a dozen or so of them). Fortunately, Keith Stanovich and Richard West simplified matters considerably when they argued that even though the technical properties and details of the various dual-process theories don't match up precisely, there are enough 'family resemblances' between the two systems to label the different aspects of the various theories as 'System 1 processing' and 'System 2 processing'.

System 1 processing

System 1 processing is highly contextually dependent, quick and inflexible. It brings together the concepts of 'associative thinking', 'heuristics', 'tacit knowledge', 'intuitive judgements' and 'implicit learning'. System 1 processes are holistic, automatic, concrete and experiential. In terms of the cognitive resources required, they are frugal. Only their final products are 'posted in consciousness'.[29] System 1 can provide a quick, low-effort evaluation and an almost instantaneous affective reaction[30] to a stimulus or set of cues. The intelligence embodied in System 1 is 'interactional'[31] and deeply contextualized (often in social settings), i.e. it enables System 1 to model others' minds, read others' intentions and make predictions and rapid social/interactional moves based on these 'readings'. Some psychologists have speculated that in evolutionary terms System 1 is comparatively ancient.

System 2 processing

System 2 processes on the other hand are abstract and independent of a particular context (i.e. they enable more general reasoning than do the System 1 processes), they are rule-based, analytic and explicit. System 2 processes make greater demands on cognitive resources than do System 1 processes.[32] Evans argues that the explicit use of mental simulations to extrapolate future possibilities by generating hypotheses is a feature of System 2 thinking (whereas intuitively doing 'what has worked well in the past' is a feature of System 1).[33] The intelligence embodied in System 2 is analytical; it enables System 2 to de-contextualize and de-personalize problems and to reason on the basis of rules and underlying general, abstract principles[34] (of the kind that are needed to solve

Table 8.2 The characteristics of System 1 and System 2 processes

System 1 processes	System 2 processes
Associative	Rule-based
Holistic	Analytic
Automatic	Controlled
Cognitively undemanding	Cognitively demanding
Fast	Slow
Involuntary	Voluntary
Acquired through biology, exposure, informal/implicit learning and experience	Acquired through cultural formation and formal/explicit learning
Interactional intelligence	Analytic intelligence
Intuiting	Analyzing

After K.E. Stanovich and R.F. West, 'Individual differences in reasoning: implications for the rationality debate?' *Behavioural and Brain Sciences*, 2000, 23: 659.

problems such as 'the Linda problem' and overcome the various computational errors which dog human reasoning in the experimental tasks used in the 'heuristics-and-biases' research programme). System 2 is believed to have evolved at a later stage in human evolution than System 1; it is also thought to be uniquely human.

The integration of the 'two minds'

As noted earlier, we see the integration of System 1 and System 2 processes in RPD. Situation awareness is often exercised quickly and with low apparent cognitive effort on the basis of the non-conscious recognition of patterns. Mental simulation (the other main 'plank' of RPD) on the other hand is more effortful and demanding of cognitive capacity. Situation awareness (a System 1 process) and mental simulation (a System 2 process) may both be used by experienced decision-makers in a seamless integration. Over the course of the development of expertise those mental elements which are under the rapid, involuntary and non-conscious control of System 1 in the expert decision-maker are likely to have been under more controlled (System 2) processing during the novice decision-maker's early learning phase. In a sense the learning (content) migrates from System 2 to System 1 – the 'logical mental processes' (as Chester Barnard would have labelled them) or 'analyses' (System 1) become 'frozen into habit' (as Herbert Simon described them) in the form of 'non logical mental processes' (System 1).

If System 1 fails to operate effectively System 2's rational analytical processes can go haywire and run amok giving rise to an explosion of possibilities or indefinite deliberation. Where the necessary computational power exists in the brain of the problem solver System 2 can over-ride the biases introduced by System 1 heuristics,[35] for example when individuals solve tasks such as the Linda problem or the Wason selection task. Where System 2 fails to override System 1 (in those instances where System 1 output is inappropriate) decisions may be infused with too much rather than an optimum level of emotion.[36] Kenneth Bowers and his colleagues argue that intuition is a relatively automatic (i.e. System 1) process of generating hunches or hypotheses which are embedded in or emerge out of the personal history or experience of an individual. The process of justifying a hunch is a much more rule-based (i.e. System 2) process that is under conscious control.[37] The implicit learning theorist Michael Polanyi described the ways in which highly-skilled mathematicians articulate analysis (computation) and intuition resulting in a harmonious integration and a synergistic effect on their reasoning powers:

> The manner in which the mathematician works his way towards discovery, by shifting his confidence from intuition to computation and back again from computation to intuition, while never releasing his hold on either of the two, represents in miniature the whole range of operations by which articulation disciplines and expands the reasoning powers of man.[38]

Each system is useful otherwise it would not have been selected for in human evolution. Rather than adopting a 'one is better than the other' view that privileges System 2 over System 1,[39] the two systems are perhaps better viewed as qualitatively different types of mutually-reinforcing modes of information processing. It is likely that System 1 processes evolved in our ancestors to solve problems in particular social domains (for example, to model others' minds, read others' intentions and make consequent predictions) and support cooperative behaviour.[40] Moreover, far from being maladapted to the modern world, System 1 processes remain attuned to supporting many of the problems and decisions faced by contemporary *Homo sapiens* in knowledge-based, technological societies. Daniel Kahneman when discussing System 1 and System 2 in the context of the 'heuristics-and-biases' research program argued that System 1 may have its own kind of 'intuitive intelligence' to the extent that:

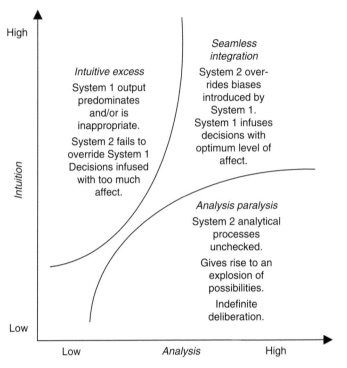

Figure 8.5 Interactions between System 1 and System 2 processes.

Some people may have particularly nuanced and subtle representations of persons and social categories. These people will make better judgements by [the] representativeness [heuristic] than others, and consequently may achieve greater predictive accuracy than others.[41]

In short: System 1 and System 2 each have their own strengths and weaknesses to the extent that the ideal condition is where the features of each system are complementary.[42] While System 1 is not synonymous with intuition, intuition draws on System 1 processes. The latter are 'quick and inflexible'[43] and as such share a number of features of intuition, i.e. 'an involuntary, difficult-to-articulate, affect-laden recognition or judgement arrived at rapidly, through holistic associations and without deliberative rational thought'.*

---

* In terms of dual-processes, the generic labels of analytic-intuitive will be adopted here, i.e. the assumption is that there is an analytic system ('rational' in Epstein's terms) and an intuitive system ('experiential') which both underlie human cognition.

THE NEURAL GEOGRAPHY OF THE 'TWO MINDS'

Neuro-scientific evidence for the operation of two separate systems of processing has emerged from research carried out by Matthew Lieberman and his colleagues at the University of California, Los Angeles.[44] They conducted an fMRI study to explore if different brain regions were activated when people make intuition-based and non-intuition-based judgements about themselves. In their experiment participants were required to make self-judgments in two areas, one where they had high levels of experience ('high experience domains'), and another where they had low levels of experience ('low experience domains'). The researchers wanted to see which brain regions were activated when quick and inflexible intuition-based judgements were made.[45]

They chose soccer and acting as the two domains and based their experiment on the idea that if an experienced soccer player or actor is asked whether or not they possess a certain attribute that characterizes soccer (for example, 'athletic') or acting (for example, 'dramatic') they would be able to make a quick, low effort judgement about themselves on the basis of their accumulated experiences. In other words they would not need to engage in effortful retrieval and analysis of explicit autobiographical evidence relating to a domain where they had high levels of experience. For example, If an experienced soccer player were asked to judge his own footballing abilities it would be unnecessary for him to engage in the effortful retrieval of specific soccer instances in order to provide autobiographical evidence, instead the self-judgement would more likely be made with little intention, effort or awareness (i.e. implicitly). On the other hand an experienced soccer player were to be asked to make a self-judgement in an area where he is not experienced (such as acting) it is more likely that he would need to search for and retrieve explicit, autobiographical memories of specific instances of any acting experience he had in order to arrive at a reasonable self-judgement. The judgement would be intentional, effortful and made with conscious awareness of the episode that was being retrieved (i.e. as an explicit memory).

In the experiment the participants were either soccer players or actors, and their task was very simple: to judge whether or not various words described them. Participants were fitted with fibre-optic goggles that had a computerized input source to in order that they could be presented with 27 soccer and acting words, one at a time for three seconds each and randomly interspersed with neutral words. They were given a two-button response box and instructed to press the right button if the displayed word described them ('Me') and to press the left button if the word it did not describe them ('Not Me'). Examples of the words used were:

Actor; Ad lib; Artist (acting words)

Active; Aggressive; Agile (soccer words)

Anxious; Bored; Caring (neutral words)

Participants were placed in an fMRI scanner and scanned over three blocks of 27 words each. Analysis of the images revealed that judgements in low experience domains produced neural activations in the lateral prefrontal cortex, posterior parietal cortex, and hippocampus. Judgements in high experience domains produced neural activations in the VMPC, basal ganglia, and amygdala. The findings suggested that:

1   intentional explicit judgements (i.e. in areas where the participants had low experience) are associated with a 'reflective' neural system (the C-system) distributed across the lateral prefrontal cortex, posterior parietal cortex and hippocampus;
2   intuition based judgments (i.e. low effort implicit judgements in areas where the participants had high experience) are associated with a reflexive system (the X-system) distributed across the VMPC, basal ganglia and amygdala.

Lieberman and his colleagues describe the reflexive system as affective, slow to form and slow to change and as being based upon generalizations about the world. As is the case with any generalization, the number of observations (i.e. the sample size) used to make the generalization is critical to how accurate and robust the inferences that are being drawn are. The reflexive system grows slowly over time in that each new experientially-based piece of knowledge adds incrementally to the growing data base that is held in long term storage. The reflexive system is slow to form new representations and also slow to change its existing representations.[46] In contrast the explicit representations in the C-system can be changed almost instantaneously in the light of a single new observation or piece of information.

IN 'TWO BRAINS'

The human brain has two distinct halves or hemispheres (the right hemisphere and the left hemisphere) which are connected by a dense

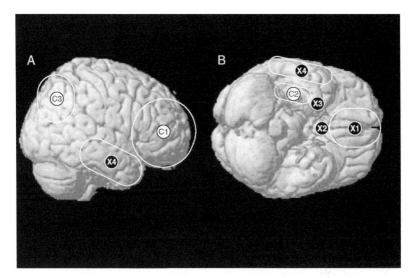

Figure 8.6 Neural correlates of reflexive and reflective systems (Based on Lieberman *et al.*, 2004, p. 423). A is the side view. B is the bottom view. C-system regions shown are: C1, lateral prefrontal cortex; C2 hippocampus and medial temporal lobe; and C3 posterior parietal cortex. X systems regions shown are: X1, ventromedial prefrontal cortex (VMPC); X2, nucleus accumbens; X3, amygdala; and X4, lateral temporal cortex.

Source: M.D. Lieberman, J.M. Jarcho A.B. Satpute, 'Evidence-based and intuition-based self-knowledge: An fMRI study', *Journal of Personality and Social Psychology*, 2004, 87: 421–35. Reproduced by permission of the American Psychological Association and the authors.

bundle of nerve fibres called the *corpus callosum*. In the 1960s psychobiologist Roger W. Sperry (1913–1994) and his colleagues pioneered 'hemispheric functional specialization' research by looking at what happens if the *corpus callosum* in cats and monkeys is severed. They extended their research programme to humans in order to explore how to control epileptic seizures (severing the *corpus callosum* enabled the patients to live a more normal life). In an ingenious set of experiments Sperry and his colleagues showed that if the two hemispheres of the brain are separated information cannot be transferred between the hemispheres; in effect the individual is left with two brains, each doing different jobs, inside one skull. Studies many years earlier of people who had sustained brain injuries to the left side of their brain had shown the dominance of that hemisphere in speech, language

208   *Inside intuition*

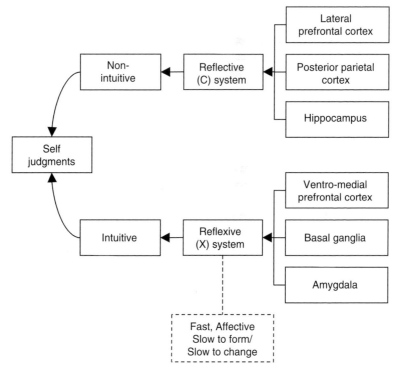

Figure 8.7 The reflexive and reflective systems.
Based on Lieberman *et al.*, 2004.

and arithmetic (damage to the left hemisphere, for example through stroke, was much more detrimental to language). Sperry's work demonstrated that the right hemisphere had its own specialisms also, including facial recognition and spatial comprehension.[47] It was for his discoveries concerning the functional specialization of the brain's hemispheres that Sperry was awarded the Nobel Prize for Physiology in 1981.

One of Sperry's colleagues the psychology professor Michael Gazzaniga summarized[48] the different aspects of thought and action that each hemisphere is responsible for:

1   *Left brain*: 'can talk', it is dominant for language and speech, it can also solve problems and is always hard at work seeking meaning in events. It looks for order and for reason even if there is none to be found. One result of this is that it tends to over-generalize,

Figure 8.8 Nobel Prize-winning psycho-biologist Roger W. Sperry (1913–1994). Copyright The Nobel Foundation (reproduced by permission).

and imagine the events that did not happen (producing 'false memories').

2   *Right brain*: while it cannot 'talk' and is deficient at problem-solving, it is dominant in visual motor tasks and 'lives in the present', and rather than confabulating, tends to give a much more truthful account of experiences.

It seems that the left hemisphere is constantly making (and some-times even making up) explanations for why things occur. One possible reason for this is that it may have evolved to anticipate the future, plan for different eventualities and make rationally-based predictions (for example, in order to avoid danger). The split brain research programme has been enormously influential in management (for example Henry Mintzberg wrote a very famous *Harvard Business Review* article in the 1970s called 'Planning on the left, managing on the right'). The split brain research programme work was elaborated on to the extent that creative abilities and intuition were often attributed to the right brain, and people even labelled as 'right brain types' and 'left brain types'. These interpretations and extrapolations may be an over-simplification and over-extension of the main findings. The indications are that processes such as insight, creativity and intuition are not exclusively located in the 'right brain' or the 'left' brain. Instead what is emerging is a picture in which different brain regions, including the RH aSTG, the VMPC, insular cortices and so forth, appear to interact in complex ways in the operation of these inter-related processes. The distinctive feature of intuition is the combined role played by neural circuitry and visceral processes in complex judgements. It is to the mechanisms by which our mind-body system generates the somatic signals which support our decision-making to which we now turn our attention.

TAKE-AWAYS FOR CHAPTER 8

Key ideas

The *intuitive system* is automatic, quick, holistic and affect-laden; it requires minimal conscious cognitive resource and only its final products are 'posted' in consciousness. The *rational system* is slower, rule-based, analytic and relatively affect-free; it makes greater demands on conscious cognitive resources. If the intuitive system fails to operate effectively the rational systems rational analytical processes can run amok giving rise to an explosion of possibilities or indefinite deliberation – one result can be *analysis paralysis*. If the rational system fails to override the intuitive system decisions may be infused with too much rather than an optimum level of gut feel – one result can be *intuitive excess*. *Explicit reflective* judgements in low-experience domains are associated with neural systems distributed across the lateral prefrontal cortex, posterior parietal cortex and hippocampus. *Implicit reflexive* judgements in high-experience domains are associated with neural systems distributed across the VMPC, basal ganglia and amygdala. Insight and intuition are *not* exclusively located in the 'right brain'; they appear to be distributed across neural systems in different brain regions which interact in complex ways in the operation of intuitive judgements and insight problem-solving processes.

Intuition quote: Chester Barnard, business executive and management thinker

'That the increasing complexity of society and the elaboration of technique and organization now necessary will more and more require capacity for rigorous reasoning is evident; but it is a super-structure necessitating a better use of the non-logical mind to support it. "Brains" without "minds" seem a futile unbalance.'

Action points

Think of an occasion in the past when you had to make a tough decision and your *analytical mind* was in the 'driving seat' when, with hindsight, perhaps it shouldn't have been. What were the consequences? Think of an occasion in the past when you had to make a tough decision and your *intuitive mind* was in the 'driving seat' when, with hindsight, perhaps it shouldn't have been. What were the consequences? How will you handle these situations more effectively in the future? Is your intuitive mind *or* your analytical mind in the 'driving seat' most of the time (have you got a 'back seat' driver)?

FURTHER READING

Chaiken, S. and Trope, Y. (eds), *Dual-process Theories in Social Psychology*. New York: Guilford Press 1999.
Jacobs, G.D., *The Ancestral Mind*. New York: Viking 2003.

9 A matter of feeling

The human understanding is no dry light, but receives an infusion from the will and affections [. . .] Numberless, in short, are the ways, and sometimes imperceptible, in which the affections colour and infect the understanding.

(Francis Bacon, 1561–1626, *Aphorism 49*)

MAIN IDEA

'Gut feelings' and 'hunches' are indispensable elements of effective decision-making; they may be induced by non-conscious pattern recognition processes and the activation of bodily states (or their surrogates) and may undergo evaluation by means of mental simulation.

Affect is a term used in psychology for a feeling or an emotion.[1] Emotions, such as fear, evolved in humans as reactive, short-term physiological (such an increased heart rate) and behavioural ('flight' or 'fight') specializations under the control of the brain, which assisted the survival of our ancestors in hostile environments. The human brain comprises three regions: the psychologically primitive hindbrain (sometimes referred to as the 'reptilian brain'), the midbrain, and psychologically complex forebrain[2] (the labels 'hind', 'mid' and 'fore' refer to the positions of these regions in the developing embryo). The forebrain, which overlies the midbrain and the hindbrain, consists of the cerebral cortex, the limbic system, the thalamus and the hypothalamus. One of the key components of the limbic system is the amygdala (its name is from the Latin *amygdala* meaning 'almond'), a structure specialized for processing emotional stimuli (electrical stimulation of it usually produces the emotion of fear). The cerebral cortex itself has two symmetrical hemispheres (the 'left' and 'right' brains) connected by a dense 'information superhighway' consisting of over 200 million axons (nerve fibres) – the *corpus callosum* (which we met in the last chapter in relation to the bisected brain). The forebrain develops comparatively late in the embryo and was also the latest part of the central nervous system to develop in the evolution of *Homo sapiens*.

Emotions involve both the limbic system (particularly the amygdala) and the higher brain regions (the cerebral cortex). A question that vexed psychologists for many years was that of the relationship between cognition (higher thinking) and emotion – essentially the question of 'which comes first?' This is the so-called 'Zajonc-Lazarus debate',

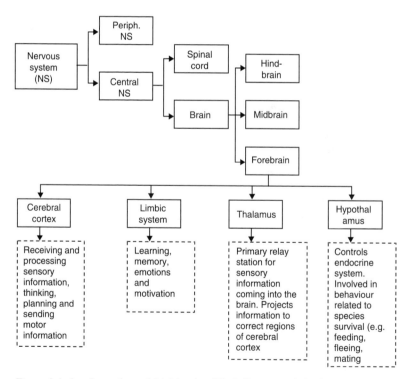

Figure 9.1 A schematic and highly simplified diagram of the human nervous system.

Based on R.J. Sternberg, *Cognitive Psychology* (Fort Worth: Harcourt Brace College Publishers, 1998) p. 47.

named after the two main protagonists – Robert Zajonc and Richard Lazarus).[3] Joseph Le Doux and his colleagues offered a resolution: they found that the initial responses to stimuli actually go via two routes, one very fast and the other somewhat slower:

1   '*Low road*': appraisal of a stimulus, such as a threat, operates via a short, very fast route in which information is transmitted from the retina to the thalamus[4] and then directly to the amygdala which induces an appropriate emotion such as fear;

2   '*High road*': appraisal operates via a slower more elaborate route involving the transmission of information from the thalamus to higher level brain regions (the sensory cortex) and then to the amygdala.

The example often given is that of an instantaneous, unfiltered reaction to a gnarled, stick on a woodland path which might be mistaken for a dangerous snake. We are very likely startled because the initial processing of the stimulus (the gnarled stick) goes along the low road from thalamus to amygdala missing out the cerebral cortex. This fast but less accurate route causes us to mistake the stick for a snake and react as we would do if it really was a snake. The comparatively slower processes are able to subsequently alter the initial reaction by processing the information more elaborately leading to the conscious realisation that the 'snake' is in fact a harmless piece of wood. All this occurs after potentially life-saving evasive action has been taken as a result of the low-road processing which is 'ahead of the game'.[5]

This system is adaptive because, as Le Doux pointed out, it is better for the organism's survival chances to make the error of mistaking a stick for a snake, than a snake for a stick. It is advantageous to have reacted in a way that would have evaded a real threat given that the subsequent processing in the sensory cortex can inhibit, correct or amplify the initial response.[6] The neural circuitry behind this, and in particular the way in which the amygdala interacts with other neural components which are specialized for cognition,[7] is a fundamental part of the human organism's 'emotional brain' and its cognitive-affective decision-making apparatus. As the proponents of emotional intelligence (EI) such as Daniel Goleman have emphasized, the amygdala can however 'hijack' our emotional responses. For example, a facial recognition experiment with young black and white male participants found that activation in the amygdala in response to faces of the same ethic group started high but declined over the course of the experiment, whilst the levels of activation in response to faces which were of the other ethnic group (black or white) stayed high. The amygdala's responses to human faces appears to be affected by the relationship between the perceived race of the stimulus face and that of the perceiver.[8]

EMOTION, FEELING AND MOOD

The American novelist Louisa May Alcott (1832–1888) knew about the distinction between emotion and feeling, when in *Little Women* (1869) she wrote: 'I am angry nearly everyday of my life . . . but I have learned not to show it; and I still hope to learn not to feel it, though it may take me another forty years to do so'. As did Wordsworth: 'Poetry is the spontaneous overflow of powerful feelings; it takes its origin from emotion recollected in tranquillity' (William Wordsworth, 1770–1850, *Lyrical Ballads*, 1802).

'Feelings of emotions' are the subjective experiences by which know our emotions.[9] William James described an emotion 'as our feeling of the [bodily] changes as they occur'.[10] Bodily changes (for example, increased heart rate, breathing, perspiration, etc.) in response to the

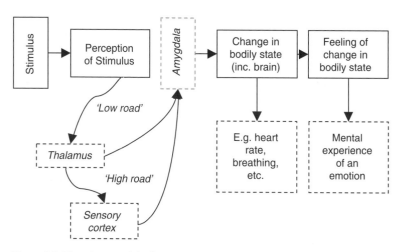

Figure 9.2 Emotions and feelings.

Based on A.R. Damasio, *The Feeling of What Happens: Body, Emotion and the Making of Consciousness* (London: Vintage, 1999) p. 37; J.E. Le Doux, *The Emotional Brain* (New York: Simon and Schuster, 1996) p. 164; J.J. Prinz, *Gut Reactions* (Oxford: Oxford University Press, 2004) pp. 5–6.

perception of a stimulus precede emotional experiences which them-selves precede feelings (of the bodily change).[11] The bodily changes are adaptive in that they prepare the organism for 'flight or fight' (for example, increased heart rate increases blood supply, and therefore oxygen supply, to muscles). In the case of the stick (or snake) on the path we met earlier the emotion involved was fear,[12] which is one of a small set of basic emotional states (e.g. anger, happiness, disgust, surprise, sadness) which have evolved in human beings. These emotional states may be publicly observable; for example from a person's physiological expression and demeanour and are underlain by particular neural systems (such as the amygdala in the case of fear).[13] Damasio describes an emotional feeling as the mental process of monitoring what the body is doing as an emotion, such as happiness, fear, anger or sadness, occurs. Damasio has suggested that one function of consciousness is so that organisms which are endowed with consciousness could 'feel their feelings', i.e. that they could know their emotions. Once established this faculty of consciousness became more generally applicable to a wider range of sensory events represented in the body. Other neuroscientists argue that consciousness 'informs us' of our brain states, and therefore is central to our understanding, but as the biologist Steven Rose notes, who is the 'us' in this statement – has a new 'ghost in the machine' suddenly appeared?[14]

Feelings may also exist as a background state of which we are not aware until our attention is drawn to it, or we make a conscious effort to notice through reflection or contemplation 'how we are feeling' about an object, event, situation or person. 'Background feelings' correspond to the body state that prevails between the feelings of emotions, and simply because we have a background feeling does not necessarily mean that we are conscious of it.[15] Damasio argues that we may realize quite suddenly that we are anxious or relaxed, but that the feeling of anxiety or relaxation did not begin at the moment of realization – it pre-existed as a 'background state' before we were consciously aware of it. Hence, the mental patterns that make up feeling states can exist below the level of conscious awareness until they emerge into consciousness or are deliberately attended to. Damasio's suggestion for imaging the background state of feeling is to try to imagine what it would be like to 'be' without the background feeling*.

---

*   According to Damasio's theory there need not be a bodily change either. An emotional response can occur in the absence of bodily changes when the brain centres that are normally associated with the bodily change become activated. It can be 'as if' there was a change in bodily state, when in fact the body is 'by-passed'. This is a point to which we shall return later in the chapter.

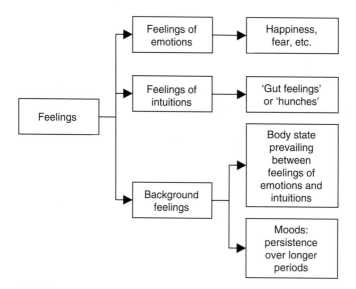

Figure 9.3 A taxonomy of feelings.
Adapted from A.R. Damasio, *Descartes' Error: Emotion, Reason and the Human Brain* (New York: HarperCollins, 1994) p. 150.

There are two important supplementary points. First, moods are part of the 'family' of emotional phenomena; they are longer-lasting states than the reactive emotions, such as fear and anger, we have been discussing so far.[16] The concept of 'mood', although related to background feeling, does not capture the state exactly.[17] Moods are affective states that become frequent or continuous over long periods of time; for example the persistent emotion of sadness is a mood disorder which is sometimes labelled as 'depression'.[18] Second, being sensitive to pre-conscious feeling states (as in the example of anxiety given above) has been described as an 'inner attunement'[19] and a number of researchers and practitioners have argued that this skill of familiarization with the feeling states in our 'body landscape' is cultivable using specific techniques[20] and could be one way of 'tuning in' to our intuitions.

We are mainly interested in the conscious experience of a feeling that accompanies an intuition (the 'hunch' or 'gut feeling'). The 'gut feelings' which attend intuitions are the product of a complex set of emotional and cognitive interactions, they are more than background feelings (they are not a subtle background state or general mood) but are less intense than emotional feelings (they are not the

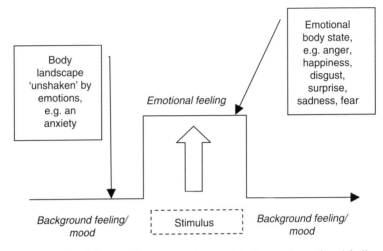

Figure 9.4 The distinction between background feeling and emotional feeling.
Based on A. R. Damasio, *Descartes' Error: Emotion, Reason and the Human Brain* (New York; HarperCollins, 1994) p. 150.

short-term, reactive bodily state perceived as a result of anger, happiness, sadness, etc.). Gut feelings are an interruption to the pervading background state – a noticeable sense of a change in the body landscape which occurs in direct response to a set of cues (stimuli) in the environment.

FEELINGS AND JUDGEMENT

Homo sapiens is thought to have evolved as an emotional, and latterly rational,[21] species, but as individuals we are often, especially in organizational life, exhorted to factor out emotions and to trust only 'hard data' which we can subject to the powers of logic and analysis using our rational mind. However, the neural scientist Joseph Le Doux amply expresses the sterility of such a view: 'minds without emotions are not really minds at all. They are "souls on ice" – cold, lifeless, creatures devoid of desires, fears, sorrows, pain or pleasures'.[22] But why and how do emotions and feelings exert such a powerful influence over our thoughts, decisions and behaviours? Consider this trivial question: 'What have Henry John Deutschendorf Jr. and Frances Ethel Gumm got in common?' The answer is that they are both very famous people who changed their names (before they became famous) – believe it or not Henry Deutschendorf became 'John Denver' and Frances Gumm became 'Judy Garland'. Fame and fortune naturally followed. Would Reg Dwight have been so successful if he had retained his original name rather than becoming 'Elton John'? What's in a name? Why do entertainers and other celebrities often change their names? One reason is to make their entertainment brand affectively 'more pleasing' in the hope that it will engender a positive disposition towards them on the part of potential fans or the buyers of their products. Entertainers and advertisers are very well aware of the power that affect can have as a short cut in human judgement and decision-making, and that it can be below the level of our conscious awareness.

The research into implicit perception or 'subliminal perception' by Zajonc and his colleagues that we met in Chapter 5 showed that a subliminally presented smiling or frowning emotional stimulus affected participants' liking or disliking for something as neutral as a Chinese ideogram (the most-preferred ideograms were preceded by smiling faces). The conclusion drawn from this was that affect, produced by the subliminal stimulus, has the power to influence preference judgements. Similarly, research has found that smiling persons may be judged as more trustworthy and honest than those who don't smile. Students accused of academic misconduct that were pictured as smiling received less punishment than those who were pictured as not smiling.[23] Further evidence of the influence that affect can have upon the way people respond is amply demonstrated in a study by in the 1980s in which researchers asked college students two questions:[24]

'How happy are you with your life in general?'
'How many dates did you have in the last month?'

When these questions were asked in the order listed above there was little correlation between the happiness rating and number of dates. However, when the order was reversed and the dating question was asked first, the correlation between the number of dates and general happiness shot up (it was around 0.66 – a strong association).[25] Thinking about our experiences, or otherwise, of dating (question 2) evokes feelings of life satisfaction, or dissatisfaction, which then affectively 'charges' the subsequent judgement (question 1).[26]

THE AFFECT HEURISTIC

In Chapter 6 a number of short cuts in reasoning (heuristics) were discussed; these were mostly cognitive short cuts that sometimes resulted in errors and biases. Affect also has an important, and sometimes essential, role to play in short-cutting decision-making and judgement processes. The decision researcher Paul Slovic has argued that affect (how we feel) is a strong conditioner of preferences and judgments, and that this holds whether the affect's cause is consciously perceived or below the level of conscious awareness.

As an illustration of this, people base their judgements of risk not only on what they think of something but on what they feel about it as well. Melissa Finucane along with Slovic and other colleagues found that giving information stating that the benefits of nuclear power technology were high led to a more positive overall affect which in turn led to lower perceived risk. Similarly, information which stated that the benefits of nuclear power technology were low led to a more negative overall affect which in turn increased the perceived risk (see Figure 9.5).

Slovic offered a number of illustrations of the power of the affect in human judgement. Marketers of affect-laden products increase consumers' impulse buying behaviour by putting on distracting displays or playing background music in the shopping environment, thus reducing potential consumers' available cognitive resources and shifting the balance of information processing away from cognition in favour of affect. The models in mail-order catalogues are always smiling in order to link positive affect to the clothes being sold. And finally, packages of food products often carry affectively-charged tag-lines such as 'new', 'natural', 'improved', 'dolphin friendly' (tuna), 'organic' or 'virtually fat free' to enhance the feeling of attractiveness of the product and thereby increase the likelihood of consumers buying it.

We each have our own bank of affect, or 'affect pool', which contains positive and negative feelings that are 'tagged' to representations of objects or events which exist in our minds.[27] Moreover, these may be 'weighted' to varying degrees of intensity of feeling.[28] In this sense any object in memory (explicit or implicit) comes with an affective 'charge' attached to it.[29] The affect pool comes into play when we make a wide variety of judgments. Affect enables a decision-maker to process information more quickly and more efficiently than weighing up the 'pros' and 'cons' of a situation.

Affect is also important in creativity and creative intuitions. In the 'emotional resonance' model of creativity Todd Lubart and his colleague

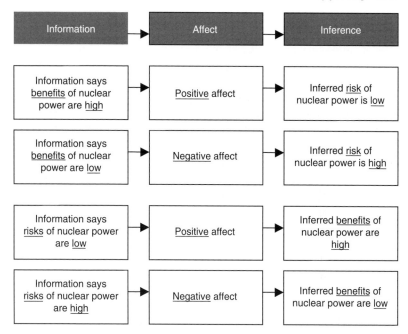

Figure 9.5 The relationship between information, affect and inference – the example of nuclear power.

Adapted from P. Slovic, M.L. Finucane, E. Peters and D.G. MacGregor, 'Risk as analysis and risk as feelings: some thoughts about affect, reason, risk and rationality', *Risk Analysis*, 2004, 24: 315.

Isaac Getz suggest that concepts and images in long term memory become linked (tagged) with particular emotions (they call 'endo-cepts').[30] When these are triggered they 'echo' though the cognitive system and resonate with other similar endocepts, there is a wide spread neural activation and association that is affectively charged. Being more open to feeling states (having lower levels of inhibition of affect) means that two things happen: first, more concepts and images get coded in this way; and second, more associations occur through the 'emotional resonance'. Because of its power, affect guides the creative process – generating more novel solutions, selecting some rejecting others and filtering the generative process down to a number of novel but viable ideas.[31] Moreover, the emotional and physiological processes that occur are rapid and out of conscious awareness and can therefore pre-select ideas even before the conscious mind is aware.

Affect is now widely acknowledged to play a crucial role in creativity and decision-making, and its use as a short cut in reasoning is known as the 'affect heuristic'. From a biological point of view the neural apparatus of rationality in the higher brain regions (the neocortex) does not work effectively without the bio-regulatory mechanisms of the lower brain regions[32] (the limbic system). A reduced capability to infuse decision-making with feelings as a result of brain damage can be detrimental to the decision-making process. Without the aid of feelings to help sift through alternatives and eliminate options, a decision-maker can be 'frozen' into 'paralysis-by-analysis'. It may appear paradoxical, but affect is often as important in decision-making as is rational analysis. When the neuro-physiological mechanisms which support the infusion of affect into decision-making are compromised the consequences for the individual can be quite devastating.

A 'MELANCHOLY AFFAIR' IN VERMONT, 1848

On 14 September 1848 the following report appeared in the *Boston Post*, shortly after a horrific accident involving a young construction foreman named Phineas P. Gage who was working for the Rutland and Burlington Railroad:

> *Horrible accident* – as Phineas P. Gage, a foreman, was yesterday engaged in preparing for a blast, the powder exploded carrying an iron instrument through his head an inch and a fourth in circumference and three feet and eight inches in length which he was using at that time. The iron entered on the side of his face, shattering the upper jaw and passing back of the left eye, and out at the top of the head.
>
> *The most singular circumstance connected with this melancholy affair, is that he was alive at two o'clock this afternoon and in full possession of his reason, and free from pain.*

Not only was Phineas Gage alive on the afternoon of the 'horrible accident', he survived for a further twelve years, dying eventually in 1861 at the age of 38, but he survived in a somewhat psychologically-altered state. His case has had significant implications for the ways in which personality, cognitive and emotional functioning and the neural circuits which underpin these within brain are understood.

Gage's job that afternoon in 1848 was to set explosive charges into holes drilled in rock by pouring gunpowder into the hole, sealing with sand and then tamping down with a three-foot iron rod weighing in at over 13 pounds. Gage's almost-fatal error that day was, through a minor distraction, to have omitted placing sand on top of the gun-powder in one of the holes before he tamped it down. Friction caused a spark which ignited the powder and propelled the rod, which had a sharp-pointed end, upwards through his cheek out and of the top of his head – the rod landed thirty yards away along with fragments of Gage's brain and skull.

The remarkable fact was that Gage was not killed, and not only that, he was able to get into an ox cart, walk from the cart to a hotel to be attended to, and to talk about the accident to the doctor and to bystanders. His language, perception and motor skill functions were unaffected. Later he made what seemed to be an amazing recovery and was, in time, able to return to work.

But even though Gage's survival was nothing short of miraculous, his story is not without its tragic aspect. Prior to his injury Gage was, by all accounts, one of Rutland and Burlington Railroad's most capable and efficient foremen. He was 'energetic and persistent', with a 'well-balanced mind' and looked upon as a 'shrewd smart businessman'.[33]

However, the remarkable two-month 'cure' that his physicians effected in healing the wound was both temporary and superficial. Shortly afterward his personality underwent a radical transformation as this account by the physician, John Martyn Harlow M.D., of Gage's behaviour and personality some years[34] after the accident illustrated:

> Gage was fitful, irreverent, indulging at times in the grossest pro-fanity (which was not previously his custom), manifesting but little deference for his fellows, impatient of restraint or advice when it conflicts with his desires, at times pertinaciously obstinate, yet capricious and vacillating, devising many plans of future oper-ations, which are no sooner arranged than they are abandoned in turn for others appearing more feasible. A child in his intellectual capacity and manifestations, he has the animal passions of a strong man ... his mind was radically changed, so decidedly that his friends and acquaintances said he was 'no longer Gage'.[35]

Gage eventually lost his job, and embarked on a series of ill-informed and capricious adventures, spending time as a sideshow freak in P.T. Barnum's New York Museum, working California's Gold Rush and eventually ending up in Chile as a coachman, returning through illness to the USA in 1859 shortly before his death in 1861 from epileptic seizure. His body was latterly exhumed and his skull and the iron rod are part of the permanent exhibition at Harvard Medical School's Warren Anatomical Museum in Boston.

What happened to Gage was summarized succinctly by the neurologist Antonio Damasio as a 'profound discrepancy' between Gage's 'normal' personality as it existed before he incurred the lesions caused by iron rod passing though his brain, and the 'nefarious' individual who was unable to make effective decisions and plan for the future that emerged after the accident. These traits plagued him for the rest of his life.

In 1993, almost 150 years after the infamous accident, neuro-imaging expert Hannah Damasio constructed computer images of Gage's brain and was able to say with some certainty that the damage he incurred was to the prefrontal cortex, and specifically to the VMPC – a brain region critical for emotion, social conduct and decision-making.[36] As we shall see, it is precisely this part of the frontal lobe which plays a significant role in the way gut feelings guide our decisions. But Gage's case is important for the study not only of intuition, but of psychology and emotion more generally. It demonstrated that a traumatic neurological event to a particular part of the brain can leave many functions unimpaired but produce dramatic changes in personality ('Gage was no longer Gage') and specifically in the ability to take effective decisions (the new 'impatient', 'capricious', 'vacillating' and 'obstinate' Gage).

The study of cases such as Gage have contributed immeasurably to the understanding of which specific brain regions contribute to human decision-making processes, including the ability to make intuitive judgements. It was in patients with brain damage similar to that incurred by Gage (but under less dramatic circumstances) that neurologists in the 1980s were able to make significant leaps forward in their understanding of the role that the VPMC plays in our judgemental and social and emotional decision-making capabilities.

THE 'IOWA GAMBLING TASK' EXPERIMENTS

Antonio and Hannah Damasio are leading neurologists whose work is shedding light on human cognitive and emotional functioning especially in the area of decision-making. A post-doctoral researcher at Damasio's Iowa research institute in the 1990s was a behavioural neurologist by the name of Antoine Bechara. He worked with the Damasios on a pioneering, and now famous, set of experiments using the 'Iowa gambling task', the results from which provided unique insights into role of the VMPC and 'gut feeling' in decision-making.

The Iowa gambling task involves participants choosing one card at a time from any of four decks of cards in order to maximize monetary profit over a one-hundred card run of selections (the number of selections is not known to the participants in advance and the game can be terminated at any time by the experimenter). Participants have $2000 in pretend money to play with. The decks of cards from which they draw are subtly different. Decks A and B yield high immediate gains, but even larger future losses. Decks C and D, on the other hand, yield lower immediate gains, but give smaller future losses. Decks A and B are the 'bad' decks – they give a long-term loss. Decks C and D are the 'good' decks – they give a modest long-term gain. The design of the experiment is summarized in Figure 9.6.

One of their experiments involved the performance of three groups of participants on the gambling task:

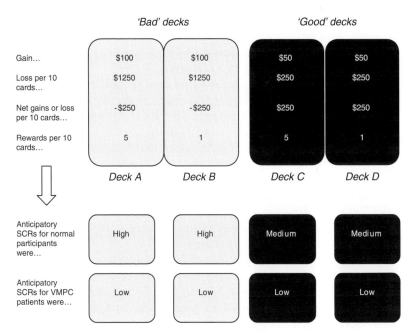

Figure 9.6 The 'Iowa gambling task' and summary of the results of the experiment.

Note: For Deck A the gain is $100; the loss per ten cards selected is $1250; the net loss per 10 cards selected is $250; and it has five smaller loss cards for every 10 cards. The skin conductance responses (SCR) designations 'high', 'medium' and 'low' are for illustrative purposes only (adapted from Bechara, Damasio, Tranel and Damasio, 2004).

1   *'normal' participants*: i.e. non-brain damaged;
2   *'VMPC patients'*: these had incurred damage to the VMPC and were included in order to explore the effect of damage to this brain region on decision-making;
3   *'controls'*: a control group of brain-damaged participants whose lesions were to the lateral occipital or lateral temporal cortex, but not to the VMPC[37] and were included to control in the design of the experiment for the effect of brain damage.

The results are both surprising and significant. At around thirty moves in to the game the 'normals' and 'controls' developed a 'hunch' that led them to avoiding Decks A and B and preferring the good decks (C and D) and eventually making a small but tidy profit. On the other hand the VMPC-damaged participants, perhaps in the way Gage behaved after he had his accident, actually preferred the bad decks, and ended up making a not insubstantial loss. They had what Bechara called 'myopia for the future' – they could not decide advantageously in choosing between immediate and delayed reward and punishment and appeared to prefer to seek the immediate gratification associated with large potential gains from the 'bad' decks. The participants with non-VMPC brain damage behaved like the normal group.

To examine the underlying neuro-physiological mechanisms Bechara and his colleagues used a polygraph to measure the skin conductance responses (SCRs or 'micro-sweating) of the normal and the VMPC patients during the gambling task. Normal participants and both groups of brain-damaged participants generated SCRs (i.e. they 'micro-sweated') when they were told that they had won or lost money with each card selection. This was a self-regulatory (autonomic) response to winning or losing; it demonstrated that all the participants were able to generate SCRs. However, as the experiment progressed the researchers found that a number of significant things occurred as far as the normal and the VMPC groups were concerned:

1   The normal participants drifted towards the good decks (C and D), whereas the VMPC patients continued to incur losses.
2   Normal participants began to generate SCRs whilst they were pondering their choice (i.e. before they selected any cards) – they exhibited 'anticipatory SCRs'.
3   The anticipatory SCRs for the normal participants were higher before picking from the bad decks (A and B) than before picking from the good decks.
4   The VMPC patients failed to generate any anticipatory SCRs –

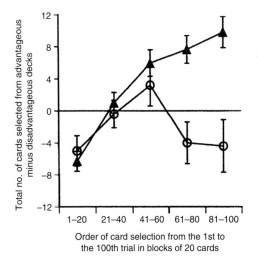

Figure 9.7 Pattern of responses for decision-making behaviour of the three groups in the 'Iowa gambling task' experiment.

Note: Filled triangles are the responses of the normal control group over the 100 trials (in blocks of 20, i.e. 1–20, 21–40, etc); open circles are the responses of the ventro-medial (VM) lesion patients over the same 100 trials.

Source: A. Bechara, D. Tranel and H. Damasio, 'Characterisation of the decision-making deficit of patients with ventro-medial prefrontal cortex lesions', *Brain*, 2000, 123: 2189–2202. Reproduced by permission of Oxford University Press.

their profile of micro-sweating across the four decks was low and flat and simply occurred as a reaction to winning or losing.

What appeared to be happening was that the normal participants responded by generating an affective signal in the form of a bodily state (micro-sweating) before they made a choice. This was even more pronounced as a marker or 'warning' before they chose from the bad decks – they were learning through feedback from a bio-regulatory system to avoid the bad decks.[38] In other words, the normal participants were generating an automatic bodily response – a somatic state activation – which signalled to them to avoid the bad decks (Damasio has referred to this as a 'non-conscious biasing step' in their reasoning).[39]

The VMPC patients did not display a lack of understanding; their verbal reasoning demonstrated that cognitively they knew what the best long-run strategy was. This did not stop them behaving against this pure reasoning in their actual decision-making behaviour which lacked the necessary emotional responsivity.[40] The damage that the VMPC patients had incurred resulted in the absence of the non-conscious, anticipatory biasing step that the normal participants had the benefit of – there was no somatic state activation. The VMPC patients continued to choose disadvantageously – they were bereft of the body's natural alarm system which, had it been functioning effectively, could have given out a marker to warn them to avoid the 'bad decks' both in the experiment and, like Gage, in their lives more generally.

Patients such as those who participated in the Iowa gambling task experiments exhibit cognitive impulsiveness, an inability to inhibit response and delay gratification. The inhibition of response observed where cognitive impulsiveness is absent (i.e. in normal individuals) is triggered by a somatic state.[41] In the condition where the VMPC is not functioning normally decisions are unable to be mediated by the appropriate emotional response. Bechara interpreted these findings as 'strong support for the notion that decision-making is guided by emotional signals (somatic states), which are generated in anticipation of future events'.[42]

THE SOMATIC MARKER HYPOTHESIS

These experiments were part of a broader research programme that led to the Damasios (Antonio and Hannah), along with Bechara and other colleagues, developing the 'somatic marker hypothesis' (shortened here to SMH). The concept of the somatic marker may also shed light on the role of gut feelings in intuitive judgement. As has been noted earlier, the term 'somatic' comes from the Greek word *soma*, which means 'body'. The term 'somatic marker' refers to a bodily marker or feeling state (an unpleasant gut feeling for example) typically associated with a bad potential outcome. Somatic markers can occur in the body (for example, respiratory and circulatory systems) but also in the levels of chemicals in the brain.[43]

Speed of processing is an important factor in the somatic marker theory. Before we can apply a rational cost/benefit analysis to a problem an unpleasant gut feeling is rapidly, involuntarily and often fleetingly experienced[44] in those circumstances where, consciously or non-consciously, we anticipate a bad outcome to be associated with an available choice. The anticipation of a negative outcome may be as a result of a number of factors, for example non-conscious pattern recognition (based on prior experience and learning) which gives rise to somatic state activation and is felt in the body as a somatic state awareness (a hunch or gut feeling). A negative somatic marker sounds an 'alarm' signalling 'danger ahead', and thus serves to reduce, by elimination, the number of options from which to choose. The anticipatory SCRs of the normal participants in the Iowa gambling task served as a negative somatic marker warning against choosing from the bad decks (A and B). Where the neural circuitry that normally supports somatic state activation is damaged decision-making is impaired. One result is that individuals will tend to show concern only for immediate outcomes and repeatedly engage in decisions that have negative longer-term consequences.[45]

THE SOMATIC MARKER IN BUSINESS DECISION-MAKING

Entrepreneurs are often on the look out for, or are approached to get involved in, new business ventures or developing new products and services. However if an opportunity generates an image of a potentially bad future outcome (for example, being 'ripped off', ending up bankrupt, etc.) the negative somatic markers may be activated. Somatic state activation may induce an unpleasant gut feeling in conscious awareness associated with the image to the extent that the affective state associated may serve to warn off the entrepreneur from the opportunity. Perhaps as a result of the operation of somatic state activation and somatic state awareness he or she is able to eliminate that particular opportunity from the available courses of action (and often within a very short time frame of seconds or minutes). This is not to say that gut feeling is necessarily accurate or infallible; it may merely help with the decision process at the time by eliminating options through the operation of the negative somatic marker. Figure 9.8 illustrates how somatic markers may act to help a decision-maker sift through the available options and make the deliberation over the costs and benefits more efficient.

Although the non-conscious pattern recognition may have evolved to be especially sensitive to negative information[46] (thus promoting the chance of avoiding threats and danger) somatic markers are not necessarily always negative. A positive somatic marker serves to highlight the favourability of an option and becomes, as Damasio puts it, a 'beacon of incentive'.[47] The way the body can respond is vividly illustrated by the experiences of Starbuck's CEO, Howard Schultz:

> It happened in the spring of 1983. I had been at Starbucks for a year, and the company had sent me to Milan to attend an international house wares show. The morning after I arrived, I decided to walk to the show. During my stroll through the centre of the city,

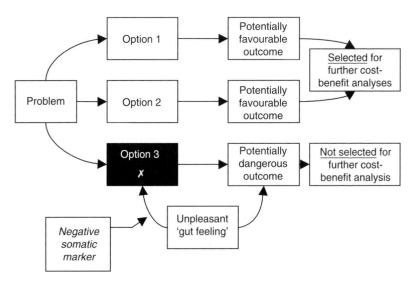

Figure 9.8 The operation of the somatic marker to reduce available choices.

I noticed espresso bars on almost every street corner. What struck me emotionally was the ritual and romance of each coffeehouse. The bartenders, called baristas, had a strong bond with customers. All kinds of people gathered and chatted at the bars, which served as extensions of the front porch in each neighbourhood. Right then it struck me like a lightning rod: Why not bring the concept to America? Starbucks could be re-created to do just that. The vision was so overwhelming, *I began shaking*.[48]

No claim is being made that a positive somatic marker is infallible – it merely plays an important role in the processes of judgement and prediction at the time. Somatic markers help decision-makers avoid the 'myopia of the future' that was observed in the VMPC patients who took part in the Iowa gambling task experiments. Somatic markers serve to constrain the number of possible courses of action to a manageable number,[49] and so prevent rational analysis from 'running riot'. Figure 9.9 illustrates how positive and negative somatic markers operate in different ways to help a decision-maker elect or eliminate available options.

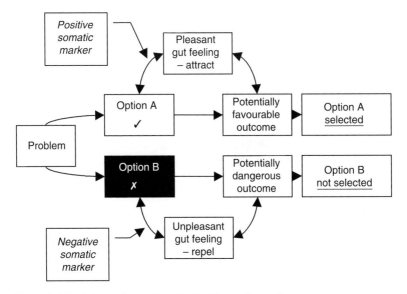

Figure 9.9 Positive and negative effects of somatic markers.

Based on A.R. Damasio, *Descartes' Error: Emotion, Reason and the Human Brain* (New York: HarperCollins, 1994) pp. 173–4.

WHEN IS A 'GUT FEELING' NOT A 'GUT FEELING'?

One answer to this question is: 'when it's "as-if" we had a gut feeling'. Damasio and Bechara describe the physiological events that accompany emotions and feelings as operating in two different ways:

1   *Via the body loop*: a pattern of activation (through chemical messages in the bloodstream and electro-chemical messages in nerve pathways) occurs in the body at the sites where the emotion is induced – for example changes in breathing, salivation or heart rate. This is also represented within the brain as a feeling of these changes in the body's state (we sense the consequences of these physiological activations, for example, a feeling that the body has become tense of heart rate increased). Damasio describes this in terms of changes in the 'body landscape' and in the representations of these in the brain (in the somatosensory structures).[50] This somatic state may act on the neural processes in the brain's working memory that influence behaviours,[51] and this is one way in which gut feelings can exert and effect on thinking and behaviour. This is system is described as the 'body loop'.

2   *Via the 'as-if' body loop*: the second way in which these physiological events occur is by the activation of representations of somatic changes in sensory 'body maps' – i.e. we have thoughts 'as if'
the body had changed when in fact it has not. Bechara explains
it thus:

> "after emotions have been experienced and expressed at least once,
> one can form representations of these emotional experiences in the
> somatosensory/insular cortices.[52] Therefore, after the emotions are
> learnt, one possible chain of events is to by-pass the body
> altogether, activate the somatosensory/insular cortices and create a
> *fainter* image of an emotional body state than if the emotion were
> actually experienced in the body" (emphasis added).

This is the 'as-if' body loop (since it is 'as if' the body had changed
when in fact it had not) where bodily feedback is 'imagined' and
cognitively represented in working memory and thereby able to
influence feelings and decisions.[53]

The body loop and 'as if' loop are shown schematically in Figure 9.10.
The body loop and the 'as-if' loop may function differently (as
suggested by Bechara[54]) on the basis of the level of uncertainty inherent
in the decision task:

1   In condition of decision-making under certainty, i.e. where the
outcome is predictable and explicit, the overall average anticipatory SCRs are lower than in decision-making under uncertainty,
i.e. where the outcome is unknown, unpredictable and cannot be
estimated.
2   In decision-making under certainty Bechara suggests that it is the
'as-if' loop which is activated (giving lower average SCRs), and we
might speculate accompanied by a fainter 'affective tag'. In decision-making under uncertainty on the other hand he suggests it is
the body loop proper (giving higher average SCRs).

PATTERN RECOGNITION (PR)-SOMATIC STATE (SS) MODEL OF INTUITIVE JUDGEMENT

The SMH helps explain the affective aspects of decision-making (intuition-as-feeling); RPD on the other hand gives an account of the role of
knowledge, learning and experience in intuitive judgement (intuition-
as-expertise).[55] For example, one of the notable features of the case

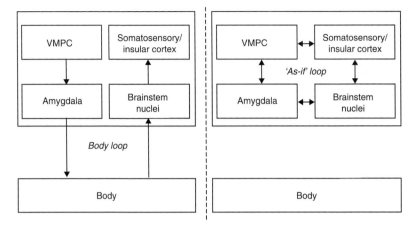

Figure 9.10 The body loop and the 'as-if' body loop.

Note: VMPC, Ventro-medial prefrontal cortex.

Based on A. Bechara, 'The role of emotion in decision-making: evidence from neurological patients with orbito-frontal damage', *Brain and Cognition*, 2004, 55: 38.

studies that RPD is based upon is the phenomenon of anomalies being sensed in conscious awareness that something doesn't 'feel right'[56] but without the decision-maker being able to offer a fully-formed rational explanation for the sense of unease. A model which brings together non-conscious pattern PR and SS activation in intuitive judgement is suggested in Figure 9.11.

Compression of prior learning and experience results in knowledge and skill which is stored as automated expertise. Non-conscious pattern recognition processes draw upon a stream of prior experiences that a related to the eliciting situation. The mechanisms by which pattern recognition operate are not entirely clear, but one process that is likely to be involved is the spread of activation through networks of associations resulting in a preliminary perception of coherence. Pattern recognition may be affect-free where a simple and straightforward match is found and the judgement arrived without the activation of the somatic marker (the matching process is below the level of conscious awareness and is not a deliberative analytical process). The second route involves the activation of a somatic state which crosses the threshold into conscious awareness and becomes an awareness of a bodily (somatic) state – a gut feeling. Intuitive judgements elicit activation within the orbito-frontal cortex, and are posted into conscious awareness as a gut feeling.[57] They may remain as intuitive judgements to be verified by subsequent experience and testing, or they may emerge fully-fledged into consciousness as an insight (activation associated with the RH aSTG region).

As was noted previously in this chapter, the representations of objects or events which exist in our minds (consciously or non-consciously) are 'tagged' to varying extents with positive or negative affect[58] (from the affect pool). Objects in memory along with their 'affective charge' come into play on the basis of pattern recognition. Antonio and Hannah Damasio, along with Bechara and Tranel suggested that in decision-making situations records of previous experiences may be accessed which have been shaped by reward or punishment along with the emotional state that attends them. Damage to the VM region of the brain inhibits access to these records thereby blocking the retrieval of the emotional state that accompanies mental records of events and thereby impairs decision-making by making it devoid of feeling.[59] Kirsten Volz and Yves von Cramon suggest that the orbito-frontal region of the prefrontal cortex (OFC) integrates information relating to the rewards associated with prior experiences. They also suggest that the associative information needed to do so is delivered by the amygdala to which the OFC has direct neuro-anatomical connections, and that this activation may be of differing magnitude dependent upon the 'value' that is associated with the observed cues. They further speculate that a brain region known as the claustrum[60] has an integrative, synchronistic function (Francis Crick likened it to the 'conductor of an orchestra'), bringing together in a holistic fashion processes which result in an affective 'charge' (they refer to this as an 'affective valence') for a specific decision choice.[61]

The RPD model has two basic elements – 'situation awareness' (by means of the non-conscious recognition of patterns) and mental simulation (the metaphor used was of a 'DVD-in-the-head') – see Chapter 7. Gut feeling can directly inform judgement; alternatively there may be the intermediate step which Klein and his colleagues suggest many experienced decision-makers perform – that of conscious mental simulation. Once a viable course of action has been identified on the basis of mental simulation, it may then be used to inform judgement and determine action as an explicit testable intuitive hypothesis or 'hunch'.

Two other possibilities arise from the marrying of the somatic state concept and the RPD model. The somatic state activation from the pattern recognition is 'real' in the sense that it is the eliciting situation (the burning building, the sick baby, the blip on the radar screen) which induces the somatic state in the body loop proper. However, in the case of the mental simulation it is an imagined situation which may induce

Pattern recognition (PR)–somatic state
(SS) model of intuitive judgement

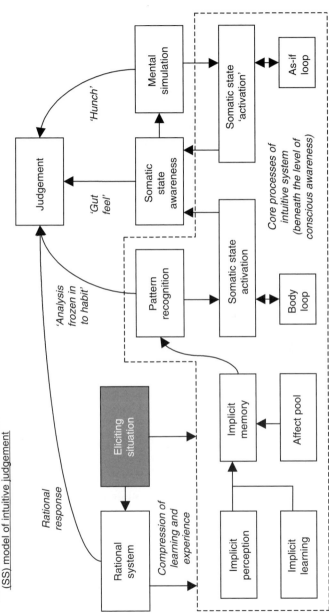

Figure 9.11 The pattern recognition (PR)–somatic state (SS) model of intuitive judgement based on core processes of recognition primed decision (PRD) making and somatic state activation (SSA).

Note: Area inside the dashed line is the intuitive system and indicates core pattern recognition and somatic state processes which are beneath the level of conscious awareness.

further somatic 'activation' but this time not in the body as such but only in the mind via the 'as if' loop (rather than the body loop itself). The model and these suggestions are speculative, but nonetheless may indicate possible mechanisms by which the SMH, RPD model and the concepts of body and 'as-if' loops may be synthesized to give an integrated picture which encompasses both 'intuition-as-expertise' (pattern recognition) and 'intuition-as-feeling' (somatic state activation and awareness).[62]

TAKE-AWAYS FOR CHAPTER 9

Key ideas

Feelings, whether consciously attended to or not, exert a strong influence on our preferences and judgments. One of the advantages of *affect* is that it enables a decision-maker to process information more *quickly* and more *efficiently* than weighing up the 'pros' and 'cons' of a situation. A *somatic marker* is a feeling state (unpleasant or pleasant) associated with a potential outcome (unfavourable or favourable); they occur in the body (for example, respiratory and circulatory systems) but also in the levels of chemicals in the brain. Intuitive judgements occur as a result of the interaction of non-conscious pattern recognition and somatic state activation, as summarized in the *pattern recognition (PR)-somatic state (SS) model* of intuitive judgement. Greater familiarity with the feeling states in our 'body landscape' can be cultivated using specific techniques and is one way of *tuning in* to our intuitions. Somatic markers are *not infallible* – they merely play a role in the processes of judgement and prediction in decision-making and problem-solving situations.

Intuition quote: Steve Jobs, Apple Computers

'Have the courage to follow your heart and intuition. They somehow already know what you truly want to become. Everything else is secondary.'

Action point

Next time you're confronted by a tough decision check it out with your *body*. Take *time out; quiet* your rational mind; *stop the*

chattering voice inside your head talking to itself; *listen* to the
'still, small voice' within – let it have its say. Does the option
you're considering *feel* right or wrong?[63] Also try extending your
'sensory modalities' through the use of metaphorical language:
kinaesthetic – 'I can't put my finger on it, but . . .'; *visual* – 'I can
really see it being a success . . .'; *olfactory* – 'It just doesn't smell
right . . .'; *gustatory* – 'I sense that it'll leave a bad taste . . .';
auditory – 'there's a little voice telling me that . . .'.[64]

FURTHER READING

Damasio, A.R., *The Feeling of What Happens: Body, Emotion and the Making
of Consciousness*. London: Vintage 1999.
Damasio, A.R., *Descartes' Error: Emotion, Reason and the Human Brain*. New
York: HarperCollins 1994.
Le Doux, J.E., *The Emotional Brain: The Mysterious Underpinnings of Emotional
Life*. New York: Simon and Schuster 1996.

10 The intuitive practitioner

> Negative Capability, that is when man is capable of being in uncertainties, mysteries, doubts, without any irritating reaching after fact and reason –
>
> (Keats, *Letter to George and Thomas Keats*, 1817)

MAIN IDEA

Intuition is a vitally important element of creativity, entrepreneurship and decision-making in business organizations. Intuitive judgements are likely to be more appropriate under certain sets of circumstances and in certain contexts (for example, complex, loosely structured, judgmental and people-oriented decisions); situation awareness can support opportunity identification; mental simulation is one way of envisioning 'possible futures'.

Intuition is of immense practical significance. We rely upon intuitions to interpret and judge people and situations, take decisions that inform immediate behaviours, and make predictions which guide future actions. If we stop and think, a moment's introspection may reveal that our pasts, presents and futures are, to varying degrees, the products of our intuitions. Our lives are the arenas in which, for better or worse, our intuitions are played out. In our occupations we are, of habit and necessity, 'intuitive practitioners'.[1]

Non-conscious pattern recognition and somatic state activation are rapid, involuntary and ubiquitous, and have the potential to exert significant effects upon our actions across personal and occupational settings. Intuitive judgement shapes both the way we perceive and the way we act, and plays a significant part in determining our futures. In this chapter we will examine the role that intuitive judgement plays in several important areas of management – creativity, entrepreneurship and business decision making.

CREATIVE INTUITION

Creativity is the ability to produce something that is original or unexpected (i.e. novel) and useful for specific task or purpose (i.e. appropriate).[2] Over the centuries there have been various interpretations of the origins and nature of human creativity. Many poets and musicians have seen themselves as 'vessels' to be filled with creative works or as channels through which a creative work emerges from a supernatural realm. In Greek mythology the Nine Muses were Goddesses of the arts and sciences that could be appealed to for inspiration and divine intervention. At the beginning of *The Iliad* Homer announces his theme and directly asks the Muse, the goddess of memory, to 'sing' through him with the invocation. 'Tell me now, you Muses who have your home on Olympus . . .'.[3] For the English romantic poet William Wordsworth (1770–1850) creativity was a manifestation of the disembodied, spiritual dimension of his being: 'In Nature's presence stood, as now I stand, a sensitive being, a *creative* soul'.[4]

From the Classical world through to the modern age the mystical origin of the 'creative spark' has been seen as extraneous, derived from some deity or supra-consciousness, and creative outputs as 'gifts from the gods'.[5] However as both Robert Sternberg and Gary Klein have noted, one of the problems with the mystical and 'magical' labelling of creativity, insight and intuition is that it relegates them to the periphery of scientific inquiry. But, as we have seen, both insight and intuition have proven amenable to scientific scrutiny, principally from the fields of cognitive psychology (through the study of mental representations and processes) and social psychology (through the study of personality, motivation and the social environment).[6] Latterly the field of cognitive neuroscience has begun to contribute to an understanding the specific brain areas involved in the creative mental processes. For example, the brain's pre-frontal neural circuits are involved in making novel ideas fully conscious, and in evaluating their appropriateness.[7] Disappointingly therefore, where magical or divine inspiration is lacking, creators have had to rely upon their own cognitive resources – their 'intuitive Muse' – and meld these with the resources in available their environments.[8]

Creative intuition favours the prepared mind

We can be pretty sure that Mozart (1756–1791) wrote the opera *Dei Zauberflöte* (*The Magic Flute*) and most of the other six hundred or so works listed in Köchel's catalogue of his music. But who do you think wrote Mozart's early piano concertos?

Mozart did of course, but this is not as bizarre a question as it first seems. For example, the first four concertos the precocious Mozart wrote are very early pieces composed astonishingly at the age of a mere 11 years in 1767. However, they are seen by some more as 'arrangements' of keyboard sonatas by various other composers (for example, C.P.E. Bach) than works of striking originality. Mozart aficionados may disagree, but these works would not score highly on novelty or innovativeness, and it was not until ten years later, in fact, in the year 1777 when Mozart produced, at the age of 21, what some have judged to be his first masterpiece in this genre, the Piano Concerto No. 9 in E flat major, K271.[9]

Cognitive psychologist Robert Weisberg cites the life of Mozart and those of other musicians and artists as diverse as Picasso and The Beatles, as evidence that early efforts at creativity often involve a preparation by deep immersion in the works of others as models of how technical and compositional problems may be handled. The period before the production of the first major works have been called an artists' 'years of silence';[10] they attest to the fact that even artistic 'geniuses' require many years of preparation (a 'deep immersion') before they begin to produce the works upon which their reputations are built and endure.[11]

But what about business, does the same hold true? The phenomenon of deep immersion as a precondition for creative invention is not confined to sublime creations such as a Mozart piano concerto or a Picasso oil painting. 3M's 'Post It Notes®', which are a ubiquitous and indispensable feature of modern home and office life, were invented by Art Fry and Spencer Silver, two scientists working at 3M in the 1960s. Novices they were not: Fry majored in chemical engineering at the University of Minnesota, and Silver had a doctorate in organic chemistry from the University of Colorado.

It was Silver who invented a novel, non-sticky ('low-tack') adhesive which could not only hold papers together, but also allowed them to be pulled apart again without tearing. Moreover the adhesive could be used repeatedly without much loss of 'stickiness'. The challenge was 'what to do with it?' – Silver's invention was one of those 'solutions waiting for a problem', so much so that 3M had difficulty finding a marketable use for it. A number of different avenues for commercial exploitation of the idea were tried including making sticky notice boards upon which ordinary paper could be posted, and also marketing it in a spray can form.[12]

The breakthrough came through a synthesis of Silver's invention and the creative insight of his colleague Art Fry. Fry was a church choir member and was frustrated by the slips of paper he used as page markers in his hymn book always fluttering to earth at inappropriate moments during the service. In parallel with this he became aware through a 3M internal seminar of Silver's low-tack adhesive that keenly awaited an application. At this juncture all the ingredients for a breakthrough were in place. Some time later, during a church sermon Fry is alleged to have experienced a classic 'Eureka!' moment: 'why not use the adhesive to make low-tack, page markers?'[13] The rest as they say 'is history'; in 1981, only one year after its introduction, 'Post-it Notes®' was given the prestigious accolade of '3M Outstanding New Product'.

The examples of Mozart and 'Post-it Notes®' illustrate the value of intense practice and preparation, and having in-depth knowledge upon which to draw. Allied to this, the combined forces of incubation and serendipity make up the vital ingredients for generating new solutions which escape the bounds of conventional thinking (see Table 10.1). Even when all of the pieces of the jigsaw are in place there is no guarantee of success. As the Austrian economist Peter Drucker noted, the 'casualty rate' amongst creative ideas is enormous but given that the volume of bright-idea innovation in business is so large even a tiny percentage of success is likely to be significant.[14] The element of chance (which does favour the prepared mind) also has an undeniable and important role to play. The Nobel Laureate in medicine, Arvid Carlson, is quoted as saying that to avoid jumping in the 'wrong direction too many times', the first thing that is needed is luck, and the second is intuition.[15] This observation is backed up at a cognitive level by the views of those psychologists who have argued that chance permutations of mental elements (concepts, emotions, episodes, etc.) are one of the ways in which the creative process operates. In this model most of these combinations have a very ephemeral existence. But from time to time chance coalescences take place which happen to form a coherent whole.[16] In the history of science, technology and business there are creative serendipitous moments when cognitive and social connections and interconnections come about. An intriguing question is if the 'tape'

Table 10.1 Some of the ingredients of insight and creative intuition

Years of silence	Major creative breakthroughs often follow 'years of silence' in which problem solver develops deep knowledge structures which feed intuition and insight.
	Not a period of inactivity; may be highly productive but outputs are more likely to be routine or incremental innovations rather than major leaps of understanding (almost like a 'calm before the storm').
Moments of silence	'Moments of silence' allow a blocked problem solver to temporarily disengage from immediate task.
	Allows 'mental breathing space' for non-conscious cognitive processes to make connections across the problem-relevant elements in long term memory.
	Environment and patterns of behaviour have to be conducive to operation of non-conscious mental processes (for example, quiet places, quiet times, meditation, contemplation, relaxation, exercise and sleep).
Shift in perception	Major upheaval in way mental elements that make up problem are perceived in themselves and in relation to each other.
	Cues, facts or data that underlie major breakthroughs may be 'mindlessly' seen many times before they are mindfully noticed[1] and come together as a creative insight.
	'Knowing how to see' (*saper vedere*) was important part of Leonardo da Vinci's approach to art and science.

[1] D.K. Simonton, 'Creativity, leadership and chance', in R.J. Sternberg (ed.) *The Nature of Creativity: Contemporary and Psychological Perspectives* (Cambridge: Cambridge University Press, 1988) pp. 386–426.

of the 'life' of a discovery, invention or innovation were rewound, wiped clean and replayed, would different contingencies and 'cascades of accumulating difference'[17] mean that it might not have taken place at that time, at that place, or even at all?

Creative insight and creative intuition

Creative intuition (based upon the activation of a somatic state) is not the same as creative insight (a fully-formed answer). A creative insight is the apocryphal 'Eureka!' moment in which the logical relations between a problem and the answer suddenly and unexpectedly become apparent and yield a novel outcome.[18] Creative intuition on the other hand is a difficult-to-articulate anticipation of a promising line of investigation which orients mental energy towards an original or unexpected (i.e. novel) outcome that is useful for specific task or purpose.[19] One might be forgiven for thinking that a 'high-tech' endeavour such as drug development would be the epitome of rationality, however creative intuition has as crucial a role to play in scientific and technical research as it does in many other areas of human endeavour.[20] The philosopher of science, Sir Karl Popper, argued that in science as well as art there is no such thing as a 'logic of creation', instead 'every discovery contains an "irrational element" or a "creative intuition" '.[21]

AstraZeneca is one of the world's leading pharmaceutical companies employing around 12,000 people in research and development at 11 centres in seven countries (Sweden, UK, US, Canada, France, India and Japan) working on the discovery, development, manufacture and marketing of prescription medicines.[22] In describing the early stages of the discovery process at AstraZeneca scientists used phrases such as:[23]

... having an intuitive feeling about this being the right way

... you feel that this is important for our work, but you don't know what. And then you can't let it go. And then sometimes the whole thing gels and you realise: 'Yes of course!'

For me, intuition is almost emotional; it's like that things 'look good' ... and I can get a feeling that 'this should work'.

These scientists at AstraZenenca used their intuition to sense how worthwhile it is to follow an idea through. Whilst creative intuitions provide much-needed motivation for continued exploration, they are not infallible; intuitions are merely the cognitive and affective 'signposts' from non-conscious processes which emerge into conscious awareness as hunches and gut feelings. They are beneficial in that they direct attention away from unfavourable outcomes and towards potentially favourable outcomes. Insight is the final posting in consciousness of the explicit and clearly delineated outputs from the non-conscious cognitive processes which may be pre-saged by an 'intimation'[24] or intuition that a breakthrough is about to occur. Not all intuitions become insights; some remain as judgements or 'hypotheses' backed up by the activation of a somatic state.

Non-conscious cognitive processes – driven by the human brain's intuitive 'hardware' and fuelled by 'software' content that has been 'uploaded' by prior learning and experience – as well as enabling the generation of novel ideas also enable a creator, inventor or entrepreneur to judge whether or not an idea or opportunity is worth pursuing. As we shall see this ability to rapidly judge between viable and non-viable ideas is one of the key cognitive attributes of the 'alertness'[25] which singles out successful entrepreneurs.

INDIVIDUAL DIFFERENCES IN INTUITION (COGNITIVE STYLE)

Our experiences attest to the fact that some people have more creative ideas than others do. In order to account for these individual differences in levels of creativity a number of researchers have proposed that some people exhibit marked preferences for intuitive processing, whilst others habituate towards analytical processing.[26] This notion, often referred as 'cognitive style' is perhaps most widely understood in terms of the notion of 'psychological type', derived from the work of Jung, and embodied in the MBTI and its sensing-intuiting (SN) distinction.[27]

A major study which summarized several decades of MBTI research in business found that 'high intuitives' ('Ns' in MBTI terminology):

- rely on 'hunches' and heuristics;
- are inclined towards idealistic, unconventional and creative behaviours;
- are more frequently encountered higher up organizational hierarchies;
- are more effective at strategic planning activities.[28]

Other research using a sample of Australian undergraduate psychology students suggests that intuition as measured by the MBTI is related to the personality traits of 'openness to experience' and 'extraversion'[29] and strongly to interests in artistic and 'adventure-seeking' activities.[30] In the same study 'high intuitives' also claimed to have had 'premonitions' that had come true.

The creativity researcher Dean K. Simonton of the University of California hypothesized that the differences between individuals in their levels of creativity can be attributed, at least in part, to structural differences in the contents of long-term memory. According to this view a low intuitive person when asked a question such as 'how many uses can you think of for a paper clip' is likely to show a rapid tailing-off in their responses after they have exhausted the most common uses (e.g. 'clipping sheets of paper together'). A 'high intuitive' on the other hand is likely to exhibit a much longer tapering-off in their suggestions, giving

Table 10.2 Sensing versus intuiting

Sensing	Intuiting
○ Realistic and sensible	○ Imaginative and reflective
○ Tends to follow instructions	○ Tends to ignore instruction
○ Notices details	○ Overlooks details
○ Literally-minded	○ Inventively-minded
○ Likes established methods	○ Likes change and variety
○ May not look for possibilities	○ May miss important facts
○ Facts and data	○ Meanings and associations
○ Concrete	○ Hunches
○ Practical	○ Speculative
○ Reality-based	○ Possibility-based
○ Present-oriented	○ Future-oriented
○ Utility	○ Novelty

Strengths and weaknesses

Pragmatic; precise; stable; results-oriented; sensible; systematic; opinions based on observations	Imaginative; conceptualises easily; creative; holistic; intellectually tenacious; idealistic
Lacks long range outlook; may overlook implications and meanings; may reject innovative ideas	Unrealistic; out-of-touch; may overlook key variables or facts; bored by routines; scattered

Adapted from P. Hedges, *Understanding your personality with Myers-Briggs and More* (London: Sheldon Press, 1993) p. 11; W.L. Gardner and M.J. Martinko, Using the Myers-Briggs Type Indicator: a literature review and research agenda' *Journal of Management*, 1996, 22(1): 47.

larger numbers of novel, unusual and even bizarre uses (e.g. 'clipping paper', 'picking a lock', 'making a fishing hook', 'making a fashion earring', and so forth). 'High intuitives' have a comparatively flat associative hierarchy (see Chapter 3), whilst 'low intuitives' have a steeper associative hierarchy.[31] For Simonton the 'intuitive geniuses'' knowledge, while having the same number of mental elements as that of an 'analytical genius', is arranged in a more 'egalitarian' fashion giving wider categories and richer interconnections between mental elements. This enables the intuitive person to generate more connections between ideas and hence devise novel combinations of ideas in those domains where they have the necessary in-depth knowledge (of course the practical utility of the ideas generated is a separate question).[32] Simonton equates this widely-focused attention to what the physicist Max Planck referred to as the 'vivid intuitive imagination'.[33]

In typecasting individuals as 'intuitive' or 'analytic' we do run some risks however. For example, we may overlook the fact that a 'creative person' might have a dense associative hierarchy of mental elements only in those areas where they have prior knowledge and experience, and therefore have the 'raw materials' for creative intuitions. In other areas they may lack creativity because they have little prior knowledge, learning or skill, hence their network of mental elements will be impoverished, and therefore will impose constraints on the level of creativity they can reach. In the latter case the individual simply would not have the raw materials to connect together in unusual or unexpected ways. Of course the intervention of chance might mean that a näive individual might just 'strike lucky' and come up with something novel, but weak contextual awareness would then make it difficult for that person to judge the value of the idea, and they might then have to rely on market research or expert opinion.

Expertise can be a double-edged sword. As well as supporting creativity, expert knowledge has the potential to inhibit idea generation if it results in 'fixedness', i.e. the expert looks only to established knowledge and established ways of using that knowledge and overlooks novel or more unusual options.[34] The notion of cognitive styles as outlined by Simonton may be one explanation for differences in creativity between people who are equals in terms of the necessary prior knowledge. 'Intuitive experts' and 'analytical experts' may have the same number of mental elements, but in the case of the intuitive expert these elements are arranged in such a way as to give wider categories, potentially richer interconnections and higher levels of creativity.[35]

A further barrier to creative intuition as a means of idea generation in collective settings, such as organizations, exists where the 'group think' or the expectations of peers is for analytical reasoning. For example, if powerful individuals (managers) or consensus-making group (the team) have an analytical cognitive style a congruent (i.e. analytical) cognitive climate is likely to be created.[36] An analytical climate is likely to support routine problem-solving, but the downside is that it will most likely impose limits on the options available and inhibit creative intuition. Group members with strong intuitions for a novel idea may be inhibited by the power of the 'in-group'. An unfortunate outcome of this is that the collective entity (the team and the organization) may lose out on exploring and exploiting the full range of potential solutions to a problem that concerns them all.[37] Intuition only flourishes where it is valued in an organization; where it is not valued it may operate covertly and perhaps dysfunctionally also.[38] This creates two problems:

1 *Weak learning*: managers are unable to refine their intuitive judgements through explicit feedback from colleagues (they might not get to know how accurate their hunches were).
2 *Convergent thinking*: focusing upon analytical methods exclusively tends to lead to convergent rather than divergent thinking, and also ideas which cannot be expressed in objective terms[39] may be dismissed ('if we can't talk about it, it doesn't exist').

As far as intuitive and analytical cognition is concerned creativity is not an 'either/or' question. Different kinds of cognitive processes may contribute to creative and innovative outcomes. For example, many creative individuals appear to begin with a private, intuitive sense of what the final product will be like, but they rely on other more explicit cognitive processes (such as analysis) to articulate a tacit idea which eventually becomes explicit, is made public[40] and materialized as an invention. This argument highlights a flaw in the theories of 'right-brain creativity'[41] which over-emphasize the generation of novel ideas through an exclusive set of 'artistic', 'imaginative', 'holistic' and 'intuitive' right-hemisphere brain processes (which, as we have seen, is an oversimplification). Creating something novel and useful requires both intuition and analysis through the integration and coordination of processes served by systems located in both hemispheres of the brain.[42] Moreover, as one of the pioneers of the original left-brain/right-brain research, Michael Gazzaniga has noted, his work and that of his colleagues became hugely distorted by the popular press in the 1970s and 1980s with little hard evidence for many of the claims being made in newspapers and magazine articles. Gazzaniga warns of similar traps that lie in wait for the unwary in the current hype that surrounds cognitive neuroscience, and which may only serve to obscure in the general public's understanding at least, the real advances that are being made.[43]

In a slightly different take on individual differences, Richard Wiseman and his colleagues undertook a major study in the UK in which they specifically looked at the attitudes of 'lucky' and 'unlucky'[44] people towards intuition. His results suggest that lucky people are more disposed towards making intuitive decisions than are unlucky people. These differences appear most pronounced in decisions relating to finance, careers and business. As well as trusting their 'lucky hunches', the lucky group were also more active in taking steps to boost their intuition, and specifically they reported greater use of meditation, returning to the problem later, 'clearing the mind' and 'finding a quiet place'.[45] The lucky people appeared to have picked up some well-known techniques[46] which can create the necessary conditions for the minds' non-conscious processes to work at a problem, for incubation to happen and insights to occur. 'Doing' is sometimes best-achieved by 'not doing':

> Do not try to stop your thinking. Let it stop by itself. If something comes into your mind let it come in, and let it go out. It will not stay for long. When you try to stop your thinking, it means you are bothered by it . . . if you are not bothered by the waves of your mind gradually they will become calmer and calmer. In five or at most ten minutes your mind will be completely serene and calm.[47]

ENTREPRENEURIAL INTUITION

Sir Richard Branson is the seen by many as the *doyen* of British entrepreneurs. Branson, as well as being famous as 'the man who signed the Sex Pistols', is the founder and driving force behind one of the world's most famous brands – Virgin. Founded in the pre-'Amazon.com' 1970s as a mail order vinyl record business in pages of the *Melody Maker* and *New Musical Express*, Virgin now has over 200 companies in 30 countries across the globe. For Branson one of the most important capabilities for running an organization is 'making decisions about people, and events *as they unfold*'. Indeed, one of the reasons that Virgin is run as so many independent businesses is to keep people focused on managing its individual companies through responsive and fluid decision-making.[48]

For any entrepreneur, the identification and judging of an opportunity and deciding whether or not it's worth following through are the foundation of developing new products and services. According to Branson, the judging of a business idea can take as little as 30 seconds on the basis of an acute business 'instinct':

> 'I make up my mind about someone within thirty seconds of meeting that person.'

> 'In the same way that I tend to make up my mind about people within thirty seconds of meeting them, I also make up my mind about a business proposal within thirty seconds and whether it excites me.'

> 'I rely far more on gut instinct than researching huge amounts of statistics.'[49]

In cognitive terms entrepreneurs of Branson's ilk appear to be able, consistently, to do at least two things:

1   *Perceive*: see meaningful coherence in patterns which may appear random, chaotic and meaningless to others;[50]
2   *Judge*: very quickly see the potential of a new commodity or service which others overlook or discount or are unable to move quickly onto.[51]

'Hunches' and opportunity

It is difficult to discuss creativity, innovation and entrepreneurship without mentioning the work of Joseph Schumpeter (1883–1950) – one of the most famous economists of the twentieth century. Among his most significant contributions was the emphasis that he accorded to the process of innovation in precipitating economic development and specifically the role of entrepreneurs in exploiting inventions, producing a new commodity or an old one in a new way.[52] Implicit in Schumpeter's work is the view that an entrepreneur is high in terms of the cognitive abilities of creativity and intuition, but also the social and emotional skills to overcome scepticism and hostility.[53] From a 'Schumpeterian' perspective, to successfully exploit an invention an entrepreneur needs to have at their disposal a blend of cognitive abilities and social skills[54], namely:

1   the creative intuition with which to develop new ideas;
2   the intuitive alertness and contextual awareness with which to recognize opportunities, select feasible ideas and reject non-feasible ones;[55]
3   the foresight and intuitive vision to be able to see beyond the present;[56]
4   the social skills and interpersonal skills to convince others of the value of an innovation.

The blend of creativity, intuition, foresight and social skill is not a recipe which guarantees success: creative ideas can fall at any number of hurdles before they are exploited commercially, an intuition may be wrong, and foresight may be blown off-course by unexpected turns of events in the business and global environment. As decision researchers Reid Hastie and Robyn M. Dawes remind us, we know a lot about the alleged 'funny bone' feelings of people such as McDonald's founder Ray Kroc which inspired entrepreneurial success, 'but how many investors had funny bone feelings that led to their ruin?'.[57] But as several writers have noted there are great business people who have made some bad 'guesses', for example, Michael Eisner (EuroDisney), Fred Smith

(ZapMail) and George Soros (Russian securities).[58] Setting too much store by a few famous examples of good or bad intuitive judgement calls is risky. Researchers need to focus their attentions on unsuccessful entrepreneurial intuitions as well as the successful ones that tend to get reported. Nonetheless, the combination of cognitive and social resources which successful entrepreneurs can marshal is likely to lead to choices that will be superior when averaged out over the longer term.[59]

One of the most commercially successful scientists and inventors of the twentieth century, Edwin Land (1909–91), is a prime example of an entrepreneurial mind that was able to quickly judge the feasibility of a novel idea and then marshal the necessary resources to exploit it. Land was the inventor of, amongst other things, the 'Land Camera'. Introduced in 1947, it made possible for the first time the immediate development of photographs.[60] It eventually became a huge commercial success as the Polaroid 'instant picture' camera. Although he did not have a science degree Land knew the value of collaboration and worked closely with scientists and technologists from the university sector and established his first laboratory in 1932 (The Land-Wheelwright Laboratories) a full 15 years before the invention of the Land Camera itself.

The creative moment for 'instant photography' is attributed to events when Land was on holiday in Santa Fe in the early 1940s with his family. The discovery was prompted by a question from his three-year-old daughter, who with the clarity, naivety and impulsiveness of a child wanted to know why couldn't she see right away the picture Land had just taken of her. The original, unexpected and innovative idea implicit in the child's question was stimulus enough for Land, and within the hour he synthesized and visualized the various elements necessary during a walk 'stimulated by the dangerously invigorating plateau air of Santa Fe'. He later recalled:

> If you sense a deep human need, then you go back to all the basic science. If there is some missing, then you try to do more basic science and applied science until you get it. So you make the system to fulfil that need, rather than starting the other way around, where you have something and wonder what to do with it.[61]

His commercial film and camera went on sale in 1948, and over half a century later it still occupies a unique and valuable niche in the market for photographic products.

Land was in possession of the basic science; his invention did not come as an inspirational 'bolt out of the blue' into an unprepared mind, rather the necessary knowledge and skill were in place for him to sense if and how the idea could be made to work. The foundation for his creative intuition was his prior learning and the extensive repositories of knowledge held in long term memory. Over and above this Land was able to realize that his daughter, with her innocent, näive and chance request, may have been onto a significant and workable idea. A sensing process was at work which was able to quickly sift out feasible from non-feasible options. This enabled Land to judge comparatively quickly whether it was merely a child's fantasy or whether 'instant photography' could be made to work, first as a viable invention and second as a commercial proposition. Once judged as feasible he and his colleagues invested the necessary cognitive, social and economic resources in the idea to make it a commercial reality. Land was able to exercise *informed intuition* to support his risky commercial venture.

We see informed intuition balanced with a healthy scepticism in other fields also. For example, in the high-tech field of aerospace the laser scientist Dr John Vetrovec is a prolific inventor with 30 inventions filed at Boeing, 16 US patents issued and pending, and four inventions that brought him the 2003 Exceptional Invention Award from the Boeing Intellectual Property Business. Vetrovec credits his inventiveness to intuition, a readiness to take on challenging problems and the constant search for opportunities to innovate: 'Often recognizing the opportunity can be more important than the technical work'; but Vetrovec has also learned to balance his intuition with a healthy scepticism which tests out and strengthens the arguments and rationales for an invention.[62]

The mechanisms behind the individual differences in analytical and intuitive thinking proposed by Simonton and others may be important in helping to explain why certain individuals are more alert than others to the potential commercial opportunity presented by a creative idea. We might anticipate for example that 'serial entrepreneurs' have finely-tuned perceptual awareness for spotting an idea that is exploitable commercially. A number of researchers have turned their attention to the role of intuition in successful entrepreneurship and business venturing. For example, a study of small and medium-sized business owner-managers in the UK found evidence to support the widely-held view that successful entrepreneurs have an intuitive approach to information processing and decision-making, and in this regard they are similar (i.e. intuitive) to that of large-firm senior executives.[63] Intuition may help to distinguish not only between how individuals generate ideas, but also the extent to which they are able to identify (and ultimately exploit) commercial opportunities. Other research in the UK has found that owner-managers of small businesses which grew consistently over several years tended to use intuition as a preferred decision-making style.[64]

'Inspiration' versus 'perspiration'

Creative intuition and insight do represent a crucial stage which many inventions pass through, however there is the danger that the romanticism of the 'Eureka!' moment can overshadow the hard work and persistence required for transforming a creative idea into an invention, and an invention into a commercial product. Most of us have used spreadsheets and appreciate the amount of mental labour that they can save; however back in the mid-1970s the laborious manual calculation of every change in a computer spreadsheet was the norm. By 1979 salvation was on its way. Dan Bricklin is the inventor of the modern computer spreadsheet which overcame this tiresome limitation and revolutionized this aspect of personal computing. He attributes his entrepreneurial success not only to prior knowledge and instinct, but perspiration and persistence:

> There had to be a better way, I figured, so I started designing a computer program to address those inefficiencies. I described my idea to Bob Frankston, whom I'd met as an undergraduate at MIT, and he agreed to try to turn my primitive prototype into a working program. After toiling for several months in the attic of Bob's home, we had a hunch that we might have something big on our hands.[65]

Instances of Thomas A. Edison's alleged maxim 'genius is one per cent inspiration and 99 per cent perspiration'[66] are legion. For example, in the popular imagination it was the Wright brothers' epoch-making flight at Kittyhawk in 1903 which ushered in the aviation age – in actual fact it took four more years of hard, secretive labour in order to persuade the sceptics that it was a viable breakthrough.[67] This pattern repeats itself many times in the history of scientific, technological and artistic discovery, and we should not be 'seduced' too much by 'Eureka!' moments alone as the 'be-all and end-all' of creativity and as a short cut to success – they are not.[68]

The concept of entrepreneurship as 'opportunity identification and exploitation' reaches beyond the traditional Schumpeterian view and applies in many diverse areas of professional life. Research by personality and social psychologists over many years has revealed that the traits of creative individuals, such as scientists or artists, tend to overlap with those of technological and commercial entrepreneurs. Both creators and entrepreneurs are independent and self-confident and have a propensity for risk-taking behaviour. Robert Sternberg and his colleague Todd Lubart couched this in terms of an 'investment' model. They argued that creative individuals in a variety of fields often deliberately engage with unknown or out-of-favour ideas in which they 'sense' growth potential. Entrepreneurial scientists, for example will invest the necessary energy in what might be seen as 'whacky' concepts in order to build up the idea, exploit the invention that follows, 'sell up' and move on to the next opportunity. This 'buy-low/sell-high' approach[69] is analogous to the strategy often used by entrepreneurs in new product development (NPD), business venturing and development, and company mergers and acquisitions.

To summarize, entrepreneurial intuition, whether it's in a commercial or non-commercial context, has three cognitive components:

1 *Creativity*: the ability to see problems in new and novel ways in order to escape the bounds of conventional thinking;[70]
2 *Contextual awareness*: being able to 'weigh up' a situation quickly and holistically;
3 *Mental simulation*: having a 'window into the future'.

Entrepreneurial intuition enables particular individuals to take in the important (salient) clues in the environment (everything from 'balance sheets' to 'body language'), process these data and make sense out of them. The outcome of the non-conscious processing of a 'constellation'[71] of environmental and contextual clues is posted in conscious awareness as a negative (that 'things don't quite fit') or positive (the situation may lead to a favourable outcome) gut feeling or hunch. A successful entrepreneur is able to make these judgements because *via* informed intuition, which incorporates thoughts, experiences, actions and feelings,[72] they are able to make sense of situations with coherent, integrated mind-body responses that feel right and, when averaged over the long run, pay dividends.

The cognitive components of entrepreneurial intuition[73] may mean that, faced with a set of clues, those who lack the crucial contextual awareness may see (and feel) nothing at all, while others who are more highly attuned may sense things differently: they may experience a 'gut reaction' with at least two possible outcomes:

1 *Negative somatic state*: the sense they arrive at is of a threat or too great a risk – the result is repulsion.

2   *Positive somatic state*: the clues may induce an emotional response which gives rise to a positive somatic marker and a sense of opportunity and promise – the result is attraction.

BUSINESS DECISIONS

The Dodge Viper has been described in the trade press as Chrysler's 'ultimate thrill machine'; with its 'roadster' lines, open cockpit and 'monster' V–10 engine[74] it is a true US 'muscle machine', with a price tag to match. When it was developed in the 1980s it was unlike anything the company, which was then facing serious problems, had ever produced. To produce something of the Viper's ilk was a departure into the unknown. The inception of the Viper is attributed to the intuitive judgement of the then company president Bob Lutz. Before he joined Chrysler in 1986 Lutz (a former US Marines aviator) did stints with General Motors, BMW and Ford. A clue to Lutz's style is to be found in some of the more forthright opinions he has expressed:

> One of the functions I hate in automobile companies is called product planning, which is a ton of 'left-brain' guys sifting through reams and reams of market data and then coming up with an elaborate numerical model of the market that to them takes on the semblance of reality. The products they come up with are bland, run absolutely counter to common sense, and almost always turn out to be disasters. Numbers are a poor surrogate for imagination, intuition, judgement, critical thinking and leaps of faith.[75]

Lutz was explicit about his preference for 'trusting his gut' in an interview for *Harvard Business Review* in 2001.[76] In recalling the experiences that led to the decision to develop the Viper, Lutz remarked: 'It was this subconscious visceral feeling. And it just felt right'.[77] That said, Lutz's intuitive intelligence is well-honed enough to realize that gut feeling itself is not enough; for example, in an interview in 1999 he argued that although it's important for an executive to have people on the team who are equally passionate about new ideas like the Viper, it's even more important to have around the person who'll say ' "Wait a minute, not so fast" [and] that's probably going to be your chief financial officer'.

   Lutz also later consciously put a check on his personal intuition when he realized that it was taking too much of a 'front seat' in the design of the Viper: 'When I saw the initial design of the car, I was disappointed because I had expected something that would more closely resemble the

Cobra.[78] Then I realized that much as I liked the Cobra, we couldn't do that car again or it wouldn't have been a Chrysler car'.[79] This time Lutz went against his own affective reaction in approving the outline design that his team had come up with. Lutz used rational analysis as a check on his intuition. Intuition and analysis exist in a sometimes delicate and dynamic balance, for example managers have also been known to turn the relationship on its head and use intuition as a check on rational analysis. This 'check-and-balance' role was one of the five functions of 'gut feeling' identified in research carried out by Daniel Isenberg in the 1980s (see Table 10.3).[80]

The 1980s was a period in which management researchers and practitioners began to take an explicit and focused interest in the role that intuition played in business. For example, in the early 1980s Weston H. Agor undertook one of the largest surveys of intuition in management ever conducted, surveying over 3,000 respondents in the USA, including CEOs, military personnel, college presidents, health managers and legislators. His finding, that the use of intuitive judgement was related to job level (senior executives were more intuitive than middle level and lower level managers), has been replicated many times.[81] Agor also found that females tended to be more intuitive than males (but closer scrutiny reveals the differences were too small to be of any practical significance) and that the use of intuition was related to occupational speciality, for example managers in human resources were more intuitive

Table 10.3 Isenberg's five functions of gut feeling

Gut feeling function	Sample quote
Sensing when a problem exists	'The data on the group were inconsistent and unfocused. I had the sense that they were talking about a future that just was not going to happen.'
To perform well-learned behaviour patterns rapidly	'It was very instinctive, almost like you have been drilled in close combat for years and now the big battle is on and you really don't have time to think.'
Synthesizing isolated bits of data	'Synergy is always non-rational because it takes you beyond the mere sum of the parts.'
Check on the results of a more rational analysis	'Intuition leads me to seek out holes in the data.'
By-passing in-depth analysis	'My gut feeling points me in a given direction then I can begin to sort out the issues.'

Source: D. Isenberg, 'How senior managers think', in W.H. Agor (ed.) *Intuition in Organizations: Leading and Managing Productively* (Newbury Park, CA: Sage) pp. 97–8.

than their colleagues in finance. Agor also examined in more depth the ways in which the most intuitive executives (those in the top ten per cent) used intuition. Situations in which these 'high intuitives' relied upon gut feeling to make their decisions included occasions when:

- a high level of uncertainty exists;
- there is little previous precedent;
- the available facts are of limited value;
- cause-and-effect relationships are not well understood;
- several plausible solutions exist;
- time is limited.[82]

Research moved on apace and the 1990s witnessed at a number of major empirical studies. For example, Jagdish Parikh and his colleagues Fred Neubauer and Adlen G. Lank conducted an international survey of intuition in management which involved over one thousand participants in nine countries.[83] They examined several aspects of intuitive judgement, including participants' perceptions of how relevant intuition was to decision-making in different areas of management, summarized in Table 10.4. In the late 1990s a more searching, in-depth qualitative study was carried out in the USA by Lisa Burke and Monica Miller in order to explore the ways experienced professionals (with at least ten years work experience) who held significant positions in major

Table 10.4 Relevance of intuition in business decision-making

Area	%
Corporate strategy and planning	80
Human resources (development)	79
Marketing	77
Research and development	72
Public relations	64
Investment and business diversification	60
Acquisitions, mergers and alliances	55
Choice of technology, plant and equipment	35
Finance	31
Production and operations management	28
Materials management	24

Source: J. Parikh, F. Neubauer and A.G. Lank, *Intuition: The New Frontier in Management* (Oxford: Blackwell Business, 1994) p. 60.

Note: Percentage (%) of respondents who thought intuition was relevant to each area of decision-making

US organizations used intuition in decision-making.[84] When asked 'what does it mean to make decisions using your intuition' the two most popular responses characterized intuition as:[85]

1   making decisions based on experience, for example: one manager said 'Individuals look through [their] experiences in their "central processing unit" [computer analogy] and make decisions based on their past experiences';
2   affect-initiated decisions, for example: 'Sometimes I've a strange feeling that something about the claim isn't quite right and then I dig for more information and find that the facts weren't absolutely accurate as reported to me'.

Nobody in Burke and Miller's study viewed intuition as a paranormal power; rather it was viewed as a process that 'kicked in' while conscious thought processes were disengaged. Their work gave strong corroboration to Agor's and Parikh's earlier findings. They found that intuition was likely to be used in situations calling for people-oriented decisions (in such situations respondents reported engaging their intuition on the basis of non-verbal signals, such as a facial expression, etc.), quick decisions, unexpected decisions, uncertain or novel situations, and situations where there was a lack of explicit clues. An overwhelming majority of respondents (over 90 per cent) said they had combined intuition with rational analysis when making decisions, and a significant majority (two-thirds) felt that they ways in which they used intuition led to better decisions.

Intuition and uncertainty

What is apparent from the research that was carried out in the 1980s and 1990s is that intuitive judgements often come to the fore when experienced business decision-makers are required to operate in uncharted territories. For many organizations in the late twentieth and early twenty-first centuries uncertainty and ambiguity are the perceived norm. Lutz, for example, with his prior experiences at BMW, Ford and GM was an informed 'intuitive explorer' in what was for Chrysler a zone of ambiguity and uncertainty.[86] Taking a leap into the unknown requires courage and a certain fortitude as this quote from a speech made by the Chief Financial Officer of Boeing in 2000 demonstrates:

'You have to feel the fear and do it anyway. That's really what I mean by courage. Companies that are succeeding in the new economy have several things in common. They didn't start with a rigid plan. Instead, they kind of started with an idea, a spark, an intuition. They had a vision of where they wanted to go, but they weren't exactly sure of how to get there. They were willing to make decisions before they had all the data. There was no paralysis by analysis going on here. And they had the courage, the *intestinal fortitude* to follow their convictions'[87]

An uncertain business environment is one in which it is difficult to identify, measure and predict key variables and explicitly understand cause-and-effect relationships – the environment may be seen by managers as 'un-analyzable'. On the other hand if managers assume that the environment that they operate in is 'hard', 'measurable' and 'determinant' they will gather intelligence with vigilance and accuracy, and use rational analysis and logic to seek solutions.[88] Faced with these different interpretations a decision-maker can endeavour to:

1   *reduce uncertainty*: invest time and resources in trying to identify, measure, understand and predict key variables and their interrelationships in order to reduce uncertainty or eliminate ambiguity;
2   *tolerate uncertainty*: recognize that there are classes of problems and situations in which the reduction of uncertainty or the elimination of ambiguity is too costly, too difficult or even impossible. Part and parcel of 'uncertainty toleration' is accepting that interpreting business environments that are un-analyzable requires a reliance on 'softer', qualitative data, as well as judgement and intuition.[89]

Uncertainty reduction

For those problems where uncertainty may be reduced or ambiguity eliminated, analysis is a tried-and-tested approach, and where this is a viable option intuition is unlikely to be necessary. Decision-makers can reduce uncertainty by establishing which data are needed, collecting the relevant facts and figures, analyzing these in terms of the overall goal and making a rational choice. For example, prices of raw materials, production technologies and rates of economic growth are knowable (as variables) and predictable (within margins of error). With the application of appropriate techniques (such as the decision trees, computer algorithms and statistical models) and the investment of the necessary resources (including time), uncertainty may be reduced to an acceptable level and a more optimal choice arrived at. Using computer-based decision tools under these circumstances can lead to much more consistent and accurate decisions than relying on a human decision-maker.[90]

Uncertainty toleration

In spite of the fact that analytical approaches are possible in many situations, to do so takes time; moreover there are difficult-to-analyse situations where as a result of novelty, complexity or time pressure the identification, measurement and prediction of key variables and an explicit understanding of cause-and-effect relationships is impossible. Situations may be un-analyzable where there are doubts about the reliability of data, inconsistencies and conflicts in data, or 'noisy' and excessive volumes of data which impose excessive cognitive demands and make interpretation exceedingly difficult.[91] Gary Klein suggests that these uncertainties can be managed by:

1   delaying a decision choice (experienced decision-makers know when it is safe to delay and when it is imperative to make a move even if they've got only 70 per cent of the required data);
2   close monitoring of the situation;
3   making reasonable assumptions or educated estimates;
4   embracing and accepting that in some situations uncertainty is a fact of life;[92]
5   building scenarios (plausible futures) which simulate the different ways that the futures could 'play out'.[93]

Scenario planning

Building plausible futures using the technique of 'scenario planning' was used with considerable success by companies such as Shell in the 1980s. In scenario planning decision-makers take into account critical uncertainties in order to produce 'pen pictures' of a range of plausible futures (this is not *a* forecast of *the* future). These 'pen pictures' are attempts to 'bound' the uncertainties that are inherent in a future which has yet to happen.[94] From a scenario planning perspective:

•   the future is seen as a multidimensional space (more than one future exists);
•   multiple scenarios are designed (these envelop and encompass the uncertainties in plausible and coherent ways).

Scenario planning was applied in Royal Dutch/Shell Group in the 1980s as a powerful tool by which senior executives in the company's Group Planning function could influence the management process throughout a very diverse organization spread across continents and time zones.[95] Typical starting points for a scenario planning exercise would be explication of issues of strategic importance but for which the current situation and potential future outcomes were not well understood,[96] for example: 'How might anticipated developments in the European community affect our business?' or 'What's going on in China? How might things turn out there, and what threats and opportunities might these outcomes represent for us?'

In Shell the scenarios, which evolved through an iterative process of interviews, research, presentations and workshops, would be used to challenge managers' mental models, identify important trends and monitor them, test out existing projects to see how well they would fit with 'Scenario X, Y or Z', and to develop new strategic thinking.

Shell's scenarios focused not on 'what *will* happen' but 'what will we do *if* X happens'. Arie de Geus, writing in 1988 as Head of Planning at Shell, described a scenario written against the backcloth of a 1984 oil price of $28 a barrel in which any future promising a $15 barrel was 'the end of the world for oil people':

> We don't know the future, but neither do you. And though none of us knows whether the price is going to fall, we can agree that it would be pretty serious if it did. So we have written a case study showing one of many possible ways in which the price of oil could fall. . . . And now [imagine] it is April 1986 and you are starting at a price of $16 a barrel. Will you please meet and give your views on these three questions: (1) What do you think your government will do? (2) What do you think your competition will do? and (3) What, if anything, will you do?[97]

When, in April 1986 the oil price did fall to $10 a barrel, the fact that Shell managers had already visited 'in their heads' a world of $15 prices helped the company through the jittery spring of a year in which average world prices for oil fell by around 50 per cent.

From a cognitive perspective, if scenarios are presented as concrete, coherent and credible stories about the future they are likely to appeal to the brain's intuitive (experiential) processing system and excite emotion and imagination. When organizations are moving into 'uncharted waters' (i.e. the future), the somatic markers that accompany informed intuitions can:

- signal 'danger' or 'opportunity' in the uncertainties that lie ahead;
- serve as a basis for identifying, reflecting on and devising problem-solving strategies to cope with the alternative futures that intuitions signal.[98]

Scenario planning and mental simulations which draw upon decision-makers' intuitions in an informed way can be an invaluable tool for generating creative ideas, dealing with uncertainty and managing yet-to-exist futures.

Mental simulation

The signals that accompany intuition point towards the future. They have a predictive or projective element which is often the basis for the creative, entrepreneurial and strategic intuitions which artists, innovators and senior company executives choose to follow when selecting viable over non-viable alternatives and in charting paths into the future. Intuitions are hypotheses which enable predictions to be made in ambiguous situations. Intuitions do not guarantee any particular future outcome – they are not infallible, but provide, as Guy Claxton notes 'a valuable source of hypotheses' which are 'capable of being interrogated'.[99]

One way in which an intuition can be interrogated is through 'mental simulation'. A mental simulation is a cognitive construction, sometimes amounting to nothing less than a 'DVD in the head' of an event or series of events that has happened or might happen.[100] Mental simulations are 'cognitive fictions' but nonetheless they have the power to affect behaviour. For example, in the USA home owners who were asked to imagine they had bought cable TV (i.e. they were 'imagining themselves in the product'[101]) were more likely to want to subscribe to cable TV than other potential consumers who were given a persuasive communication which related the benefits of cable TV.[102] Edwin Land was an innovator who was able to mentally simulate his inventions, rewinding from the vision back through the necessary sub-goals: 'You always start with a fantasy. Part of the fantasy technique is to visualize something as perfect. Then with the experiments you work back from the fantasy to reality, hacking away at the components.'[103]

One of the key features of successful mental simulations is that, rather than being fantastical, preposterous or magical they tend to be constrained by what is feasible, realistic and possible; for this reason they have the potential to be a practical guide for anticipating the future.[104] One of the reasons they are able to exert considerable influence on thoughts and actions stems from the fact that they can be affect-laden. Mental simulations can evoke positive or negative feeling states[105] which can even manifest themselves as elevations in heart rate, blood pressure and electro-dermal, or SCRs.[106] Consequently, a particularly vivid mental simulation may have enormous potency to induce the 'as-if' loop and the associated feelings which may influence decision-making. Mental simulations are also as flexible as a DVD, helping us to look backwards as well as forwards – they have a retrospective (rewind) function and a prospective (fast-forward) function.[107]

Counterfactuals are a mental representation of alternatives to what has actually happened. Counterfactual thinking[108] allows a decision-maker to re-experience and re-process events 'virtually' in the mind's eye, enabling them to cope with or regulate emotional responses (for example, a mental simulation may assist with the restoration of self-esteem and make help to us 'feel better').[109]

Mental simulations also enable us to 'fast-forward' both in the short term (tactically) or in the longer term (strategically). At a tactical level fast-forward mental simulations allow decision-makers to anticipate scenarios that are to be faced in the immediate or short-term and thereby visualize problem-solving strategies (for example, in the negotiation with clients of a pricing structure for a new product or service – 'what to say if . . .'). Mental simulations also have a prospective strategic value – they allow a decision-maker to fast-forward events by weeks, months and years. For example, an entrepreneur might use mental simulation to anticipate whether or not, on the basis of their informed intuition (i.e. prior learning, knowledge and experience) a business opportunity is a viable means of meeting desired goals.[110] Research shows that mentally simulating the steps involved in progressing towards a realistic objective through goal-appropriate behaviours[111] is more effective than merely conjuring up unrealistic, 'pie-in-the-sky' fantasies.

One of the drawbacks of mental simulations is that the easier it is to mentally simulate an event (i.e. the less surprising the chain of events is) the more likely its occurrence is judged to be. On the other hand the more difficult it is to imagine, the less likely it is judged to be.[112] This can serve to exclude very novel occurrences from mental simulations. One means of guarding against this is to be open to the possibility of, or actively seek out, unlikely or surprising events.[113] Wider categories and richer interconnections between mental elements may enable some individuals to be more proficient than others at imagining unexpected occurrences. Because their ease of generation is not equated with their likelihood of occurrence, mental simulations need to be treated with a degree of caution. The sharing of one's personal mental simulations and collectively creating mental simulations within a team may serve to enhance the degree novelty generated and to expose mental simulations to a constructive critique. It may even be possible for a group to generate a collective intuition with which to navigate an uncertain future.

Mental simulations are useful cognitive tools which can be employed as a means not only to generate novel and potentially valuable ideas, but also to put intuitions and other predictive judgements 'under the microscope' and subject them to a critical scrutiny. Mental simulations which imagine in detail the steps leading to a goal which intuitively 'feels right' can help guard against false optimism or wishful thinking. As with the case of Edwin Land's 'fantasy', imagining the steps needed to make a creative intuition into a reality allows its feasibility to be rigorously scrutinized and tested.[114]

As well as highlighting whether an intuitively sensed outcome is feasible, mental simulation may help with the very concrete step of developing problem-solving strategies and the regulation of associated emotions,[115] thereby improving the chances of success. On the other hand, mental simulations which focus solely on a highly and anxiously sought-after goal ('riches', 'fame', 'fortune', 'losing weight', 'giving up addiction' or 'achieving happiness' – as many 'self help' programmes exhort us to do) may induce a temporary 'feel-good' factor but can lead to the mundane practical constraints being overlooked or brushed aside on a tide of self-belief, self-delusion and unfounded optimism.[116] As far as intuitive predictions and mental simulation are concerned, analysis and intuition can be mutually reinforcing:

* Rational analysis can be used to test out an intuitive hypothesis (see Table 10.5[117]).
* Using an informed 'intuitive awareness' to scan an analytically-driven solution is a way of sensing its viability ('does it feel right?').

There are unambiguous situations in which intuition and analysis both give affirmation to a particular choice. For example where the figures 'stack up' and our gut feeling says 'yes' the judgement is likely to be to 'go for it'; on the other hand where the figures don't hold water and our inner alarm bell says 'no!', again the choice is an easy one – steer clear. More ambiguity arises where intuition strongly says 'no' but analysis strongly says 'yes' – in this situation if it's possible to get more data to allay the fears that our intuitive system is alerting us to this may be a prudent thing to do. In the situation where our analysis firmly says 'no' and our intuition gives a firm 'yes' this might be a good time to get some

Table 10.5   Putting intuitive hypotheses to the test

Remembering	Recalling what happened on past occasions in similar situations
Multiple thought experiments	Do thought experiments, imagining variants of the intuitive hypothesis and what might occur in each variant
Stand the intuition on its head	Juxtaposing the intuitive hypothesis with an opposite scenario, examining the potential outcomes of each.
Go to the edge	Push the intuitive hypothesis to an implausible extreme.
Multiple modalities	Re-express the intuitive hypothesis in modalities other than that which it is currently expressed (for example, from words to pictorial, diagrammatic, tabular or auditory)
Stonewall	Stonewall in defence of an intuitive hypothesis in order to test it to the limit

Adapted from W.J. McGuire, 'Creative hypothesis testing in psychology: some useful heuristics', *Annual Review of Psychology*, 1987, 48: 1–30.

Analysis strong 'yes'	Get more data to bolster analysis	**Unambiguously 'yes'**
Analysis strong 'no'	**Unambiguously 'no'**	Seek good feedback on intuition
	Intuition strong 'no'	Intuition strong 'yes'

Figure 10.1   Intuition-analysis decision matrix.

searching feedback on the intuitive judgement call before acting. Of course under time-pressured situations it may not be possible to get more data or to seek feedback, and in these circumstances building strong 'intuitive muscle power'[118] can give greater confidence in intuitive judgements when they arise. As we found out earlier two of the best 'work outs' for building intuitive muscle power are first, immersion in learning and experience and data and analysis over extended periods so that rational analyses become 'compressed'; and second getting candid and constructive feedback on intuitive judgements (in what Robin Hogarth terms a 'kind' learning environment).

Intuition and strategic decisions

Strategic decisions can change the whole course of a company's history; they are complex judgemental problems that demand informed intuition, the foresight to imagine a more desirable future state and the ability to act in goal-directed ways.[119] They also require courage. Does intuition equip managers to tolerate uncertainty and manage their enterprises more effectively in unstable conditions?

The levels of uncertainty or instability that managers have to tolerate vary across different industry types and derive from the interplay of a variety of factors (for example, levels of competition, technological development and government intervention and regulation). Researchers Naresh Khatri and Alvin Ng looked at the relationship between industry instability, intuitive decision-making and firm performance amongst 433 US firms in computing (which they classified as a 'highly unstable' industry), banking (moderate instability) and utilities (least unstable). They found that the use of intuition in strategic decision-making was much greater in the computer industry than in banking and the utilities and that intuition was positively associated with performance in this unstable environment (computing), but was negatively associated with company performance in the stable environments.

They concluded that intuition needs to be used cautiously and in combination with rational analysis in business environments that are stable or moderately stable, but may be used 'more often in a highly unstable context'.[120] US intuition researchers Erik Dane and Mike Pratt attribute this to the fact that decision-making in uncertain environments needs to be less routine than in stable situations. This means that decision-makers under uncertainty have to shift away from treating problems as structured and resolvable using standard procedures.[121] Instead Dane and Pratt argued that decision-makers are likely to be faced with a 'multitude of plausible alternative solutions' rather than a single clearly-articulated, quantitatively-specified, objective criterion for success. As a consequence decision-making becomes less analytical (they use the term 'intellective') and much more judgemental, with a reliance upon informed intuitions.

The problems that confront decision-makers range from those which are 'tightly structured' (i.e. there is 'hard' data available which is amenable to analysis and the criteria for success are explicitly stated) to those which are 'loosely structured' (i.e. available data is 'soft', is un-analyzable and the criteria for success are not explicitly stated). Intuition is unlikely to be necessary or effective in tightly-structured situations especially where the level of computational complexity is high (in this situation computers can usually do a better job than humans). On the other hand, in loosely-structured situations informed intuitive judgements may be better placed to take into account the subtleties, novelties, nuances and dynamism of the problem as it changes or takes shape. As the structure of the task becomes 'tighter' the balance is likely to shift in favour of analytical approaches; conversely, intuitive judgments are likely to become more effective as the structure of the task becomes 'looser'[122] (see Table 10.6). The human brain's intuitive mind did not evolve to solve probabilistic judgement tasks or tightly-structured intellective tasks, the latter are best left to the rational analytical mind which is thought to have evolved later and which is better suited to objective, computationally complex tasks. The intuitive mind on the other hand is better adapted to complex judgemental tasks involving sensing, synthesising, strategising, creativity, pattern recognition, and people-oriented decisions.

At a strategic level creative intuition can be a unique and valuable source of competitive advantage. For example, companies move into uncharted territories when they market a product or service that consumers aren't aware of the existence of, let alone their need for it. A proactive marketing orientation involves developing novel products or services to meet 'latent needs' (i.e. needs that consumers aren't aware they have). The converse situation is a reactive marketing orientation – a

Table 10.6   Problem structure and intuitive judgement

Tightly-structured (favouring analysis)	*Loosely-structured (favouring intuition)*
Intellective	Judgemental
Tasks for which there are explicit and objective criteria for success	Judgments for which there is no explicit or objective criterion of success
Conflict resolution; optimization; justification; computational complexity*	Time pressure; ill-defined goals; dynamic conditions; experienced participants*
Examples†	*Examples†*
Finance	Corporate strategy and planning
Production and operations management	Human resources

Sources: * G. Klein, *Intuition at Work* (New York: Doubleday Currency, 2002) p. 57; P. Laughlin, 'Social combination processes of cooperative problem-solving groups on verbal intellective tasks', in M. Fishbein (ed.) *Progress in Social Psychology, Vol. 1* (Hillsdale, NJ: Lawrence Erlbaum Associates, 1980);† J. Parikh, F. Neubauer and A.G. Lank, *Intuition: The New Frontier in Management* (Oxford: Blackwell Business, 1994).

business responds to what customers say they want. The specification of the key variables which need to be identified, measured and predicted, while not impossible, is more difficult in the proactive orientation than where the customers themselves have a clearly-articulated need. Pro-activity requires the anticipation of unexpressed customer needs and a tolerance of uncertainty.[123] Proactive marketing relies more upon inference and informed intuition and these softer sources of data may be as important as feedback from potential customers. Moreover, the use of creative intuition in these circumstances is a resource that it is extremely difficult, if not impossible, for a competitor to copy.[124] As a 2007 *Harvard Business Review* article noted: 'a gut is a personal, non-transferable attribute' and even if we pore over every word that a Richard Branson or Jack Welch writes in the hope of replicating their success we 'cannot replicate the experiences, thought patterns and personality traits that inform those leaders' distinctive choices'.[125]

AI – 'ARTIFICIAL INTUITION'?

In 1954 the psychologist Paul Meehl (1920–2003) shook many in the scientific world when he published a book (*Clinical Versus Statistical Prediction: A Theoretical Analysis and a Review of the Evidence*)[126] demonstrating that human clinical judgements were inferior to statistical models. This research and the extensive programme of work which followed compared the informal, difficult-to-specify, subjective methods used by clinicians (including applied psychologists and physicians) with computational methods that employed statistical models, algorithms, and 'hard' data. The research did not explicitly investigate intuitive judgement as such, nonetheless, since the arguments pertain to expertise and its effectiveness they have more than a passing relevance.

In 2000 William Grove and his colleagues from the University of Minnesota used the techniques of meta-analysis[127] to look back over four decades of this research in applications as diverse as predicting college academic performance, diagnosis of heart disease and the assessment of supervisory potential.[128] They concluded that prediction by statistical models and other 'mechanical' methods is typically more accurate than clinical prediction by a human being (overall around 10 per cent more accurate than the predictions made by clinicians). However, they also noted that statistical prediction is not uniformly superior – there are areas where the clinical method is as good as the statistical method and in a few instances the clinical method is more accurate. What was it that made human judgement inferior?

Researchers have attributed it to several sources of error, a number of which will be familiar to us, including:

1   ignoring base rates (see Chapter 6);
2   errors associated with the representativeness and availability heuristics (see Chapter 6);
3   lack of feedback for clinicians on their judgements giving them little opportunity to learn and improve.

Surely if computational tools are better than human judges the case for intuitive judgement is undermined? Are those executives and others who use intuition simply deluding themselves (as some critics have forcefully argued[129])? There is no doubt that in certain situations humans may make better judges than do computational tools, but because of human frailties – their cognitive limitations, fatigue and the role of affect – they are unable to apply the same 'formula' consistently and subjectively across all cases.[130] Contrast this with a 'machine' – it is capable of being perfectly consistent, unemotional and robust indefinitely across a limitless number of cases. Even though they may break down now and again, computers don't suffer from fatigue and have hugely superior analytical processing power; therefore on average a computerised model is bound to outperform a human.[131]

The story doesn't end there however. As the decision researcher Robin Hogarth has pointed out in order to build statistical models it is necessary both to have indicator variables (for example, patient symptoms) and a criterion variable (chances of survival).[132] In the case of creative intuitions, entrepreneurial intuition, strategic visioning or the judgements of another person's emotional state it is difficult to envisage what the criterion variable (or indeed indicator variables) might be and how it might be assessed. Hogarth also makes the telling point that human input and professional judgement are necessary to build a model in the first place;[133] moreover, expert human judges are alert and able to take into account aberrant or novel data that may not have been specified in the original model.

Nonetheless, some of the critics of intuitive and expert human judgement see great future promise in building better machines.[134] In those cases where it is possible to build a computational decision support tool the potential exists to save on a substantial amount of the human resource that is being 'squandered' on judgements that could be performed more effectively and efficiently by statistical models.[135] Doing so might not only free humans from some of the drudgery, it would also free up their professional judgement for the important, complex, judgemental tasks for which a statistical model cannot currently be built, such as generating novel ideas, sifting viable from non-viable inventions, deciding whether to evacuate a burning building, visioning alternative futures, fantasizing and reading another human being's intentions.

Co-founder of Sony and the driving force behind the Sony Walkman, Akio Morita was sceptical about the value of machines in the creative domain and optimistic about the role that human beings will always play in industrial creativity and innovation: 'Machines and computers cannot be creative in themselves, because creativity requires something more than the processing of existing information. It requires human thought, spontaneous intuition and a lot of courage'.[136]

In the foreseeable future, even when the situation arrives where it is possible to build computers that can impose 'left brain discipline on right brain hunches',[137] for the majority of decision-makers who find themselves in everyday situations which are complex, ambiguous, uncertain or time-pressured they will have few alternatives but to rely upon a reasoned interpretation and application of their informed intuitions.[138]

TAKE-AWAYS FOR CHAPTER 10

Key ideas

An entrepreneur needs to have at his or her disposal the *creative intuition* with which to develop new ideas, the intuitive alertness and contextual awareness with which to recognize opportunities, select feasible ideas and reject non-feasible ones, and the foresight and intuitive vision to be able to see beyond the present. Faced with the same set of clues, those who lack the crucial *contextual awareness* may see (and feel) nothing at all, whilst others who are more highly attuned may feel a *negative somatic state* (indicating a threat or too great a risk) or a *positive somatic state* (indicting a sense of opportunity and promise). Intuition is *more likely* to be used in people-oriented decisions, quick decisions, unexpected decisions, uncertain or novel situations, and situations where there is lack of explicit clues. *Mental simulations* can generate novel and potentially valuable ideas, and also put intuitions and other predictive judgements 'under the microscope' and subject them to a critical scrutiny. Analysis and intuition can be *mutually reinforcing*: rational analysis can be used to test out an intuitive hypothesis; informed intuitive awareness can be used to scan an analytically-driven solution as a way of sensing its viability ('does it feel right?'). Intuition is unlikely to be necessary or effective in *tightly-structured* situations; in *loosely-structured* situations informed intuitive judgements may be better placed to take into account the subtleties, novelties, nuances and dynamism of the problem as it changes or takes shape.

Intuition quote: Herbert Simon, scholar, researcher and Nobel prize-winner

'The effective manager does not have the luxury of being able to choose between "analytic" and "intuitive" approaches to problems.'

Action point

Tough decisions can be intuitively driven or they can be analytically driven. If *analysis* is the route you've taken check out with your intuition the choice you've made *before* taking action. Does it *feel* right? If *intuition* is your guiding light check out the choice you've made by running the 'rational ruler' over it. Does it 'stack up'? If intuition says 'no' when rational analysis says 'yes' – *get more data*. If rational analysis says 'no' when your intuition says 'yes' – *get good feedback* on your intuitive judgement call.[139]

FURTHER READING

Hogarth, R.M., *Educating Intuition*. Chicago: The University of Chicago Press 2001.
Klein, G., *Intuition at Work*. New York: Currency/Double Day 2003.
Wilson, T.D., *Strangers to Ourselves: Discovering the Adaptive Unconscious*. Cambridge, MA: Belknap/Harvard 2002.

11 Emotional, social and moral intuition

Below the surface stream, shallow and light,
Of what we say we feel – below the stream,
As light, of what we think we feel – there flows
With noiseless current strong, obscure and deep,
The central stream of what we feel indeed.
(Matthew Arnold, *St Paul and Protestantism*, 1870)

MAIN IDEA

Among the most important areas in which human beings utilize their capability to arrive at fast and accurate intuitive judgements (both in personal and work settings) are in reading others' feelings, motives and intentions and in exercising affectively-infused moral judgements.

The 1990s was a decade of phenomenal scientific and technological progress; innovations such as the internet, e-commerce, mobile phones and DVDs have all changed the ways in which we live our twenty-first century personal and working lives. Alongside these technological leaps forward George Bush declared it 'The Decade of the Brain'. In the cognitive and neurosciences the 1990s saw the publication of two highly influential works: Joseph Le Doux's *The Emotional Brain: The Mysterious Underpinnings of Emotional Life* (1996), and two years previously Antonio R. Damasio's *Descartes Error: Emotion, Reason and the Human Brain*. At the end of the decade Lakoff and Johnson in *Philosophy in the Flesh* (1999) summarized the position that cognitive science had reached with the stark assertion that 'the mind is inherently embodied; thought is mostly unconscious; [and] reason is not dispassionate, but emotionally engaged'.[1]

If any confirmation were needed that emotions were looming large in the scientific and public imagination, the popular social science 'blockbuster' of the 1990s was Daniel Goleman's *Emotional Intelligence: Why it Can Matter More Than IQ* (1995). It popularized scientific research in the field of EI, became a 'Number One Bestseller', was the *Time Magazine* cover story 'What's your EQ?',[2] and had a major impact on consulting and management practice. From a cognitive and social science perspective the 1990s was 'the decade of the emotions', the effects of which are still very much with us today, not least because of the continued interest in and ongoing controversy surrounding EI but also because of the increasing level of interest in the role of intuition in social and moral judgement.

EMOTIONAL INTELLIGENCE AND INTUITION

The term EI itself has been traced back to a doctoral thesis by Wayne L. Payne entitled 'A study of emotion: developing emotional intelligence' in 1985. It is generally acknowledged that the first scientists to publish EI articles in peer-reviewed, scholarly journals were Jack Mayer, Peter Salovey and their colleagues. In the 1990s the dam burst and there was an explosion in the number of publications on the subject. At the time of writing there are over 300 research journal articles with term 'emotional intelligence' in the title alone, and almost 2000 that mention it somewhere in the body of the text.[3] The scientific status of EI is controversial and hotly debated. Vociferous claims are made for EI's contribution over-and-above that made by IQ to academic achievement and occupational success, as well as to life and job satisfaction and emotional and health adjustment.[4] Some in the research community, such as the applied psychologist Frank Landy, are trenchant in their criticisms of it, arguing that these claims made on behalf of the concept require much more searching scientific scrutiny.[5] The concept of EI is generally taken to span five domains:

(1) knowing one's emotions, i.e. recognizing a feeling as it happens;
(2) managing and coping with one's emotions;
(3) using emotions to motivate oneself in pursuit of a goal;
(4) being attuned to and recognizing emotions in others;
(5) having the skills to 'manage' emotions in others.[6]

According to the theory of EI people differ in their 'abilities' in each of these areas, and for assessment, self-development, guidance and counselling purposes there are various questionnaire and inventories available (such as Reuven Bar-On's *Emotional Quotient Inventory*, or *EQi*).

The debates within and between the scientific community and consultants, practitioners and popularizers of EI about its status and value show few signs of abating, and this is not the place for a recapitulation of the arguments 'for' and 'against'. Neal Ashkanasy and Catherine Daus offer a balanced view and their assurance that it is 'safe' to work on the assumptions that EI:

1   involves the ability to identify and perceive emotions in the self and others and the skills to understand and manage them;
2   is an individual difference which is distinct from, but positively related to, other 'intelligences';
3   develops over the life span and is 'trainable'.

Taking these points as a conservative and constructive basis for engaging with EI, what do its proponents have to say about its relationship to intuition? In *Emotional Intelligence* Goleman appeals to Damasio's

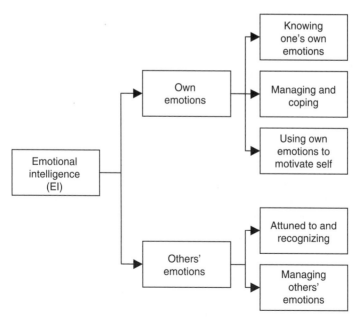

Figure 11.1 Simplified representation of the components of EI.

SMH as a scientific explanation of 'gut feeling' which he sees as a 'key' to sounder personal decision-making: 'formal logic alone can never work as the basis for deciding whom to marry or trust or even what job to take; these are realms where reason without feeling is blind'.[7] Goleman argues that awareness of one's emotions (i.e. sensing and interpreting changes in the body landscape), how they affect behaviour and performance and the underlying goals and values which they reflect are part of the competence of 'emotional awareness' – which he refers to as an 'inner rudder'. People who are emotionally aware (to say that they have 'a firmer hand on the tiller' perhaps stretches the metaphor too far) are able to recognize:

- what they are feeling and why;
- the connections between their feelings and their thoughts and behaviours;
- the connections between their feelings and the way they perform;
- the goals and values that guide their lives.[8]

Emotion and its regulation (and therefore EI) may have an effect upon problem-solving, insight, creativity and intuition. The spread of neural activation was discussed previously in Chapters 3 and 7 as a possible explanation for the ways in which people are able to non-consciously judge the coherence in a pattern of cues such as word triads or visual stimuli. Research suggests that if a person is able to self-regulate their moods (for example by being able to induce more positive feelings) he or she may gain access to wider semantic fields and thereby increase the likelihood of creative intuitive judgements. When 'action-oriented individuals'[9] are confronted by potentially stressful situation they are able to intuitively regulate ('get a grip on') their feelings and thereby cope with stressors and maintain access to wider semantic networks. By contrast 'state-oriented' (i.e. non-action oriented) individuals are at the mercy of their feelings (they become hijacked by them) because they lack the skills to intuitively regulate affect with negative consequences for coping ability and general effectiveness in stressful situations.[10] Intuitively accessing positive affective states has the potential therefore to foster creative insights and intuitions through a wider spread of activation.

Does EI have any biological basis? Joint investigations by psychologists and neurologists suggest that EI may be an aspect of the brain's control system for the regulation of emotions, the location of which appears to be the frontal cortex.[11] The overlap between the neural systems that serve emotional intelligence and somatic state activation ('gut feeling') was investigated by Reuven Bar-On, the developer of the *EQi*, and Daniel Tranel, Antoine Bechara and Natalie Denburg (colleagues of Damasio).[12] Twenty-three neurological patients participated in a joint emotional intelligence-somatic marker hypothesis experiment. The group was made up of:

- those that did not have damage to the neural circuitry thought to be involved in somatic state activation – these were the control group;
- those with damage to the amygdala, VMPC and insular/somato-sensory cortices – these were the experimental group.

As well as being assessed with regard to EI (using the *EQi*) and social functioning (data were gathered on employment status, social function-ing, interpersonal relationships and social standing), participants also took part in the well-known 'Iowa (Bechara) Gambling Task' which assesses decision-making behaviour. The results showed that partici-pants with damage to the somatic marker circuitry (i.e. the experimental group):

- scored significantly lower EI;
- scored lower on all aspects of social functioning;
- exhibited poor judgement in the decision-making task.

The researchers interpreted their findings as evidence that the neural systems which support EI overlap with the systems which support som-atic state activation and judgement in decision-making. Moreover, there were no significant differences between the two groups in terms of cog-nitive intelligence (IQ), suggesting that the systems which support EI and somatic state activation are separate from the neural systems that support cognitive intelligence (i.e. the higher cortical structures).

In common with the feeling of an emotion, the 'receipt' of a gut feeling (a bodily signal) in conscious awareness is involuntary and automatic. The emotions, such as fear, anger, sadness, happiness, etc. with which EI is concerned, differ from intuition not only in terms of their reactive and short-lived nature, but also in terms of the extent to which the eliciting cause can be explicitly reasoned. With gut feeling, while we may be able to recognize what we are feeling (for example, excitement, foreboding, anxiety, or anticipation) we are unlikely to be able say explicitly why we are conscious of the feeling apart from the fact that there is an eliciting situation (such as a job candidate at interview, a sick infant, a burning building, a business deal, etc.) which has precipitated the non-conscious pattern recognition and associated somatic state activation. Unlike the feeling of an emotion (for example, fear) for which the eliciting cause is usually pretty obvious (a threatening object or situation) the causes of feelings which arise as a result of intuitions are not as easily reasoned. For example, I do not feel anger or fear as a result of a complex combination of cues the reasons of which elude explanation; rather I know that, for instance, a dangerous driver has made me feel angry or scared – the reason is clear. Like the feelings of an emotion, gut feelings arise into conscious awareness, but unlike the feelings of an emotion the reasons why a particular set of cues set off a gut feeling are not clear. The cues themselves may have been perceived implicitly and the processes and evaluations which induce gut feelings operate below the level of conscious awareness. It is the output (the bodily signal or somatic marker) and not the reasoning which is posted in conscious awareness.

Whether or not we experience somatic markers in the first instance appears to be tied to the functioning of specific brain regions. Impairment of those brain regions that support the emotional aspects of decision-making may have a detrimental effect upon an individual's ability to:

- experience and be aware of their gut feelings;
- generate feelings necessary to behave in goal-directed ways;
- cope flexibly with the immediate situation;
- make the decisions necessary to solve personal and interpersonal problems.[13]

As the receiver of an intuitive signal we are left to ponder why we feel the way we do, and whether or not the judgement that the feeling predisposes us towards should be heeded. The intensity of the somatic signal in the body landscape (its 'affective charge') may vary (a hunch can be weak or strong) and thereby exert differing degrees of repulsion or attraction upon possible courses of action. The extent to which we

Table 11.1 Emotion and gut feeling

Emotion	*Gut feeling*
Reaction to an identifiable stimulus	Involuntary response to a set of cues
Clear-cut cause(s)	Cause(s) less clear cut
Shorter-lived	Longer-lived
Finite and distinct (happiness, sadness, etc.)	General and less distinct (harder to 'pin down')
More intense	Less intense

can trust a hunch in those situations that lend themselves to intuitive judgement is likely to be influenced by:

- whether or not the hunch is informed by prior knowledge and experience;
- the effective functioning of the body's somatic state activation mechanisms.

Given that intuition, like rational analysis, is not infallible we are presented with a dilemma – to trust or not to trust our gut. The essence of being 'intelligent' about one's intuitions lies in balancing circumspection with risk. We need to be confident that a hunch can be trusted, and having decided to trust it also acknowledged that there are attendant risks and uncertainties. We have to accept that our intuitions are limited and fallible. We have expectations of our intuitive judgements that might be met, but that they never come with any kind of guarantee.

SOCIAL INTUITION

The psychologist David G. Myers calls social intuition an 'ancient biological wisdom'. The logic of natural selection behind it goes like this: those who could read social situations and motives accurately were more likely to survive, reproduce and pass on the capability for recognizing whether the 'stranger on the savannah' was a friend or foe.[14] The 'stranger on the savannah syndrome' is an example of reading 'thin slices' of behaviour in social settings. We met this concept in a previous chapter in the case of the students who were able to accurately judge lecturers from video-clips only a few seconds in length. Evaluation on the basis of thin slices is one of the processes that support social intuition. Other processes include[15]:

Mere exposure

The concept of 'mere exposure' was introduced previously in relation to Zajonc's experiments in which seeing a stimulus on one occasion, even if one is not consciously aware of it, can generate a preference for it on future occasions.[16] 'Mere exposure' effects operate in social settings. Being favourably predisposed to people with whom we expect to interact and the desire for harmony and agreement within a social group tends to have a strong biasing effect on judgements in ways that maintain relatedness, group cohesion and social stability.[17] It appears that evolution has 'hard-wired' us with an intuitive tendency to bond with those familiar to us (the in-group), and to be more wary of those who are unfamiliar (the out-group).[18]

Emotional contagion

We are 'social chameleons'[19] tending to mimic other peoples' facial expressions, tone of voice and postures (so-called 'mood linkage'), and not only that, most of us prefer to be around reasonably happy, lively people whose moods can be so contagious as to make us 'feel good' ourselves. Myers argues that non-conscious mimicry smoothes social interaction and that via mood linkage we are more able to 'intuit what the other person is feeling, and it [helps] the other person sense your empathy'.[20]

Empathic accuracy

Our intuitions help us to read the intentions and motives of others, especially those people with whom we are familiar. For example, we are likely to have a fairly well-developed mental representation of our close friends and family members, and are able therefore to run 'mental simulations' of their behaviour or infer their intentions and motives from clues they give out via their body language, facial expressions, tone of voice and behavioural patterns. Moreover, Myers also notes that:

- With experience and training empathic accuracy, and the related skill of lie detection, can be improved.
- There are individual differences in that certain people are easier to 'read', and there are also people who are better 'readers'.

Spontaneous trait inference

Humans automatically infer the traits of others within a very few seconds of meeting with them. For example we may erroneously infer a host of attributes from the affluence or otherwise of the social setting in which we encounter somebody – spacious luxury apartment, 'flashy' car, expensive jewellery, and designer clothes create particular impressions and beliefs. Moreover, positive evaluations of a trait such as physical attractiveness can lead to the belief that the person has corresponding positive traits in other domains such as morality,[21] and job competence.

It isn't only explicit cues that can have this effect; subliminally-presented stimuli can influence our spontaneous inferences. In an experiment in the 1980s John Bargh and Paula Pietromonaco presented trait information in the form of 15 hostile words (such as 'insult', 'unkind', 'inconsiderate', 'hurt', etc.) subliminally (i.e. outside of conscious awareness) to a group of psychology undergraduates. The participants then judged a written description of a hypothetical person called 'Donald'. Exposure to the hostile words subsequently skewed participants' construal of how hostile 'Donald' was on nothing more than a pretty ambiguous description of him: 'A salesman knocked at the door, but Donald refused to let him enter. He also told me that he was refusing to pay his rent until the landlord repaints the apartment'.[22] The more hostile words people were subliminally exposed to, the more negatively (i.e. hostile) they rated the ambiguous 'Donald'. As the social psychologist Timothy D. Wilson has noted, the unconscious is not only a 'gatekeeper' of social information, it's our own personal 'spin doctor' as well.[23] Whilst evolution may have equipped *Homo sapiens* to quickly make attributions, judgements, evaluations and categorizations of others, many of the categories themselves are culturally and socially constructed – we make the 'boxes'; all that is left is for our unconscious to do is automatically assign people to them.

Activation in 'mirror neurons'

The actions performed by others in our social group present us with an almost constant stream of visual and auditory stimuli. These stimuli not only have to be interpreted and understood to 'oil the wheels' of social organization and functioning, they also provide a huge repertoire of stimuli for learning. Mirror neurons are neurons that fire in response to performing an action (such as a gesture) and also fire in response to seeing another person perform the same action (see Chapter 1). The activation in mirror neurons 'reflects' the actions of another person (e.g. raising a hand) in the absence of the corresponding motor activity in the 'receiver' of the visual stimulus (i.e. the receiver's hand does not move but the neurons fire). Giacomo Rizzolatti and his colleagues have suggested that in humans (which he maintains is one of the few species that learns through imitation):[24]

- learning by imitation is the basis of human culture and adaptation;
- learning by imitation and the understanding of the actions of others is under-pinned by the neuro-physiological mechanism of the mirror neuron.[25]

That mirror neurons play a role in imitation and the way in which we understand the actions of others has significant implications for our understanding of non-conscious cognition and intuition. For example, research since has gone beyond the study of simple grasping movements and hand gestures and looked at quite complex motor behaviours. Scientists in Rizzolatti's lab have investigated the ways in which novice guitarists learn guitar chords through observation and imitation of expert guitarists. Using fMRI techniques they found:

- activation of mirror neurons in novices' brains when they were asked to observe experts' hand movements in forming guitar chords;
- new motor patterns formed for the actual playing of the chord which corresponded to the mirror neurons activated during observation.

Social learning is made possible by imitation and social interaction is enhanced by an intuitive understanding of the actions of others.

Much non-verbal communication (as aspect of social intuition) occurs without conscious effort and is under the control of the intuitive system rather than the rational system. As social cognitive neuroscientist Matt Lieberman has argued mirror neurons may play a particularly important role in these processes: 'there is evidence for a complex reciprocal non-verbal "dance" that occurs between interaction partners' the dynamics of which provide each partner with a basis for their judgement about an interaction.[26] Research into the role played by mirror neurons promises to be an exciting new avenue of investigation for researchers of unconscious cognition, implicit learning and intuition.

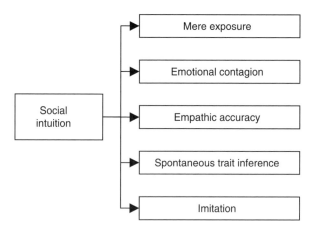

Figure 11.2 Components of social intuition.

After D.G. Myers, *Intuition: Its Powers and Perils* (New Haven: Yale, 2002).

Female intuition

In 1997 a report in a respected British newspaper ran the following story:

> Nature, not nurture, is responsible for feminine intuition and men's lack of tact scientists argue. The sensitive sex was born that way. And boys are oafish because they can't help it. Blame nature not nurture. The gene machine switches on feminine intuition long before birth. The same mechanism 'switches-off' in boy babies after conception, leaving them to grow up awkward, gauche and insensitive.[27]

The research that was being reported was carried out by David Skuse of London's Institute of Child Health and six medical and applied psychology colleagues. They were researching a human female disorder known as Turner's Syndrome in which all or part of one X chromosome is deleted. Intelligence is normal but social adjustment problems are common. Under normal circumstances females have two X chromosomes; males have an X and a Y. In Turner's syndrome females who have only one X chromosome derived their X from the paternal source – X^p, and some derived it from the maternal source – X^m. Eighty females with Turner's syndrome participated in Skuse's study; they differed in that 55 of them derived their X from their mother (X^m) and 25 from their father (X^p).

The parents of the Turners' Syndrome females and of age-matched normal male and female comparisons filled out a 'social cognition questionnaire' which assessed the child's social functioning (for example: 'awareness of other's feelings', 'does not pick up on body language', 'very demanding of people's time', etc.). The X^m girls were significantly less socially well-adjusted, whereas the X^p girls had significantly better verbal and higher-order executive functioning which exercises control over social interactions. Because males invariably inherit their single X chromosome from their mothers (X^m) the genetic locus for social adjustment would be silenced in boys.[28] These results were taken by the popular press to suggest that feminine intuition is genetically-based and moreover, that it comes from the X^p (i.e. paternal) chromosome rather than the X^m (i.e. maternal).

As might be expected the results caused a mini furore. For some, such as the newspaper 'agony aunt' Clare Rayner there was nothing new in any of this: 'We've always known that women are more verbally-gifted, nurturing and empathetic than men'; whilst the psychotherapist and writer Susie Orbach thought it 'completely preposterous. What this evidence describes is social reality in the West. Go and look at other cultures and you'll see intuition is the preserve of male elders [. . .] Gender roles are culturally prescribed – they've nothing to do with genetics'.[29] One unfortunate feature of the reporting of the research was that the contribution made by the environment in shaping social behaviours was 'underplayed almost to the point of omission'.[30] More-over, even casual scrutiny of the social cognition questionnaire that the researchers used reveals it to be more akin to a measure of EI (e.g. one question reads 'Does not realize when others are upset or angry') than of intuition as such.

What does other research tell us about female intuition? In a study involving almost one thousand participants and using a more focused measure of intuition (a short questionnaire called 'Faith in intuition') Seymour Epstein and his colleagues failed to observe any significant differences between males and females. Other studies have found small differences which in practical terms are insignificant.[31] If Skuse and his colleagues did find a genetic explanation for 'social cognition' as they defined it, perhaps it was for some facet of EI rather than 'general intuition' as we understand it. If there is a substantive gender difference in intuition it will probably require a more fine-grained approach to measuring the distinctions between different types of human intuition. The question also remains of whether or not 'female intuition', if it exists, is innate, a personality trait, a learned skill or a product of the social context. Researchers have argued that high interpersonal sensitiv-ity ('rapport') when two individuals are highly attuned can vary, being more pronounced at certain times, in particular situations or when deal-ing with specific people.[32] It is likely social intuition (including reading intentions and 'rapport') is a product of the interaction of non-conscious pattern recognition, somatic state activation, learning, experience and the social context rather than the product exclusively of genes or environment.

Leadership and intuition

Leadership is one of the 'buzz words' of management in the early twenty-first century. It is offered both as a contrast to what is often seen as the 'mundane drudgery' of management, and as a panacea to organizational and societal ills. Marry the *gravitas* of 'leadership' to the mystique of 'intuition' and a heady mix is formed. Leadership is a subtle process of mutual influence, and 'effective leadership' has been defined as that which produces actions that serve a set of values and purposes which are mutually embraced by the leader and the led.[33] To achieve this mutual-ity of purpose requires 'authenticity' on the part of the leader – a quality singled out by London Business School's Rob Goffee and Gareth Jones as one of the cardinal features of leadership. Authenticity by its very nature reflects aspects of a leader's 'in-side', of their 'inner-self' and their 'in-tuition':

> Authentic leaders remain focused on where they are going but never lose sight of where they came from. Highly attuned to their environments, they rely on an intuition born of formative, sometimes harsh experiences to understand the expectations and concerns of the people they seek to influence.[34]

In a similar vein the EI community argue that 'the smart guess' born of a 'life wisdom' in making business decisions is important for leaders in complex and uncertain business environments. The 'smart guess' enables charismatic, wise and transformational leaders to make what looks to others like a 'leap of faith' and takes them and their followers beyond the data[35] and into uncharted territories. Authenticity, honesty, integrity and wisdom are the raw materials which allow leaders to build the levels of trust and the strength of relationships which engage follower-ship. To make transformational leaps into the unknown requires the ability to anticipate events and make decisions on the basis of compressed and crystallized experience – an intuitive ability that accumulates with age.[36] That said, leadership which transforms individuals and institutions must be grounded in the moral foundations and the moral character of the leader.[37]

MORAL INTUITION: DON'T ASK ME WHY – I JUST KNOW IT'S WRONG!

Consider the following story:

> A family's pet dog, which was healthy and well-cared for, was killed by a car on the road outside their house. The house owners had heard that some people have been known to enjoy eating dog meat, and so being willing to experiment, they decided to try it out for themselves. They cooked their dog in a stew and ate it.[38]

Often when people from particular cultural backgrounds read vignettes like this their immediate reaction is a feeling of revulsion and disgust followed by moral condemnation; when asked to explain their moral judgement the response of 'don't ask me why I just know it's wrong!' is not uncommon. Read the vignette below and rate how morally wrong you feel the politician's behaviour is on a scale of one (low) to 10 (high):

> Member of Parliament Mr X frequently gives speeches condemning corruption and arguing for the reform of the financing of political parties and their election campaigns. But he is just trying to cover up the fact that he himself will take bribes from the tobacco lobby, and other special interest groups, to promote their legislation.

Social psychologists Thalia Wheatley and Jonathan Haidt gave this vignette to 64 highly-hypnotizable participants, half of whom were hypnotized to feel disgust when they read the innocuous word 'take' in the final sentence of the vignette. Having read through the 'politician' and five other vignettes, participants were asked to rate how morally wrong the people in the stories were. Participants for whom hypnotic disgust was absent (i.e. they weren't instructed to feel disgust at the word 'take') scored around 7.8 for the politician vignette, whereas participants where hypnotic disgust was present scored around 9.1.[39] When the results across all six vignettes were averaged out the ratings where induced hypnotic disgust was present were significantly higher (i.e. judged more immoral) than where hypnotic disgust was absent. When disgust is induced the direct link to moral indignation appears to be amplified.

By testing whether or not an arbitrarily-induced gut level response would be used to inform moral judgement the researchers were aiming to test if and how peoples' bodily reactions might affect their moral judgements. The researchers' interpretation was that people do 'listen to their gut' when judging moral transgressions. When Haidt and colleagues in a separate experiment used stories intended to elicit disgust but which were construed so that no plausible harm could be found (like the dog-eating vignette), they found that although participants agreed that nobody was harmed the actions of the people in the stories were nevertheless deemed, almost universally, to be very wrong.[40]

The Scottish philosopher David Hume (1711–1776) in his *Treatise of Human Nature* (1739/1740) argued that we are fundamentally creatures of instinct and habit and that our mental lives are dominated by passion over reason. It is our 'passionate' nature which enables us through the ability of 'sympathy' to share in the emotions we infer to be present in others.[41] In Hume's philosophy reason has a reduced but not unimportant role: 'Reason is, and ought only to be the slave of the passions, and can never pretend to any other office than to serve and obey them'. Hume acknowledged that his view 'may appear somewhat extraordinary' and thus 'it may not be improper to confirm it by some other "considerations" '.[42] Here is not the place to go into Hume's 'considerations', however almost 300 years after his birth, the workings of the 'intuitive mind' and somatic state activations are modern day 'considerations' which offer an explanation of why 'passions' should exert so strong a hold on moral judgment.

In the rationalist model of moral judgement a situation (such as eating your dead pet dog) may elicit a moral emotion, but a process of reasoning and reflection, weighing up the 'rights and wrongs' ('the dog was loved family pet', on the other hand 'nobody was harmed') leads to a judgement (e.g. 'it is wrong to eat your dog'). Jonathan Haidt offers an alternative to the rationalist model in which moral judgement is caused by quick 'moral intuitions' through which approval or disapproval is almost instantaneously invoked, followed (where necessary) by slower more effortful moral reasoning. In the case of the affectively-charged situation of dog-eating for example:

1   *Rationalist approach*: moral emotion may be an indirect input (A) – dashed line, Figure 11.3; *but* issues of harm, etc are weighed-up rationally and fairly (B); moral judgement (for example, indignation at 'dog eating') is arrived at (C).
2   *Intuitionist approach*: the situation elicits automatically and effortlessly a moral intuition that eating your dog is wrong (D); the judgement of moral indignation at the dog-eaters is arrived at (E); and arguments are constructed (for example: 'a loved family pet', 'dogs are intelligent animals', 'how could they do that?', etc.) to support the judgement already made by gut reaction (F).

In those situations where affect, such as disgust, is induced the intuitionist rather than the rationalist model holds sway; however, Haidt goes further to argue that, in keeping with dual-process theories, intuition is used for quick, economical and holistic everyday moral judgements.[43] In a sense he argues that intuitive moral judgement, not rational moral judgement, is the 'default setting', and the moral reasoning route served by System 2 (analytic) processes only works well under circumstances where the person has sufficient time, mental capacity and motivation, and they are without an *a priori* position or a relatedness motivation to defend. Moral judgements involve not only reason but affect also. Indeed, patients with damage to the VMPC exhibit what Damasio refers to as 'acquired sociopathy'[44]: the tendency not to have any somatic response to stimuli that evoke very strong SCRs in normal individuals. Pictures of earthquakes, gory accidents, and burning buildings are understood cognitively but elicit no feeling – these patients are

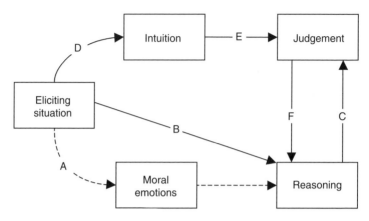

Figure 11.3 Simplified rationalist (A, B, C) and social intuitionist (D, E, F) models of moral judgement.

Adapted from J. Haidt, 'The emotional dog and its rationalist tail: a social intuitionist approach to moral judgement', *Journal of Personality and Social Psychology*, 1999, 76: 815.

able 'to know but not to feel'.[45] Somatic state activation it seems affects not only decision-making but moral judgement also. Neither reason nor 'gut feel' is slave to the other, but they are partners in human reasoning, judgement and action.

TAKE-AWAY

Key ideas

Unlike the feeling of an *emotion* for which the eliciting cause is usually obvious, the causes of feelings which arise as a result of intuitions are not so easily reasoned. The essence of any intuitive intelligence lies in *balancing* circumspection with risk. We need to: be *confident* that a hunch can be trusted; acknowledge that there are attendant *risks* and uncertainties; accept that intuitions (like analyses) are limited and fallible. The *evolutionary logic* behind social intuition is that those who could read social situations and motives accurately were more likely to survive, reproduce and pass on the capability for recognizing whether the 'stranger on the savannah' was a friend or foe. Moral judgements are not reasoned purely rationally, they are strongly influenced by affect, so much so that some psychologists have argued that that *intuitive moral judgement*, not rational moral judgement, is the 'default setting' and is used day-in, day-out for quick, economical and holistic moral judgements.

Intuition quote: Jonas Salk, discoverer of the polio vaccine

'Our subjective intuitional responses are more sensitive than our objective reasoned responses.'

Action points

Next time you're confronted by a tough decision and an intuition arises *spontaneously* let the gut feeling come in without any *attachment* to the outcome, ask yourself how much *certitude* does the intuitive judgement have; does it *resonate* with your deepest values?[46]

FURTHER READING

Myers, D.G., *Intuition: Its Powers and Perils*. New Haven: Yale 2002.

12 The intuitive ape

[. . .] it seems to me, that man with all his noble qualities, with sympathy which he feels for the most debased, with benevolence which extends not only to other men but to the humblest living creature, with his god-like intellect which has penetrated into the movements and constitution of the solar system – with all these exalted powers – Man still bears in his bodily frame the indelible stamp of his lowly origin.

(Charles Darwin, *The Descent of Man and Selection in Relation to Sex*,
London: John Murray, 1882, second edition, p.619)

MAIN IDEA

It is likely that human beings evolved the capacity to exercise intuitive judgement for a purpose which was advantageous to survival in their evolutionary past. Intuition continues to be an important and invaluable aspect of the way in which *Homo sapiens* functions in industrial and post-industrial societies.

Decision-makers in companies large and small, in organizations of every type, across languages and national cultures share in the experience of 'gut feeling' and testify to the value of informed intuition in solving judgemental problems in ill-structured or time-pressured situations. If intuition is so powerful and pervasive, what's nature's purpose – what advantages do non-conscious pattern recognition, somatic state activation and mental simulation confer? Can the brain be 'reverse-engineered' to figure out what gut feeling was designed to accomplish?[1] Why has evolution endowed *Homo sapiens* with intuition?

A VERY BRIEF HISTORY OF HUMAN EVOLUTION

The first members of the genus *Homo* (*Homo habilis*, or 'handy man') are thought to have emerged about 2 million years ago at the beginning of the Pleistocene epoch in what is now Tanzania. The oldest fossil evidence for anatomically modern humans, *Homo sapiens*, is currently about 160,000–195,000 years old from Ethiopia.[2] Between *Homo habilis* and *Homo sapiens* three important developments gathered pace: bipedalism, 'big brains' and sophistication of tools and their use.

The particularly upright stance ('striding bi-pedalism'[3]) that modern humans exhibit first appeared in *Homo erectus* about 1.8 million years ago (possibly as an adaptation for freeing the hands for tasks such as hunting and gathering, improved vision in the topography of East Africa, or reducing the body's exposure to heat from the tropical sun).[4] The first undisputed evidence for the deliberate manufacture of tools is to be found with *Homo habilis*; much later there was a burst of very sophisticated weaponry construction (for example, arrowheads and spearheads) around 50,000 years ago.[5] Brain size increased exponentially from the time of *Homo habilis* to the emergence of *Homo sapiens*. Compared to its direct ancestors and to the other great apes (chimpanzee, gorilla and orang utan) *Homo sapiens* has a gracile, lightly-built physique, a high domed cranium with a flat forehead, and a large brain space inside the skull.[6] The cranial capacity for *Homo sapiens* is about 1300 cubic centimetres (compared to around 400cm^3 for our Australopithecine[7] ancestors and modern chimpanzees). *Homo sapiens* has a smaller brain size than did the Neanderthals (*Homo neanderthalensis*, cranial capacity of around 1500 cm^3), and it is something of a mystery as to why this species became extinct about 30,000 years ago.

Ancestral *Homo sapiens* were the most gregarious of the great apes, probably living in quite large extended families of two to three dozen individuals. The fact that there is a strong relationship between brain size and size of a primate's social group[8] suggests that the increase in brain size witnessed in the evolution from the Australopithecines to *Homo sapiens* was related to changes in the complexity of human social organization and relationships.[9] As well as being adapted to cope with the threats from their natural environment and find food, water and shelter, *Homo sapiens* was also adapted to the world of social groupings which hunted and gathered cooperatively, ate communally and camped together, and who from time to time would interact with other social groups in their immediate environment.[10]

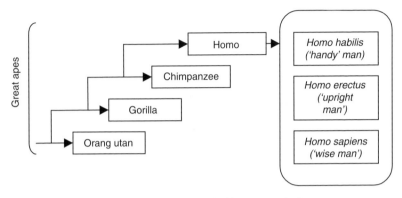

Figure 12.1 Highly simplified 'family tree' of human evolution.

COGNITION AND EVOLUTION

A number of evolutionary psychologists have argued that progress in the social sciences has been hampered by the assumption that humans are born as 'blank slates' predisposed to nothing and onto which social and cultural values are subsequently etched, and which then determine behaviour.[11] The psychologist Gregory J. Feist argues that the problem with this view is that it is 'probably wrong' because:

> Empirically there are now thousands of studies in psychology, neuroscience, linguistics, anthropology, and cognitive science that support the evolutionary view that the human brain structure is not vague and general at birth but rather consists of many specific evolved mechanisms designed to solve problems.[12]

The neuro-philosopher Patricia Smith Churchland has argued that an important purpose of the development of cognition (the faculty of perceiving, knowing and conceiving) in our species' evolutionary past was to enable individuals to make predictions that guided decisions, which in turn may have enhanced their chances of survival. Evolution is driven by random mutations, the majority of which turn out to be disadvantageous in a particular environmental setting. However, where a mutation turns out to be advantageous it may increase the individual's chances of survival and the opportunity to reproduce and thereby pass on its adaptive features to its offspring via its genes.

As far as cognitive functioning is concerned the mutation which led

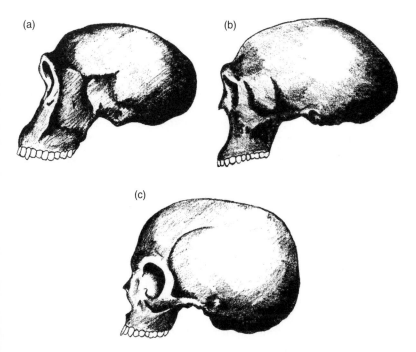

Figure 12.2 Reconstruction drawings of the skulls (lower jaw absent):
(a) *Homo habilis*; (b) *H. erectus*; (c) *H. sapiens*.

to the capability to make predictions turned out to confer a net advantage – in Churchland's words it enabled the individual to be 'predictively adoit' rather than 'predictively clumsy'. The advantages conferred by 'predictive adroitness' in the environment in which our ancestors found themselves created the opportunity for reproduction (i.e. they did not starve, nor were killed by enemies or eaten by predators) and the passing on of the genetic material which conferred this competitive edge.[13] Prediction in relation both to the physical environment and the social world would have been an essential requirement for survival. As a social species, *Homo sapiens* has evolved not only to recognize members of its own species and its own kin but also to be able to predict their behaviour in a variety of situations based upon analyses, insights[14] and intuitions. To predict requires conscious awareness not only of the future (to see into) and the past (to reflect upon),[15] but also of the positive or negative feeling states in our bodies that arise as a result of somatic state activation. Consciousness therefore not only allows us our own 'crystal ball', it also allows us to 'hear' the 'alarm bells' that our unconscious mind 'sounds off' in the body.

Homo sapiens' cognitive inheritance includes implicit perception, learning and memory systems, the original functions of which were to monitor the environment for regularities and reliable relationships between phenomena and to encode these into patterned thinking[16], particularly in social settings[17]. In all likelihood this capability allowed our ancestors to quickly recognize similar patterns in similar situations (with cognitive economy and at great speed), make predictions (especially about others' intentions) and take decisions (informed by the signals from positive or negative somatic markers but with a bias toward evading threats) that enhanced their chances of survival and reproduction. The implicit memory system[18] tends to be automatic rather than controlled, it is context-specific, is not easily tapped into through introspection, and is robust over time and in the face of psychological disorder. Some of the biases which we encountered in Chapter 6 occur as a result of the speed and rigidity of the intuitive system. When it does manifest in conscious awareness it is often in the form of insights and intuitions. Seymour Epstein has speculated that this implicit 'experiential' system is not only older in evolutionary terms than the rational system but that it may, unlike the rational system, be present in non-human animals also.

In keeping with the claims of many cognitive scientists (i.e. that most thought is unconscious) Pawel Lewicki and his colleagues have argued that the 'real work' in human cognition is done at a level to which we do not have conscious access, and that this work is concerned with much more than low-level 'housekeeping' operations. This non-conscious cognitive machinery, which is 'whirring away behind the scenes' without our being aware of it, can be directly involved in high-level operations such as interpretation and inference, things traditionally associated with conscious control.[19] And as Guy Claxton reminds us, the contents of conscious awareness can be likened to the dashboard of a car which shows only the read-outs of processes which are going on 'under the bonnet'. The 'read-outs' are the things that the brain, during the moment we are conscious of them, happens to be treating as novel, useful or important[20] and therefore come under the spotlight of consciousness.

The downside is that these non-conscious processes often have been automatized through extensive learning, experience and practice,[21] to the extent that they may be relatively inflexible and applied in similar ways across contexts even when it's inappropriate to do so. One of the advantages of the conscious control which the later addition of the rational mind endowed *Homo sapiens* with was that it allowed cognition to be adapted quickly to changed situations.[22] The evolutionarily more recent rational analytical system has been described as a 'long-leash' system which allows humans to pursue their own consciously- and rationally-determined goals. As a result they are able to exercise what Jonathan Evans refers to as a 'higher level of rationality' in reasoning and decision-making[23] rather than being 'slavish vehicles of their genes'.[24]

In addition to having conscious and non-conscious problem-solving 'machinery', most human beings also acquire in the course of their development a 'theory of mind' with which they can instinctively and intuitively understand that other human beings have minds of their own and that the having of such a mind is not unlike what they themselves experience.[25] A 'theory of mind' develops at around four years of age and allows one human being to make inferences about another human mind's intentions. Without a theory of mind social behaviour can be disrupted (for example, people with severe autistic disorders are impaired in their ability to understand mental states) and social cooperation may break down.[26] A lack of the instinctive and intuitive ability to have insights into the minds of others can result in 'mind-blindness'.[27]

One possible location for the mechanisms which allow us to make assumptions about others' intentions may be the mirror neurons which are to be found in the brain's prefrontal cortex and which were first identified by Giuseppe di Pellegrino, Gaicomo Rizzolatti and colleagues[28] in the brains of monkeys (see also Chapter 1). These are neurons which fire in response to the actions of others and may help an individual to map meanings associated with its own actions (for example a gesture or expression) onto the actions and intentions of others.[29] Mirror neurons may have evolved to assist *Homo sapiens* in intuitively making assumptions and predictions about how other members of its species are likely to behave on the basis of non-verbal signals.

More generally the neural circuitry which underlies somatic state activation (ventromedial prefrontal region (VM) → amygdala → body → somatosensory/insular cortices → brain stem nuclei) enacts a somatic state which influences, consciously or non-consciously, a decision-maker's behavioural choices (Bechara and his colleagues call this the 'body loop', see Chapter 9).[30] This system operates across a range of decision-making situations affecting the quality of decisions in daily life and therefore does not appear to be narrowly confined to a small set of decision-making tasks. Once such an emotion has been expressed and experienced at least once it becomes 'learned' to the extent that the body can then be 'by-passed' and the insular/somatosensory cortices activated directly giving a fainter image ('as-if' we had a gut feeling). The circuitry of the body and as-if loops may be part of a set of general adaptations to support intuitive decision-making and learned intuitive responses across variety of domains.

INTUITIVE NATURE OR NURTURING INTUITION?

Informed intuition is the outcome of the interaction between non-conscious pattern recognition and somatic state activation. It assists with the taking of decisions and reaching certain types of judgements rapidly and accurately without conscious awareness of the processes involved. This capability to intuitively make predictions that guide successful behaviours may have been one of many advantageous capabilities that random mutations conferred upon our ancestors in our evolutionary past. Those who were less well adapted to their physical and social environments died out. For example, intuition would have equipped our ancestors us to recognize a dangerous 'stranger on the savannah' as a foe rather than as a friend on the basis of 'thin slices' of behaviour.[31] This capability has been selected for through evolutionary mechanisms, and helps us to infer, predict and decide in a wide range of social settings and situations.

In the modern world, even if social intuitions are part of a genetic inheritance, experts don't come 'pre-loaded' with the knowledge and skill which enables them to come to speedy, accurate judgements. An expert's 'intuitive grasp' operates via non-conscious pattern recognition acquired through the workings both of the rational system and of non-conscious cognitive processes such as (implicit perception and learning) and the 'compressing' of experience. Experienced decision-makers' judgements are guided by pattern recognition and somatic state activation, and are supported by mental simulation. This is manifested most typically in the adroit ways in which experienced decision-makers are able to solve problems quickly and with little apparent effort. If nature provided the hardware upon which such intuitive judgements were able to 'run', then this hardware is probably the same in the *Homo sapiens* who roamed the savannahs of the Pleistocene as it is in those who now inhabit the floor of the London Stock Exchange. If informed intuition works equally well on the floor of the Stock Exchange as it did on the savannah perhaps non-conscious pattern recognition and somatic state activation are general adaptations. General adaptations are a set of rules that govern behaviour. These rules can be applied differently in the different settings which a decision-maker can find themself and result in an almost infinite range of behaviours[32] co-determined by biology and the environment.

If human beings' potential to non-consciously recognize patterns, experience somatic state activation and engage in mental simulation is an outcome of evolution, what we intuit and how we act is shaped by our experiences and learning, and the social and cultural settings which we inhabit. To use a computer analogy: perhaps nature provided the cognitive and affective neural circuitry, whilst nurturing (provided by learning, experiences, society and culture) 'uploaded' the software. This does not preclude the possibility of some 'software' (such as 'cheater detection') being 'pre-loaded'. As the psychologist David Myers argues nature and nurture 'co-evolve'; for example, evolutionary pressures may have selected for female abilities in decoding non-verbal expressions (one facet of social intuition), but the outcome of a gene-culture co-evolution has meant that not only were females more likely to be better than males at certain aspects of social intuition, they were 'expected', 'assumed' and 'supposed' to be so.[33] Similarly, the dynamic executive at the head of a business empire might have a less kudos if they did not meet shareholders' or society's expectations as someone who can 'manage from the gut'.

Homo sapiens is a habitual 'classifier' most often on the basis of physical appearance;[34] in doing so we reduce complexity and the demands upon our scarce cognitive resources. Moreover, the faster our ancestors were able to make these categorizations in threatening situations and err on the side of caution, the better – the more likely their survival was; as Nigel Nicholson has noted 'sitting around doing calculus was not a recipe for a long and fertile life'[35] on the savannahs. However, if we are hardwired to merely 'categorize' intuitively, then many of the categories we employ rather than being determined, are fluid, social constructions over which we are able to exercise our free will and our 'longer leash' conscious reasoning processes.[36]

RATIONALITY RE-RECONSIDERED

When asked to judge the probability of the two events: (A) the occurrence of an earthquake in California causing a flood in which more than 1000 people drown, and (B) the occurrence of a massive flood somewhere in North America in which more than 1000 people drown, heuristics and biases researchers have found that people tend to judge Event A (the conjunction of flood and earthquake) as more likely than event B (the flood alone).[37] In fact the probability of event A is necessarily lower than event B (see Chapter 6). The (logically-flawed) line of reasoning is based on a vivid mental prototype of a region of the world (California) which is earthquake-prone (because of the well-known San Andreas fault-line) and a mechanism in which earthquakes can cause tidal waves (*tsunamis*). The philosophers Lakoff and Johnson are unsurprised by this because the concrete, prototypical reasoning which gives the 'wrong' judgement in the earthquake (and the Linda) problem are quick cognitive mechanisms which have evolved over the course of human evolution to allow *Homo sapiens* to function as effectively and efficiently as possible in everyday life. In their view to not use non-conscious, prototypical reasoning would be irrational; moreover it's a good thing that we don't reason exclusively using the probability theory that would enable us to get the earthquake and Linda problem 'right' because this type of conscious reasoning is of limited value and largely inappropriate to many of the situations we find ourselves in.[38]

In management we tend to concern ourselves with rational processes (as embodied in the traditional 'define', 'diagnose', 'design' and 'decide' model[39] of decision-making). However, as well as being concerned with the *process* of rationality the limits of which were reconsidered in Chapter 2, rationality may also be reconsidered in terms of its *purpose*, or 'rationality of response'. A 'rationality of response' involves thinking or acting 'in a way that maximises the attainment of your own goals'[40]. Arguably rationality of purpose is aspired to not only in *Homo sapiens*' analytical system, but in its intuitive system also. If intuition evolved to assist the organism in achieving its goals then at the core of informed intuitive thinking is 'rationality of response' as a means of achieving a given purpose:

> It was the experiential [intuitive] system, after all, that enabled human beings to survive during their long period of evolution. Long before there was probability theory, risk assessment and decision analysis, there were intuition, instinct and gut feeling to tell us whether an animal was safe to approach or whether the water was safe to drink.[41]

It is only with human cultural and technological progress that, in the view of Paul Slovic and others, analytical 'tools' were invented to boost the rationality of our intuitive thinking. A number of threads run through this argument: in business and management, at least overtly, analysis has been privileged over intuition; rationality and analysis are often taken to be synonymous; rationality and intuition are portrayed as being at antithetical; a false corollary of this is that intuition is 'irrational'. While intuition may not be 'analytical' it is not 'irrational'.

There are echoes here of three precepts set out by Herbert Simon in *Administrative Behavior*. First, Simon assumed that the processes of conscious and non-conscious judgement 'were essentially the same',[42] namely that they drew upon factual premises and value premises (we might say they both had rationality of purpose). This is one of the basic assumptions of 'intuition-as-expertise' or 'intuition-as-non-conscious pattern recognition'. Second, the non-rational intuitive decisions of experts must not be confused with the irrational decisions in which intense emotion may precipitate ('intuitive excess' – see Chapter 8, Figure 8.5) or the uninformed intuitive decisions which a novice is likely to make. Finally, it bears repetition, good intuitive judgements 'are [according to Simon at least] simply analyses frozen into habit and into the capacity for rapid response through the recognition of familiar kinds of situations' (note that Simon does not say 'rationality frozen into habit' but 'analyses frozen into habit'). There may therefore be a 'rationality-of-sorts' in intuition as well as in analysis; it is the kind of rationality which differs in each case.

There has been general trend towards embracing affect within the scientific study of cognition[43] and along with this there has been the acceptance that affect is a vital component of human decision-making. As Nigel Nicholson has noted employees are all to often urged to dispense with emotions and substitute analytical techniques like 'decision trees' and 'algorithms'; he argued that the dispensing with feelings can never work because emotions evolved to aid *Homo sapiens*' survival and as such our 'emotional radar' is always active and can never be fully 'turned off'.[44] Nicholson describes the intuitive system and its processes as merely a 'gift out of place' which evolved in *Homo sapiens* to deal with the complexities of the natural world, but which our species now needs to harness to cope with the complexities of dealing with our own kind in post-industrial society.[45] The challenge faced by *Homo sapiens* in the twenty-first century is to reconcile the mind's analytical and intuitive intelligences in the context of a sustainable modern world.[46]

A few very rough calculations illustrate the fact that modern humans have occupied a small proportion, about $1/10^{th}$ (10 per cent), of the time that the genus *Homo* itself has existed (195,000 out of 2,000,000 years); the period during which sophisticated tools have existed (from spear heads to space shuttles) is a minuscule $1/40^{th}$ (two and half per cent) of the existence of the genus. The time that has elapsed since the beginning of industrial revolution occupies a vanishingly small 1/10,000 (0.01 per cent) of the period since the first big-brained hominids appeared. Against this backcloth consider the following report which appeared in the *The Times* on 3 February, 2007.

> In February 2007 the Inter-governmental Panel on Climate Change (IPCC) released its bleakest and most confident assessment yet of the science behind global warming. Its report, prepared by more than 2500 scientists form 113 countries, predicted that average temperature are likely to rise by 4°C by the end of the century and that human activities were 'very likely' responsible.

In the bigger picture of the evolutionary path followed by the genus *Homo*, how effective has that evolutionary 'Johnny-come-lately',[47] the rational system been at the level of the whole ecosystem and its viability? Compelling evolutionary arguments for the utility of *Homo sapiens*' intuitive system are to be found in the work of Seymour Epstein and Rosemary Pacini. In their view the rational system's evolutionary history is relatively brief, but given that we live in era in which technology and industrialisation (the manifestation of rationality *par excellence*) threatens not only humanity but the whole ecosystem, the long term adaptability in biological terms of the rational system has some question marks hanging over it.[48] A salutary thought perhaps is that 195,000 years (roughly one four thousandth of a per cent of the period of the Earth's existence) is not very long at all in the geological time frame for a mutation to prove maladaptive by destroying the habitability of an organism's own environment. Epstein and Pacini argue that, by contrast, the 'experiential system' (what I and others would call the 'intuitive system') has a much longer evolutionary history and that it has proven itself to be an efficient system, placing minimal demands upon cognitive resources. It enabled successful adaptation to the savannah-like environment in which *Homo* evolved and thrived and from which it spread over a period of two thousand millennia. The question which remains is 'what place does intuition occupy in the modern world which *Homo sapiens* created and finds itself in?'

CONCLUSION

The ancestors of *Homo sapiens* who hunted and gathered during the Pleistocene epoch on the plains of what is now East Africa would have been constantly confronted with decisions and dilemmas: 'is this stranger a friend or foe?', 'is this a good place to hunt?', 'what are their motives?', 'is this sick infant going to die?', 'can water be found over there?', or 'is this person a viable and willing mate?' In the question of 'what to do?' our ancestors, like ourselves, most likely had the sometimes disconcerting experience of the combined processes of nonconscious pattern recognition and somatic state activation beating their conscious minds to the decision-making finishing line 'hands down'. These processes helped to minimize threats and maximize chances of survival.

Fast-forward one hundred millennia to modern times. Many CEOs in major companies claim to have made multi-million dollar decisions based on their 'gut instincts'. Nor is this behaviour confined to senior executives in multi-national companies who have the power to wield intuition: composers, artists and scientists, teachers and doctors, firefighters, neonatal nurses, HR managers, chief financial officers, students, biomedical and aerospace scientists, entrepreneurs, and inventors across organizations and national cultures testify to the role that intuition plays in creative, entrepreneurial, professional, social and moral judgements. When 'gut feelings' and 'hunches' are accurately informed by prior experience, learning and feedback, the integration of pattern recognition, somatic state activation and mental simulation can indeed confer upon *Homo sapiens* an adroitness for trusting 'to ourselves and our own intuitions'[49] and for minimizing risks and maximizing opportunities. Intuition research is in its infancy, and there is a multitude of questions to be identified and explored using the theories and methods of traditional psychology as well as the emerging insights from newer areas such as evolutionary psychology and cognitive neuroscience, but that said there is also ancient wisdom which teaches us that: 'what we are today comes from the thoughts of yesterday; our present thoughts build our life of tomorrow: our life is the creation of our mind'.[50]

FURTHER READING

Claxton, G.L., *The Wayward Mind: An Intimate History of the Unconscious.* London: Abacus 2005.
Dunbar, R., *The Human Story.* London: Faber, 2004.

Notes

1 The view from inside

1 Adapted from M. Boucouvalas, 'The concept and the experience', in R. Davis-Floyd and P.S. Arvidson (eds) *Intuition: The Inside Story* (New York: Routledge, 1997, pp. 3–18), p. 3.

2 R. Rowan, *The Intuitive Manager* (Aldershot: Wildwood House, 1987) pp. 7–8.

3 http://www.fbi.gov/publications/leb/2006/sept2006/sept2006leb.htm (accessed 09/02/07).

4 http://www.northwestern.edu/newscenter/stories/2007/02/romantic.html; *The Times: Body and Soul*, 'Love in the fast lane', 10/02/2007; P.W. Eastwick, E.J. Finkel, D. Mochon and D. Ariely, 'Selective vs. unselective romantic desire: not all reciprocity is created equal', *Psychological Science*, 2007 (in press).

5 Latin: *intueri* [in-*tueri* (look)]. See: *The Oxford Encyclopaedic English Dictionary*, edited by J.M. Hawkins and R. Allen (Oxford: Clarendon Press, 1991) p. 745.

6 I am grateful to Erella Shefy (Israel), Ioanna Theodoulou (Cyprus), Dr George Papageorgiou (Surrey), Dr. YingFei Gao (China) Victoria Eichorn (Germany) and Dr. Laura Constanzo (Italy) for these helpful insights.

7 L.A. Burke and M.K. Miller, 'Taking the mystery out of intuitive decision-making', *Academy of Management Executive*, 1999, 13(4): 91–99.

8 D. Isenberg, 'How senior managers think', in W.H. Agor (ed.) *Intuition in Organisations: Leading and Managing Productively* (Newbury Park, CA: Sage Publications, 1989) pp. 91–110.

9 J. Parikh, F. Neubauer and A.G. Lank, *Intuition: The New Frontier in Management* (Oxford: Blackwell Business, 1994) p. 57.

10 *Blink* by Malcolm Gladwell topped bestseller lists in 2005. George van Dearborn writing in the prestigious scientific journal *Psychological Review* declared in an article entitled simply 'Intuition' that 'there is no acceptable reason for denying that this popular concept, intuition, is a live one [. . .], worthy therefore of at least brief scientific discussion' – the date was 1916.

11 G.P. Hodgkinson, J. Langan-Fox and E. Sadler-Smith, 'Intuition: a fundamental bridging construct in the behavioural sciences', *British Journal of Psychology*, 2008 (in press).

12 A. Moskowski, *Conversations with Einstein*, translated by Henry L. Bose (London: Sidgwick and Jackson, 1972).

13 J. Welch and S. Welch, *Winning* (London: Harper Collins, 2006) pp. 63, 83–4 and 72.

14 For example: M. Sinclair and N. Ashkanasy, 'Intuition: myth or a decision-making tool?', *Management Learning*, 2005, 36: 353–70.

15 P.S. Churchland, *Brain-wise: Studies in Neurophilosophy* (Cambridge, MA: Bradford Book MIT Press, 2002) p. 48.

16 Ibid.

17 A.S. Reber, *Implicit Learning and Tacit Knowledge: An Essay on the Cognitive Unconscious* (New York: Oxford University Press, 1993).

18 G. Rizzolatti and L. Craighero, 'The mirror neuron system', *Annual Review of Neuroscience*, 2004, 27: 169–92.

19 M. Eysenck, *Simply Psychology* (Hove: Psychology Press, 1996).

20 T.D. Wilson, *Strangers to Ourselves: Discovering the Adaptive Unconscious* (Cambridge, MA.: Belknap) p. 21.

21 G. Lakoff and M. Johnson, *Philosophy in the Flesh: The Embodied Mind and its Challenge to Western Thought* (New York: Basic Books, 1999) pp. 10–13.

22 Positivism is the theory that every rationally justifiable assertion is scientific-ally verifiable or capable of logical or mathematical proof; in the words of Scottish Philosopher David Hume (1711–76) we should ask of any 'volume' [argument]: 'Does it contain any abstract reasoning concerning quantity or number?'; 'Does it contain any experimental reasoning concerning matter of fact or existence?'. If the answer to these questions is 'no' we should 'commit it then to the flames: for it can contain nothing but sophistry and illusion'.

23 E. Bonabeau, 'Don't trust your gut', *Harvard Business Review*, 2003, 81(5): 116–23.

24 The Nobel prize-winner Herbert Simon's (1916–2001) path-breaking work on the concept of 'bounded rationality' was first published in the 1940s. See: H.A. Simon, *Administrative Behaviour* (New York, NY: Macmillan, 1947).

25 'The elephant in the room' is an English figure of speech which refers to an issue, problem or question that many people are aware of but which is ignored (an elephant would be very conspicuous in any normal room). The reluc-tance to discuss a problem, issue or question may serve only to reinforce the denial of its existence.

26 D. Cappon, 'The anatomy of intuition', *Psychology Today*, 1993, May/June: 40–5 and 86–94.

27 The ideal of perfect knowledge as a foundation for an all-powerful rational-ity was encapsulated in the French astronomer Laplace's notion of the fic-tional super-intelligence or *demon* which is a 'secularised version of God, knows everything about the past and present, and can deduce the future with certitude'. See: G. Gigerenzer, 'Bounded and rational', in R.J. Stainton (ed.) *Contemporary Debates in Cognitive Science* (Oxford: Blackwell, 2006) p. 116.

28 G.P. Hodgkinson and P.R. Sparrow, *The Competent Organization: A Psy-chological Analysis of the Strategic Management Process* (Buckingham: Open University Press, 2002); M.R. Louis and R.I. Sutton 'Switching cognitive gears: from habits of mind to active thinking', *Human Relations*, 1991, 44: 55–76.

29 The French painter Henri Matisse dreamt of 'an art of balance, of purity and serenity . . . a soothing, calming influence on the mind' (1908). E. Knowles

302   *Notes*

(ed.) *Oxford Dictionary of Quotations* (Oxford: Oxford University Press, 1999) p. 501.

30 M.A. Boden, *The Creative Mind: Myths and Mechanisms* (London: Routledge, 2004) p. 31.

31 Cartesian (i.e. René Descartes') dualism: the human mind is separate from and independent of the human body. See Lakoff and Johnson, op. cit., p. 5.

32 Ibid.

33 M. Ray and R. Myers, *Creativity in Business* (New York, NY: Doubleday, 1989).

34 http://www.the-intuitive-self.org (accessed 11/02/07).

35 P.M. Senge, *The Fifth Discipline: The Art and Practice of the Learning Organisation* (London: Century, 1990) pp. 167–8.

36 P.Wright, 'Strategies to overcome information overload', *Strategic Communication Management*, 1998, October/November: 10–14.

37 D. McCormick, 'Hooked on a feeling', *Money Management*, 2006, 2 November: 20–2.

38 http://www.boeing.com/news/frontiers/archive/2006/august/ts_sf09.pdf (accessed 07/01/07).

39 http://www.virgingalactic.com/ (accessed 11/01/07).

40 Interview: 'King bean', *Your Company*, 1998, April/May, 8(3).

41 See W.H. Agor (ed.), *Intuition in Organisations: Leading and Managing Productively* (Newbury Park, CA.: Sage Publications, 1989); L.A. Burke and M.K. Miller, 'Taking the mystery out of intuitive decision-making', *Academy of Management Executive*, 1999, 13(4): 91–9; J. Parikh, *Intuition: The New Frontier of Management* (Oxford: Blackwell Business, 1994).

42 G. Pappas, 'George Berkley', in S.M. Emanuel (ed.) *The Blackwell Guide to the Modern Philosophers: From Descartes to Nietzsche* (Oxford: Blackwell, 2001) p. 141.

43 *de facto*: in fact.

44 T. Maunter (ed.), *Penguin Dictionary of Philosophy* (London: Penguin Books, 1997) p. 258.

45 E. Sosa and J. van Cleve, 'Thomas Reid', in S.M. Emanuel (ed.) *The Blackwell Guide to the Modern Philosophers: From Descartes to Nietzsche* (Oxford: Blackwell, 2001) p. 188.

46 R. Bowie, *Ethical Studies* (Cheltenham: Nelson Thornes, 2004) pp. 67–8.

47 R.H. Popkin and A. Stroll, *Philosophy* (Oxford: Butterworth-Heinemann, 1996) pp. 141–2.

48 *The Stanford Encyclopaedia of Philosophy*, http://plato.stanford.edu/entries/plato-metaphysics/ (accessed 31/12/06).

49 T. Maunter (ed.), *The Penguin Dictionary of Philosophy* (London: Penguin Books, 1996) p. 426.

50 J. Harvey, *Music and Inspiration* (London: Faber, 1999) p. 3.

51 Ibid. (emphases added)

52 S. Walsh, *Igor Stravinsky: A Creative Spring – Russia and France, 1882–1934* (London: Jonathan Cape, 1999).

53 I. Stravinsky, *Apropos of Le Sacre: Recorded Commentary by Igor Stravinsky About the History of a Musical Landmark*, Colombia Records Inc.: USA (CBS-72054), 1960.

54 H. Carpenter, *Benjamin Britten: A Biography* (London: Faber and Faber, 1992) pp. 200–1.

55 F. E. Vaughan, *Awakening Intuition* (New York: Doubleday, 1979) p. 4.

56 M. Tippett, 'Aspects of belief', in M. Bowen (ed.) *Tippett on Music* (Oxford: Clarendon Press, 1995) p. 242.

57 K. Popper, *Conjectures and Refutations* (London: Routledge and Kegan Paul, 1963) p. 47. Cited in B. Magee, *Popper* (London: Fontana/Collins) p. 34.

58 From the Sanskrit word *mándala* meaning 'disc'.

59 C.G. Jung ed., *Man and his Symbols* (London: Penguin Books, 1964) p. 242.

60 M. Kemp, 'Kemp's conclusions', *Nature*, 1998, 392: 875–6.

61 'Spiral formations' are used by Don Beck and his colleagues as the bases of the concept of 'spiral dynamics' which Beck and Cowan describe as 'the forces inside the human spirals that wind through individual minds, drive organisations to new plateaus, and push societies to evolve through layers of complexity'. See: D.E. Beck and C.C Cowan, *Spiral Dynamics: Mastering Values, Leadership and Change* (Oxford: Blackwell, 1996) p. 27.

62 A. Moskowski, *Conversations with Einstein*, trans. Henry L. Bose, Sidgwick and Jackson (London, 1972) p. 96.

63 In the field of music the ability to improvise is not at all a naïve skill; it represents a very high level of proficiency founded upon extensive learning and practice. Beethoven and Bach as well as being consummate musicians and composers were also reputed to be outstanding improvisers because of the keyboard skills they had acquired. Similarly, jazz musicians can improvise convincingly and well only after they have acquired a very high level of technical command of their instrument.

64 Cited in H. Gardner, *Frames of Mind: The Theory of Multiple Intelligences* (New York: BasicBooks, 1983) p. 148.

65 F.E. Vaughan, *Awakening Intuition* (New York: Doubleday, 1979) p. 73.

66 E.H. Monsay, 'Intuition in the development of scientific theory and practice', in R. Davis-Floyd and P.S. Arvidson (eds) *Intuition: The Inside Story* (Routledge: New York, 1997) p. 105.

67 Ibid.

68 H. Gruber, 'Insight and affect in the history of science', in R.J. Sternberg and J.E. Davidson (eds) *The Nature of Insight* (Cambridge, MA: MIT Press, 1995) pp. 414–15.

69 C.I. Barnard, *The Functions of the Executive* (Cambridge: Harvard University Press, 1938/1968) p. 305.

70 Barnard, op. cit., p. 306.

71 Barnard, op. cit., p. 284.

72 http://www.macvideo.co.uk/downloads/Steve%20Speaks[1].qxd.pdf (accessed 18/01/07).

73 P.M. Senge, *The Fifth Discipline: The Art and Practice of the Learning Organisation* (London: Century, 1990) p. 168.

74 P. Senge, C.O. Scharmer, J. Jaworksi and B.S. Flowers, *Presence: Exploring Profound Change in People, Organisations and Society* (London: Nicholas Brealey Publishing, 2005) p. 87.

75 R.W. Revans, *The Origins and Growth of Action Learning* (Bromley: Chartwell-Bratt, 1982) p. 10. Action learning relies on facilitating inquiry that enables managers to ask insightful questions about real world 'here-and-now' problems in order to move towards their resolution. Action learning is a method of collaborative reflection, inquiry and learning. See: E. Sadler-Smith, *Learning and Development for Managers: Perspectives from Research and Practice* (Oxford: Blackwell, 2006) pp. 190–3.

76 D.A. Schön, *The Reflective Practitioner: How professional Think in Action* (Aldershot: Gower, 1983).
77 Ibid., p. 17.
78 J. Furlong, 'Intuition and the crisis in teacher professionalism', in T. Atkinson and G. Claxton (eds) *The Intuitive Practitioner: On the Value of Not Always Knowing What One is Doing* (Buckingham: Open University Press, 2000) p. 19.
79 S.H. Davis and P.B. Davis, *The Intuitive Dimensions of Administrative Decision-making* (Lanham: Scarecrow, 2003) p. 168.
80 D.A. Schön, *The Reflective Practitioner: How Professional Think in Action* (Aldershot: Gower, 1983) p. 49.
81 Ibid.
82 P. Benner, C.A. Tanner and C.A. Chesla, *Expertise in Nursing Practice: Caring, Clinical Judgement and Ethics* (New York: Springer, 1996) p. 10.
83 J. Dewey, 1960, p. 132, cited in P. Benner, C.A. Tanner and C.A. Chesla, *Expertise in Nursing Practice: Caring, Clinical Judgement and Ethics* (New York: Springer, 1996) p. 269.
84 H.H.I. McCutcheon, and J. Pincombe 'Intuition: an important tool in the practice of nursing', *Journal of Advanced Nursing*, 2001, 35: 346.
85 J. Cioffi, 'Heuristics, servants to intuition, in clinical decision-making', *Journal of Advanced Nursing*, 1997, 26: 205.
86 Buddhism is a philosophy which originated in the teachings of Siddhartha Gautama in India in the 5th century BC. Gautama attained enlightenment at the age of 35 after which he was referred to as Buddha ('the enlightened one'). A fundamental understanding in Buddhism is that 'All mental states have mind as their forerunner, mind is their chief and they are mind-made.' See: W.S. Rahula, *What the Buddha Taught* (Bedford: Gordon Fraser, 1958). Selections 1 and 2 from *The Dhammapda*, p. 125. James Austin is a neurologist who has integrated a scientific understanding of the brain and its functioning with Zen Buddhist theory and practice; see: J.H. Austin, *Zen and the Brain* (Cambridge, MA: MIT Press, 1998).
87 Or *viypashyana* (Sanskrit).
88 S.A. Goenka, 'Moral conduct, concentration and wisdom', in S. Bercholz and S.C. Kohn (eds) *The Buddha and his Teachings* (Boston, MA: Shambala, 1993) pp. 96–121.
89 F.J. Varela, E. Thompson and E. Rosch, *The Embodied Mind* (Cambridge, MA: MIT Press, 1991) p. 255.
90 Sogyal Ringpoche, *The Tibetan Book of Living and Dying* (London: Rider, 2002) p. 53.
91 When mental objects such as thoughts, ideas, emotions or recollections come into contact with the mind sensations arise and these are accompanied by corresponding sensations within the body. See: Goenka, op. cit., p. 115.
92 F. Vaughan, *Awakening Intuition* (New York: Anchor Books/Doubleday, 1979).
93 S.A. Goenka, op. cit.
94 See: www.vri.dhamma.org
95 F.J. Varela, E. Thompson and E. Rosch, *The Embodied Mind: Cognitive Science and Human Experience* (Cambridge, MA: MIT Press, 1991) p. 22.
96 C. Laughlin, 'The nature of intuition: a neuro-psychological approach', in

R. Davis-Floyd and P.S. Arvidson (eds) *Intuition: The Inside Story* (Routledge: New York, 1997) pp. 19.

97 A shaman is a person in certain traditional cultures who it is claimed has access to and influence in the spiritual world and who is empowered through trance-like states to cure illnesses and so forth.

98 Vaughan, op. cit., p. 143.

99 K.-E. Sveiby and T. Skuthorpe, *Treading Lightly: The Hidden Wisdom of the World's Oldest People* (Crows Nest, NSW: Allen and Unwin, 2006) p. 154.

100 Vaughan, op. cit.

101 E. Shefy and E. Sadler-Smith, 'Applying holistic principles in management development', *Journal of Management Development*, 2006, 29(4): 368–85.

102 L. Burke and E. Sadler-Smith, 'Instructor intuition in the educational context', *Academy of Management Learning and Education*, 2006, 5(2): 169–81.

103 M. Fisher, *Intuition: How to Use it in Your Life* (Green Farms, Conn.: Wildcat Publishing Company Inc. 1981).

104 A. Revonsuo, 'The reinterpretation of dreams: an evolutionary hypothesis of the function of dreaming', *Behavioral and Brain Sciences*, 2000, 23: 877–901.

105 A. Pascual-Leone, D. Nguyet, L.G. Cohen, J.P. Brasil-Neto, A. Cammarota and M. Hallett, 'Modulation of muscle responses evoked by trans-cranial magnetic stimulation during the acquisition of new fine motor skills', *Journal of Neurophysiology*, 1995, 74: 1037–45.

106 M.S. Franklin and M.J. Zyphur, 'The role of dreams in the evolution of the human mind', *Evolutionary Psychology*, 2005, 3: 59–78; R.B. Zajonc, 'Feeling and thinking: preferences need no inferences', *American Psychologist*, 1980, 35: 151–75.

107 Proponents of remote viewing (a kind of 'natural television') argue that it allows the 'viewer' to gather information on a target object (for example a person) that is separated from the viewer usually through a considerable physical distance. It may also involve precognition, i.e. perceiving the contents of a stimulus (such as a drawing) before being exposed to that stimulus. It is alleged that in the 1970s the United States Central Intelligence Agency (CIA) explored whether such phenomena as remote viewing might have any utility for intelligence collection. For a further discussion of this and related phenomena by one of its proponents see: R. Sheldrake, *The Sense of Being Stared at and Other Aspects of the Extended Mind* (New York: Crown Publishers, 2003) pp. 215–24.

108 L. Nadel, *Sixth Sense: How to Unlock your Intuitive Brain* (London: Prion, 1996) pp. 25 and 193.

109 M.L. Schulz, *Awakening Intuition: Using your Mind-body Network for Insight and Healing* (New York: Three Rivers Press, 1998) p. 20.

110 From Arthur Conan-Doyle, *The Adventures of Sherlock Holmes: A Study in Scarlet*, 1887.

111 www.channel4.com/entertainment/tv/microsites/M/mindcontrol (accessed 17/01/07).

112 B.R. Forer, 'The fallacy of personal validation: a classroom demonstration of gullibility', *Journal of Abnormal and Social Psychology*, 1949, 44: 118–23.

113 R. Wiseman and E. Greening, 'The Mind Machine: a mass participation experiment into the possible existence of extrasensory perception', *British Journal of Psychology*, 2002, 93: 487–99. Note: clairvoyant trails – coin

tossed prior to participant choosing; pre-cognition trail – coin tossed after the participant made their choice.

114 J. Musch and K. Ehrenberg, 'Probability mis-judgement, cognitive ability, and belief in the paranormal', *British Journal of Psychology*, 2002, 93: 169–77.

115 B. Way, *Living Intuitively: Reaping Life's Rich Benefits* (Berkley, CA: Celestial Arts) p. 13.

116 For example one piece of advice that has been offered is that 'the most confusion you will ever experience will come as a result of not listening to your intuition. And the most help you will ever have will come to you because you did' in S.A. Klingler, *Intuition and Beyond: A Step-by-step Approach to Discovering your Inner Voice* (London: Rider, 2002) p. 7.

117 It must be borne in mind that rational analysis never claims, nor is it expected, to be 100 per cent correct all of the time – and nor does intuition. Intuition and rationality have their limits – rationality and intuition may both be considered as 'bounded' under different sets of circumstances.

118 This is the essence of Gary Klein's Recognition-Primed Decision (RPD) model.

119 See G.L. Claxton, *The Wayward Mind* (London: Abacus, 2005).

120 H.A. Simon, 'Making management decisions: the role of intuition and emotion', *Academy of Management Executive*, 1987, February: 57–64 (p. 63).

121 A.R. Damasio, *Descartes' Error: Emotion, Reason and the Human Brain* (New York: HarperCollins, 1994).

122 A.M. Hayashi, 'When to trust your gut', *Harvard Business Review*, 2001, February: 59–65.

123 D. Cappon, 'The anatomy of intuition', *Psychology Today*, 1993, May/June: 40–5 and 86–94.

124 P.S. Arvidson, 'Looking intuit', in R. Davis-Floyd and P.S. Arvidson (eds) *Intuition: The Inside Story* (Routledge: New York, 1997) p. 41.

125 See: R.M. Hogarth, *Educating Intuition* (Chicago and London: University of Chicago Press, 2001) pp. 250–1.

126 Adapted from: E.I. Dane and M.G. Pratt, 'Exploring intuition and its role in managerial decision-making', *Academy of Management Review*, 2007, 32(1): 33–54.

127 Ibid.

128 I am grateful to Dr Jane Mathison for alerting me to the concept of 'de-nominalization' in this respect, i.e. intuit (verb) rather than intuition (noun).

2 Analysis paralysis

1 R. Olby, *Charles Darwin* (Oxford: Oxford University Press, 1967) p. 7.

2 J. Browne, *Charles Darwin: Voyaging* (London: Jonathan Cape, 1995) p. 543.

3 A. Desmond and J. Moore, *Darwin* (London: Penguin, 1992) p. 257.

4 *quod erat demonstrandum*: that which was to be proved.

5 R. Hastie and R.M. Dawes, *Rational Choice in an Uncertain World: The Psychology of Judgement and Decision-making* (Thousand Oaks, CA: Sage, 2001) p. 236–7.

6 A. Lock and H. Thomas, 'An appraisal of multi-attribute utility models in marketing', *European Journal of Marketing*, 1979, 13(5): 294–307.

7 R.L. Daft and D. Marcic, *Management: The New Workplace* (Mason, OH: Thomson South-Western, 2007) p. 216.
8 S.J. Miller, D.J. Hickson and D.C. Wilson, 'Decision-making in organizations', in S.R. Clegg, C. Hardy, and W.R. Nord (eds) *Managing in Organizations: Current Issues* (London: Sage, 1999) p. 43; 'Optimize' refers to making the best or most effective use of a situation.
9 H.R. Arkes and K.R. Hammond (eds), *Judgement and Decision-making: An Interdisciplinary Reader* (Cambridge: Cambridge University Press, 1986).
10 See: G. Klein, *Sources of Power: How People Make Decisions* (Cambridge, MA: MIT Press, 1998) p. 29.
11 Arkes and Hammond, op. cit., p. 7.
12 Arkes and Hammond, op. cit., p. 6.
13 J.C. Sisson, E.B. Schoomaker and J.C. Ross, 'Clinical decisions: the hazards of using additional data', in H.R. Arkes and K.R. Hammond, op. cit., pp. 354–63.
14 R. Davis-Floyd and E. Davis, 'Intuition as authoritative knowledge in midwifery and homebirth', in R. Davis-Floyd and P.S. Arvidson (eds) *Intuition: The Inside Story* (New York: Routledge, 1997) pp. 145–76.
15 *Ratiocination* is from the Latin *rationcinatio* 'to compute, to calculate, to reason'. http://dictionary.reference.com (accessed 14/09/06).
16 J. Cioffi, 'Heuristics, servants to intuition, in clinical decision-making', *Journal of Advanced Nursing*, 1997, 26: 205.
17 P. Benner and C. Tanner, 'Clinical judgement: how expert nurses use intuition', *American Journal of Nursing*, 1987, 87: 23–31; P. Benner and J. Wrubel, 'Skilled knowledge: the value of perceptual awareness' *Nurse Educator*, 1982, 7: 11–17.
18 T. Greenhalgh, 'Intuition and evidence: uneasy bed-fellows?', *British Journal of General Practice*, 2002, 52: p. 395.
19 G.P. Hodgkinson and P. Sparrow, *The Competent Organization* (Buckingham: Open University Press, 2002).
20 For a discussion of the learning-related issues, see: S. Fineman, 'Emotion and learning', in Clegg *et al.* (eds) op. cit., p. 545.
21 D. Hume, *Treatise of Human Nature*. Most frequently cited is the edition by L.A. Selby-Bigge (Oxford: Oxford University Press, 1740/1978).
22 The lecture is contained as the Appendix to: C.I. Barnard, *The Functions of the Executive* (Cambridge, MA: Harvard University Press, 1938/1968) pp. 301–22.
23 A number of changes in supervisory style and 'human relations' were attributed to be the causes of increased productivity in the Hawthorne Plant of the Western Electric company in the USA during the 1920s and 1930s.
24 Behaviourism was the pre-eminent school of psychological thought at the time (the inception of behaviourism is often dated at around 1913) and is most often associated with work in the USA of J.B. Watson and B.F. Skinner. Its goal was the prediction and control of behaviour. Its adherents considered introspection and the study of mental processes to be unscientific. See: A.M. Colman, *Oxford Dictionary of Psychology* (Oxford: Oxford University Press, 2003) p. 83.
25 Barnard, op. cit., pp. 302–3.
26 Ibid.
27 Normative is used the sense here to mean 'to be pursued'.

308   *Notes*

28 R. Frantz, 'Herbert Simon: Artificial intelligence as a framework for under-
    standing intuition', *Journal of Economic Psychology*, 2003, 24: 265–77.
29 H.A. Simon, *The Sciences of the Artificial* (Cambridge, MA: MIT Press,
    1969) p. 69.
30 H.A. Simon, 'Making management decisions: the role of intuition and
    emotion', *Academy of Management Executive*, 1987, February: 57–64 (p. 57).
31 J.G. March and H.A. Simon, *Organizations* (New York: John Wiley and
    Sons, Inc., 1958) p. 12 (cited in Little *et al.* 2002, 127).
32 H.A. Simon, 'Theories of bounded rationality', in H.A. Simon (ed.) *Models
    of Bounded Rationality: Behavioral Economics and Business Organization*,
    Volume 2 (Cambridge, MA: MIT Press, 1989) p. 415.
33 See Hastie and Dawes, op. cit., p. 241.
34 H.A. Simon, *Administrative Behaviour: A study of Decision-making Processes
    in Administrative Organisations* (4th edn) (New York: The Free Press, 1997)
    p. 118.
35 See: G.P. Hodgkinson and P.R. Sparrow, op. cit.
36 G. Gigerenzer, P.M. Todd and the ABC Research Group, *Simple Heuristics
    that Make us Smart* (Oxford: Oxford University Press, 1999).
37 Simon 1987, op. cit., p. 63.
38 Ibid., pp. 57–64.
39 D.A. Schön, *The Reflective Practitioner: How Professionals Think in Action*
    (Aldershot: Gower, 1983) p. 21.
40 D.A. Schön, op. cit., pp. 39–40.
41 D.A. Schön, *The Reflective Practitioner: How Professionals Think in Action*
    (Aldershot: Gower, 1983) p. 16. Here Schön is borrowing terminology from
    the American philosopher, psychologist and educational reformer, John
    Dewey.
42 Schön describes Auguste Comte's (1798–1857) positivist doctrine thus:
    (a) empirical science is the only source of positive knowledge about the
    world; (b) men's minds should be cleansed of mysticism; (c) the extension of
    scientific knowledge to society. See: DA Schön, op. cit., p. 32.
43 M. Polanyi, *The Tacit Dimension* (London: Routledge and Kegan Paul,
    1966).
44 These discussions are not intended to imply any one-to-one correspondence
    between the arguments of Simon and Schön; indeed Schön argues that
    Simon attempts to preserve technical rationality by proposing a science of
    design which depends on having well-formed instrumental problems to
    begin with. For Schön, part of the artistry of professional practice lies in the
    ways in which the problems themselves are framed. See page 48 of Schön's
    The Reflective Practitioner.
45 C.I. Barnard, *The Functions of the Executive* (Cambridge, MA: Harvard
    University Press, 1938/1968) p. 322.
46 G. Klein, *Sources of Power: How People Make Decisions* (Cambridge, MA:
    MIT Press, 1998) p. 32.
47 G. Klein, 'The recognition-primed decision (RPD) model: looking back,
    looking forward', in C.E. Zsambok and G. Klein (eds) *Naturalistic Decision-
    making* (Mahwah, NJ: Lawrence Earlbaum Associates, 1997) p. 285–92.
48 Klein, 1998, op. cit., p. 26.
49 Ibid., p. 21.
50 M.D. Lieberman, J.M. Jarcho and A.B. Satpute, 'Evidence-based and

intuition-based self-knowledge: an fMRI study', *Journal of Personality and Social Psychology*, 2004, 87: 421–35.

51 A.R. Damasio, *The Feeling of what Happens: Body, Emotion and the Making of Consciousness* (London: Vintage, 1999) pp. 60–1.

52 A.R. Damasio, *Descartes' Error: Emotion, Reason and the Human Brain* (New York: Quill, 1994) p. 194.

53 H.A. Simon, *Administrative Behaviour: A study of Decision-making Processes in Administrative Organisations* (4th edn) (New York: The Free Press, 1997) p. 91.

54 Schön, op. cit., p. 49.

55 Sylvia Plath, *The Bell Jar* (London: Faber, 1963) p. 73.

3 Eureka! moments

1 'Eureka' has the same etymological root in Greek as does the term 'heuristic' – both are derived from *heurisko* – 'find'. Heuristics and biases are the subject of Chapter 5.

2 Adapted from A. Koestler, *The Act of Creation* (London: Pan Books, 1964) p. 105.

3 H. Gruber, 'Insight and affect in the history of science', in R.J. Sternberg and J.E. Davidson (eds) *The Nature of Insight* (Cambridge, MA: MIT Press, 1995) p. 406.

4 C.M. Seifert, D.E. Meyer, N. Davidson, A.L. Patalano and I. Yaniv, 'Demystification of cognitive insight: opportunistic assimilation and the prepared-mind perspective', in R.J. Sternberg and J.E. Davidson (eds) *The Nature of Insight* (Cambridge, MA: MIT Press, 1995) pp. 65–124.

5 R.E. Mayer, 'The search for insight', in Sternberg and Davidson, op. cit., p. 3.

6 J.W. Schooler, M. Fallshore and S.M. Fiore, 'Epilogue: putting insight into perspective', in Sternberg and Davidson, op. cit., p. 578.

7 L.R. Novick and M. Bassock, 'Problem solving' in K.J. Holyoak and R.G. Morrison (eds) *The Cambridge Handbook of Thinking and Reasoning* (Cambridge: Cambridge University Press, 2005) p342.

8 From P.G. Wodehouse's *The Code of the Woosters*: 'That brief monosyllable "you" [a loud exclamation uttered by his Aunt] had accomplished what a quarter of an hour's research had been unable to do – *viz*. the unsealing of the fount of memory. Jeeve's [Bertram's butler] words came back to me with a rush. One moment the mind a blank: the next the fount of memory spouting forth like nobody's business. It often happens this way'. This insight was prompted by Bertie's Aunt Dahlia's exclamation of 'Here you!' to his enemy Roderick Spode – like much of Wodehouse, the plot is complex and not easy to summarize succinctly. The significance is that Bertie has been non-consciously searching his semantic memory (which had failed him up until this moment) for the name of a female former acquaintance of Spode's – a lady by the name of Eulalia. The monosyllable 'You!' was the cue.

9 F. Marton, P. Fensham, and S. Chaiklin, 'A Nobel's eye view of scientific intuition', *International Journal of Science Education*, 1994, 16(4): 457–73. Cited in: L.V. Shavinina, 'Explaining high abilities of Nobel laureates', *High Ability Studies*, 2004, 15(2): 246.

10 M. Csikszentmihalyi, *Creativity* (New York: HarperPerennial, 1996). Cited in: Shavinina, op. cit., p. 249.

11 Marton, Fensham and Chaiklin, op. cit., p. 248.
12 M.A. Schilling, 'A "small world" network model of cognitive insight', *Creativity Research Journal*, 2005, 17(2&3): 131–54.
13 See: C. Pettimengin-Peugeot, 'The intuitive experience', *Journal of Consciousness Studies*, 1999, 6(2&3): 43–77; R. Henley, 'Distinguishing insight from intuition', in F. Varela and J. Shear (eds) *The View from Within* (Thoverton, UK: Imprint Academic, 1999) pp. 287–90.
14 L. Jaroff, 'Paul MacCready', *Time*, 30 December 2005. http://www.time.com/time/magazine/article/0,9171,90512-1,00.html (accessed 15.05.07).
15 A. Rothenberg, 'Creative cognitive processes in Kekulé's discovery of the structure of the benzene molecule', *American Journal of Psychology*, 1995, 108(3): 419–38.
16 M.A. Boden, *The Creative Mind: Myths and Mechanisms* (London: Routledge, 2004) p. 62.
17 Some have challenged this story, see: J.H. Wotiz and S. Rudofsky, 'Kekulé's dream: fact or fiction?', *Chemistry in Britain*, 1984 August: 720–3.
18 F.R. Japp, 'Kekulé's memorial lecture, 1897', *Memorial Lectures Delivered before the Chemical Society, 1893–1900* (London: Gurney and Jackson, 1898) p. 100.
19 Japp, op. cit.
20 A. Koestler, *The Act of Creation* (London: Pan Books, 1964) p. 210.
21 S. J. Henderson, 'Product inventors and creativity', *Creativity Research Journal*, 2004, 16(3&4): 293–312.
22 T. Singer, 'Your brain on innovation', *Inc Magazine*, 1987, September: 86–8.
23 http://www.kurzweilai.net/ (accessed 18/01/07).
24 H. Gruber, 'Insight and affect in the history of science', in Sternberg and Davidson, op. cit., p. 406; Rothenberg, op. cit.
25 P. LoPiccolo, 'Eureka moments', *Computer Graphics World*, 2003, 26(11): 4.
26 C.G. Jung, M.-L. von Franz, J.L. Henderson, J. Jacobi and A. Jaffe, *Man and his Symbols* (London: Arkana Penguin Books, 1964).
27 For example: M. Sinclair and N. Ashkanasy, 'Intuition: myth or a decision-making tool?', *Management Learning*, 2005, 36: 353–70.
28 These quotes are from Henri Poincaré's lecture at the *Societé de Psychologie*, Paris in Koestler, op. cit., pp. 114–18.
29 J. Wright and N. Pye, 'From concept to product', *Brand Strategy*, 2006, February: 32–3.
30 G. Wallas, *The Art of Thought* (New York: Franklin Watts, 1926) p. 87. Cited in J. Dorfman, V.A. Shames and J.F. Kihlstrom, 'Intuition, incubation and insight: implicit cognition and problem solving', in G. Underwood (ed.) *Implicit Cognition* (Oxford: Oxford University Press, 1996) p. 258.
31 Wallas, op. cit., p. 97.
32 F.T. Durso, C.B. Rea and T. Dayton, 'Graph-theoretic confirmation of restructuring during insight', *Psychological Science* 1994, 5: 94–8; E.M. Bowden and M. Jung-Beeman, 'Aha! insight experience correlates with solution activation in the right hemisphere', *Psychonomic Bulletin and Review*, 2003, 10: 730–7.
33 B.W. Mattimore, 'Eureka: how to invent a new product', *The Futurist*, 1995, March–April: 34–8.
34 M. Michalko, 'Lights on!', *Across the Board*, 1998, 35(7): 41–5.

35 These five key views of insight are from the comprehensive and authoritative account by Richard E. Mayer. See Mayer, op. cit., pp. 3–32.

36 Ibid., pp. 3–32.

37 Mayer, op. cit., p. 13.

38 N.R.F. Maier, 'Reasoning in humans: II. The solution of a problem and its appearance in consciousness', *Journal of Comparative Psychology*, 1931, 12: 181–94.

39 Mayer, op. cit., p. 15.

40 Mayer, op. cit., pp. 13–14

41 Adapted from: G. Mosler, *The Puzzle School* (New York: Abelard-Schuma, 1977). Cited in C.M. Seifert, D.E. Meyer, N. Davidson, A.L. Patalano and I. Yaniv, 'Demystification of cognitive insight: opportunistic assimilation and the prepared-mind perspective', in Sternberg and Davidson, op. cit., pp. 65–124.

42 A.M. Colman, *Oxford Dictionary of Psychology* (Oxford: Oxford University Press) p. 653.

43 K.J. Holyoak, 'Analogy', in K.J. Holyoak and R.G. Morrison (eds), *The Cambridge Handbook of Thinking and Reasoning* (Cambridge: Cambridge University Press, 2005) p. 117.

44 M.L. Gick and K.L. Holyoak, 'Schema induction and analogical transfer', *Cognitive Psychology*, 1983, 15: 1–38; P.N. Johnson-Laird, *The Computer and the Mind: An Introduction to Cognitive Science* (London: Fontana Press, 1988).

45 B.T. Christensen and C.D. Schunn, 'Spontaneous access and analogical incubation effects', *Creativity Research Journal*, 2005, 17(2&3): 207–20; C.M. Seifert, D.E. Meyer, N. Davidson, A.L. Patalano and I. Yaniv, 'Demystification of cognitive insight: opportunistic assimilation and the prepared-mind perspective', in Sternberg and Davidson, op. cit., pp. 65–124.

46 K.J. Holyoak, op. cit., p. 131.

47 Boden, op. cit., p. 113.

48 Johnson-Laird, op. cit., p. 267.

49 D.K. Simonton, 'Foresight in insight?', in R.J. Sternberg and J.E. Davidson (eds) *The Nature of Insight* (Cambridge MA: MIT Press, 1995) p. 467.

50 M.A. Schilling, 'A "small world" network model for cognitive insight', *Creativity Research Journal*, 2005, 17(2&3): p. 136.

51 C.M. Seifert, D.E. Meyer, N. Davidson, A.L. Patalano and I. Yaniv, 'Demystification of cognitive insight: opportunistic assimilation and the prepared-mind perspective', in Sternberg and Davidson (eds), op. cit., pp. 65–124.

52 U. Kraft, 'Unleashing creativity', *Scientific American Mind*, 2005, 16(1): 16–23.

53 S.H. Carson, J.B. Peterson and D.M. Higgins, 'Decreased latent inhibition is associated with increased achievement in high-functioning individuals', *Journal of Personality and Social Psychology*, 2003, 85(3): 499–506.

54 J.R. Anderson, *The Adaptive Character of Thought* (Hillsdale, NJ: Lawrence Earlbaum Associates Inc. 1990).

55 J. Dorfman, V.A. Shames and J.F. Kihlstrom, 'Intuition, incubation and insight: implicit cognition and problem solving', in Underwood, op. cit., p. 284.

56 E. Segal, 'Incubation in insight problem solving', *Creativity Research Journal*, 2004, 16(1): p. 143.

57 The effect of incubation being exclusively a result of 'no-activity' (thus allowing recovery from mental exertion and fatigue) is not tenable as an explanation. This is because taking a break has been shown to have a positive effect upon problem-solving even if participants are given tasks to do in the break, be they demanding tasks, such as working on a crossword puzzle or undemanding ones such as leafing through a newspaper. See: Segal, op. cit.

58 I. Yaniv and D.E. Meyer, 'Activation and meta-cognition of inaccessible stored information: potential bases of incubation effects in problem solving', *Journal of Experimental Psychology: Learning, Memory and Cognition*, 1987, 13: 187–205.

59 Koestler, op. cit., pp. 122–3.

60 Dorfman, Shames and Kihlstrom, op. cit., p. 282.

61 J.W. Schooler and S. Dougal, 'Why creativity is not like the proverbial typing money', *Psychological Inquiry*, 1999, 10(4): 351–6.

62 Dorfman, Shames and Kihlstrom, op. cit., p. 284.

63 C. Martindale, 'The biological bases of creativity', in R.J. Sternberg (ed.) *Handbook of Creativity* (Cambridge: Cambridge University Press, 1999) p. 139.

64 For a discussion of coarse versus fine semantic coding see: M. Jung Beeman *et al.*, 'Neural activity when people solve problems with insight', *Public Library of Science (Biology)*, 2004, 2(4): 500–10. It was Mednick in 1962 who proposed that people with richer associative hierarchies are creative – they are able to generate unusual associations (chair – elbow) once they have run out of the more usual ones (chair – table). See: S.A. Mednick, 'The associative basis of the creative process', *Psychological Review*, 1962, 69: 220–32.

65 E. Fromm, 'Primary and secondary process in waking and in altered states of consciousness', *Journal of Altered States of Consciousness*, 1978, 4: 115–28.

66 Michalko, op. cit., pp. 41–5.

67 U. Kraft, 'Unleashing creativity', *Scientific American Mind*, 2005, 16(1): 16–23.

68 L.R. Novick and S.J. Sherman, 'On the nature of insight solutions: evidence from skill differences in anagram solution', *The Quarterly Journal of Experimental Psychology*, 2003: 56A(2): 351–82.

69 Ibid.

70 M.A. Schilling, 'A "small world" network model of cognitive insight', *Creativity Research Journal*, 2005, 17(2&3): p. 133.

71 B. Foster, 'Einstein and his love of music', *Physics Today*, 2005, January: 1.

72 K.A. Ericsson, 'Creative expertise as superior reproducible performance: innovative and flexible aspects of expert performance, *Psychological Inquiry*, 1999, 10(4): 329–61.

73 G.L. Claxton, *Hare Brain, Tortoise Mind: Why Intelligence Increases When You Think Less* (London: Fourth Estate, 1997) p. 47.

74 E. Shefy and E. Sadler-Smith, 'Applying holistic principles in management development', *Journal of Management Development*, 2006, 29(4): 368–85. See for example: J.H. Austin, *Zen and the Brain: Toward an Understanding of Meditation and Consciousness* (Cambridge, MA: MIT Press, 1999).

75 E. Chaline, *The Book of Zen* (Gloucester, MA: Fair Winds Press, 2003).

76 E. de Vita, 'Space to think', *Management Today*, 2003, November: 64–71.

77 S. Salzberg, *Loving-kindness: The Revolutionary Art of Happiness* (Boston; Shambala, 1995).
78 J. Austin, *Zen and the Brain* (Cambridge, MA: MIT Press, 1999).
79 H. Wenk-Sormaz, 'Meditation can help reduce habitual responding', *Advances* 2005, 21(3&4): 33–49.
80 J. Metcalfe and D. Wiebe, 'Intuition in insight and non-insight problem solving', *Memory and Cognition*, 1987, 15(3): 238–46.
81 Examples of problems used by Metcalfe and Wiebe (p. 245): (1) insight problem: 'A prisoner is attempting to escape from a tower. He found in his cell a rope which was half long enough to permit him to reach the ground safely. He divided the rope in half and tied the two parts together and escaped. How could he have done this?'; (2) non-insight problem: $(3x^2 + 2x + 10)(3x) = ?$
82 N. Jausovec and K. Bakracevic, 'What can heart rate tell us about the creative process?', *Creativity Research Journal*, 1995, 8(1): 11–24.
83 Schilling, op. cit.
84 See Jung-Beeman *et al.*, op. cit., p. 500.
85 For a discussion of the 'nothing special view' of insight offered by Weisberg and colleagues, see: Mayer., op. cit., p. 7.
86 M.S. Gazzaniga, R.B. Ivry and G.R. Mangun, *Cognitive Neuroscience: The Biology of the Mind* (New York: W.W. Norton and Co., 2002) p. 129.
87 P.S. Churchland, *Brain-wise: Studies in Neurophilosophy* (Cambridge, MA: MIT Press, 2002) p. 18.
88 Jung-Beeman *et al.*, op. cit.; these researchers also used EEG in a second study which supported the findings of the FMRI study.
89 These terms have quite specific meanings in neuroanatomy: 'anterior' means front; 'posterior', back; 'superior', top; 'inferior, 'bottom'. 'Gyri' are protruding rounded surfaces of the cerebral cortex. See: Gazzaniga, Ivry and Mangun, op. cit., p. 78.
90 Shefy and Sadler-Smith, op. cit.
91 Gazzaniga *et al.*, op. cit., p. 129.
92 K.S. Bowers, G. Regehr and C. Balthazard, 'Intuition in the context of discovery', *Cognitive Psychology*, 1990, 22: 72–110.

4 Intuitive expertise

1 N. Ambady and R. Rosenthal, 'Half a minute: predicting teacher evaluations from thin slices of nonverbal behaviour and physical attractiveness', *Journal of Personality and Social Psychology*, 1993, 64: 431–41.
2 This is typical of the kind of information which universities and colleges in the USA, UK and elsewhere routinely collect (for example, 'Rate the overall effectiveness of _____ as a teacher'). Ratings are important in the assessment of the performance of individual teaching staff and of institutions.
3 The correlation coefficients (*r*) between confidence and optimism and teacher effectiveness were all in excess of 0.80 ($p < 0.001$).
4 Not content with this in the next step Ambady and Rosenthal slimmed the ten second slices down further on two subsequent trials to five seconds, and then to two seconds. They had eight judges rate the teachers. The more remarkable finding this time was that the judgements based on the ten

314   *Notes*

second exposures were not significantly more accurate than the five or the two second clips, and all correlated with teaching effectiveness.

5 See also: S.E. Asch, 'Forming impression of personality', *Journal of Abnormal and Social Psychology*, 1946, 41: 258–90.

6 For a discussion of the impact of learning environments and feedback upon intuitive judgement, see: R.M. Hogarth, *Educating Intuition* (Chicago: University of Chicago Press, 2001) pp. 184–5.

7 H.A. Simon, *Administrative Behaviour: A Study of Decision-making Processes in Administrative Organisations* (4th edn) (New York: The Free Press, 1997) p. 134.

8 For a discussion of the neural circuitry involved in 'as-if' loops see Chapter 9 and also: A. Bechara, 'The role of emotion in decision-making: evidence from neurological patients with orbito-frontal damage', *Brain and Cognition*, 2004, 55: 30–40.

9 Simon, op. cit., p. 88.

10 R. Frantz, 'Herbert Simon artificial intelligence as a framework for understanding intuition', *Journal of Economic Psychology*, 2003, 24: 265–77.; H.A. Simon, 'Making management decisions: the role of intuition and emotion', *Academy of Management Executive*, 1987, February: 57–64. An alternative description to that of a 'static store' of knowledge might be a 'dynamic mental model' or mental simulation which undergoes continuous refinement through learning and experience – the subject of mental models and simulations will be returned to in Chapter 5.

11 K.A. Ericsson and N. Charness, 'Expert performance: its structure and acquisition', *American Psychologist*, 1994, 49: 725–47.

12 K.A. Ericsson and A.C. Lehman, 'Expert and exceptional performance: evidence of maximal adaptation to task constraints', *Annual Review of Psychology*, 1996, 47: 273–305; K.A. Ericsson and N. Charness, 'Expert performance: its structure and acquisition', *American Psychologist*, 1994, 49: 725–47.

13 H.L. Dreyfus and S.E. Dreyfus, *Mind over Machine: The Power of Human Intuitive Expertise in the Era of the Computer* (New York: Free Press, 1986).

14 P. Batalden, D. Leach, S. Swing, H.L. Dreyfus and S.E. Dreyfus, 'General competencies and accreditation in Graduate Medical Education: an antidote to over-specification in the education of medical specialists', *Health Affairs*, 2002, 21(5): 103–11.

15 H.L. Dreyfus and S.E. Dreyfus, op. cit., p. 31.

16 B. Herbig, A. Büssing and T. Ewert, 'The role of tacit knowledge in the context of nursing,' *Journal of Advanced Nursing*, 34(5): 687–95.

17 K.W. Eva, G.R. Norman, A.J. Neville, T.J. Wood and L.R. Brooks, 'Expert-novice differences in memory: a reformulation', *Teaching and Learning in Medicine*, 2002, 14: 257–63.

18 A.M. Hayashi, 'When to trust your gut', *Harvard Business Review*, 2001, February: 59–65.

19 K.A. Ericsson, 'Recent advances in expertise research: a commentary on the contributions to the special issue', *Applied Cognitive Psychology*, 2005, 19: 233–41.

20 M. Csikszentmihalyi, *Flow: The Classic Work on How to Achieve Happiness* (London: Rider, 2002) p. 71.

21 M. Csikszentmihalyi, *Good Business: Leadership, Flow and the Making of Meaning* (London: Hodder and Stoughton, 2003) p. 48.

22 L. Porter, *John Coltrane: His Life and Music* (Ann Arbor: University of Michigan Press, 1998) p. 64.
23 In jazz music 'wood shedding' means to cloister oneself away for a period of intense practice.
24 J.C. Thomas, *Chasin' the Trane: The Music and Mystique of John Coltrane* (Garden City, N.Y: Double Day, 1975).
25 Ericsson and Lehman, op. cit., p. 297.
26 In this book the term 'practitioner' is sometimes used as a 'catch-all' for professionals who exercise judgement in complex real world situations (such as managers, nurses and teachers).
27 See: K.E. Weick, *Making Sense of the Organisation* (Oxford: Blackwell Publishing, 2001) p. 286. In his discussion of improvisation and intuition Weick cites: P.F. Berliner, *Thinking in Jazz: The Infinite Art of Improvisation* (Chicago, IL: University of Chicago, 1994).
28 G. Kaufmann, 'Creativity and problem solving', in J. Henry (ed.) *Creative Management* (London: Sage, 2001) p. 58.
29 R.H. Bennett, 'The importance of tacit knowledge in strategic deliberations and decisions', *Management Decision*, 1998, 36(9): 593; L.A. Burke and M.K. Miller, 'Taking the mystery out of intuitive decision-making', *Academy of Management Executive*, 1999, 13(4): 91–9.
30 B. Kleinmuntz, 'Why we still use our heads instead of formulas: towards an integrative approach', *Psychological Bulletin*, 1990, 107: 296–310.
31 H.A. Simon, 'Making management decisions: the role of intuition and emotion', *Academy of Management Executive*, 1987, 1: 57–64, p. 60; P. Benner and C. Tanner, 'How expert nurses use intuition', *American Journal of Nursing*, 1987, January: 23–31; D.J. Isenberg, 'How senior managers think', *Harvard Business Review*, 1984, November/December: 81–90.
32 See: C.W. Allinson and J. Hayes, 'The Cognitive Style Index: A measure of Intuition-Analysis for organizational research', *Journal of Management Studies*, 1996, 33(1): 119–35; G.P. Hodgkinson and E. Sadler-Smith, 'Complex or unitary? A critique and empirical reassessment of the Allinson-Hayes Cognitive Style Index', *Journal of Occupational and Organizational Psychology*, 2003, 76: 243–68; E. Sadler-Smith, D.P. Spicer, and F. Tsang, 'Validity of the Cognitive Style Index: replication and extension', *British Journal of Management*, 2000, 11: 175–81.
33 The direction of the causality in this relationship is not clear, for example: (1) are senior managers intuitive 'by nature'; (2) does being a senior manager make one become more intuitive; (3) or does one have to behave in a more intuitive fashion to move up through the organizational hierarchy? It may be that finding themselves in situations that do not allow for structured, rational analysis means that managers are able to rely upon or legitimize the use of intuition.
34 Eva *et al.*, op. cit.
35 *Boeing Flight Test Journal*, 19 December 2005 http://www.boeing.com/commercial/777family/200LR/flight_test/archives/2005/12/where_it_all_co.html (accessed 07/01/07).
36 Ericsson and Lehman, op. cit., p. 283.
37 H. Mintzberg, *Managers not MBAs: A Hard Look at the Soft Practice of Management and Management Development* (San Francisco, CA: Berrett-Koehler, 2004) pp. 384–5.

38 N. Khatri and A. Ng, 'The role of intuition in strategic decision-making', *Human Relations*, 2000, 53(1): p. 77.
39 R.M. Hogarth, *Educating Intuition* (Chicago: Chicago University Press, 2001) p. 93.
40 S. Pyles and P. Stern, 'Discovery of nursing *gestalt* in critical care nursing: the importance of the gray gorilla syndrome', *The Journal of Nursing Scholarship*, 1983, 15: p. 54.
41 E. Sadler-Smith and E. Shefy, 'The intuitive executive: understanding and applying "gut feeling" in decision-making', *The Academy of Management Executive*, 2004, 18(4): 76–92.
42 B. Bird, 'Implementing entrepreneurial ideas: the case for intention', *Academy of Management Review*, 1988, 13(3): 447. H.H. Stevenson, 'A new paradigm for entrepreneurial management', in J.J. Kao and H.H. Stevenson (eds), *Entrepreneurship: What it is and How to Teach it* (Boston: Harvard Business School, 1985) pp. 30–61.
43 Accessed from L'Oreal's web site (http://www.en.loreal.ca/_en/_ca/news/) on 14/09/06.
44 Ericsson and Lehman, op. cit.
45 K.A. Ericsson and N. Charness, 'Expert performance: its structure and acquisition', *American Psychologist*, 1994, 49: 725–47.
46 Ericsson and Charness, op. cit.
47 Ericsson and Lehman, op. cit., p. 280.
48 Ericsson and Charness., op. cit., p. 744.
49 See: R. Hastie and R.M. Dawes, *Rational Choice in an Uncertain World: The Psychology of Judgement and Decision-making* (Thousand Oaks, CA: Sage, 2001) pp. 54–5.
50 W. Starbuck, 'Learning by knowledge intensive firms', in M.D. Cohen and L.S. Sproull (eds) *Organizational Learning* (London: Sage, 1996) pp. 484–515; G.P. Hodgkinson and P.R. Sparrow, *The Competent Organization: A Psychological Analysis of the Strategic Management Process* (Buckingham: Open University Press, 2002) pp. 161–2.
51 P. Benner, *From Novice to Expert: Excellence and Power in Clinical Nursing Practice* (Menlo Park, CA: Addison-Wesley, 1984).
52 P. Benner, C.A. Tanner and C.A. Chesla, *Expertise in Nursing Practice: Caring, Clinical Judgement and Ethics* (New York: Springer, 1996) p. 44.
53 J.W. Schooler and S. Dougal, 'Why creativity is not like the proverbial typing money', *Psychological Inquiry*, 1999, 10(4): 351–6.
54 D.A. Schön, *The Reflective Practitioner: How Professionals Think in Action* (Aldershot: Ashgate, 1983).
55 K.A. Ericsson, 'Creative expertise as superior reproducible performance: innovative and flexible aspects of expert performance', *Psychological Inquiry*, 1999, 10(4): 329–61.
56 T.D. Wilson, *Strangers to Ourselves: Discovering the Adaptive Unconscious* (Cambridge, MA: Belknap Press, 2002) p. 21.
57 R. Baumeister, 'The championship choke', *Psychology Today*, 1985, April: 49–53.
58 Csikszentmihalyi 2003, op. cit.; R. Masters, 'Knowledge, nerves and know-how: the role of explicit versus implicit knowledge in the breakdown of a complex skill under pressure', *British Journal of Psychology*, 1992, 83: 343–58.

59 K.E. Weick, *Making Sense of the Organisation* (Oxford: Blackwell Publishing, 2001) pp. 112–13.
60 J.A. Meacham, 'Wisdom and the context of knowledge', in D. Kuhn and J.A. Meacham (eds) *Contributions in Human Development* (Basel: Karger, 1983) Vol. 8, pp. 111–34, cited in Weick op. cit.
61 Weick, op. cit. pp. 112–13.
62 K.A. Ericsson, 'Creative expertise as superior reproducible performance: innovative and flexible aspects of expert performance', *Psychological Inquiry*, 1999, 10(4): 329–61.
63 E. Goldberg, *The Wisdom Paradox: How your Mind can Grow Stronger as your Brain Grows Older* (London: Simon and Schuster, 2005) p. 78.
64 J. Dorfman, V.A. Shames and J.F. Kihlstrom, 'Intuition, incubation, and insight: implicit cognition and problem solving', in G. Underwood (ed.) *Implicit Cognition* (Oxford: Oxford University Press, 1996) pp. 259–96.

5 All in the mind?

1 G. Lakoff and M. Johnson, *Philosophy in the Flesh: The Embodied Mind and its Challenge to Western Thought* (New York: Basic Books, 1999).
2 E. Goldberg, *The Wisdom Paradox: How your Mind can Grow Stronger as your Brain Grows Older* (London: Simon and Schuster, 2005) p. 117.
3 R.L. Gregory (ed.) *The Oxford Companion to the Mind* (Oxford: Oxford University Press, 1987) pp. 21–2.
4 S. Baxendale, 'Memories aren't made of this: amnesia at the movies', *British Medical Journal*, 2004, 329 (7840): 1480–3.
5 J.F. Kihlstrom, 'Conscious versus unconscious cognition', in R.J. Sternberg (ed.) *The Nature of Cognition* (Cambridge, MA: MIT Press, 1999) pp. 173–204.
6 Long term memory (LTM) is modelled as consisting of two separate storage systems: (1) an explicit (declarative) system and; (2) an implicit (non-declarative) system. Episodic long term memory (memory for events), and semantic LTM (memory for facts) are sub-systems of explicit (declarative) memory, whilst procedural memory is a component of implicit (non-declarative) memory. These concepts are discussed more fully later in this chapter.
7 E. Claparede, 'Experiences sur la memoire dans un cas de psychose de Korsakoff (Experiments on memory in a patient suffering from Korsakoff's psychosis)', *Revue Medicale de la Suisse Romande*, 1907, 27: 301–3. Translated by Serge Nicholas and Gila Walker.
8 Kihlstrom, op. cit.
9 The hippocampus (named thus because of its 'sea-horse'-shaped form, from the Greek *hippos* – horse) is part of the limbic system and influence learning and memory.
10 M.S. Gazzaniga, R.B. Ivry and G.R. Mangun, *Cognitive Neuroscience: The Biology of the Mind* (New York: W.W. Norton and Co., 2002) p. 332.
11 J.E. Le Doux, *The Emotional Brain: The Mysterious Underpinnings of Emotional Life* (New York: Simon and Schuster, 1996).
12 P.M. Merikle and M. Daneman, 'Memory for unconsciously perceived events: evidence from anesthetized patients', *Consciousness and Cognition*, 1996, 5: 525–41.

13 Observations were based upon ten patients interviewed one month after surgery.

14 T.D. Wilson, *Strangers to Ourselves: Discovering the Adaptive Unconscious* (Cambridge, MA: Belknap Press, 2002) p. 25.

15 P.M. Merikle and M. Daneman, 'Memory for unconsciously perceived events: evidence from anesthetized patients', *Consciousness and Cognition*, 1996, 5: 525–41.

16 C.I. Barnard, *The Functions of the Executive* (Cambridge: Harvard University Press, 1938/1968) p. 284.

17 A.S. Reber, *Implicit Learning and Tacit Knowledge: An Essay on the Cognitive Unconscious* (New York: Oxford University Press, 1993) p. 5.

18 C.A. Seger, 'Implicit learning', *Psychological Bulletin*, 1994, 115(2): 163–96.

19 K.J. Holyoak and B.A. Spellman, 'Thinking', *Annual Review of Psychology*, 1993, 44: 265–315. H. Krist, E.L. Fieberg and F. Wilkening, 'Intuitive physics in action and judgement: the development of knowledge about projectile motion', *Journal of Experimental Psychology: Learning, Memory and Cognition*, 1993, 19: 952–66.

20 From Professor Arthur S. Reber's website: http://academic.brooklyn.cuny.edu/userhome/psych/areber/index.htm (accessed 12/12/06).

21 D. Leonard and S. Sensiper, 'The role of tacit knowledge in group innovation', *California Management Review*, 1998, 40(3): 65–72.

22 G. Underwood and J.E.H. Bright, 'Cognition with and without awareness', in G. Underwood (ed.) *Implicit Cognition* (Oxford: Oxford University Press, 1996) pp. 1–40.

23 J. Dorfman, V.A. Shames and J.F. Kihlstrom, 'Intuition, incubation and insight: implicit cognition and problem solving', in G. Underwood (ed.) *Implicit Cognition* (Oxford: Oxford University Press, 1996) pp. 257–96.

24 T.D. Wilson, *Strangers to Ourselves: Discovering the Adaptive Unconscious* (Cambridge, MA: Belknap Press, 2002) p. 29.

25 See: Le Doux, op. cit.

26 R.F. Bornstein, 'Subliminal mere exposure effects', in R.F. Bornstein and T.S. Pittman (eds) *Perception Without Awareness: Cognitive, Clinical and Social Perspectives* (New York: Guilford, 1992) pp. 191–210.

27 D.G. Myers, *Intuition: Its Powers and Perils* (New Haven: Yale University Press, 2002) p. 40.

28 T.J. Perfect and C. Askew, 'Print adverts: not remembered but memorable', *Applied Cognitive Psychology*, 1994, 8: 693–703.

29 P.J. Whalen, S.L. Rauch, N.L. Etcoff, S.C. McInerney, M. Lee and M.A. Jenike, 'Masked presentations of emotional facial expressions modulate amygdala activity without explicit knowledge', *Journal of Neuroscience*, 1998, 18: 411–18.

30 The amygdala is a small almond shaped structure in the limbic system which influences emotions (including anger and aggression).

31 fMRI works on the principle of hemodynamics (the tracking of blood flow in the brain) on the basis that localized increases in blood flow are associated with increases in neuronal activity. See: P.S. Churchland, *Brain-wise: Studies in Neurophilosophy* (Cambridge, MA: MIT Press, 2002) p. 18.

32 The concept of 'procedural knowledge' is discussed in the next section.

33 P. Lewicki, T. Hill and M. Czyzewska, 'Non-conscious acquisition of information', *American Psychologist*, 1992, June: 796–801.

34 M.T.H. Chi and S. Ohlsson, 'Complex declarative learning', in K.J. Holyoak and R.G. Morrison (eds) *The Cambridge Handbook of Thinking and Reasoning* (Cambridge: Cambridge University Press, 2005) pp. 371–99.

35 G.A. Miller, 'The magical number seven, plus or minus two: some limits on our capacity for processing information', *Psychological Review*, 1956, 63: 81–97.

36 This teaching exercise is from M. Cardwell, L. Clark and C. Meldrum, *Psychology for 'A' level* (London: Collins Educational, 1996) p. 325.

37 A.D. Baddeley, *Human Memory: Theory and Practice* (Hove: Psychology Press, 1997); M.S. Gazzaniga, R.B. Ivry and G.R. Mangun, *Cognitive Neuroscience: The Biology of the Mind* (New York: W.W. Norton and Co., 2002) p. 311.

38 R.G. Morrison, 'Thinking in working memory', in Holyoak and Morrison, op. cit, pp. 457–73.

39 Le Doux, op. cit., p. 278.

40 Wilson, op. cit., p. 21.

41 K. Koedinger and J.R. Anderson, 'Abstract planning and perceptual chunks: elements of expertise in geometry', *Cognitive Science*, 1990, 14: 511–50.

42 Gazzaniga *et al.*, op. cit., pp. 551.

43 A. Damasio, *Descartes Error: Emotion, Reason, and the Human Brain* (New York: Harper Collins (Quill), 1994) pp. 197–8.

44 Gazzaniga *et al.*, op. cit.

45 D. Berry and Z. Dienes, 'Towards a working characterisation of implicit learning', in D. Berry and Z. Dienes (eds) *Implicit and Explicit Knowledge in Human Performance* (Erlbaum: Hove, 1993) pp. 1–18; W. Schneider and R. Schiffrin, 'Controlled and automatic human information processing: 1. Detection, search and attention', *Psychological Review*, 1977, 84: 1–66.

46 Berry and Dienes, op. cit. Schneider and Schiffrin, op. cit.

47 J.R. Anderson, *The Architecture of Cognition* (Cambridge, MA: Harvard University Press, 1983).

48 K. Van Lehn, 'Cognitive skill acquisition', *The Annual Review of Psychology*, 1996, 47: 513–39.

49 J.R. Anderson, *Rules of the Mind* (Hillsdale, NJ: Erlbaum, 1993).

50 A. Newell, *Unified Theories of Cognition* (Cambridge, MA: Harvard University Press, 1990); A. Newell and P. Rosenbloom, 'Mechanisms of skill acquisition and the law of practice', in J.R. Anderson (ed.) *Cognitive Skills and Their Acquisition* (Hillsdale, NJ: Erlbaum, 1981) pp. 1–56.

51 Ibid.

52 P.C. Kyllonen and V.J. Shute, 'A taxonomy of learning skills', in P.L. Ackerman, R.J. Sternberg and R. Glaser (eds) *Learning and Individual Differences: Advances in Theory and Research* (New York: W.H. Freeman and Co., 1989) pp. 117–63.

53 The list is taken from: Gazzaniga, Ivry and Mangun, op. cit., p. 330.

54 Gazzaniga, Ivry and Mangun, op. cit., pp. 314 and 330.

55 Berry and Dienes, op. cit., pp. 1–18.

56 Gazzaniga *et al.*, p. 332.

57 A.S. Reber, R. Allen and P.J. Reber, 'Implicit versus explicit learning', in R.J. Sternberg (ed.) *The Nature of Cognition* (Cambridge, MA: MIT Press, 1999) pp. 173–202.

58　S. Epstein, 'Integration of the cognitive and the psychodynamic unconscious', *American Psychologist*, 1994, 49: 709–24.

59　Reber *et al.*, op. cit., pp. 173–202.

60　The findings of the AG studies have not been free of critical scrutiny. For example, some researchers have suggested that it may be merely the physical similarity of the stimulus and test strings in terms of groups, repeats, beginnings, endings and so forth which are surface features (abstract analogies) of the strings rather than the deep structure of the grammar. See for example: L.R. Brooks and J.R. Vokey, 'Abstract analogies and abstracted grammars: a comment on Reber, and Mathews *et al.*', *Journal of Experimental Psychology: General*, 1991, 120: 316–23.

61　R.C. Mathews, R.R. Buss, W.B. Stanley, F. Blanchard-Fields, J.-R. Cho and B. Druhan, 'The role of implicit and explicit processes in learning from examples: a synergistic effect', *Journal of Experimental Psychology: Learning, Memory and Cognition*, 1989, 15: 1083–100.

62　Reber *et al.*, op. cit.

63　Myers, op. cit., p. 52; Wilson, op. cit., p. 26.

64　P. Lewicki, T. Hill and E. Bizot, 'Acquisition of procedural knowledge about a pattern of stimuli that cannot be articulated', *Cognitive Psychology*, 1998, 20: 24–37.

65　Lewicki *et al.*, op. cit.

66　Lewicki explained this general phenomenon in terms of what a process he called 'conditional elimination'. A learned algorithm based upon a simple co-variation between two stimuli (for example, X not in same square twice in succession) can be abandoned or replaced by a new one when it fails to fit current stimuli, however rather than being lost completely the learned algorithm is merely de-activated (conditionally eliminated) but can be re-activated when stimuli consistent with it are re-encountered. P. Lewicki, T. Hill and M. Czyzewska, 'Non-conscious acquisition of information', *American Psychologist*, 1992, 47: 796–801.

67　Lewicki *et al.*, op. cit., p. 801.

68　Wilson, op. cit., p. 27.

69　Lewicki *et al.*, op. cit.

70　A. Dijksterhuis, 'Think different: the merits of unconscious thought in preference development and decision-making', *Journal of Personality and Social Psychology*, 2004, 87: 586–98; A Dijksterhuis and T. Meurs, 'Where creativity resides: the generative power of unconscious thought', *Consciousness and Cognition*, 2006, 15: 135–46.

71　In his foreword to French and Cleerman's 2002 edited book *Implicit Learning and Consciouness* Reber refers to the 'polarity fallacy' (that something is one thing or the other rather than being a little of each) as one of psychology's worst conceptual errors.

72　L. Litman and A.S. Reber, 'Implicit cognition and thought', in K.J. Holyoak and R.G. Morrison (eds) *The Cambridge Handbook of Thinking and Reasoning* (Cambridge: Cambridge University Press, 2005) pp. 431–53.

73　A. Bandura, *Social Learning Theory* (Englewood Cliffs, NJ: Prentice Hall, 1977).

74　J. Nadler, L. Thompson, L. and L. van Boven, 'Learning negotiation skills: four models of knowledge creation and transfer', *Management Science*, 2003, 49: 529–40.

75 The three other methods were: didactic; information revelation; and analogical learning.
76 A.S. Reber, *Implicit Learning and Tacit Knowledge: An Essay on the Cognitive
Unconscious* (New York: Oxford University Press, 1993); E. Sadler-Smith,
*Learning and Development for Managers: Perspectives Form Research and
Practice* (Oxford: Blackwell, 2006).
77 Wilson, op. cit.

6 The 'least effort' principle

1 R.M. Hogarth, *Educating Intuition* (Chicago: University of Chicago Press,
2001) p. 125.
2 A. Tverskey and D. Kahneman, 'Judgement under uncertainty: heuristics
and biases', in H.R. Arkes and K.R. Hammond (eds) *Judgement and Decision
making: An inter-disciplinary Reader* (Cambridge: Cambridge University
Press, 1986) pp. 38–55.
3 http://www.national-lottery.co.uk/player/p/gaming/lotto
(accessed 22/01/07).
4 Tverskey and Kahneman, op. cit.
5 Base rate in this context has nothing to do with interest rates or finance – in
this case it is being used to refer to the percentage of a particular occupational group in the population as a whole.
6 It is a law of probability that specification can only reduce probability, i.e.
the probability of A and B (P(A&B)) cannot be greater than the probability
of A or B alone (P(B)), that is: P(A&B) < P(B). See: A. Tversky and D.
Kahneman, 'Judgement of and by representativeness', in D. Kahneman,
P. Slovic and A. Tversky (eds), *Judgement Under Uncertainty: Heuristics and
Biases* (Cambridge: Cambridge University Press, 1982) pp. 84–98.
7 In this version of the problem six of the eight alternatives are 'fillers' and
only (6) and (8) make up the true experiment. Some interesting variations in
the results were found when the numbers of responses was pared down to
(6) and (8) alone.
8 Hogarth, op. cit., p. 126.
9 P. Slovic, M. Finucane, E. Peters and D.G. MacGregor, 'The affect heuristic',
in Gilovich, *et al.*, op. cit., pp. 397–420.
10 D. Kahneman and S. Frederick, 'A model of heuristic judgment', in K.J.
Holyoak and R.G. Morrison (eds) *The Cambridge Handbook of Thinking
and Reasoning* (Cambridge: Cambridge University Press, 2005) p. 279.
11 S.J. Gould, *Bully for Brontosaurus: Further Reflections in Natural History*
(London: Penguin, 1991) p. 469.
12 S. Epstein, V. Denes-Raj and R. Pacini, 'The Linda problem revisited
from the perspective of cognitive experiential self theory', *Personality and
Social Psychology Bulletin*, 1995, 12: 1124–38; E. Epstein and R. Pacini,
'Some basic issues regarding dual process theories from the perspective of
cognitive-experiential self theory', in S. Chaiken and Y. Trope (eds) *Dual-
process Theories in Social Psychology* (New York: The Guilford Press, 1999)
p. 469.
13 R. Hastie and R.M Dawes, *Rational Choice in an Uncertain World: The
Psychology of Judgement and Decision Making* (London: Sage, 2001).
14 Ibid. p. 81.

15 B. Glassner, *The Culture of Fear: Why Americans are Afraid of the Wrong Things* (New York: Basic Books, 1999).

16 P. Slovic, B. Fischhoff and S. Lichtenstein, 'Behavioral decision theory', *Annual Review of Psychology*, 1977, 28: 1–39.

17 A. Tverskey and D. Kahneman, 'Judgement under uncertainty: heuristics and biases', in H.R. Arkes and K.R. Hammond (eds), *Judgement and Decision making: An Inter-disciplinary Reader* (Cambridge: Cambridge University Press, 1986) p. 47.

18 Tverskey and Kahneman, op. cit., p. 49.

19 D. Kahneman and A. Tversky, 'The simulation heuristic', in D. Kahneman, P. Slovic and A. Tversky (eds) *Judgement under Uncertainty: Heuristics and Biases* (Cambridge: Cambridge University Press, 1982) pp. 201–8.

20 K. Fielder and J. Schmid, 'Heuristics', in A.S.R. Manstead and M. Hewstone (eds) *The Blackwell Encyclopaedia of Social Psychology* (Oxford: Blackwell, 1995) pp. 296–300.

21 C.M. Gaglio, 'The role of mental simulations and counter-factual thinking in the opportunity identification process', *Entrepreneurship Theory and Practice* 2004, winter: 533–52.

22 N.J. Roese *et al.* 'Sex differences in regre*t all* for love or some for lust', *Personality and Social Psychology Bulletin*, 2006, 32: 770–80.

23 J.E. Escalas, 'Imagine yourself in the product: mental simulation, narrative transportation, and persuasion', *Journal of Advertising*, 2004, 33: 37–48.

24 The concepts of 'heuristics and biases' has not been immune from criticism from other psychologists and decision researchers. Stanovich and West offered the view that 'perhaps no finding in the heuristics and biases literature has been the subject of as much criticism' (p. 657) as that levelled at the conjunction fallacy in the Linda problem. For example, they noted that some have argued that the phrase 'Linda is a bank teller' might be construed (because from the amount the experimenter seems to know about Linda) as not containing the phrase 'and is not active in the feminist movement'. If this is the inference that is made rating (8) higher than (6) is no longer a conjunction fallacy. For a more detailed discussion see: K.E. Stanovich and R.F. West, 'Individual differences in reasoning: implications for the rationality debate?' *Behavioral and Brain Sciences*, 2000, 23: 645–726; E. Shafir and A. LeBouef, 'Rationality', *Annual Review of Psychology*, 2002, 53: p. 504.

25 In the previous version of the problem five of the eight alternatives were 'fillers' and only (3), (6) and (8) made up the true experiment.

26 D. Kahneman and S. Frederick, 'Representativeness revisited: attribute substitution in intuitive judgment', in T. Gilovich, D. Griffin, and D. Kahneman (eds) *Heuristics and Biases: The Psychology of Intuitive Judgment* (Cambridge: Cambridge University Press, 2002) p. 62.

27 D. Kahneman and S. Frederick, 'A model of heuristic judgement', in K.J. Holyoak and R.G. Morrison (eds) *The Cambridge Handbook of Thinking and Reasoning* (Cambridge: Cambridge University Press, 2005) p. 270.

28 G. Gigerenzer, 'How to make cognitive illusions disappear: beyond 'heuristics and biases', in W. Stroebe and M. Hewstone (eds) *European Review of Social Psychology*, Vol. 2 (Chichester: John Wiley, 1991) pp. 83–115.

29 D. Kahneman and A. Tversky, 'On the reality of cognitive illusions: a reply to Gigerenzer's critique', *Psychological Review*, 1996, 103: 582–91.

30 T.D. Wilson, *Strangers to Ourselves: Discovering the Adaptive Unconscious*, (Cambridge, MA: Belknap/Harvard, 2002) p. 50.
31 K.S. Bowers, G. Regehr and C. Balthazard, 'Intuition in the context of discovery', *Cognitive Psychology*, 1990, 22: 72–110.
32 G.P. Hodgkinson and P.R. Sparrow, *The Competent Organization: A Psychological Analysis of the Strategic Management Process* (Buckingham: Open University Press, 2002).
33 It should be noted that there has been some debate between the 'heuristics-and-biases' research and the 'fast-and-frugal' perspective. See: T. Gilovich and D. Griffin, 'Introduction – heuristics and biases: then and now' in T. Gilovich, D. Griffin, and D. Kahneman (eds) *Heuristics and Biases: The Psychology of Intuitive Judgment* (Cambridge: Cambridge University Press, 2002) pp. 1–18.
34 G. Gigerenzer and P.M. Todd, 1999, 'Fast and frugal heuristics: the adaptive toolbox', in G. Gigerenzer, P.M. Todd and the ABC Research Group (eds) *Simple Heuristics that Make us Smart* (Oxford: Oxford University Press, 1999) pp. 3–36.
35 D.G. Goldstein and G. Gigerenzer, 'The recognition heuristic: how ignorance makes us smart', in Gigerenzer, *et al.*, op. cit. pp. 37–58.
36 Gigerenzer and Todd, op. cit. *Note*: this form of the heuristic is based on the assumption that there is a positive relationship between recognition and the criterion (population size). If there was a negative relationship between recognition and the criterion the heuristic should be stated as: 'If one of two objects is recognised and the other is not, then infer that the recognised object has a lower value'.
37 P.M. Todd and G. Gigerenzer, 'Bounding rationality to the world', *Journal of Economic Psychology*, 2003, 24: p. 161.
38 B. Borges, D.G. Goldstein, A. Ortmann and G. Gigerenzer, 'Can ignorance beat the stock-market?', in Gigerenzer *et al.*, op. cit., p. 65.
39 Borges *et al.*, op. cit., p. 61.
40 The recognition approach in this context begs one obvious question: what are the criteria for well known-ness – 'well-known for what?', moreover, what if the experiment had been conducted in 2004, might Enron have been amongst the most well known of US companies?
41 For a fuller discussion of each of these see: G. Gigerenzer and D.G. Goldstein, 'Betting on one good reason: take the best heuristics', in Gigerenzer *et al.*, op. cit., pp. 75–95.
42 Gigerenzer and Todd, op. cit., p. 30.
43 Gigerenzer and Todd, op. cit., p. 33.
44 Todd and Gigerenzer, op. cit.
45 M.S. Gazzaniga, R.B. Ivry and G.R. Mangun, *Cognitive Neuroscience: The Biology of the Mind* (New York: W.W. Norton and Co., 2002) p. 596.

7 Intuitive 'muscle power'

1 G. Klein, *Intuition at Work: Why Developing Your Gut instincts Will make you Better at What you Do* (New York: Doubleday, 2003) pp. xx–xxi.
2 G. Klein, *Sources of Power: How People Make Decisions* (Cambridge, MA: MIT Press, 1990).

3   I. Janis and L. Mann, *Decision Making: A Psychological Analysis of Conflict, Choice and Commitment* (New York: Free Press, 1977).
4   R.O. Besco, D. Maurmo, M.H. Potter, B. Strauch, R.B. Stone and E. Wiener, 'Unrecognised training needs for airline pilots', in *Proceedings of the Human Factors and Ergonomics Society 38th Annual Meeting*, Santa Monica, CA.: Human Factors and Ergonomics Society, 1994, pp. 41–5. Cited in A.F. Stokes, K. Kemper and K. Kite, 'Aeronautical decision making, cue recognition, and expertise under time pressure', in C.E. Zsambok and G. Klein (eds) *Naturalistic Decision Making* (Mahwah, NJ: Lawrence Erlbaum Associates Publishers, 1997) p. 184.
5   Klein, *Sources of Power*, op. cit.
6   G. Klein, S. Wolf, L. Militello and C. Zsambok, 'Characteristics of skilled option generation in chess', *Organisational Behavior and Human Decision Processes*, 1995, 62(1) 63–9.
7   G. Klein, 'The recognition primed decision (RPD) model: looking back, looking forward', in Zsambok and Klein, op. cit.
8   Klein, *Sources of Power*, op. cit., p. 11.
9   Klein, *Sources of Power*, op. cit., p. 21.
10   W.L. Waag and H.H. Bell, 'Situation assessment and decision making in skilled fighter pilots', in C.E. Zsambok and G. Klein (eds) *Naturalistic Decision Making* (Mahwah, NJ: Lawrence Erlbaum Associates Publishers, 1997) pp. 247–54.
11   A.F. Stokes, K. Kemper and K. Kite, 'Aeronautical decision making, cue recognition, and expertise under time pressure', in Zsambok and Klein, op. cit., p. 184.
12   Klein, *Sources of Power*, op. cit., p. 24.
13   Klein, *Sources of Power*, op. cit., p. 33.
14   The method often employed is known as Applied Cognitive Task Analysis (ACTA). See: L.G. Militello R.J.B. Hutton, 'Applied cognitive task analysis (ACTA): a practitioner's toolkit for understanding cognitive task demands', *Ergonomics* 1998, 41: 1618–41.
15   K.S. Bowers, G. Regehr and C. Balthazard, 'Intuition in the context of discovery', *Cognitive Psychology* 1990, 22: 72–110.
16   Ibid.
17   N. Baumann and J. Kuhl, 'Intuition, affect and personality: unconscious coherence judgements and self-regulation of negative affect', *Journal of Personality and Social Psychology*, 2002, 83(5): 1213–23.
18   J.F. Kihlstrom, 'Conscious versus unconscious cognition', in R.J. Sternberg (ed.) *The Nature of Cognition* (Cambridge, MA: MIT Press, 1999) pp. 173–203.
19   There may be exceptions in domains in which human beings come 'hardwired' to make certain intuitive judgements – see Chapter 11.
20   K.G. Volz and D.Y. von Cramon, 'What neuroscience can tell about intuitive processes in the context of perceptual discovery', *Journal of Cognitive Neuroscience*, 2006, 18(12): 2077–87.
21   M. Bar, K. S. Kassam, A.S. Ghuman *et al.*, 'Top-down facilitation of visual recognition', *Proceedings of the National Academy of Sciences, USA*, 2006, 103, pp. 449–54.
22   Volz and von Cramon, op. cit.
23   As Volz and von Cramon note (p. 2081), they did not observe activation

within the aSTG region (as was observed by Jung-Beeman and his colleagues – see Chapter 3); one reason for this may be because Volz and Cramon were concerned with activations that took place in relation to intuitive perceptions of coherence, whilst Jung-Beeman and his colleagues were concerned with the activation which occurred at the moment of insight (Eureka! moments).

24 A. Bolte, T. Goschke and J. Kuhl, 'Emotion and intuition: effects of positive and negative mood on implicit judgements and semantic coherence', *Psychological Science*, 2003, 14(5): 416–21.

25 M. Jung-Beeman, R.B. Friedman, J. Grafman, E. Perez, S. Diamond and M. Beadle Lindsay, 'Summation priming and coarse semantic coding in the right hemisphere', *Journal of Cognitive Neuroscience*, 1994, 6: 26–45.

26 Psychologists have been somewhat divided for a number of years on the extent to which implicit learning and non-conscious processing are complex. As we have already seen Lewicki and his colleagues are of the view that non-conscious processing of information can be much more than merely confined to mundane, automated operations. Loftus and Klinger and Greenwald on the other hand, whilst agreeing that unconscious cognition exists, are of the opinion that that it is not very sophisticated (for example, they argue that there is little evidence for unconscious processing of verbal stimuli at a higher level than a single word). See: A.G. Greenwald, 'New look 3: unconscious cognition reclaimed', *American Psychologist*, 1992, 47: 766–79. C.A. Seger, 'Implicit learning', *Psychological Bulletin*, 1994, 115(2): 163–96.

27 S.E. Taylor, L.B. Pham, I.D. Rivkin and D.A. Armor, 'Harnessing the imagination: mental simulation, self regulation and coping', *American Psychologist*, 1998, 53(4): p. 430.

28 J. Nicklaus, *Play Better Golf* (New York: King Features, 1976).

29 Klein, *Sources of Power*, op. cit., p. 45.

30 Klein, *Sources of Power*, op. cit., p. 68.

31 P.C Wason, 'Reasoning about a rule', *Quarterly Journal of Experimental Psychology* 1968, 20: 273–81.

32 P.N. Johnson-Laird, *The Computer and the Mind: An Introduction to Cognitive Science* (London: Fontana, 1988) pp. 241–2.

33 The Popperian method urges scientists to look for evidence that will disconfirm a theory rather than accumulate confirmatory evidence. See: K. Popper, *The Logic of Scientific Discovery* (London: Hutchinson, 1959).

34 K. Dunbar and J. Fugelsang, 'Scientific thinking and reasoning', in K.J. Holyoak and R.G. Morrison (eds) *The Cambridge Handbook of Thinking and Reasoning* (Cambridge: Cambridge University Press, 2005) p. 710.

35 M.S. Cohen, J.T. Freeman and B.B. Thompson, 'Training the naturalistic decision maker', in C.E. Zsambok and G. Klein (eds) *Naturalistic Decision Making* (Mahwah, NJ: Lawrence Erlbaum Associates Publishers, 1997) pp. 257–68; J. Shanteau, 'Competence in experts: the role of task characteristics', *Organizational Behavior and Human Decision Processes*, 1992, 53: 252–66.

36 Besides which we may be thinking about them (consciously or nonconsciously) for a particular reason with which their phone call is connected.

37 J.E. Le Doux, *The Emotional Brain: The Mysterious Underpinnings of Emotional Life* (New York: Simon and Schuster, 1996) p. 212.

38 From: G. Klein, *Intuition at work* (New York: Currency Doubleday, 2003) p. 31.

8 In two minds?

1 S. Epstein, 'Integration of the cognitive and the psychodynamic unconscious', *American Psychologist*, 1994, 49: 718.
2 R. Pacini, and S. Epstein, 'The relation of rational and experiential information processing styles to personality, basic beliefs, and the ratio-bias phenomenon', *Journal of Personality and Social Psychology*, 1999, 76: 972–87.
3 V. Denes-Raj and S. Epstein, 'Conflict between experiential and rational
   processing: when people behave against their better judgement, *Journal of
   Personality and Social Psychology*, 1994, 66: 819–29; L.A. Kirkpatrick and
   S. Epstein, 'Cognitive experiential self theory and subjective probability:
   further evidence for two conceptual systems', *Journal of Personality and
   Social Psychology*, 1992, 63: 535–44.
4 Kirkpatrick and Epstein, op. cit., p. 539.
5 For example, the Yin aspect of human nature is nurturing and self-effacing;
   the Yang aspect is harsh and domineering – see *The Tao te Ching: A New
   Translation by Stephen Hodge* (Arlesford: A Godsfield Book, 2002) p. 55;
   Thinking (T) versus feeling (F) is one of the dimensions upon which the
   Myers-Briggs Type Indicator (MBTI) personality inventory is based, which
   itself was derived from the work of the Swiss psycho-analyst Carl Gustav
   Jung. Another dimension is sensing (S) versus intuiting (N).
6 W. James, *The Varieties of Religious Experience: A Study in Human Nature*
   (New York: Penguin Books USA Inc., 1902/1985) p. 73.
7 S. Epstein, R. Pacini, V. Denes-Raj and H. Heir, 'Individual differences
   in intuitive-experiential and analytical-rational thinking styles', *Journal of
   Personality and Social Psychology*, 1996, 71: p. 392.
8 R. Pacini, F. Muir and S. Epstein, 'Depressive realism from the perspective
   of cognitive-experiential self theory', *Journal of Personality and Social
   Psychology*, 1998, 74: 1056–68.
9 S. Epstein and R. Pacini, 'Some basic issues regarding dual-process theories
   from the perspective of Cognitive Experiential Self Theory', in S. Chaiken
   and Y. Trope (eds) *Dual-process Theories in Social Psychology* (New York:
   The Guilford Press, 1999) pp. 462–82.
10 S. Epstein, R. Pacini, V. Denes-Raj and H. Heir, 'Individual differences in
   intuitive-experiential and analytical-rational thinking styles', *Journal of
   Personality and Social Psychology*, 1996, 71: p. 391.
11 Epstein and Pacini, op. cit., p. 473.
12 Epstein cites a US Gallup poll in the early 1990s in which one in four people
   reported belief in ghosts, one in seven attested to the fact that they had
   'seen' a UFO and one in two believed in ESP. See: S. Epstein, 'Integration of
   the cognitive and psychodynamic unconscious', *American Psychologist*, 1994,
   August: 709–24.
13 Epstein and Pacini, op. cit., p. 467.
14 A.R. Damasio, *Descartes' Error: Emotion, Reason and the Human Brain*
   (New York: HarperCollins, 1994) p. 192.
15 The sub-title for this section is from: J.St.B.T. Evans, 'In two minds: dual-
   process accounts of reasoning', *Trends in Cognitive Sciences*, 2003, 7(10): 458.
16 S.A. Sloman, 'The empirical case for two systems of reasoning', *Psychological Bulletin*, 1996, 119: 3–22; E.R. Smith and J. DeCoster, 'Associative
   and rule-based processing', in S. Chaiken and Y. Trope (eds) *Dual-process
   Theories in Social Psychology* (New York: Guilford Press, 1999) 323–36.

17 H.L. Dreyfus and S.E. Dreyfus, 'Expertise in real world contexts', *Organization Studies*, 2005, 26(5): 779–92.
18 Sloman, op. cit.
19 E.R. Smith and J. DeCoster, 'Associative and rule-based processing', in S. Chaiken and Y. Trope (eds) *Dual-process Theories in Social Psychology* (New York: Guilford Press, 1999) pp. 323–36.
20 E. Sadler-Smith, *Learning and Development for Managers: Perspectives from Research and Practice* (Oxford: Blackwell, 2006).
21 This is the region of the greatest visual acuity.
22 J.St.B.T. Evans, 'In two minds: dual-process accounts of reasoning', *Trends in Cognitive Sciences*, 2003, 7(10): 454–9.
23 A number of researchers attribute this to a heuristic that the experiential system is prone to – that of the 'matching bias' – which results in a strong tendency to chose items that have a perceptual match to the those named in the rule (irrespective of whether to do so is logically correct or not).
24 R.M. Hogarth, *Educating Intuition* (Chicago: University of Chicago Press, 2001) pp. 118–19.
25 L. Cosmides and J. Tooby, 'Cognitive adaptations for social exchange', in J.H. Barkow, L. Cosmides and J. Tooby, *The Adapted Mind: Evolutionary Psychology and the Generation of Culture* (New York: Oxford University Press, 1992) pp. 163–228.
26 J.A. Fodor, *The Modularity of Mind: An Essay in Faculty Psychology* (Cambridge, MA: MIT Press, 1983).
27 D. Evans and O. Zarate, *Introducing Evolutionary Psychology* (New York: Totem Books, 1999).
28 J.St.B.T. Evans, 'In two minds: dual-process accounts of reasoning', *Trends in Cognitive Sciences*, 2003, 7(10): 454.
29 Ibid.
30 E.R. Smith and J. DeCoster, 'Associative and rule-based processing', in S. Chaiken and Y. Trope (eds) *Dual-process Theories in Social Psychology* (New York: Guilford Press, 1999) pp. 323–36.
31 C.S. Levinson, 'Interactional biases in human thinking', E. Goody (ed.) *Social Intelligence and Interaction* (Cambridge: Cambridge University Press, 1995) pp. 221–60.
32 W. Schroyens, W. Schaeken and S. Handley, 'In search of counter-examples: deductive rationality in human reasoning', *Quarterly Journal of Experimental Psychology*, 2003, 56: 1129–45; K.E. Stanovich, *Who is Rational? Studies of Individual Differences in Reasoning* (Hillsdale, NJ: Lawrence Erlbaum Associates, Inc. 1999); K.E. Stanovich and R.F. West, 'Individual differences in reasoning: implications for the rationality debate?', *Behavioral and Brain Sciences*, 2000, 23: 645–726.
33 Evans, op. cit.
34 K.E. Stanovich and R.F. West, 'Individual differences in reasoning: implications for the rationality debate?', *Behavioral and Brain Sciences* 2000, 23: 659.
35 Stanovich and West, op. cit., p. 660.
36 K.E. Stanovich, 'Rationality, intelligence and levels of analysis in cognitive science', in R.J. Sternberg, *Why Smart People can be so Stupid* (New Haven: Yale University Press, 2002) 145.
37 K.S. Bowers, G. Regehr and C. Balthazard, 'Intuition in the context of discovery', *Cognitive Psychology*, 1990, 22: 72–110.

38 M. Polanyi, *Personal Knowledge: Towards a Post-critical Philosophy* (New York: Harper Row, 1958) p. 131. Cited in R.M. Hamm, 'Moment-by-moment variations in experts' analytical and intuitive cognitive activity, *IEEE Transactions on Systems, Man and Cybernetics*, 1988, 18(5): 757.

39 See: A. Wozniak, 'Managerial intuition across cultures: beyond a "West-East dichotomy" ', *Education and Training*, 2006, 48(2&3): 84–96.

40 Stanovich and West, op. cit., p. 661.

41 D. Kahneman, 'A psychological point of view: violations of rational rules as diagnostic of mental processes', *Behavioral and Brain Sciences*, 2000, 23: 683. For a more detailed discussion of the representativeness heuristic see Chapter 6.

42 This is not to say that the two systems do not conflict; as Stanovich and West noted: 'these conflicts may be rare, but the few occasions on which they occur might be important ones. This is because knowledge-based technological societies often put a premium on abstraction and de-contextualisation, and sometime require that the fundamental computation bias of human cognition be over-ridden by System 2 processes' (Stanovich and West, op. cit., p. 661).

43 J.L. Pollock, *Cognitive Carpentry: A Blueprint for How to Build a Person* (Cambridge, MA: MIT Press, 1995); Stanovich, op. cit., p. 145.

44 M.D. Lieberman, J.M. Jarcho A.B. Satpute, 'Evidence-based and intuition-based self-knowledge: an fMRI study', *Journal of Personality and Social Psychology*, 2004, 87: 421–35.

45 On the basis of the hemodynamic principles upon which fMRI techniques are founded, these areas would show up in the scan as increased blood flow. See: P.S. Churchland, *Brain-wise: Studies in Neurophilosophy* (Cambridge, MA: MIT Press, 2002).

46 S.B. Klein, J. Loftus, J.G. Trafton, and R.W. Fuhrman, 'Use of exemplars and abstractions in trait judgments: a model of trait knowledge about the self and others', *Journal of Personality and Social Psychology*, 1992, 63: 739–53.

47 Adapted from: http://nobelprize.org/nobel_prizes/medicine/laureates/1981/ (accessed: 24/01/07).

48 M.S. Gazzaniga, 'The split brain revisited', *Scientific American*, 2002, 12(1): 27–31.

9 A matter of feeling

1 R.L. Gregory (ed.), *The Oxford Companion to the Mind* (Oxford: Oxford University Press, 1987) p. 12.

2 J.E. Le Doux, *The Emotional Brain* (New York: Simon and Schuster, 1996) p. 82.

3 R.W. Buck, 'The epistemology of reason and affect', in J.C. Borod (ed.) *The Neuro-psychology of Emotion* (Oxford: Oxford University Press, 2000) pp. 31–55.

4 The thalamus is the 'gateway to the cortex': information normally passes from the senses through the thalamus and onto the sensory receiving areas in the cortex. See: M.S. Gazzaniga, R.B. Ivry and G.R. Mangun, *Cognitive Neuroscience: The Biology of the Mind* (New York: W.W. Norton and Co., 2002) p. 86.

5 Le Doux, op. cit., p. 164.

6 K.N. Ochsner and D.L. Schacter, 'A social cognitive neuroscience approach to emotion and memory', in Borod, op. cit., pp. 163–193.
7 Gazzaniga *et al.*, op. cit., p. 545.
8 A.J. Hart, P.J., Whalen, L.M. Shin, S.C. McInerney, H. Fischer and S.L. Rauch 'Differential response of the human amygdala to racial out-group versus in-group face stimuli', *Neuroreport*, 2000, 11: 2352–4.
9 Le Doux, op. cit., p. 329.
10 W. James, 'What is an emotion?', *Mind*, 1984, 9: 188–205. Cited in J.J. Prinz, *Gut Reactions* (Oxford: Oxford University Press, 2004) p. 5.
11 A.R. Damasio, *The Feeling of What Happens: Body, Emotion and the Making of Consciousness* (London: Vintage, 1999), p. 37.
12 Le Doux, op. cit., p. 40.
13 Gazzaniga, *et al.*, op. cit., p. 539.
14 S. Rose, 'Thinking allowed', *The Guardian (Review)*, 17 February 2007, p. 8. Book review by S. Rose of: G.M. Edelman, *Second Nature: Brain Science and Human Knowledge* (New Haven: Yale, 2007).
15 A.R. Damasio, *Descartes' Error: Emotion, Reason and the Human Brain* (New York: HarperCollins, 1994), pp. 145 and 149–151.
16 K. Oatley, *Emotions: A Brief History* (Oxford: Blackwell, 2004).
17 A.R. Damasio, *Descartes' Error: Emotion, Reason and the Human Brain* (New York: HarperCollins, 1994) p. 150.
18 Damasio, op. cit., p. 341.
19 The term 'inner attunement' is from: D. Goleman, *Emotional Intelligence: Why it can Matter More than IQ* (London: Bloomsbury, 1996) p. 54. For a discussion of 'attunement' techniques see: G.L. Claxton, *Hare Brain, Tortoise Mind* (London: Fourth Estate, 1997); G.L. Claxton and B. Lucas, *Be Creative*, (London: BBC Audio Books, 2004); E. Sadler-Smith and E. Shefy, 'Developing intuitive awareness in management education', *Academy of Management Learning and Education*, 2007, 6 (in press); and finally, Professor Bill Taggart's web site: http://www.the-intuitive-self.org/
20 E.T. Gendlin, *Focusing* (New York: Bantam, 1981).
21 Damasio argues that 'Nature appears to have built the apparatus of rationality not just on top of the apparatus of biological regulation, but also *from* it and *with* it'. See: A.R. Damasio, *The Feeling of what Happens: Body, Emotion and the Making of Consciousness* (London: Vintage, 1999) p. 128.
22 Le Doux, op. cit., p. 25
23 M. La France and M.A. Hecht, 'Why smiles generate leniency', *Personality and Social Psychology Bulletin*, 1995, 21: 207–14.
24 F. Strack, L.L. Martin and N. Schwarz, 'Priming and communication: the social determinants of information use in judgments of life satisfaction', *European Journal of Social Psychology*, 1988, 18: 429–42.
25 For studies of this nature a correlation (*r*) of 0.66 is deemed to be 'high' (it represents about 44 per cent shared variance), and is highly statistically significant ($p < 0.001$).
26 D. Kahneman and S. Frederick, 'Representativeness revisited: attribute substitution in intuitive judgment', in T. Gilovich, D. Griffin, and D. Kahneman (eds) *Heuristics and Biases: The Psychology of Intuitive Judgment* (Cambridge: Cambridge University Press, 2002) p. 53.
27 P. Slovic, M.L. Finucane, E. Peters and D.G. MacGregor, 'Risk as analysis

and risk as feelings: some thoughts about affect, reason, risk and rationality', *Risk Analysis* 2004, 24: 311–22.

28 Le Doux, op. cit., p. 314

29 This parallels Le Doux's argument that for a memory to appear in consciousness: 'The associative network has to reach a certain level of activation, which occurs as a function of the number of components of the memory that are activated and the weight of each activated component'. Le Doux, op. cit., p. 212.

30 I. Getz and T. Lubart, 'The emotional resonance model of creativity: theoretical and practical extensions, in S.W. Russ (ed.) *Affect, Creative Experience and Psychological Adjustment* (Philadelphia: Brunner/Mazel, 1999) pp. 41–55.

31 S.W. Russ, 'An evolutionary model for creativity: does it fit?', *Psychological Inquiry*, 1999, 10(4): 359–61.

32 Damasio 1994, op. cit., p. 128.

33 M. Macmillan, *An Odd Kind of Fame: Stories of Phineas Gage* (Cambridge, MA: MIT Press, 2000).

34 Harlow's account was written 20 years after the accident. This time lag has led some critics to question the reliability of the many subsequent analyses based on it of the changes in Gage's personality.

35 Macmillan, op. cit.

36 Damasio, 1994, op. cit., p. 32.

37 The human orbitofrontal cortex is the part of the pre-frontal cortex which forms the base of the frontal lobe, leaning against the upper wall of the orbit above the eyes. It is often divided into the VMPC and the lateral orbitofrontal cortex. It has been inferred that Gage incurred trauma to the VMPC. See: Gazzaniga *et al.*, op. cit., p. 546.

38 Damasio, 1994, op. cit., pp. 220–2.

39 A. Bechara, H. Damasio, D, Tranel and A.R. Damasio, 'Deciding advantageously before knowing the advantageous strategy', *Science* 1997, 275: 1293–5.

40 P.S. Churchland, *Brain-wise: Studies in Neurophilosophy* (Cambridge, MA: MIT Press, 2002) p. 224.

41 A. Bechara, D. Tranel and H. Damasio, 'Characterisation of the decision-making deficit of patients with ventro-medial prefrontal cortex lesions', *Brain*, 2000, 123: 2189–202.

42 A. Bechara, 'The role of emotion in decision-making: evidence from neurological patients with orbito-frontal damage', *Brain and Cognition*, 2004, 55: 30–40.

43 J.J. Prinz, *Gut Reactions* (Oxford: Oxford University Press, 2004) p. 5.

44 Damasio, 1994, op. cit.

45 Bechara *et al.*, op. cit.

46 T.D. Wilson, *Strangers to Ourselves: Discovering the Adaptive Unconscious* (Cambridge, MA: Belknap/Harvard, 2002) p. 63.

47 Damasio, 1994, op. cit., p. 174.

48 'Interview: King bean', *Your Company*, 1998, April/May, 8(3) (emphases added).

49 K.E. Stanovich, 'Rationality, intelligence and levels of analysis in cognitive science', in R.J. Sternberg, *Why Smart People can be so Stupid* (New Haven, CT: Yale University Press, 2002) pp. 124–58.

50 Damasio, 1999, op. cit., p. 80.
51 Bechara, op. cit., p. 38.
52 The somatosensory/insular cortices are cortical regions that receive and represent information abut touch, pain, temperature and limb position. See: Gazzaniga *et al.*, op. cit., p. 75.
53 Le Doux, op. cit., p. 295.
54 Bechara, op. cit., p. 39.
55 See: M. Sinclair, E. Sadler-Smith, G.P. Hodgkinson, 'The role of intuition in strategic decision making', in L.A. Costanzo and R.B. McKay (eds) *The Handbook of Research on Strategy and Foresight* (Cheltenham, UK: Edward Elgar, 2008 in press)
56 G. Klein, *Intuition at Work* (New York: Doubleday, 2003) p. 98.
57 K.G. Volz and D.Y. von Cramon, 'What neuroscience can tell about intuitive processes in the context of perceptual discovery', *Journal of Cognitive Neuroscience*, 2006, 18(12): 2077–87.
58 P. Slovic, M.L. Finucane, E. Peters and D.G. MacGregor, 'Risk as analysis and risk as feelings: some thoughts about affect, reason, risk and rationality', *Risk Analysis*, 2004, 24: 311–22.
59 A. Bechara, H. Damasio, D, Tranel and A.R. Damasio, 'Deciding advantageously before knowing the advantageous strategy', *Science*, 1997, 275: pp. 1293–5.
60 The claustrum (meaning 'hidden away') is a thin, irregular sheet of grey matter beneath the inner surface of the neo-cortex. It receives inputs from almost all regions of the cortex and projects back to almost all regions of the cortex; however its function is 'enigmatic'. Francis Crick and Christof Koch speculated on its relationship to the processes that give rise to integrated consciousness. See: F.C. Crick and C. Koch, 'What is the function of the claustrum?', *Philosophical Transactions of the Royal Society, Series B*, 2005, 360: 1271–9.
61 K.G. Volz and D.Y. von Cramon, 'What neuroscience can tell about intuitive processes in the context of perceptual discovery', *Journal of Cognitive Neuroscience*, 2006, 18(12): 2077–87.
62 Intuition-as-expertise and intuition-as-feeling is a basic distinction that a number of authors have drawn, for example: E. Sadler-Smith and E. Shefy, 'The intuitive executive: understanding and apply 'gut feeling' in decision making', *Academy of Management Executive*, 2004, 18: 76–91.
63 Based on: L.A. Robinson, *Trust your Gut: How the Power of Intuition can Grow your Business* (Chicago: Kaplan Publishing, 2006) p. 34.
64 M. Emery, *Powerhunch: Living an Intuitive Life* (Hillsboro, OR: Beyond Words Publishing, 2001) p. 7.

10 The intuitive practitioner

1 The term 'practitioner' is used here as a generic term to refer to a person in an occupational role. Many of the examples are drawn from practice in the 'professions', and hence the term 'professional' or 'professional practitioner' could equally have been used as a 'catch-all' for executives, managers, doctors, lawyers, teachers, entrepreneurs and so forth (many of to whom what is written, I hope, pertains). Instead I use 'practitioner'.
2 R.J. Sternberg and T.I. Lubart, 'An investment theory of creativity and its development', *Human Development*, 1991, 34: 1–32; R.J. Sternberg and T.I.

Lubart, 'The concept of creativity: prospects and paradigms', in R.J. Sternberg (ed.) *Handbook of Creativity* (Cambridge: Cambridge University Press, 1999) pp. 3–15.

3 Homer, *The Iliad*, originally translated by E.V. Rieu (London: Penguin Books, 1950) p. 186.

4 From: Wordsworth's *The Prelude* (1850), Book 12, Line 204, (original emphasis).

5 Sternberg and Lubart, 1999, op. cit.

6 Sternberg and Lubart, 1999, op. cit. Also, see for example: R.J. Sternberg and J.E. Davidson (eds) *The Nature of Insight* (Cambridge, MA: The MIT Press); T.M. Amabile, *The Social Psychology of Creativity* (New York: Springer Verlag 1983).

7 A. Dietrich, 'The cognitive neuroscience of creativity', *Psychonomic Bulletin and Review*, 2004, 11(6): 1011–26.

8 M.A. Boden, *The Creative Mind: Myths and Mechanisms* (London: Routledge, 2004).

9 J.R. Hayes, 'Cognitive processes in creativity', in J.A. Glover, R.R. Ronning and C.R. Reynolds (eds) *Handbook of Creativity* (New York: Plenum, 1989) pp. 135–45. (Cited in Weisberg – see below).

10 Ibid.

11 R.W. Weisberg, 'Creativity and knowledge: a challenge to theories', in Sternberg, op. cit.

12 From: http://www.3m.com/about3m/pioneers/fry.jhtml (accessed 29/12/06).

13 From: http://web.mit.edu/invent/search.html (accessed 29/12/06).

14 P.F. Drucker, *Innovation and Entrepreneurship* (Oxford: Butterworth-Heinemann, 1985) p. 121.

15 M. Sundgren and A. Styhre, 'Intuition and pharmaceutical research', *European Journal of Innovation Management*, 2004, 7(4): 276.

16 D.K. Simonton, 'Foresight in insight: a Darwinian answer?', in R.J. Sternberg and J.E. Davidson (eds) *The Nature of Insight* (Cambridge, MA: MIT Press, 1995) pp. 465–94.

17 S.J. Gould, *Wonderful Life: The Burgess Shale and the Nature of History* (London: Hutchinson Radius, 1989) p. 287.

18 E. Dane and M.G. Pratt, 'Exploring intuition and its role in managerial decision making', *Academy of Management Review*, 2007, 32(1): 33–54.

19 See: E. Policastro, 'Creative intuition: an integrative review', *Creativity Research Journal*, 1995, 8(2): 99.

20 One AstraZeneca scientist is quoted as saying: 'The drug development process is not so damned rational as a lot of people would like it to be, instead intuition can prove to be extremely significant'. See: M. Sundgren and A. Styhre, 'Intuition and pharmaceutical research', *European Journal of Innovation Management*, 2004, 7(4): 274.

21 K. Popper, *The Logic of Scientific Discovery* (London: Hutchinson, 1959) p. 32. Cited in B. Magee, *Popper* (London: Fontana/Collins) p. 32.

22 See: http://www.astrazeneca.com/article/11155.aspx (accessed 31/12/06).

23 Sundgren and Styhre, op. cit., pp. 273, 274 and 275.

24 'Intimation' is the term used by Wallas in his model of the creative process. See Chapter 3.

25 I. Kirzner, *Perception, Opportunity and Profit* (Chicago: University of Chicago Press, 1979).

26 These differences are often referred to as 'cognitive styles'. See: R.J. Stern-berg, *Thinking Styles* (Cambridge: Cambridge University Press, 1997). For an empirical study of the effects of differences in intuitive and analytical cognitive styles on task performance, see: L.S. Woolhouse and R. Bayne, 'Personality and the use of intuition: individual differences in strategy and performance on an implicit learning task', *European Journal of Personality*, 2000, 14: 157–69. There is strong evidence to suggest that intuition and analysis are independent rather than opposing modes of thinking; see: G.P. Hodgkinson and E. Sadler-Smith, 'Complex or unitary? A critique and empirical reassessment of the Allinson-Hayes Cognitive Style Index', *Journal of Occupational and Organizational Psychology*, 2003, 76: 243–68.

27 P. Hedges, *Understanding your Personality with Myers-Briggs and More* (London: Sheldon Press, 1993) p. 11. A caveat is in order: Robert Sternberg has argued that, although the Myers-Briggs theory is the most widely-applied model of cognitive style, the underlying theory is open to question as are the purposes to which the test is often put. See: R.J. Sternberg, *Thinking Styles* (Cambridge: Cambridge University Press, 1997) p. 144.

28 W.L. Gardner and M.J. Martinko, 'Using the Myers-Briggs Type Indicator: a literature review and research agenda', *Journal of Management*, 1996, 22(1): 45–83.

29 Openness to experience and extraversion are two of the 'Big Five' personal-ity dimensions (the others are conscientiousness, agreeableness and neuroti-cism). Openness to experience includes having wide interests, and being imaginative and insightful, whilst extraversion encompasses traits as talka-tive, energetic, and assertive. See: P.T. Costa and R.R. McCrae, *NEO PI-R Professional Manual* (Chicago: Psychological Assessment Resources, 1992).

30 J. Langan-Fox and D.A. Shirley, 'The nature and measurement of intuition: cognitive and behavioural interests, personality and experiences', *Creativity Research Journal* 2003, 15(2 and 3): 207–22. For 'artistic' $t(4,40) = 5.74$ ($p < 0.001$); for 'adventure seeking' $t(4,40) = 4.78$ ($p < 0.001$) (see Langan-Fox and Shirley, op. cit., p. 215).

31 The concept of associative hierarchy was encountered previously (Chapter 4). See: S.A. Mednick, 'The associative basis of the creative process', *Psycho-logical Review*, 1962, 69: 220–32.

32 D.K. Simonton, 'Creativity, leadership and chance', in R.J. Sternberg (ed.) *The Nature of Creativity: Contemporary and Psychological Perspectives* (Cambridge: Cambridge University Press, 1988) p. 403.

33 M. Planck, 'Scientific autobiography and other papers', translated by F. Gaynor (New York: Philosophical Library, 1949). Cited in Simonton op. cit., p. 403.

34 H.A. Simon and W. Chase, 'Skills in chess', *American Scientist*, 1973, pp. 394–403; M. Runco, 'Creativity', *Annual Review of Psychology*, 2004, 55: 668.

35 Simonton, op. cit.

36 M.J. Kirton, *Adaption-innovation in the Context of Diversity and Change* (Hove: Routledge, 2003) pp. 237–8.

37 D. Leonard and S. Sensiper, 'The role of tacit knowledge in group innov-ation', *California Management Review*, 1998, 40(3): 65–72.

38 E. Sadler-Smith and E. Shefy, 'Developing intuitive awareness in manage-ment education', *Academy of Management Learning and Education*, 2007, 6(2): 186–205.

39 L.A. Burke and M. Miller, 'Taking the mystery out of intuitive decision making', *Academy of Management Executive*, 1999, 13(4): 91–8.

40 E. Policastro, 'Creative intuition: an integrative review', *Creativity Research Journal*, 1995, 8(2): p. 104.

41 A. Katz, 'Creativity in the cerebral hemispheres', in M.A. Runco (ed.) *Creativity Research Handbook* (Creskill, NJ: Hampton Press, 1997) pp. 203–26.

42 M. Runco, 2004, op. cit.

43 M.S. Gazzaniga, 'The brain as boondoggle', *Harvard Business Review*, 2006, February, p. 66.

44 People were classified on the basis of their responses to a self-report questionnaire as 'lucky', 'neutral' or 'unlucky'. See: R. Wiseman, *The Luck Factor: Change your Luck – and Change your Life* (London: Century, 2003) p. 75 and pp. 29–30.

45 Wiseman, op. cit., pp. 75 and 86.

46 See for example: G. Claxton and B. Lucas, *Be Creative: Essential Steps to Re-vitalize your Work and Life* (London, BBC Books, 2004) pp. 144–67; E. Sadler-Smith and E. Shefy, 'Developing intuitive awareness in management education', *Academy of Management Learning and Education*, 2007 (forthcoming).

47 S. Suzuki, *Zen Mind, Beginner's Mind: Informal Talks on Zen Meditation and Practice* (New York & Tokyo: Weatherhill Inc., 2002) p. 34.

48 See: http://www.virgin.com/aboutvirgin/allaboutvirgin/richardreplies/default.asp (accessed 29/12/06).

49 R. Branson, *Losing my Virginity: How I've Survived, Had Fun and Made a Fortune Doing Business my Way* (London: Virgin Books, 2005) pp. 120 and 152.

50 K.S. Bowers, S.G. Regehr, C. Balthazard and K. Parker, 'Intuition in the context of discovery', *Cognitive Psychology*, 1990, 22: 72–110.

51 D.K. Simonton, 'Creativity, leadership and chance', in Sternberg, op. cit., p. 396.

52 J.A. Schumpeter, *Capitalism, Socialism and Democracy* (New York: Harper, 1942).

53 This is an inference that Dutta and Crossan draw from their reading of Schumpeter. See: D.K. Dutta and M. Crossan, 'The nature of entrepreneurial opportunities: understanding the process using the 4i organisational learning framework, *Entrepreneurship Theory and Practice*, 2005, July: 425–49.

54 E. Mosakowski, 'Entrepreneurial resources, organisational choices, and competitive outcomes', *Organization Science*, 1998, 9(6): 625–43.

55 Dutta and Crossan, op. cit.

56 B. Bird, 'Implementing entrepreneurial ideas: the case for intention', *Academy of Management Review*, 1988, 13(3): 442–53.

57 R. Hastie and R.M. Dawes, *Rational Choice in an Uncertain World: The Psychology of Judgement and Decision Making* (Thousand Oaks, CA: Sage Publications, 2001) p. 66.

58 L. Buchanan and A. O'Connell, 'A brief history of decision-making', *Harvard Business Review* 2006, January: 32–41.

59 Mosakowski, op. cit., p. 630.

60 P.C. Wensberg, *Land's Polaroid: A Company and the Man Who Invented It* (Boston: Houghton Mifflin, 1987).

61 From: http://www.nap.edu/readingroom/books/biomems/eland.html (accessed 29/12/06).

62 G. Golightly, 'Deflecting the sceptics', *Boeing Frontiers Online* 2003, 2(7) http://www.boeing.com/news/frontiers/archive/2003/november/i_people3. html (accessed 29/12/06).

63 C.W. Allinson, E. Chell and J. Hayes, 'Intuition and entrepreneurial performance', *European Journal of Work and Organizational Psychology*, 2000, 9(1): 31–43.

64 E. Sadler-Smith, 'Cognitive style and the performance of small and medium sized enterprises', *Organization Studies*, 2004, 25: 155–82.

65 D. Bricklin, 'Natural-born entrepreneur', *Harvard Business Review*, 2001, September, 79(8): p. 53.

66 According to *The Edisonian* (available in the Rutgers Edison Archive) these words – probably the most famous ever associated with Edison – are now in question. Edison Papers editors recently discovered a fragment penned by Edison in 1915 in which he placed doubt upon his own famous quote: '[T]hey attribute this saying to me,' he wrote, 'but I cannot remember that I ever said it'! See: http://edison.rutgers.edu/pdfs/The%20Edisonian%20-%20Volume%203.pdf (accessed 11/01/07).

67 H. Evans, 'The eureka myth', *Harvard Business Review*, 2005, June: 18–20.

68 Evans, op. cit.

69 R.J. Sternberg and T.I. Lubart, 'The concept of creativity: prospects and paradigms', in Sternberg, op. cit., p. 10.

70 Sternberg and Lubart, op. cit., p. 11.

71 S.H. Davis and P.B. Davis, *The Intuitive Dimensions of Administrative Decision Making* (Lanham, Maryland: The Scarecrow Press Inc., 2003).

72 K.E. Weick, *Making Sense of the Organization* (Oxford: Blackwell, 2001) p. 449.

73 For a further discussion of the cognitive aspects of 'alertness' see: N.F. Krueger, 'The cognitive infrastructure of opportunity emergence', *Entrepreneurship Theory and Practice*, 2000, Spring: 5–23.

74 'Follow the Leaders', *Adweek Midwest Edition* 11/29/99, 40 (48): 34–42.

75 'Got guts?', *Inc* 1999, March: 54.

76 A.M. Hayashi, 'When to trust your gut', *Harvard Business Review*, 2001, February: 59–65.

77 Hayashi, op. cit., p. 60.

78 The 'Cobra', with its Ford V-8 engine, was the car that inspired the vision Lutz had for the Viper.

79 Hayashi, op. cit., p. 65.

80 D. Isenberg, 'How senior managers think', in W.H. Agor (ed.), 1989 *Intuition in Organizations: Leading and Managing Productively* (Newbury Park, CA: Sage Publications) pp. 91–110.

81 See: C.W. Allinson and J. Hayes, 'The Cognitive Style Index: a measure of intuition-analysis for organizational research', *Journal of Management Studies*, 1996, 33: 119–35; G.P. Hodgkinson and E. Sadler-Smith, 'Complex or unitary? A critique and empirical reassessment of the Allinson-Hayes Cognitive Style Index', *Journal of Occupational and Organizational Psychology*, 2003, 76: 243–68; E. Sadler-Smith, D.P. Spicer and F. Tsang, 'The Cognitive Style Index: a replication and extension', *British Journal of Management*, 2000, 11: 175–81.

82 W.H. Agor, 'The logic of intuition: how top executives make important decisions, in W.H. Agor (ed.) *Intuition in Organisations: Leading and Managing Productively* (Newbury Park, CA: Sage Publications) p. 159.

83 J. Parikh, F. Neubauer and A.G. Lank, *Intuition: The New Frontier in Management* (Oxford: Blackwell Business, 1994); The countries were: Austria; France; Netherlands; Sweden; UK; USA; Japan; Brazil and India.

84 Burke and Miller, op. cit.

85 56 per cent and 40 per cent of participants respectively. The other responses were: cognitively-based decisions, 23 per cent; sub-conscious mental processing, 11 per cent; and values or ethics-based decisions, 10 per cent. See Burke and Miller, op. cit., p. 92.

86 Chet Miller and Duane Ireland argue for a distinction, between 'uncertainty' and 'ambiguity'. If something is uncertain it's 'not known with certainty' but decision-makers know what the issues are, what questions need to be asked and which data need to be collected and analyzed. In these situations an analytical approach is likely to yield benefits and conventional rational approaches to decision-making can be adopted. Contrast this situation with that of 'ambiguity', the literal meaning of which is from the Latin *ambi* meaning 'both ways' and *agere* meaning 'drive'. See: C.C. Miller and D.R. Ireland, 'Intuition in strategic decision-making: friend or foe in the fast-paced 21st century', *Academy of Management Executive*, 2005, 19(1): 19–30.

87 D. Hopkins, Chief Financial Officer, The Boeing Company, 'Architects of the future', *The IBM Lectureship in Business and Finance*, Westminster College, Fulton, Missouri, 4 April 2000, http://www.boeing.com/news/speeches/2000/hopkins_000404.html (accessed 07/01/07). Emphases added.

88 R.L. Daft and K.E. Weick, 'Toward a model of organizations as interpretation systems', *Academy of Management Review*, 1984, 9(2): 287.

89 Daft and Weick, op. cit., 1984.

90 E. Bonabeau, 'Don't trust your gut', *Harvard Business Review*, 2003, May: 116–23; W.M. Grove, D.H. Zald, B.S. Lebow, B.E. Snitz and C. Nelson, 'Clinical versus mechanical prediction: a meta-analysis', *Psychological Assessment*, 2000, 12(1): 19–30.

91 G. Klein, *Intuition at Work* (New York: Currency/Double Day, 2003) p. 112.

92 Klein notes that there are certain people (personality types) that tend to thrive on uncertainty, while others crave certainty (see, Klein op. cit., p. 117). There may also be cultural differences in that particular national cultures tend towards the avoidance of uncertainty. For example, in Hofstede's model of national culture one of the dimensions is uncertainty avoidance, defined as the extent to which a society attempts to cope with anxiety by reducing uncertainty. Mediterranean countries, such as Greece, tend to score highly on the uncertainty avoidance index (UAI), whilst Scandinavian countries such as Denmark and Sweden, and the UK are low on UAI. See: G. Hofstede, *Culture's Consequences: Comparing Values, Behaviors, Institutions and Organizations Across Nations* (2nd edn) (Thousand Oaks, CA: Sage Publications, 2001).

93 Klein, op. cit., pp. 113–18.

94 K. van der Heijden, R. Bradfield, G. Burt, G. Cairns and G. Wright, *The Sixth Sense: Accelerating Organisational Learning with Scenarios* (Chichester: John Wiley and Sons, Ltd.) p. 63.

95 See: P. Wack, 'Scenarios: uncharted waters ahead', *Harvard Business Review*, 1985, 63(5): 73–89.

96 G.S. Kaler and K. van der Heijden, 'Scenarios and their contribution to organisational learning: from practice to theory', in M. Dierkes, A. Berthoin Antal, J. Child and I. Nonaka (eds) *Handbook of Organisational Learning and Knowledge* (Oxford: Oxford University Press, 2001) p. 853.

97 A.P. de Geus, 'Planning as learning', *Harvard Business Review*, 1988, March–April: pp. 72–3.

98 'An update classic: scenario planning re-considered', *Harvard Management Update*, 2006, May: 3–4.

99 G.L. Claxton, 'The anatomy of intuition', in G.L. Claxton and T. Atkinson (eds) *The Intuitive Practitioner: On the Value of Not Always Knowing What one is Doing* (Buckingham: Open University Press, 2000) p. 43.

100 L.J. Sanna, 'Mental simulation, affect and personality: a conceptual framework', *Current Directions in Psychological Science*, 2000, 9(5): 168–73.

101 J.E. Escalas, 'Imagine yourself in the product: mental simulation, narrative transportation, and persuasion', *Journal of Advertising*, 2004, 33: 37–48.

102 L.W. Gregory, R.B. Cialdini and K.M. Carpenter, 'Self-relevant scenarios as mediators of likelihood estimates and compliance: does imagining make it so?', *Journal of Personality and Social Psychology*, 1982, 43: 89–99.

103 From: http://www.nap.edu/readingroom/books/biomems/eland.html (accessed: 29/12/06).

104 S.E. Taylor, L.B. Pham, I.D. Rivkin and D.A. Armor, 'Harnessing the imagination: mental simulation, self regulation and coping', *American Psychologist*, 1998, 53(4): 429–39.

105 Taylor *et al.*, op. cit., p. 431.

106 F. Strack, N. Schwarz and E. Gschneidinger, 'Happiness and reminiscing: the role of time perspective, affect and mode of thinking', *Journal of Personality and Social Psychology*, 1985, 49: 1460–9.

107 S.E. Taylor, 'Coping and the simulation of events', *Social Cognition*, 1989, 7: 174–94.

108 Counterfactuals are 'mental representations of alternatives to the past'. See: N.J. Roese, 'Counterfactual thinking', *Psychological Bulletin*, 1997, 121(1): 133.

109 C.M. Gaglio, 'The role of mental simulations and counterfactual thinking in the opportunity identification process', *Entrepreneurship Theory and Practice*, 2004, 28(6): 533–52.

110 Gaglio, op. cit.

111 Taylor *et al.*, op. cit.

112 D. Kahneman and A. Tversky, 'The simulation heuristic', in D. Kahneman, P. Slovic and A. Tversky. (eds) *Judgement under Uncertainty: Heuristics and Biases* (Cambridge: Cambridge University Press, 1982) 201–08.

113 Gaglio, op. cit.

114 G. Oettingen, 'Positive fantasy and motivation', in P.M. Gollwitzer and J.A. Bargh (eds) *The Psychology of Action: Linking Cognition and Emotion to Behaviour* (New York: Guilford Press, 1995) pp. 219–35.

115 Taylor *et al.*, op. cit.

116 Taylor *et al.*, op. cit.

117 W.J. McGuire, 'Creative hypothesis testing in psychology: some useful heuristics', *Annual Review of Psychology*, 1987, 48: 1–30.

338   *Notes*

118 G. Klein, *Intuition at Work* (New York: Doubleday Currency, 2002).
119 M. Sinclair, G.P. Hodgkinson and E. Sadler-Smith, 'The role of intuition in strategic decision making', in L.A. Costanzo and R.B. McKay (eds) *The Handbook of Research on Strategy and Foresight* (Cheltenham: Edward Elgar, 2007).
120 N. Khatri and A. Ng, 'The role of intuition in strategic decision making', *Human Relations*, 2000, 53(1): 57–86.
121 E. Dane and M.G. Pratt, 'Exploring intuition and its role in managerial decision making', *Academy of Management Review*, 2007, 32(1): 33–54.
122 G. Klein, *Intuition at Work* (New York: Doubleday Currency, 2002) p. 57; P. Laughlin, 'Social combination processes of cooperative problem-solving groups on verbal intellective tasks', in M. Fishbein (ed.) *Progress in Social Psychology, Vol. 1* (Hillsdale, NJ: Lawrence Erlbaum Associates 1980) pp. 127–55;
123 J.C. Narver, S.F. Slater and D.L. MacLachlan, 'Responsive and proactive market orientation and new-product success', *Journal of Product Innovation Management*, 2004, 21(5): 334–47.
124 http://uwnews.washington.edu/ni/public/article.asp?articleID=5771 (accessed 05/01/07).
125 L. Buchanan and A. O'Connell, 'A brief history of decision-making', *Harvard Business Review*, 2006, January: 41.
126 P.E. Meehl, *Clinical Versus Statistical Prediction: A Theoretical Analysis and a Review of the Evidence* (Minneapolis: University of Minnesota Press, 1954).
127 Meta analysis combines the results of several, usually large numbers of, studies which address the same or similar research questions and often focusing on effect sizes (the magnitude of a treatment effect).
128 W.M. Grove, D.H. Zald, B.S. Lebow, B.E. Snitz and C. Nelson, 'Clinical versus mechanical prediction: a meta-analysis, *Psychological Assessment*, 2000, 12(1): 19–30.
129 See for example: E. Bonabeau, 'Don't trust your gut', *Harvard Business Review*, 2003, May: 116–23.
130 R.M. Hogarth, *Educating Intuition* (Chicago: The University of Chicago Press, 2001).
131 W.M. Grove, D.H. Zald, B.S. Lebow, B.E. Snitz and C. Nelson, 'Clinical versus mechanical prediction: a meta-analysis', *Psychological Assessment*, 2000, 12(1): 19–30.
132 R.M. Hogarth, *Educating Intuition* (Chicago: The University of Chicago Press, 2001) p. 145.
133 Hogarth, op. cit.
134 Bonabeau, op. cit.
135 R. Hastie and R.M. Davies, *Rational Choice in an Uncertain World: The Psychology of Judgement and Decision Making* (Thousand Oaks, CA: Sage Publications, 2001) p. 70.
136 A. Morita, 'Selling to the world: the Sony Walkman story', in J. Henry and D. Walker (eds) *Managing Innovation* (London: Sage Publications, 1991) p. 191.
137 Bonabeau, op. cit., p. 123.
138 Edwin Locke, in a critique of emotional intelligence, argues that it is not possible to reason *with* emotion, only to reason *about* emotion. See: E.A.

Locke, 'Why emotional intelligence is an invalid concept', *Journal of Organizational Behavior*, 2005, 26: 425–31.

139 Based on: M. Fisher, *Intuition: How to Use it in Your Life* (Green Farm, CT: Wildcat Publishing 1995), p. 104.

11 Emotional, social and moral intuition

1 G. Lakoff and M. Johnson, *Philosophy in the Flesh: The Embodied Mind and its Challenge to Western Thought* (New York: Basic Books, 1999) pp. 3–4.

2 Subsequent Daniel Goleman publications in the same vein have included *Working with Emotional Intelligence, Primal Leadership* (with Richard Boyatzis and Annie McKee) and *Destructive Emotions: A Dialogue with the Dalai Lama.*

3 EBSCO search 25/01/07. Search terms 'emotional intelligence' (title); and emotional intelligence (all text).

4 G. Matthews, M. Zeidner and R.D. Roberts, *Emotional Intelligence: Science and Myth* (Cambridge, MA: A Bradford Book, MIT Press, 2004).

5 F.J. Landy, 'Some historical and scientific issues related to research on emotional intelligence', *Journal of Organizational Behavior*, 2005, 26: 411–24. See also: Locke, op. cit.

6 D. Goleman, *Emotional Intelligence: Why it Can Matter More Than IQ* (London: Bloomsbury, 1996) p. 43.

7 Ibid., p. 53.

8 D. Goleman, *Working with Emotional Intelligence* (New York: Bantam Books, 1998) p. 54.

9 An example of a question which assessed an individual's 'action orientation' is: 'When I know I must finish something soon I find it easy to get it over and done with'. An example of the opposite orientation is: 'When I have a boring assignment I sometimes just can't get moving on it'. See Koole and Jostman (note 10).

10 S.L. Koole and N.B. Jostman, 'Getting a grip on your feelings: effects of action orientation and external demands in intuitive affect regulation', *Journal of Personality and Social Psychology*, 2004, 87(6): 974–90.

11 Matthews *et al.*, op. cit., p. 282.

12 R. Bar-On, D. Tranel, N. Denburg and A. Bechara, 'Exploring the neurological substrate of emotional and social intelligence', *Brain*, 2003, 126: 1790–800.

13 Bar-On *et al.*, op. cit.

14 D.G. Myers, *Intuition: Its Powers and Perils* (New Haven: Yale, 2002) p. 33.

15 Myers, op. cit.

16 R.B. Zajonc, 'Feeling and thinking: preferences need no inferences', *American Psychologist*, 1980, 35: 151–75.

17 J. Haidt, 'The emotional dog and its rationalist tail: a social intuitionist approach to moral judgement', *Psychological Review*, 2001, 108(4): 821.

18 Myers, op. cit., pp. 42–3.

19 T.L. Chartrand and J.A. Bargh, 'The chameleon effect: the perception-behaviour link and social interaction', *Journal of Personality and Social Psychology*, 1999, 76: 893–910.

20 Myers, op. cit., pp. 42–3.

21 Haidt, op. cit., p. 820.

22 J.A. Bargh and P. Pietromonaco, 'Automatic information processing and social perception: the influence of trait information presented outside of conscious awareness on impression formation', *Journal of Personality and Social Psychology*, 1982, 43(3): 441.

23 T.D Wilson, *Strangers to Ourselves: Discovering the Adaptive Unconscious* (Belknap/Harvard, 2002) p. 31.

24 There are controversies about the extent to which other great apes (for example chimps and gorillas) can exhibit true imitation. See: D. Chiappe and K. MacDonald, 'The evolution of domain general mechanisms in intelligence and learning', *The Journal of General Psychology*, 2005, 132(1): 5–40.

25 G. Rizzolatti and L. Craighero, 'The mirror neuron system', *Annual Review of Neuroscience*, 2004, 27: 169–92.

26 M.D. Lieberman, 'Social cognitive neuroscience: a review of core processes', *Annual Review of Psychology*, 2007, 271.

27 T. Radford, 'Genes say boys will be boys and girls will be sensitive', *The Guardian*, 12 June, 1997, p. 1.

28 D.H. Skuse, R.S. James, D.V.M. Bishop *et al.*, 'Evidence from Turner's syndrome of an impaired X-linked locus affecting cognitive function', *Nature*, 1997, 387: 705–8. Note: the internal consistency for Skuse *et al.*'s social cognition measure (12 items) was 0.94 (Cronbach's α).

29 Radford, op. cit.

30 J. Scourfield and P. McGuffin, 'Imprinted X-linked genes, "feminine intuition" and the public (mis)understanding of science', *Molecular Psychiatry*, 1997, 2: 386.

31 G.P. Hodgkinson and E. Sadler-Smith, 'Complex or unitary? A critique and empirical reassessment of the Allinson-Hayes Cognitive Style Index', *Journal of Occupational and Organizational Psychology*, 2003, 76: 243–68. Other research, such as Allinson and Hayes (1996) found females to be more analytical than males. The picture is confused.

32 S.E. Snodgrass, 'Women's intuition: the effect of subordinate role on interpersonal sensitivity', *Journal of Personality and Social Psychology*, 1985, 49(1): 146–55. Snodgrass argues in this paper that what is commonly referred to as 'women's intuition' may in fact be better termed 'subordinate intuition' – a manifestation of an individual's subordinate role in a social setting.

33 L.G. Bolman and T.E. Deal, *Reframing Organisations: Artistry, Choice and Leadership* (San Francisco: Jossey-Bass, 2003) p. 339.

34 R. Goffee and G. Jones, 'Managing authenticity: the paradox of great leadership', *Harvard Business Review*, 2005, December: 86–94.

35 D. Goleman, R. Boyatzis and A. McKee, *The New Leaders: Transforming the Art of Leadership into the Science of Results* (London: Time Warner, 2003) p. 53.

36 E. Goldberg, *The Wisdom Paradox: How your Mind can Grow Stronger as your Brain Grows Older* (London: Free Press, 2005).

37 B.M Bass and P. Steidlmeier, 'Ethics, character and authentic transformational leadership,' *Leadership Quarterly*, 1999, 10(2): 181–217.

38 This is an adaptation of the dog-eating vignette to be found in: J. Haidt, S. Koller and M. Dias, 'Affect morality and culture, or is it wrong to eat your dog?', *Journal of Personality and Social Psychology*, 1993, 65: 613–28.

39 T. Wheatley and J. Haidt, 'Hypnotic disgust makes moral judgements more severe', *Psychological Science*, 2005, 16(10): 780–4. Note: the vignette as presented here has been anglicized.
40 Haidt *et al.*, op. cit.
41 T. Maunter (ed.) *Penguin Dictionary of Philosophy* (London: Penguin Books, 1997) p. 258.
42 D. Hume, *Treatise of Human Nature*. Most frequently cited is the edition by L.A. Selby-Bigge, (Oxford: Oxford University Press, 1740/1978).
43 These moral judgements may be culturally-specific – for example, eating a dead pet dog may not meet with moral repugnance in particular cultural settings.
44 A.R. Damasio, D. Tranel, and H. Damasio, 'Individuals with sociopathic behaviour caused by frontal damage fail to respond autonomically to social stimuli', *Behavioral Brain Research*, 1990, 41: 81–94. Blair and Cipolotti reported a study of a patient who, following trauma to the right frontal region, including the orbito-frontal cortex, presented with 'acquired socio-pathy' manifested as behaviour that was aberrant and marked by high levels of aggression and a callous disregard for others. See: R.J.R. Blair and L. Cipolotti, 'Impaired social response reversal: a case of acquired socio-pathy', *Brain*, 2000, 123(6): 1122–41.
45 A.R. Damasio, *Descartes Error: Emotion, Reason and the Human Brain* (New York: Harper Collins, 1994) p. 45.
46 From: M. Emery, *Power-hunch: Living an Intuitive Life* (Hillsborough, OR: Beyond Words Publishing, 2001) p. 23.

12 The intuitive ape

 1 The term 'reverse-engineer the brain' is from the interview with the cogni-tive scientist Steven Pinker in: M.S. Gazzaniga, R.B. Ivry and G.R. Mangun, *Cognitive Neuroscience: The Biology of the Mind* (New York: W.W. Norton and Co., 2002) p. 580.
 2 K. Wong, 'The morning of the modern mind', *Scientific American*, 2005, 292(6): 86–95.
 3 D.M. Bramble and D.E. Lieberman, 'Endurance running and the evolution of *Homo*', *Nature*, 2004, 432: 345–52.
 4 http://www.mnh.si.edu/anthro/humanorigins/ (accessed 26/01/07).
 5 R. Dunbar, *The Human Story* (London: Faber, 2004) p. 143.
 6 R. Dunbar, *The Human Story* (London: Faber, 2004).
 7 The Australopithecines were small-brained upright hominids with very human-like characteristics. The oldest of these, *Australopithecus afarensis* flourished in Africa 3.0 million and 3.75 million years ago. See: C. Willis, *The Runaway Brain: The Evolution of Human Uniqueness* (London: Harper Collins, 1994) p. 331.
 8 R.A. Barton, 'Neocortex size and behavioural ecology in primates', *Pro-ceedings of the Royal Society of London*, 1996, B. 263: 173–7.
 9 D.C. Geary, 'What is the function of mind and brain?', *Educational Psych-ology Review*, 1998, 10(4): 377–87.
10 K. Oatley, *Emotions: A Brief History* (Oxford: Blackwell, 2005) p. 27.
11 J. Barkow, J. Tooby and L. Cosmides, *The Adapted Mind* (New York: Oxford, 1992).

12 G.J. Feist, 'Is the theory of evolution winning the battle of the survival of the fittest in the social sciences?', *Psychological Inquiry*, 1999, 10(4): 334–41.

13 P. S. Churchland, *Brain-wise: Studies in Neurophilosophy* (Cambridge, MA: MIT Press, 2002) pp. 40–1.

14 See: M. Thomasello, 'The human adaptation for culture', *Annual Review of Anthropology*, 1999, 28: 509–29.

15 T.D. Wilson, *Strangers to Ourselves: Discovering the Adaptive Unconscious* (Cambridge, MA: Belknap/Harvard, 2002) p. 51.

16 L. Litman and A.S. Reber, 'Implicit cognition and thought', in K.J. Holyoak and R.G. Morrison (eds) *The Cambridge Handbook of Thinking and Reasoning* (Cambridge: Cambridge University Press, 2005) pp. 431–53.

17 D. Berry and Z. Dienes, 'Practical implications', in D. Berry and Z. Dienes (eds) *Implicit and Explicit Knowledge in Human Performance* Hove: Erlbaum, 1993) pp. 129–44.

18 D. Berry and Z. Dienes, 'Towards a working characterisation of implicit learning', in Berry and Dienes, op. cit., pp. 1–18.

19 P. Lewicki, T. Hill and M. Czyzewska, 'Non-conscious acquisition of information', *American Psychologist*, 1992, 47: 796–801.

20 G.L. Claxton, *The Wayward Mind: An Intimate History of the Unconscious* (London: Abacus, 2005) p. 341.

21 J.F. Kihlstrom, T.M. Barnhardt and D.J. Tataryn, 'The psychological unconscious: found, lost, and regained', *American Psychologist*, 1992, 47: 788–91.

22 E.F. Loftus and M.R. Klinger, 'Is the unconscious smart or dumb?' *American Psychologist*, 1992, 47: 761–5.

23 J.St.B.T. Evans, 'In two minds: dual process accounts of reasoning', *Trends in Cognitive Sciences*, 2003, 7(10): 458.

24 K.E Stanovich, *The Robot's Rebellion: Finding Meaning in the Age of Darwin* (Chicago, IL: Chicago University Press, 2004).

25 Dunbar, op. cit., p. 43.

26 A.M. Colman, *Oxford Dictionary of Psychology* (Oxford: Oxford University Press, 2003) p. 739.

27 For detailed discussion of 'mindblindness' see: S. Baron-Cohen, *Mindblindness: An Essay on Autism and Theory of Mind* (Cambridge, MA: MIT Press, 1995).

28 G. Rizzolatti and L. Craighero, 'The mirror neuron system', *Annual Review of Neuroscience* 2004, 27: 169–92.

29 M.S. Gazzaniga, R.B. Ivry and G.R.Mangun, *Cognitive Neuroscience: The Biology of the Mind* (New York: W.W. Norton and Co., 2002) p. 577.

30 A. Bechara, 'The role of emotion in decision-making: evidence from neurological patients with orbito-frontal damage', *Brain and Cognition*, 2004, 55: 30–40.

31 For a discussion of 'social intuitions', see: D.G. Myers, *Intuition: Its powers and Perils* (New Haven, CT: Yale, 2002); Wilson, op. cit.

32 Gazzaniga *et al.*, op. cit., p. 581

33 Graham and Ickes cited in Myers, op. cit., p. 48.

34 Dunbar, op. cit., p. 43.

35 N. Nicholson, 'How hardwired is human behaviour?', *Harvard Business Review*, 1998, July–August: 140.

36 Timothy D. Wilson argues that when we meet someone for the first time we are prone to categorize them on the basis of stereotypes (for example based

on race, age or gender) which we are not born with but once learned from our immediate culture they tend to come into operation unconsciously and effortlessly and bias our thinking. See: Wilson, op. cit., p. 53. Stephen Pinker argues that it's very difficult to lie about our intentions because intentions come from emotions, emotions have evolved displays on the face and body, and 'they probably evolved *because* they are hard to fake'. See: S. Pinker, *How the Mind Works* (New York: W.W. Norton, 1997) p. 421 (original emphases).

37 A. Tversky and D. Kahneman, 'Extensional versus intuitive reasoning,: the conjunction fallacy in probability judgement', *Psychological Review*, 1983, 90(4): 293–315.
38 G. Lakoff and M. Johnson, *Philosophy in the Flesh: The Embodied Mind and its Challenge to Western Thought* (New York: Basic Books, 1999) pp. 527–8.
39 H. Mintzberg and F. Westley, 'Decision-making: it's not what you think', *MIT Sloan Management Review*, 2001, 42(3): 89–93.
40 S.A. Sloman, 'Rational versus Arational models of thought', in R.J. Sternberg (ed.) *The Nature of Cognition* (Cambridge, MA: MIT Press, 1999) p. 557.
41 P. Slovic, M.L. Finucane, E. Peters and D.G. MacGregor, 'Risk as analysis and risk as feelings: some thoughts about affect, reason, risk and rationality', *Risk Analysis*, 2004, 24: 311–22.
42 H.A. Simon, *Administrative Behaviour* (New York: Macmillan, 1997) p. 131.
43 For example: J.E. Le Doux, *The Emotional Brain* (New York: Simon and Schuster, 1996).
44 Nicholson, op. cit., pp. 135–47.
45 N. Nicholson, *Managing the Human Animal* (London: Texere, 2000).
46 For a discussion of the 'thinking mind' and the 'ancestral mind' see: G.D. Jacobs, *The Ancestral Mind* (New York: Viking, 2003).
47 This is the term used by Arthur Reber – see Chapter 5.
48 S. Epstein and R. Pacini, 1999, 'Some basic issues regarding dual process theories from the perspective of Cognitive Experiential Self Theory', in S. Chaiken and Y. Trope (eds) *Dual Process Theories in social Psychology* (New York: The Guilford Press, 1999) p. 473.
49 Plato, *Phaedo* 66 (360 BC).
50 *Dhammapada*, V. I.

An intuition reading list

With apologies in advance for the inevitable omissions, listed here is an eclectic selection of books about intuition along with book chapters and a small selection of the available academic papers. The latter are mostly from business, management and organization studies and have appeared since the awakening of a stronger interest in intuition among scholars in mainstream management from the early 1980s onwards, and especially in the wake of the 'intuitive pioneers' Bill Taggart and Weston Agor. The current generation of researchers owes them an immense debt of gratitude for their courage, imagination and intellectual contribution.

A SELECTION OF BOOKS

Agor, W. H. (ed.), *Intuition in Organizations: Leading and Managing Productively*. Newbury Park, CA: Sage Publications 1989.

Bastick, T., *Intuition: How We Think and Act*. New York, NY: John Wiley & Sons 1982.

Cappon, D., *Intuition and Management: Research and Application*. Westport, CT: Quorum Books 1994.

Davis, S.H. and Davis, P.B., *The Intuitive Dimensions of Administrative Decisionmaking*. Lanham: Scarecrow 2003.

Davis-Floyd, R. and Arvidson, P.S. (eds), *Intuition: The Inside Story*. Routledge: New York 1997.

Emery, M., *Powerhunch: Living an Intuitive Life*. Hillsboro, OR: Beyond Words Publishing 2001.

Gawain, S., *Developing Intuition: Practical Guidance for Daily Life*. Novato, CA: New World Library 2000.

Gladwell, M., *Blink: The Power of Thinking without Thinking*. London: Allen Lane 2005.

Goldberg, P., *The Intuitive Edge*. Los Angeles: Tarcher 1985.

Hogarth, R.M., *Educating Intuition*. Chicago: University of Chicago Press 2001.

Klein, G., *Sources of Power: How People Make Decisions*. Cambridge, MA: MIT Press 1998.

Klein, G., *Intuition at Work*. New York: Currency/Double Day 2003.

Klingler, S.A., *Intuition and Beyond: A Step-by-Step Guide to Discovering your Inner Voice*. London: Rider 2002.

Myers, D.G., *Intuition: Its Powers and Perils*. New Haven: Yale University Press 2002.

Nadel, L., *Sixth Sense: How to Unlock your Intuitive Brain*. London: Prion 1996.

Parikh, J., *Intuition: The New Frontier of Management*. Oxford: Blackwell Business 1994.

Rowan, R., *The Intuitive Manager*. Boston: Little Brown 1986.

Schulz, M.L., *Awakening Intuition: Using your Mind Body Network for Insight and Healing*. New York: Three Rivers Press 1999.

Vaughan, F.E., *Awakening Intuition*. New York: Doubleday 1979.

Weintraub, S., *The Hidden Intelligence: Innovation through Intuition*. Woburn, MA.: Butterworth Heinemann 1998.

Wilson, T.D., *Strangers to Ourselves: Discovering the Adaptive Unconscious*. Cambridge, MA: Belknap Press 2002.

A SELECTION OF ACADEMIC PAPERS AND BOOK CHAPTERS

Allinson, C.W. and Hayes, J., 'The Cognitive Style Index: a measure of intuition-analysis for organizational research', *Journal of Management Studies*, 1996, 33(1): 119–35.

Behling, O. and Eckel, N.L., 'Making sense out of intuition', *Academy of Management Executive*, 1991, 5(1): 46–54.

Burke, L.A. and Miller, M.K., 'Taking the mystery out of intuitive decision making', *Academy of Management Executive*, 1999, 13(4): 91–9.

Burke, L.A. and Sadler-Smith, E., 'Instructor intuition in the educational context', *Academy of Management Learning and Education*, 2006, 5(2): 169–81.

Claxton, G., 'Investigating human intuition: knowing without knowing why', *The Psychologist*, 1998, 11(5): 217–20.

Dane, E. and Pratt, M.G., 'Exploring intuition and its role in managerial decision making', *Academy of Management Review*, 2007, 32(1): 33–54.

Epstein, S., 'Integration of the cognitive and the psychodynamic unconscious', *American Psychologist*, 1994, 49: 709–24.

Hodgkinson, G.P., Langan-Fox, J. and Sadler-Smith, E., 'Intuition: a fundamental bridging construct in the behavioural sciences', *British Journal of Psychology*, 2008 (in press).

Hodgkinson, G.P. and Sadler-Smith, E., 'Complex or unitary? A critique and empirical re-assessment of the Allinson-Hayes Cognitive Style Index', *Journal of Occupational and Organizational Psychology*, 2003, 76: 243–68.

Isenberg, D.J., 'How senior managers think', *Harvard Business Review*, 1984, November/December: 81–90.

Khatri, N. and Ng, H.A., 'The role of intuition in strategic decision making', *Human Relations*, 2000, 53: 57–86.

Lieberman, M.D., 'Intuition: a social cognitive neuroscience approach', *Psychological Bulletin*, 2000, 126(1): 109–37.

Lieberman, M.D., Jarcho, J.M. and Satpute, A.B., 'Evidence-based and intuition-based self-knowledge: an fMRI study', *Journal of Personality and Social Psychology*, 2004, 87: 421–35.

Miller, C.C. and Ireland, D.R., 'Intuition in strategic decision making: friend or foe in the fast-paced 21st century', *Academy of Management Executive*, 2005, 19(1): 19–30.

Sadler-Smith, E. and Shefy, E., 'The intuitive executive: understanding and applying "gut feeling" in decision making', *The Academy of Management Executive*, 2004, 18(4): 76–92.

Sadler-Smith, E. and Shefy, E., 'Developing intuitive awareness in management education', *Academy of Management Learning and Education*, 2007, 6(2): 186–205.

Sadler-Smith, E. and Sparrow, P.R., 'Intuition in organisational decision-making', in Hodgkinson, G.P. and Starbuck, W.H. (eds), *The Oxford Handbook of Organizational Decision-making*. Oxford: Oxford University Press 2007.

Simon, H.A., 'Making management decisions: the role of intuition and emotion', *Academy of Management Executive*, 1987, 1: 57–64.

Sinclair, M. and Ashkanasy, N.M., 'Intuition: myth or a decision-making tool?', *Management Learning*, 2005, 36(3): 353–70.

Sinclair, M., Sadler-Smith, E., and Hodgkinson, G.P., 'The role of intuition in strategic decision making', in Costanzo, L.A. and McKay, R.B. (eds), *The Handbook of Research on Strategy and Foresight*. Cheltenham, UK: Edward Elgar 2008.

Taggart, W. and Robey, D., 'Minds and managers: on the dual nature of human information processing and management', *Academy of Management Review* 1981, 6: 187–95.

Index

intuition 108; limits of expert performance
118; practitioners 10
extra sensory perception (ESP) 5, 27, 30, 56,
177, 178, 196

failure indices 89
Fangio, M. 2
fast-and-frugal heuristics 163–168
fear 4, 11, 126, 196, 212–218, 257, 263,
275–276; irrational 196
feedback 105, 122, 145, 170, 188, 227, 232,
247, 264, 267–270
feelings of warmth (FOW) 96
Feist, G. 290
female intuition 281–282 (see also social
intuition)
Feynman, R. 19
Finding Nemo 20, 125
'flow' experiences 110–111
Fodor, J. 200
forebrain 212–213
Forer, R.B. 27
forms (Plato) 14–15
Four Quartets (TS. Eliot) 17
foveal vision (analogy) 198
Franklin, B. 34–36, 60, 173
Frederick, S. 154
Freud, S. 8
Fromm, E. 90
Fry, A. 240, 241
functional magnetic resonance imaging
(fMRI) 6, 97, 99, 131, 179, 205–206, 280
'funny bone' instinct (McDonalds) 2

Gage, P. 222–228
Galileo 66
Garland, J. 219
Gazzaniga, M. 168, 180, 208, 247
gene-culture co-evolution 295
Gestalt 79, 179
Getz, I. 221
Ghandi 117
Gigerenzer, G. 163–166, 168–169
Gladwell, M. 4, 32
globalisation 2
Goffee, R. 283
Goldberg, P. 11, 123
Goleman, D. 214, 272
Gould, SJ. 154
great apes 8, 289
Greenhalgh, T. 40, 115
Greening, E. 27
Grove, W. 267
gut feel 1–2, 12, 20, 23, 39, 113, 135–136, 147,
150, 169, 187, 217, 233, 253–256, 263, 286,
294
gut feeling 3–4, 29–30, 32, 61, 110, 114–115,
144, 189, 198, 224, 228–229, 231, 233, 243,
274–276, 287, 288, 296, 299

Haidt, J. 284–285

Hammond, K. 37
Hastie, R. 48, 169, 249
heuristics and biases 148–69, 172, 182–183,
204, 222; limitations 161, 171
Hill, T. 142
hindbrain 212
hippocampus 126, 206, 210
hiring-and-firing 22
HMS Gloucester 56, 177
Hockney, D. 117
Hogarth, R. 153–154, 199, 264, 268, 270
holistic 23, 31–32, 110, 121, 154, 174, 179,
181, 189, 201, 204, 210, 234, 247, 285, 287
Holmes, Sherlock 26–27
Homer 239
Homo erectus, habilis, neanderthalensis 289
Homo sapiens (evolution) 6, 202–203, 289,
296
Hume, D. 14, 284–285
hunch 3, 20, 23, 32, 40, 169, 186–188, 203,
217, 226, 228, 234, 252–253, 276–277, 286
hunches 29, 40, 101, 198, 203, 212, 243–244,
247, 269, 299
hypnagogic state 71
hypothalamus 59, 212

implicit: cognition 127, 146; knowledge 7,
128, 139, 143, 144, 145, 198, 201, 203, 280;
memory 133, 138, 292; perception 129, 131
improvisation 51, 111, 116
individual differences (in cognition) 89–90
information overload 12
informed intuition 10, 12, 22–23, 28–29,
31–32, 57, 62, 121, 143, 251–253, 262, 265,
267, 288, 294
innovation 4, 9, 20, 66–67, 71, 76, 85, 87,
241–242, 247, 249–250, 269
insight: alpha wave 99; autonomous
activation 88; bottom-up reformulation
81; box problem 82; expertise 90; fortress
problem 85; functional fixedness 78, 82,
83, 122; grind-out 74, 93, 96; illumination
75, 76, 78, 101; incubation 74–75, 85–89,
94, 97, 99, 101, 125, 179, 241, 248;
interactive activation 88; intimation 67, 75,
101, 243; narrowly-focused attention 89;
neuro-physiology 96; pop-out 93;
preparation 74; problems 96; radiation
problem 81; random recombination 87;
scientific discovery 69; spread of activation
88, 90, 97, 179, 181, 233, 274; top-down
reformulation 81; verification 76; visual
restructuring 78–79, 88; Wallas model 72;
warmth ratings 96
instinct 9, 13, 14, 30, 248, 252, 284, 296
intueri (Latin) 3, 32, 299
intuition and insight (Buddhist perspective)
23
intuition: alarm bell 1, 28, 29, 171, 263;
artificial 267; business management 20;
creative 239, 240, 242, 252; definition 30;